THE MANAGEMENT OF MONEY

THE MANAGEMENT
OF MONEY

A Survey of American Experience

HAROLD ⌐BARGER

COLUMBIA UNIVERSITY

RAND McNALLY & COMPANY · CHICAGO

Rand McNally Economics Series

WALTER W. HELLER, ADVISORY EDITOR

To the chairmen and members of the
Joint Economic Committee
of the
Congress of the United States
through whose enterprise and public spirit
so much of the material in this book
was first brought to light

Preface

Writing this book has been fun. If its scope and content are thought capricious by some, no defense is offered except to say that the reader will find discussed here the questions that seemed to me interesting and worth inquiry. Inevitably the first century and a half of central banking in the United States is a subject so vast that no single volume could do it justice. Selection of topics and of emphasis proved essential. First, I have confined myself to the domestic management of money and have said no more than appeared absolutely necessary about the external relations of the dollar. Second, I have said little about monetary management—such as it was— during the Civil War and two world wars. The political constraints upon monetary policy in wartime are so great that such periods have few lessons for time of peace. Third, I have neglected as of secondary interest such side conditions affecting the money market as banking structure, bank failures, rules governing check collection, regional distribution of the money supply, and variation in money-using habits. It is to be hoped that these self-imposed limitations have allowed major issues of monetary—and fiscal—policy to occupy the center of the stage.

A note is in order regarding the comparative absence of statistical data. This is deliberate. Monetary statistics for the period since 1914 are so readily available in publications of the Federal Reserve System that it would be absurd to reproduce them here. I have therefore confined myself to presenting leading series in graphic form (Figs. 1–3) in a manner to render intelligible the narrative of the text.

Unpublished data for the maturity distribution of System holdings of governments for 1932–1936 and a tabulation of member-bank reserve requirements since 1914 are given in Appendix III.

A word about source materials for a study such as this. The earlier period of Federal Reserve history is rich in unpublished collections available to the scholar, and is becoming richer still with the gradual opening of the papers of Henry Morgenthau, Jr. For recent years none but published material is available; yet this deficiency is largely compensated by the rich veins uncovered in the many hearings of the Joint Economic Committee.

In addition to canvassing the sources listed in footnotes and in Appendix I, I interviewed a goodly number of former officials and some officials still connected with the System. With few exceptions my experiences were disappointing. Despite the current fashion for "oral history," the recollections of events by those who participated in them frequently were belied by the written record. Reminiscences long after the event can no doubt convey the atmosphere of the time; but it would appear that a reliable account of how and why things happened can seldom be constructed except from contemporary documents. Too often we forget embarrassing occurrences and re-member only those in which we triumphed. As an extreme example I cite the following. Shortly before his death I interviewed Eugene Meyer with a view to learning something of the background sur-rounding the open-market purchases of the Spring of 1932 and why they were discontinued so abruptly. On this subject—perhaps the most important issue that arose during his governorship—Meyer's mind was a complete blank. On the other hand he had no difficulty in recalling with much circumstantial detail how, when he had only just been appointed governor, Miller came into his office and de-manded that he fire Goldenweiser even before he had had a chance to make the latter's acquaintance! Such is the stuff of oral history.

Research on which this book is based was facilitated by my tenure in 1954 of a Schuyler Fiske Seager Fellowship awarded by Colum-bia University and in 1957–1958 of a Faculty Research Fellow-ship awarded by the Ford Foundation.

Numerous colleagues and other friends have placed me in their debt. Mildred Adams and Robert D. Calkins helped me locate source material, and David Wilkofsky did research. The manuscript was read in whole or in part, and useful criticisms were made, by James

W. Angell, Benjamin Haggott Beckhart, Marriner S. Eccles, George Garvy, Peter B. Kenen, the late Harold V. Roelse, Robert V. Roosa, Ira O. Scott, Jr., and Allan Sproul. I am also grateful to Mr. Eccles and Mr. Sproul for permission to quote from unpublished letters and memoranda; and to the Library of Congress with respect to the diary of Charles S. Hamlin. For permission to quote from published works I am indebted to the following: to Columbia University Press for quotation from Margaret G. Myers, *The New York Money Market*, Vol. I; to Carter Glass III and other heirs of Senator Glass for quotation from *An Adventure in Constructive Finance*; to the Brookings Institution for quotation from Lester V. Chandler, *Benjamin Strong, Central Banker*, and Wilfred Lewis, Jr., *Federal Fiscal Policy in the Postwar Recessions*; to the Macmillan Co. for quotation from Herbert Hoover, *Memoirs*, Vol. III, and from a paper by Allan Sproul in *Money, Trade and Economic Growth*; to Harper and Brothers for quotation from Benjamin Strong, *Interpretations of Federal Reserve Policy*; to the American Economic Association for quotation from Adolph C. Miller, "Responsibility for Federal Reserve Policies, 1927–1929," *American Economic Review*, XXV; to Marriner S. Eccles for quotation from *Beckoning Frontiers*; to Yale University Press for quotation from Kenneth D. Roose, *The Economics of Recession and Revival, An Interpretation of 1937–1938*; to the McGraw-Hill Book Co. for quotation from Henry C. Murphy, *National Debt in War and Transition*; to Time, Inc., for quotation from Harry S. Truman, *Memoirs*, Vol. II; to Theo R. Goldsmith for quotation from the *Goldsmith Washington Service*, No. 365; to the University of Chicago for quotation from Milton Friedman, *Essays in Positive Economics*; to Fordham University Press for quotation from Arthur F. Burns, *Prosperity without Inflation*; to Harvard University Press for quotation from papers by Otto Eckstein and Alvin H. Hansen in the *Review of Economics and Statistics*, XLIV; and to Alfred A. Knopf for quotation from George L. Bach, *Federal Reserve Policy-Making*.

H. Irving Forman drew the illustrations with more than his customary skill. Romayne Ponleithner edited the manuscript. My wife, Gwyneth, gave unstinted attention to points of style and accuracy. The errors and obscurities are my own.

HAROLD BARGER

Contents

List of Tables

List of Charts

Part One

Historical

Chapter 1

The Public Aspects of the Banking Business

> *I would say that banking appears to most*
> *people as one of the most inexplicable busi-*
> *nesses in which human beings engage.*
> —Governor RANSOM
>
> *". . . you said nothing of the cheque,"*
> *pleaded the dean. "I don't suppose I did,"*
> *said Mrs. Arabin. "I thought that cheques*
> *were like any other money; but I shall*
> *know better for the future."*
> —ANTHONY TROLLOPE,
> The Last Chronicle of Barset

From the earliest times the business of banking has invited public concern on one score or another. Originally concern stemmed from the fact that the failure of a bank could cause far more—and more widespread—distress and disorganization than the failure of any other type of business. Especially was this true of banks of issue whose "bills of credit" circulated from hand to hand, but losses suffered by depositors could also be a serious matter.

To be sure, neither banknotes nor checks drawn against bank deposits were legal tender; but this fact was no real help. The power of the individual to protect himself by refusing to accept payment in these commonly-used media, and to insist on receiving coin, was seldom exercised and did not lessen appreciably the desirability of having banks that were sound. In the United States holders of banknotes have been secure against loss through default since the Civil War, when special legislation was passed to protect national banknotes, and state banks gave up their issues. Bank depositors received similar protection when federal deposit insurance was introduced in 1933. The rocky road whereby bank failure was rendered innocuous is a fascinating story, but its interest lies in the past. The safety of banks against risk of default may now, at least in western countries, be taken as assured. That problem is solved.

The Creation and Destruction of Purchasing Power

As the nineteenth century advanced, public concern over banks developed on quite other grounds—grounds that still exist. For we came gradually to realize that, in the course of furnishing the promises to pay by which we all live, the banks unwittingly exercise tremendous power for good or evil. When they lend, they create purchasing power; when they contract their lending, they destroy it. How much purchasing power do we need? Too much causes rising prices and inflation; too little leads business to stagnate. How can we make sure that the banks create just the right amount of purchasing power, neither too much nor too little? With this problem we are still wrestling.

The topic of this book is the far-reaching social consequences of the creation and destruction of purchasing power by banks. Public concern first arose from the periodic general suspension of specie payments, as in 1837–1839 and again in 1857. Such suspensions perhaps should have been, but were not in fact, treated as defaults: the banks remained open for business, and eventually resumed redemption of their paper. Accompanied by very high rates of interest and panic conditions, these occurrences were early identified with the overissue of bank paper, i.e., the excessive creation of purchasing power. Yet it did not seem that individual banks could well be blamed, for even the most conservative and apparently well-managed institutions succumbed at such times to the same disease that plagued the notorious "wildcat banks" of the western frontier.

Such panics were an extreme manifestation of what has since been called the "inherent instability of credit." Remedies have indeed been sought in many different directions, but the taming of paper money has proved a more difficult enterprise than was at first supposed. It would be premature even now to claim that its domestication has been achieved. In most countries a partial solution was found through the gradual emergence of a sort of superbank, known as a central bank. Because of what were popularly thought to have been unfortunate experiences with the First and Second Banks, the United States was slow to imitate these experiments, but it eventually did so in 1914 with the establishment of the Federal Reserve System. To what extent the System has solved the problems of credit instability, and whether or not it is capable of solving them completely, are the major questions to which this book is addressed.

Accordingly, Part I (Chapters 1–8) is a review of the origins of central banking in the United States and a study of the development of credit policy under the Federal Reserve System. Part II (Chapters 9–16) sets forth what seem to me to be the main lessons of this experience and discusses the leading controversial issues to which it has given rise. It is sometimes helpful to the reader for an author to disclose the main directions of his thinking at the outset. In the few brief paragraphs which follow I shall try to summarize my argument.

Is Central Banking the Answer?

Let me say at once that I agree with majority opinion that central banking in one form or another, necessarily involving administrative discretion in the management of credit, is the most hopeful approach to a solution of our problems in this area. I agree with the majority in holding that the general line and direction which institutional development has taken is a sound one. Among those who share this viewpoint, there remain, of course, wide divergences of opinion as to just how much can eventually be achieved through central banking, and to just how much progress toward that potential of achievement the Federal Reserve System may fairly lay claim. Yet from the very beginnings of central banking a noteworthy current of dissent has found expression. Claiming kin with the economic liberals of the eighteenth century, the writers in this tradition have argued for a monetary constitution that would eliminate the need for the exercise of discretion by any central authority.

In this tradition are to be found alike the exponents of "free banking" of early last century, the adherents of an "automatic gold standard" in more recent times, and in our own day the advocates of "100% money" and similar nostrums. In an earlier age the dissenters decried the need for a central bank, or attacked it as an irresponsible monopoly—which in Europe it very often was. Today in this country they appeal to experience with the Federal Reserve System as proof that central banking cannot achieve what it promises. The strength of their position is that they attack concentration of power— albeit concentration in a public body—and the possibilities of uncertainty and disorder that can follow an abuse or misuse of administrative discretion. But in truth the tradition of opposition to central banking rests, in its modern expression, upon nostalgia for an era long since departed—the era that preceded the coming of paper money. The fatal weakness of this opposition is that today no conceivable monetary constitution could eliminate the need for the exercise of discretion, except through the total abolition of banking— an attempt to set the clock back which even the most extreme opponents of centralized control have hesitated to advocate. Indeed, even so drastic a measure might not achieve the desired result. European experience in the sixteenth century suggests that, although free from the worst excesses of inflation and deflation of which paper money is capable, in behavior even a purely metallic currency may fall well short of the ideal.

The viewpoint of this study is that in the management of money discretion is a necessary evil, inherent in paper money if paper money is not itself to produce worse evils. Yet discretionary control can take many different forms and be pursued in widely varying degrees. As we shall see, the design of an efficient and workable system of monetary control, embodying no more discretion than strictly necessary, is a complex and controversial task.

The lessons of our central-banking experience, analyzed in Part II of this book, therefore begin with a justification of the majority (or orthodox) view that a monetary authority, possessing wide discretion, is a necessary element if paper money is to be made to work. I have called the dissenters on this issue Nihilists, because they believe that central banking is undesirable and unnecessary, and would abolish it altogether. Having disposed of this minority view in Chapter 10, I turn in the later chapters of Part II to the more interesting question, what should be the scope of central banking, granted it is to exist. Among the majority, who agree that money needs managing, wide divergences of course exist as to what instruments are necessary for its management, and how they should be used. It is here, I believe, that our experience with central banking, and especially with the Federal Reserve System, can throw much useful light. We need to inquire what are reasonable and desirable objectives for monetary policy in the sort of world in which we live today, whether the System possesses the kind of weapons needed to attain these objectives, what should be the relations between the System and the Treasury Department, and above all how monetary policy should be related to fiscal policy. On all these questions Federal Reserve experience has something to say.

Some Prejudices and a Point of View

Some doctrinal positions taken in this book, and the evidence for them, will become entirely clear to the reader only when he arrives at the later chapters, especially those in Part II. Nonetheless, a preliminary sketch of the way I believe money works may be useful at this point. In view of the prevailing confusion, I would hesitate to claim merit either as a Keynesian or an anti-Keynesian. Yet much of the most convenient—not to say the standard—terminology and taxonomy for the discussion of monetary problems derives from Keynes' chief work, *The General Theory of Employment, Interest and Money;* in this sense "we are all Keynesians" by sheer necessity. The Keynesian rubrics and concepts are now firmly embedded in conventional discussion: their employment, here as elsewhere, is by no means to be taken as endorsement of particular theoretical positions or policy recommendations to be found in the *General Theory.*

Historically, central bankers have been concerned about and influenced by many different policy criteria, but within the past thirty years, especially in this country, they have become more and more exclusively concerned with the effect of their policies on the state of business, or the level of business activity. There is perhaps no more difficult and complex question in this area than the precise mechanism by which and the degree to which, in given institutional surroundings, the monetary authority can influence business activity. I shall here outline the framework which seems to me to make sense, in the light of our own experience.

The classical analysis suggested by the Quantity Theory runs as follows. The central bank can vary the quantity of money (which let us define as checking accounts, i.e., demand deposits, plus currency outside banks). This it does by encouraging or discouraging commercial banks from seeking accommodation (use of discount rate), and by buying or selling assets in the open market. Thereby it raises or lowers the cash reserves of the commercial banks. But the commercial banks vary the amount of assets they hold, by lending to customers or by purchase in the open market, in response to the state of their reserves. The volume of demand deposits varies with the amount of commercial-bank assets, since whenever banks acquire an asset they create a deposit in favor of the seller, and vice versa. Moreover, currency outside banks varies with demand deposits. Hence—so the argument runs—the central bank can control demand deposits plus currency outside banks, i.e., the amount of money. But an increase in the amount of money will raise commodity prices (according to the Quantity Theory) and increase profits, since costs (factor prices) do not rise immediately. Levels of employment and business activity will be higher in consequence. Conversely, a cut in the amount of money will lower commodity prices and the level of business.

On the strictly practical side this analysis failed to jibe with experience. For instance, the quantity of money might increase without any corresponding effect upon commodity prices or business activity, as happened during the Great Depression when the nexus seemed completely shattered. And, apart from a mere appeal to the Quantity Theory, the mechanism whereby more money was supposed to raise commodity prices remained quite vague.

By importing the rate of interest into the analysis, Wicksell, Robertson, and others took a considerable step forward. The full significance of this advance had to await Keynes' *General Theory*. To summarize briefly: the increase in the quantity of money lowers the rate of interest. This it does because banks are more liquid and more willing to lend, or (which is really the same thing) people's preference for illiquid assets rather than money can be overcome only by diminishing the yield on the former (in accordance with their "liquidity preference" schedule). Next, a decline in the rate of interest encourages investment spending, and thereby total spending. (Total spending = gross national product (GNP) = investment spending plus consumer spending plus government spending for goods and services.) Furthermore, increments of investment spending raise consumer spending (via the "multiplier"), and increments of consumer spending raise investment spending (via the "accelerator"), so that the expansion tends to feed on itself or cumulate. Reverse statements apply to a decline in the volume of money. If more money fails to increase spending (as it failed during the Great Depression), either preference for liquidity is so extreme that the rate of interest fails to decline; or, if the rate of interest declines, entrepreneurial pessimism is so great that investment fails to respond.

But the *General Theory* does not go far enough. Couched in terms of "the" rate of interest, it fails to distinguish adequately between short- and long-term interest rates, and between the cost of borrowing to the government and to private industry. Traditionally, central banks buy little but government paper, and both they and commercial banks operate primarily in the short-term market. If arbitrage were effective, and particularly if risk premiums did not vary greatly from one period to another, this might not matter much: changes in short-term rates and rates on government paper would communicate themselves rather rapidly and smoothly to the market for other types of capital, e.g., long-term corporate obligations. But this does not happen. For instance, during the Great Depression short-term rates fell to very low levels through central-bank action, but long-term rates, both for public and for private borrowers, remained high. Accordingly, the failure of the increased quantity of money to expand spending can be explained equally well in either fashion. (1) We may say that the preference for liquidity was so extreme that arbitrage from the short- to the long-term market failed to produce a fall in the long-term rate, and (arguing that the long-term rate is critical for investment spending) we conclude that entrepreneurs simply were not offered capital cheap enough. Alternatively, (2) believing with Hawtrey that short-term rates powerfully influence investment in working capital, and observing the very low level to which such rates declined during the Great Depression, we conclude that entrepreneurial pessimism was at the root of the trouble.

Plainly, as an explanation of the failure of monetary policy to have any observable impact in inducing recovery from the Great Depression, the two possibilities envisaged are by no means mutually exclusive, and each may contain some truth. Yet evidence accumulates that long-term rather than short-term investment is responsive to the rate of interest. Here indeed lies a dilemma both for theory and for policy. The traditional contact between money and business —via bank lending—is essentially short term in character. Open-market operations by the central bank, too, are customarily confined to short maturities and to prime risks; even when made, medium- or long-term purchases are confined strictly to Treasury obligations. The monetary authority, therefore, as things now stand, has no way of influencing directly the cost of long-term capital to private industry, yet this may be the most critical factor of all in determining the state of business. As things now stand, it must rely on arbitrage: either or both (1) arbitrage from rates of interest on government to rates on private obligations; and (2) arbitrage from rates on short-term private obligations (bank lending) to rates on long-term private borrowing. Our historical review suggests that sometimes this arbitrage could be relied upon to produce the desired result, and that at other times it could not.

To alter the volume of means of payment; to vary the cost and availability of short-term commercial credit—these may be, and upon occasion undoubtedly should be, proximate aims of monetary policy. But they do not begin to describe the nature of the responsibility which rests upon whatever agency is charged with the task of managing our money. Whatever the ultimate objectives desired by society—whether they be stabilization of business activity, stabilization of commodity prices, economic growth, minimization of monetary interferences (neutral money) or some other—the monetary authority must proceed, in the nature of things, by influencing the level of aggregate demand (or current-dollar national product, GNP). To alter the supply of money and to vary the cost and availability to business of short-term credit, are means to control spending—in some situations, effective means; in others, not so effective. Other means also exist: varying the cost and availability of long-term capital, and perhaps even, if necessary, selective credit controls. Unless and until, in given situations, all such means have been used and found ineffective in controlling aggregate spending, it cannot truthfully be said that monetary policy has been tried—still less that it has been found wanting. Certainly, as we shall see, there is no basis in the record for concluding that monetary policy is ineffective or inadequate to reach such desired objectives as those just mentioned.

Chapter 2

Monetary Management Before 1914

> *We must, in a word, use a bank to unbank the banks, to the extent that may be necessary to restore a safe and stable currency— just as we apply snow to a frozen limb in order to restore vitality and circulation.*
>
> —JOHN C. CALHOUN

> *. . . the separation of the financial interests of the government from those of the rest of the country was as impossible of accomplishment as it was dangerous to attempt.*
>
> —MARGARET G. MYERS

At no time in recorded history has the adjustment between the stock of money and the desire to obtain it, or to hold it, been entirely happy. The adjustment—or lack thereof—has at some times shown itself through persistent long-run changes in the level of prices; at other times through short and sharp fluctuations in that level. We need only recall the steady decline in the purchasing power of European currencies that followed the flood of precious metals from "New Spain" during the sixteenth and seventeenth centuries. Or we may remember the sudden changes in the purchasing power of money that accompanied the commercial crises of the eighteenth and nineteenth centuries.

The Instability of Credit

During the whole of the four centuries between 1500 and 1900, the supply of goods increased with only temporary setbacks. The stock of money increased also, but much more erratically. During the first three of the four centuries mentioned, and with minor qualifications even during the nineteenth century, the supply of money was governed directly by the supply of the precious metals; and, in turn, the supply of the precious metals was governed by individual initiative operating along well-known profit-making lines. To the supply of money, that is to say, there was applied no central direction or control. The necessary qualification to this statement when we reach the nineteenth century is, as we shall see, very minor in character. Only after 1900 was the money supply tamed, and perhaps even yet it has not been fully domesticated. The founders of the Federal Reserve System believed that in their time the regulation of the money supply was, and indeed would continue to be even under the regime they were then establishing, almost wholly automatic.

To say that until a few decades ago monetary management was undreamed of is accurate enough. But to say that the supply of money was governed by the supply of the precious metals is of course an oversimplification. As first paper currency and later bank deposits became important, the stock of money expanded far beyond what it would have been, had it continued to consist merely of coin and bullion. But no clear-cut set of rules or well-developed tradition, still less any central direction, governed the relationship between paper on the one hand and metal on the other. Sometimes paper money burgeoned to supply the sinews of war or the greed of a monarch: a more pervasive reason was that banking proved a profitable endeavor to those engaged in it.

The role of credit continually broadened. The ratio of bank money to metallic base increased. But it did not increase steadily. Again and again during the nineteenth century the expansion of bank money led, under a regime of convertibility, to a shortage of metallic reserves, a rise in interest rates, a contraction of paper, and a commercial crisis. Sometimes the crisis amounted to a panic, and the convertibility of the bank money into specie was suspended.

The continued need for such painful readjustments between the stock of money and the desire to hold it shows up most clearly in the rather sharp fluctuations in short-term interest rates that were a feature of nineteenth-century money markets. Just as the price of wheat reflects the balance between supply and demand, so interest rates reflect the balance between the amount of money and the desire to hold it. Variations in the stock of money were so wayward that we may be sure some of the instability in interest rates and in the price level came from the side of supply. Yet it seems likely, if only because of fluctuations in the inducement to invest, that the desire to hold money was also extremely variable, so that the instability came from both sides of the market.

There are, however, two very good reasons for concentrating our attention upon the supply of, rather than upon the demand for money. In the first place, we possess some degree at least of control over the supply of money, and so have some hope of adjusting supply to demand, whereas the reverse procedure is not promising. In the second place, it is believed that changes in people's desire to hold money often are induced by prior changes in its supply. This means there is some hope that a more stable supply of money may contribute to lessened fluctuations in the demand for money.

To clarify these two points let us look at the principles on which the money supply expanded, or occasionally contracted, during the nineteenth century. Consider a banking system with no central bank, i.e., with no reserve supply of cash. In such a system, since banking is a profit-making affair, all banks will tend to be "fully loaned up."[1] In a search for profits, that is to say, all banks will expand their assets and liabilities to the point where their cash ratio is reduced to the minimum consonant with custom or legal requirements. This will be true whether a bank's primary function is to issue notes or to create deposits (although the cash ratio may differ in the two cases).

In such a situation several possible happenings could (and did) increase the supply of cash. First, an increment in the metallic base, from the mines or from abroad, could furnish reserve cash for credit creation. Second, a decline in customary or legal reserve ratios of the banks would have the same effect. Third, the substitution of checking deposits for currency in the hands of the public would work in the same manner. If any one, or a combination, of these things happened, monetary expansion could start. All of these causes were in operation at one time or another during the nineteenth century.

But monetary expansion proceeded by fits and starts. The reins, long too loose, often had suddenly to be tightened. Monetary expansion might outrun the growth of production, so that prices rose,

---

[1] Although this term has become customary, "fully expanded" might be a more accurate description, since banks hold investments as well as loans.

the demand for money increased on this account, and money became tight. Or the stringency might arise through a transfer of funds from areas using bank deposits to areas preferring currency, as commonly occurred in the United States and other countries during the crop-moving season. Or, finally, the "pressure on the money market" might be caused by the accumulation of Treasury deposits in the banks or of currency in the Treasury. How tight money became on such occasions depended upon how sharp was the induced increase in the demand for the existing supply of money, and what were the possibilities of increasing its supply.

The Elements of Monetary Management

We can now identify the elements of monetary management, whether the manager be a central bank or some other institution. First, there is the supply of additional cash—at a price—at moments when the demand for money has suddenly and temporarily swollen. During the nineteenth century such moments were heralded by a sharp rise in short-term interest rates and sometimes by the onset of a commercial crisis involving widespread liquidation. Indeed, the rise in interest rates and the crisis aspects of the situation reflected the absence of any agency prepared to supply (sufficient) additional cash —the absence, that is to say, of a central bank or other "lender of last resort."

The second element of monetary management is the avoidance or offsetting of changes in the supply of cash to the banks and to the public occasioned by the flow of cash into and out of the Treasury. In part this is a problem that the Treasury itself can solve, although today the assistance of the central bank is commonly invoked. Since, by assumption, the Treasury can influence the supply by absorbing or releasing cash, it follows that the Treasury can act as a stabilizing as well as a destabilizing agent, and therefore can itself exercise central-banking functions, i.e., monetary management.

Third, there is the question of continuous control. If last-resort lending is needed in time of crisis, why—it will be asked—was the crisis allowed to develop in the first place? We have seen that the trouble arises because credit tends normally to expand to the point where bank reserves are no more than adequate to meet conventional or legal requirements for banking liquidity, i.e., the point where commercial banks are fully loaned up. The crisis occurs because, this having happened, an increase occurs in the demand for money. Commonly (1) the bank expansion (an increase in the *supply* of money) sets in motion forces leading to an induced increase in the *demand* for money. This cumulative or feedback effect occurs because more money leads to higher prices; higher prices mean larger business profits, increased investment spending, and a greater desire to borrow.

More rarely, (2) once the banks are fully loaned up, an autonomous or accidental increase takes place in the demand for money—as with crop-moving or a Treasury surplus. In either case, if the supply of money is limited, tightness develops in the money market. So long as commercial banks are operated with a view to profits, it is needless to expect them to husband their lending power for emergency use. This being so, the situation under (2), autonomous or accidental increases in the demand for money, can be relieved only through the existence of a lender of last resort.

So far as concerns (1) above, however, the effects of the inherent instability of credit might be obviated if bank expansion could be prevented, or could be prevented from assuming its cumulative character, where prices rise and the *demand for* as well as the *supply of* credit expands. Such continuous control of credit in the interest of stability, as we shall see below at length, constitutes the third and today the main element in monetary management.

The management of money is thus a matter of three more or less distinct elements. The first two may be described as negative or therapeutic: last-resort lending and the neutralizing of autonomous disturbances. They were developed during the nineteenth century. Much later came the third, which we may call positive or prophylactic: continuous control of the volume of credit with a view to avoiding runaway movements resulting from credit's unstable nature.

The avoidance of cumulative expansion and contraction of credit is at once a modest and an ambitious aim. It stemmed during the nineteenth century from a desire to do away with financial panics and the hardships they entailed. This aim proved modest and was not too difficult to attain. Later came the desire, more ambitious, to smooth out the business cycle by monetary means.

For others management had still other meanings. To proponents of the gold standard it meant policies that would smooth out specie movements and prevent sudden and catastrophic drains on the nation's metallic reserve. Still other writers and propagandists have seen in monetary management a means to yet grander objectives: a stable value of money, continuous full employment, maximum use of resources, or a rapid rate of growth.

It will be part of our task to trace these differing concepts, each put forward by a different group among those who have proposed to manage money.

The Origins of Last-Resort Lending

Since commercial banks, being profit-making institutions, ordinarily are fully loaned up, the provision of emergency cash obviously must come from some source outside the commercial-banking system. Today the Federal Reserve Banks stand ready to furnish additional cash when needed. Prior to the establishment of the Federal Reserve System in 1914, there existed three possible sources of additional liquidity: (1) foreign money markets, especially London; (2) the Treasury; and (3) the clearing-house associations, after their establishment beginning in the 1850's. In addition, for a brief spell of years, we must include the First and Second Banks of the United States.

The first examples of practical attempts to relieve commercial banks when under pressure are to be found in the operations of the Treasury, and run right back to Alexander Hamilton. In 1792 the Treasury, not yet three years old, refrained from drawing on its deposit with the Bank of New York in order to help that bank. The nation possessed at that time only six banks, and but one of these was in New York. When Albert Gallatin became Secretary of the Treasury, he followed the precedent set by Hamilton. In 1801 he arranged to make a deposit in the Bank of Columbia in Washington to help it cope with a run, and in 1802 he had the Treasury give similar assistance to the Bank of Pennsylvania. In the latter case it is known that Gallatin suggested that aid also be sought from the First Bank of the United States, which had been founded in 1791. The First Bank undoubtedly made loans upon occasion to the state-chartered banks, and the purpose of their borrowing must have been to ease their cash position: but Hammond thinks the practice was exceptional. Unfortunately the records of the First Bank have not survived, so we cannot be certain. That the Treasury should help out in this fashion, even though the banks were private businesses, must have appeared altogether natural and sensible, for they were its de-positories and it had a lively interest in their operations.[2]

Between the closing of the First Bank in 1811 and the opening of the Second Bank in 1817, state-chartered banks with Treasury deposits grew from 15 to 94, and the total numbers of state banks were of course larger still. Many banks failed during and immediately after the War of 1812, and the notes of many others became inconvertible. During this period the Treasury itself was short of cash, and does not seem to have assisted even the largest and longest-established of the banks. On the contrary, the general suspension of specie payments in 1814 was obviously due in large measure to excessive borrowing from the banks by the Treasury.

In 1817 and again in 1819 the Treasury made deposits in banks in Washington, Georgetown, and Alexandria to help them to maintain specie payments. If the threat of suspension was not general, was the result of overissue, and was confined to a few banks, such measures might prove effective. But in the crisis of 1837 no aid was given and the suspension became general. By that time the Second Bank had lost its federal charter and no longer had charge of the government deposits.[3]

The First and Second Banks and the Treasury

In a well-organized money market with a central bank, lack of correspondence between the flow of funds into and out of the Treasury may be readily neutralized by open-market operations. Prior to the establishment of the Federal Reserve, the Treasury had to rely for the most part on its own devices to prevent its operations from disturbing the money market. Common enough in later years, the Treasury's solicitude for the inconvenience it could cause commercial banks goes back at least to 1792, when Hamilton arranged for an extremely gradual transfer of the Treasury's funds from the three existing commercial banks to the First Bank of the United States.

Probably the First Bank helped to ease Treasury disturbances, but again we have few details. In February 1805 Albert Gallatin

[2] Esther R. Taus, *Central Banking Functions of the U.S. Treasury* (New York: Columbia University Press, 1943), Ch. II; Bray Hammond, *Banks and Politics in America* (Princeton: Princeton University Press, 1957), Chs. 5 and 8.
[3] Margaret G. Myers, *The New York Money Market* (New York: Columbia University Press, 1931), I, 160, 172–73.

wrote to Thomas Willing, president of the Bank, suggesting that he make deposits in (i.e., lend to) the New York banks as a means of affording them relief; but whether the need for relief was caused by Treasury operations, or because the banks had overissued, is not clear.[4]

The Second Bank undoubtedly paid attention to the effects of Treasury operations on the money market. A common problem soon became the accumulation of surplus funds within the Treasury. In 1824, for instance, the Treasury took pains to use the surplus promptly to repay debt.[5]

Serious difficulties occurred as a result of Treasury operations after the Second Bank was no longer available to exercise any central-banking functions. In 1836 the Treasury made difficulties for itself and for the banks by issuing the Specie Circular which prohibited payment for land in state banknotes. In the same year Congress passed an act making illegal the transfer of public funds "for the purpose of accommodating the banks to which the transfers may be made." The circular ensured an increase in specie held by the Treasury and the new law made it illegal to return the specie to banks that might feel the pressure. These measures resulted in an extremely tight situation in 1837, and the crisis of that year was thereby rendered unusually severe.

These examples are enough to show that the early uses of monetary management were negative or therapeutic. The Treasury and the First and Second Banks early felt a responsibility to help out in time of need, and also to refrain themselves from engaging in what today we would call "destabilizing" actions.

The First and Second Banks and the Money Supply

The uses of monetary management for positive or prophylactic purposes came later. The first desire actively to promote stability seems to have originated with concern to prevent the notes of state-chartered banks from losing their convertibility into specie. This purpose does not appear to have been in mind when the First Bank of the United States was established. But experience with the operations of that bank tended to the belief that it restrained overissue by the state banks. Certain it is that the first general suspension by the

[4] Taus, Ch. II; Hammond, Ch. 8.
[5] Myers, p. 161.

state banks occurred during the War of 1812 and was in part occasioned by the war: nevertheless it was the opinion of so competent
an observer as Albert Gallatin that the suspension would not have
occurred, but for the fact that the First Bank was out of business, its
charter having expired the previous year.

Gallatin reviews the statistics of note circulation for the period,
and then proceeds:

> Under these circumstances, the alarm caused by the capture of Wash-
> ington, and the threatened attack on Baltimore, was sufficient to cause
> a suspension of specie payments. It took place at that particular crisis,
> and appears to have originated in Baltimore. The example was im-
> mediately followed in Philadelphia and New-York; and it is indeed
> known, that an attack was apprehended on both those places, and that
> some of the banks of Philadelphia had sent their specie to Lancaster.
> We have stated all the immediate and remote causes within our
> knowledge, which concurred in producing that event; and although the
> effects of a longer continuance of the war cannot be conjectured, it is
> our deliberate opinion, that the suspension might have been prevented,
> at the time it took place, had the former Bank of the United States
> been still in existence. The exaggerated increase of state banks, oc-
> casioned by the dissolution of that institution, would not have occurred.
> That bank would, as before, have restrained within proper bounds, and
> checked their issues: and, through the means of its offices, it would have
> been in possession of the earliest symptoms of the approaching danger.
> It would have put the Treasury Department on its guard; both acting
> in concert, would certainly have been able at least to retard the event;
> and, as the treaty of peace was ratified within less than six months after
> the suspension took place, that catastrophe would have been altogether
> avoided.[6]

The desire to have an agency which might restrain the state banks
was perhaps the main reason for the chartering of the Second Bank.
The existence of a bank the convertibility of whose notes was assured, Calhoun argued in 1816, would enable the Treasury to refuse
dealings with the state banks and would lead the latter—partly by
pressure and partly by example—to resume and subsequently to
maintain the convertibility of their circulation. Later, in 1834, he
reported that the Bank had in fact proved "an indispensable agent
in the restoration [and presumably thereafter in the maintenance]
of specie payments" by the state banks.[7]

[6] Albert Gallatin, *Considerations on the Currency and Banking System of the U.S.*
(Philadelphia: Carey and Lea, 1831), p. 46.
[7] John C. Calhoun, *Works* (New York: Appleton, 1854–60), II, 153–62, 325.

Gallatin was of the same opinion. Writing in 1831 he said:

[The statistics] show, that the Bank of the United States, wherever its operations have been extended, has effectually checked excessive issues on the part of the state banks, if not in every instance, certainly in the aggregate. . . . [Between 1819 and 1829] the whole amount of the paper currency has . . . increased about forty-five, and that portion which is issued by the state banks only twenty-two and a half per cent. We have indeed a proof, not very acceptable perhaps to the bank, but conclusive of the fact, that it has performed the office required of it in that respect. The general complaints, on the part of many of the state banks, that they are checked and controlled in their operations by the Bank of the United States, that, to use a common expression, it operates as a screw, is the best evidence that its general operation is such as had been intended. It was for that very purpose that the bank was established. We are not, however, aware that a single solvent bank has been injured by that of the United States, though many have undoubtedly been restrained in the extent of their operations, much more than was desirable to them. This is certainly inconvenient to some of the banks, but in its general effects is a public benefit to the community.[8]

How was the Second Bank, with neither monopoly of note issue nor much in the way of special privilege, enabled to perform this function? Gallatin's answer is as follows:

The manner in which the Bank checks the issues of the state banks is equally simple and obvious. It consists in receiving the notes of all those which are solvent, and requiring payment from time to time, without suffering the balance due by any to become too large. . . . It is obvious, that it is only by keeping its discounts at a lower rate than those of the state banks, that these can be its debtors; and that it is only by enforcing the payment of the balances, that it can keep them within bounds, and thus regulate the currency. A contrary course will induce the state banks to enlarge their own discounts, and will engender excessive issues, followed by necessary contractions and unavoidable distress. . . . It is only as an additional dealer, with greater funds and facilities than any other, [that it has the power to regulate.][9]

Evidently the ability of the Second Bank to restrain the state banks depended on its willingness to refrain from expanding its discounts when the other banks expanded, that is, to renounce some of the profits which might accrue were it always fully loaned up.

[8] *Considerations*, pp. 82–83.
[9] *Considerations*, p. 84; *Suggestions on the Banks and Currency of the Several United States* (New York: Wiley and Putnam, 1841), pp. 34, 91.

Such a policy would yield it a measure of control in normal times, and also furnish reserve lending power in time of crisis. For success a further necessary condition was of course its size: although less than half the nation's total circulation, the Second Bank's note issue was far larger than that of any single state bank.

As the other banks overissued, the failure of the Second Bank to do likewise would ensure that they lost specie to it through what today would be called "the clearing." Nicholas Biddle explained that this mechanism was enforced by a policy on the part of the Bank of paying out only its own notes, and returning the notes of other banks for redemption. This was of course precisely the practice that led to complaints by the state banks, and caused Senator Benton and others to accuse the Bank of "disparaging" the notes of the state banks. What was to prevent the state banks from retaliating by the adoption of a similar policy? In the first place, by assumption, they had expanded their note circulation while the Second Bank had not, so that relatively more of their notes would be held by the latter as hostages than vice versa. In the second place, I suspect that a preference on the part of the public for notes of the Second Bank made it difficult for them to retaliate: the existence of such a preference would be natural in view of the country-wide acceptability of the Second Bank's notes, and is suggested by the more rapid growth of the latter in comparison with the state banks' circulation, upon which Gallatin remarks in the above quotation. However, if the Second Bank could tighten the money market in this fashion, it could and did ease the market on occasion by keeping state bank notes in its vaults and refraining from presenting them for redemption for the time being.[10]

We have here the elements of a deliberate regulation of the money market with some criterion of stability in mind. The criterion in this case was a rather modest and none too definite one: to prevent such overexpansion as might lead to a *general* lapse into inconvertibility (such as had occurred in 1814 and was to occur again in 1837), yet at the same time to allow credit to expand with the growth of the country as far as was compatible with the regular maintenance of specie payments. During the period of the Second Bank's central-banking activity (1817–1833), the nation was on a

[10] Hammond, pp. 307, 308; Ralph C. H. Catterall, *The Second Bank of the United States* (Chicago: University of Chicago Press, 1903), Ch. XVIII.

limping bimetallic—in fact, a silver—standard, since gold was undervalued at the mint.[11] The highest objective of monetary management by the Second Bank was the effective maintenance and smooth working of this standard. Compared with the conflicting management objectives and proliferation of instruments of central-banking control since World War I, the picture of Mr. Biddle and his Bank has a simple but undeniable charm.

The record suggests that down to the First World War the Treasury did not engage in deliberate regulation of the money market with a view to stability or the avoidance of crises. Instead it left the market pretty much to its own devices, interfering only when critical conditions developed. The Treasury, that is, confined its central-banking functions to mitigating the money-market effects of its own, often extensive, operations and of other autonomous disturbances (such as seasonal pressure), and to occasional last-resort lending. After the Second Bank's wings were clipped in 1833 by the removal of the deposits, there was no central-banking activity in the United States until 1914, except that of an emergency character performed by the Treasury.

Were the First and Second Banks True Central Banks?

The First Bank of the United States was chartered as a result of Alexander Hamilton's submission to Congress in December 1790 of his *Report on a National Bank*. Its prime purpose was, as Hamilton makes clear, its prospective usefulness to the Treasury in transferring public funds. Influence upon the primitive money market of the time, regulatory action to prevent crises, last-resort lending in time of trouble—such central-banking functions were not contemplated or understood. Yet the First Bank alone was the public depository and had branches in more than one city. The exigencies of day-to-day operations soon led it to practice rudimentary central-banking techniques. Its ability to develop such techniques was indeed sharply limited by the absence of a bill market and by the fact that it was prohibited from dealing in the public debt. Moreover, the entire operation was of so experimental a nature, and ideas about reserve ratios were so vague, that the notion of emer-

[11] In minting coins the United States treated 1 ounce of gold as equivalent to 15 ounces of silver, but the ratio in world markets was closer to 1:15½. The mint ratio was changed to 1:16 in 1834.

gency lending power could scarcely arise. During the life of the First Bank, the Treasury itself seems to have been at least as active as the Bank in exercising management functions.

As we have seen, the Second Bank, unlike the First, was established chiefly as a remedy for the currency disorder that followed the War of 1812. In fact, under Nicholas Biddle the Second Bank came to exercise a more conservative lending policy than the state banks, and this fact, coupled with its size and its possession of the Treasury's deposits, made it easy for it to develop a regulatory function.

Yet we should not make too great a claim. The management operations of the Second as of the First Bank were supplemented by —if indeed not secondary to—those of the Treasury. No clear example of last-resort lending in time of crisis is to be found. Modern instruments of monetary policy were of course unknown. Neither Bank varied its discount rate. Instead, publishing no standards for the eligibility of the paper they would accept, it was easy for them to be more or less open-handed according to the situation as they judged it. Thus both banks protected themselves by what was really a form of rationing. No doubt this practice, as with the contemporary Bank of England, discouraged emergency lending by the Banks. For the characteristic feature of a crisis is the large demand for loans—a demand which can be brought within manageable bounds only by raising the price at which credit is supplied. So long as rationing was practiced there was no scope for the emergence of what later became the traditional central-banking doctrine: "Lend freely, if necessary at a high rate."

I am therefore inclined to answer the question, Were the First and Second Banks true central banks? in the negative. No more, of course, was the Bank of England at that period. The Bank of England developed true last-resort lending in the crises of 1848, 1857, and 1866. Had the Second Bank not been killed, it probably would have followed a similar development. The makeshifts to which the Treasury was forced to resort, and the use of clearing-house certificates as a crisis measure, would no doubt have been rendered unnecessary. Once last-resort lending had become clearly understood, the general regulation of credit would no doubt have followed without difficulty, for had it not already begun in relation to state note issues during the lifetime of the Second Bank?

Central-Banking Functions after the Demise of the Second Bank

During the eighty years between 1833 and 1914 the three pressing problems of monetary management—alleviation of stringency
caused by Treasury operations, seasonal variation in the supply of
currency, and last-resort lending in time of crisis—were solved in
a partial and very inefficient manner without the help of any institution that could be called a central bank. Commonly the Treasury
possessed specie or other legal-tender currency that it could and
did supply to the market when necessary. This it did by making
deposits in commercial banks or by repaying Treasury obligations.
And in time of crisis the clearing-house associations created emergency cash in the shape of clearing-house certificates that, although
not legal tender, proved acceptable to banks in satisfying their
needs for reserve money. I shall now review the use made of these
devices prior to the establishment of the Federal Reserve System in
1914. It will be apparent that the devices in question proved entirely
inadequate to handle the problem. In particular, the Treasury came
to feel a responsibility which it was increasingly unable to discharge.

Released from such control as the Second Bank had exercised,
the state-chartered banks rapidly expanded their note issues between
1834 and 1837. In July 1836 the Treasury issued the celebrated
Specie Circular, requiring payment in specie for all sales of public
land. The intention was to encourage the movement of coin to the
West, but the distribution of the federal surplus in the early months
of 1837, chiefly to the more populous states, had just the opposite
effect. In the Spring of 1837, hoarding of specie became common
and general suspension followed, beginning with the New York
banks on May 10. So far from being able to ease the crisis, the
Treasury itself was now in a difficult situation, for it could not legally
make deposits in nonspecie-paying banks, nor could it accept irredeemable paper in making withdrawals. Among the 86 banks in
which the Treasury owned deposits, only four maintained specie
payments throughout the crisis.[12]

These evils led some to advocate a total prohibition of paper
currency. At the very least,

---

[12] "Report on the Finances, September, 1837," in *Reports of the Secretary of the
Treasury* (Washington, D.C.: John C. Rives, 1851), IV, 10, 18, 57–58.

nothing but gold and silver should be received in payment of dues to the government. The state banks would then be obliged to provide a sufficient fund of specie to meet the demands of the merchants having payments to make to government. This would force them to diminish the amount of notes in circulation. The government receiving and paying nothing but gold and silver, the people generally would begin to distinguish between paper and specie—between cash and credit.[13]

However, the immediate concern of the Administration was less with the state of the currency and the regulation of credit than with the safety and transferability of Treasury balances. The establishment of yet another federal bank was politically out of the question. An extension of the principle of the Specie Circular seemed the only course open. In September 1837 President Van Buren proposed to Congress that the federal government should collect, keep, and disburse its own funds exclusively in specie, without exception, even for the notes of specie-paying banks. This plan came to be known as the "Independent Treasury."

The struggle over this proposal was long and bitter. Meanwhile, dissatisfaction with the state banks as depositories led the Administration to revert to some extent to the primitive plan whereby funds were left with collectors, upon whom drafts were made directly.[14] Finally in July 1840 Congress established the first Independent Treasury.

From Van Buren's standpoint the victory must have seemed an empty one. Within a few months the Whigs, who now came into office, had reverted to the practice of keeping public funds in state banks. The case against the Independent Treasury was eloquently stated by Gallatin:

> Whenever the revenue shall exceed the expenditure . . . if the excess should . . . be considerable, the drain of specie this would occasion, might indeed break any bank, and render the suspension of specie payments universal. It cannot be perceived, in what manner the measure can, in any way whatever, have a tendency towards restoring a general sound currency. It is utterly impossible to substitute, otherwise than very gradually, a currency consisting exclusively of the precious metals, for that which now pervades the whole country. . . . Any great ac-

[13] William M. Gouge, *Short History of Paper Money and Banking: Inquiry into the Principles of the System* (Philadelphia: T. W. Ustick, 1833), p. 113.

[14] For instance, in November 1838, Jesse Hoyt, Collector of the Port of New York, had $65,296.24 in his possession—presumably in coin in an ordinary office safe ("Report on the Finances, December, 1838," in *Reports of the Secretary of the Treasury*, IV, 193, 227.

cumulation of the public monies . . . if consisting of gold and silver accumulated in the Treasury chest . . . is an active capital taken from the people and rendered unproductive.[15]

In August 1841 the Act of the previous year establishing the Independent Treasury was repealed, though the inconvenience of relying on the state banks for the safekeeping of public funds had not diminished. Accordingly, bills to establish a national bank were introduced by Clay and others, apparently with the approval of President Tyler. Yet a bill to set up a national bank, not unlike the Second Bank but with strict rules about specie reserve and lending power, was vetoed by the President on constitutional grounds.

In 1846, however, the Democrats, once again in office, decided on a second experiment with the Independent Treasury (Act of August 6). From this point until the Civil War the collection, safekeeping, and disbursement of public funds were on a strictly specie basis. Initially the practical difficulties were considerable:

> Custody of the money is . . . forced upon [disbursing officers] without any provision for its convenience, or even safety. . . . If they adopt the usual and customary mode of keeping and transferring money [i.e., depositing it in a bank] they violate the law. If they undertake themselves its custody and carriage, they incur great risk and responsibility. The actual carriage of coin from place to place, in the same town, is burdensome, especially in those southern parts where silver is the coin chiefly in use. . . . The insecurity of the actual custody of the public money—confided, as it is, at several points, to the vigilance and fidelity of one assistant treasurer, and he inadequately compensated—is a subject which should attract the serious attention of Congress.[16]

Gradually vaults were built in all major centers, and by an Act of 1857 all disbursing officers were required to keep their funds on deposit with these subtreasuries.

Disturbance to the money market was a more serious matter. In periods of deficit, the Treasury would of course borrow in the market, but unless it overborrowed, no unwelcome accumulation of specie would occur. As Gallatin had pointed out, difficulties might rather be expected in periods of surplus when, unless debt were promptly repaid, specie drained from circulation or from bank reserves would accumulate in the Treasury, causing tightness in

---

[15] *Suggestions*, pp. 87–88.

[16] "Report on the Finances, December 1849," in *Reports of the Secretary of the Treasury*, VII, 20–21.

the money market. The difficulty proved to be particularly acute in years of surplus, but also showed itself when existing debt had to be refinanced: the modern "roll over" was unknown, and the practice was for the Treasury to raise fresh money in the market well before existing securities matured, thus locking up cash for weeks or months.

For a few years the system worked smoothly, largely because the Mexican War created fresh debt, but in the early 1850's surpluses led to the situation which Gallatin had foreseen. The relatively small federal debt of around $60 million had now to be repaid, whether or not it had reached maturity. Fortunately an Act of 1849 permitted the Secretary of the Treasury to buy bonds in the market, if necessary at a premium.

The European crisis of 1848, which in England led to the suspension of the Bank Charter Act, did not result in noticeable difficulties on this side of the Atlantic. But the crisis of 1856–1857, fed by railroad speculation, was by contrast quite severe. The role of the Treasury has been debated. In 1856 Secretary Guthrie and in 1857 Secretary Cobb used the Treasury surplus to buy bonds with the intention of easing the money market, but it has been said that they did so too far in advance of the crisis, thus feeding the flames of bank expansion.[17] On October 13, 1857, the New York City banks suspended specie payments. By the time the panic occurred, the Treasury's ability to supply cash had been exhausted. Resort was now made for the first time to an issue of clearing-house certificates.

The New York Clearing House had been established in 1853. In accordance with a proposal by Gallatin,[18] the participating banks had deposited specie with the Bank of America, as agent for the Clearing House, in return for which they had received clearing-house deposit certificates of relatively large denomination, to be used for convenience in settling interbank indebtedness. In time of crisis, by an obvious extension of this procedure, the managing

---

[17] David Kinley, *The Independent Treasury of the United States* (New York: Crowell, 1893), p. 179. In claiming virtue for the Independent Treasury, Guthrie argued that the accumulation of currency in the Treasury as a result of growing revenues during a business expansion would have a stabilizing effect on the economy: see *Report of the Secretary of the Treasury for 1856*, 34th Cong. 3rd Sess., Ex. Doc. No. 3 (Washington, D.C.: O. P. Nicholson, 1856), p. 32. Kinley, reviewing experience down to 1890, concluded that the over-all stabilizing effect was in practice negligible.
[18] *Suggestions*, p. 64.

committee of the Clearing House could readily issue such certificates, not against specie, but against a note executed by a commercial bank. This was done for the first time in 1857, and again on
frequent occasions until the establishment of the Federal Reserve
System in 1914. The New York banks to which clearing-house loan
certificates were issued paid 6% for the accommodation, and they
used the certificates as reserve money or for settling balances due
to other banks. The use of the certificates, while it enabled the
banks to stay open, did not prevent a general suspension of specie
payments; nor, on account of their novelty and large denomination,
were the certificates suitable for general circulation among the
public.

In 1857 the Clearing House does not seem to have made any
conditions for granting assistance, but after the crisis was over it
asked the New York banks to pledge themselves as a regular practice to hold specie of at least 20% of their deposits as well as of
their notes in circulation, a figure raised to 25% in 1861. When
the device was used again in 1860, the Clearing House demanded
collateral in the shape of government obligations or bills payable
by a bank. Further, the banks were required to furnish daily statements of condition, to agree to part with specie if assessed by the
Clearing House, and to bear a proportionate share of any losses.
These obligations, although temporary in character, were more onerous than those imposed today by most central banks.

Although the role of the Independent Treasury in the crisis of
1857 was equivocal, and the need for emergency cash was supplied
by the New York Clearing House, one improvement over 1837 must
be noted: the Treasury was able throughout to meet its own obligations in specie, as it had not been able to do in 1837. This may
have helped the general resumption of specie payments by the
banks late in 1857 and early in 1858.

The Civil War brought an end to note issues by state-chartered
banks, for Congress subjected them to a prohibitive tax. Their place
was taken by Treasury notes ("greenbacks") and notes of the new
national banks. The former were a direct obligation of the Treasury
and the latter were secured by the deposit of specified issues of
Treasury bonds. The obligation to redeem in specie had now to be
met by the Treasury instead of the banks. For the extreme elasticity
that had led so often to overissue there was substituted a virtual

ceiling on paper-money circulation—a ceiling imposed by statute. By contrast, deposit banking, growing yearly more important, remained a very elastic affair.

During the Civil War the operation of the Independent Treasury was suspended. The Treasury's need to borrow from the banks made it inevitable that they would once more be used for the deposit of public funds. Inconvertibility—of banknotes and Treasury notes alike—made it impossible to maintain all Treasury receipts and disbursements on a specie basis; however, customs revenue continued to be collected, and debt interest to be paid in specie.

The course of the wartime inflation has been often described and analyzed and need not be treated here. After the surrender of the Confederacy, the Treasury, with a view to eventual resumption, concentrated on reducing the discount at which the new greenbacks and national banknotes circulated. Under President Grant, Secretary Boutwell sold large amounts of gold with the intention of reducing its premium in the market. Since gold did not circulate and could not become a basis for additional currency, and since the gold was paid for in currency, the result was to tighten the money market. Sometimes, however, the Secretary felt he had overdone the contraction, in which case he redeposited the currency in banks, issued additional greenbacks, or bought bonds for redemption.

With the rise of grain production, especially for export to Europe, the need for seasonal variation in the volume of currency (as distinct from currency plus bank deposits) became acute. Secretary Boutwell described the problem:

> The crops cannot be moved generally by the aid of bank balances, checks, and letters of credit, but only by bank notes and United States notes paid at once to the producers. This money finds its way speedily into the channels of trade and to the commercial centres; but if it be allowed to remain for general use, after the reason for its issue has ceased, the volume of currency would be increased permanently and the year following the same process would be repeated with the same results, and thus would the country depart more and more widely from the policy of resumption.
>
> The problem is to find a way of increasing the currency for moving the crops and diminishing it at once when that work is done. This is a necessary work, and, inasmuch as it cannot be confided to the banks, where, but in the Treasury Department, can the power be reposed?
>
> While the currency revenue was in excess of the currency expenses

it was practicable to accumulate large balances in the Treasury during the summer, to be used, if necessary, in the purchase of bonds in the autumn, thereby meeting the usual demand for currency at that season of the year.

Hereafter such accumulations must be made by the sale of gold, and the sale of gold in large quantities during the summer, when business is the least active, may not always be consistent with the best interests of the country. Reliance cannot, therefore, be placed upon the ability of the Treasury to accumulate a currency balance each year for the purpose indicated.[19]

Nevertheless it became the general practice for Secretaries of the Treasury to hoard currency in the Spring and release it in the Fall— a practice not discontinued until the foundation of the Federal Reserve System in 1914.

Linked with, but more serious than, the seasonal problem was the inability of the Treasury to supply anything like the volume of currency required at cyclical peaks in business if panics were to be prevented. At the height of the panic of 1873, after the failure of Jay Cooke and Company in September, call rates went to 1½% *per day*. Secretary Richardson proceeded to buy bonds, but the action came late and the relief was slight. As in 1856–1857 the New York banks resorted to the use of clearing-house loan certificates, which were issued up to 75% of the value of bills, or the par value of bonds, pledged as collateral. The Clearing House charged interest at 7% and received the power to equalize legal-tender reserves among banks, by assessment or otherwise. These conditions were again far more onerous than a central bank would have imposed. The New York plan was imitated by clearing houses in other cities.

Resumption of specie payments was achieved on January 1, 1879, through a modest contraction in greenback currency, at a time when the nation's demand for currency was expanding with the growth of the economy. The required reduction was easily made by using Treasury surpluses to retire greenbacks instead of bonds.

In the panic of 1884, Secretary Folger arranged for the prepayment of debt which was soon to mature, and in New York clearing-house certificates were again issued to banks desiring them. The Treasury was seldom able to make sufficient currency available in time of crisis, and what it could do depended largely upon the acci-

[19] *Annual Report of the Secretary of the Treasury for 1872,* p. xxi.

dent of its situation at the time. Clearing-house certificates, on the other hand, could be furnished as needed and practically without limit: they satisfied the need for bank reserves, although they could not circulate. Such certificates had in fact now become a standard remedy, and were used successively in the crises of 1890, 1893, and 1907.

As the 1880's advanced, federal surpluses continued to accumulate. Coinage of silver under the Act of 1878 somewhat eased the situation, but increasingly the Treasury was forced into bond purchases as a means of returning currency to circulation. Moreover, as interest rates declined, the Treasury had to pay substantial premiums for its bonds. Secretary Manning complained:

> The present premium on the four and a half per cents of 1891 is about 11 per cent. The present premium on the four per cents of 1907 is about 28 per cent. To continue our present surplus taxation, and to employ its proceeds now or for some years to come in giving to the bondholder any such, or still higher, premiums by anticipatory purchase of those bonds before they are due and payable at par, is a fiscal policy . . . unnecessary, extravagant, and merciless to the industrial toilers of our land, from whose earnings, profits, or capital are deducted and taken all the revenues of the Treasury. . . .[20]

By 1888 the Treasury surplus was so large that it could not be disbursed through bond purchases without risk of diminishing the national banknote circulation which was based on bonds. The law required that customs revenue be deposited directly in the Treasury in specie. Although internal revenue might legally be deposited in banks (secured by collateral pledged with the Treasury), such deposits had been practically confined to the proceeds of Treasury borrowing. Transfers of currency from the Treasury to banks for deposit were of questionable legality, for customs revenue was not segregated within the Treasury. The situation was equivocal and Secretaries of the Treasury interpreted the extent of their discretion variously. To deal with the surplus of 1887–1888, Secretary Fairchild largely increased deposits in national banks and relaxed requirements for collateral.[21]

By the time the Baring crisis broke in London in November 1890,

[20] Annual Report of the Secretary of the Treasury for 1886, I, xli.
[21] Taus, pp. 80–82. See also Annual Report of the Secretary of the Treasury for 1902, pp. 67–68.

the Treasury, which had been buying bonds all Fall, had no surplus cash with which to ease the market.[22] During the years of severely depressed trade which followed, the Treasury experienced deficits. Moreover, the temporary cessation of capital imports and the agitation for free coinage of silver led to the export of gold, much of which was sought from the Treasury. Because of the deficits, the Treasury became dependent upon the New York banks, both for operating funds and for gold. In the renewed panic of 1893, as in 1890, the Treasury was again without spare cash with which to ease the market. Bank failures were numerous. In February 1895 the Treasury's helplessness reached an extreme: the intervention of President Cleveland with a group of New York bankers headed by J. P. Morgan and H. P. Belmont was necessary before the Treasury was able to sell an issue of 4% 30-year bonds.

The period of deficits came to an end in 1899, after which buoyant revenues produced an overflowing Treasury and again posed the perennial problem of how to return currency to circulation. Successive Secretaries now found themselves more crippled than ever by legal restrictions remaining from the pre-Civil War Independent Treasury system. Congress still refused to change the law: as a result great ingenuity had to be devoted to circumventing it. For instance the effectiveness of bond purchases in supplying the market with currency was limited by the need for bonds as collateral for national banknotes and as security for government deposits in national banks. Congress refused Secretary Shaw permission to make unsecured deposits, even after special examination of the banks concerned, but in 1902 he found a measure of relief by ruling that state and municipal, as well as federal, obligations might be used as collateral for Treasury deposits.[23] He obtained further relief by announcing that where such deposits were secured by federal obligations they would no longer be subject to reserve requirements under the National Banking Act. Although of doubtful legality, these rulings were not challenged.

Past practice had allowed internal revenue receipts to accumulate in depository banks before transfer to the Treasury in the shape of currency, but doubt existed as to whether in case of need cur-

[22] As an ironic consequence Secretary Windom was able to claim convincingly that this panic at least was not due, as had been alleged, to locking up funds in the Treasury: see *Annual Report of the Secretary of the Treasury for 1890*, pp. xxxi–xxxii.
[23] *Annual Report of the Secretary of the Treasury for 1903*, p. 127.

rency could legally be moved in the reverse direction, i.e., from the Treasury to the banks. To enable this to be done, yet still show some respect for tradition, since here too Congress refused to amend the law, Secretary Shaw segregated these receipts in the Treasury during the Spring and Summer of 1903, depositing them in the Fall against expected stringency. He further announced his willingness to advance currency to banks on the security of government bonds. Still another device, introduced by Secretary Shaw in 1906, was to make deposits against gold imports as soon as the gold was shipped from the place of origin abroad, so that the Treasury bore the interest cost.[24] Admittedly these measures conflicted with the spirit of the Independent Treasury, were mere palliatives, and did little to lessen the need for thoroughgoing reform. Yet judgment has not always been kind. For example, Parker Willis makes these points and then criticizes Secretary Shaw vigorously, and as I think most unfairly, for allowing the Treasury to "play the market":[25] rather, Shaw should be praised for making the most of what little elbow room Congress gave him.

In 1907 Congress, at last relenting, confirmed the Secretary's right to specify the collateral required of depository banks, and permitted public funds without distinction (including customs receipts) to be deposited in national banks. A year later Congress confirmed the Secretary's view that no reserve need be required against Treasury deposits.

Thus at long last, partly through administrative ingenuity and partly through legislation, the Independent Treasury was buried, and the Treasury Department furnished with means to prevent its fiscal operations from disturbing the money market. These various changes also implied some leeway in offsetting disturbances originating elsewhere, such as the seasonal drain of currency into and out of circulation. Yet, as the panic of 1907 showed, it still was not possible for the Treasury—without large additional powers that might be better given to a central bank—to furnish adequate emergency supplies of liquidity to the market, i.e., to develop into an effective lender of last resort. It was one thing to avoid the locking up of currency, or to husband currency in March against an easily

---

[24] Annual Report of the Secretary of the Treasury for 1906, pp. 37–40.
[25] H. Parker Willis, The Federal Reserve System (New York: Ronald Press, 1923), p. 32.

anticipated drain in September. It was quite another to be able to furnish the really large supplies of additional cash needed to stave off a panic: such supplies just were not yet available. Issues of greenbacks and national banknotes were narrowly limited by law (the celebrated "inelasticity" of the currency), and it would have required quite extraordinary self-discipline (and some degree of deflation) for the Treasury to have locked up enough cash in ordinary times, under existing currency laws, to deal with such a panic as that of 1907. The need for additional bank cash was indeed satisfied by clearing-house certificates on such occasions, but additional currency for general circulation or hoarding by the public did not exist.

The general complaint of successive Secretaries of the Treasury of the period between the demise of the Second Bank and the coming of the Federal Reserve was perhaps most aptly summarized by Secretary Carlisle in 1893:

> While the laws have imposed on the Treasury Department all the duties and responsibilities of a bank of issue, and to a certain extent the functions of a bank of deposit, they have not conferred upon the Secretary any part of the discretionary powers usually possessed by the executive heads of institutions engaged in conducting this character of financial business.[26]

The same judgment is echoed by a more recent critic:

> When money rates were high, when gold was being exported, and in half a dozen other contingencies, the Treasury was expected to step in. It was supposed to supply elasticity for the currency on the one hand and to prevent inflation on the other, to ward off panics and to assist in maintaining prosperity—and all under a law which had as its foremost purpose the complete separation of the Treasury from the money market. Of those powers by which the central banks of other countries assisted the banks, the Treasury possessed none with the possible exception of the purchase of securities. It could not issue notes, rediscount commercial paper, or lend on securities, and so it was put to all sorts of shifts. The wonder is, not that it was obliged to resort to such devious methods, but that it managed to survive at all.[27]

Thus the limited ability of the Treasury to help in time of crisis, and the makeshift character of the clearing-house certificate, made

---

[26] *Annual Report of the Secretary of the Treasury for 1893*, p. lxxiii.
[27] Myers, pp. 390–91.

it ever plainer that drastic reform was needed. But first more palliatives were to be adopted. Clearing-house certificates were useful in
settling balances between banks in the same city, and could be—
and were—used temporarily for bank reserves, releasing vault cash.
But being in large denominations and unfamiliar to the public, they
could not be paid out to depositors for general circulation: more
important, they could not in general be used for settling balances
with out-of-town banks—a serious limitation, at least in New York.
In 1908 Congress passed the Aldrich-Vreeland Act, which permitted
national banks to form local "national currency associations." These
associations were to supply member banks with emergency currency
against the deposit with the Treasury of state and municipal bonds
and—for the first time—commercial paper, up to 75% of the value
deposited. Aldrich-Vreeland currency, essentially an extension of
the clearing-house certificate, was used only once—in 1914 when
the outbreak of war in Europe produced a panic in New York.
Thereafter it was supposed that the elasticity of the Federal Reserve
note issue would be adequate to supply emergency currency, but in
the Fall of 1931 (as we shall see) this proved not to be the case.
Authority to issue Aldrich-Vreeland currency had lapsed June 30,
1915, and liberalization of Federal Reserve issues by the Glass-
Steagall Amendment was achieved only after some months' delay.
But I am running ahead of my story.

The Pyramiding of Bank Reserves and Other Troubles

Since the Civil War, paper currency had consisted of national
banknote issues and greenbacks. But national banknotes were limited in amount by the need to deposit U.S. bonds with the Treasury
to obtain them, and greenback issues were rigidly restricted within
a legal maximum. These limitations on the issue of paper currency
and the growing popularity of the checkbook encouraged commercial banks to expand their facilities for deposit banking.

Even before the Civil War, an elaborate system of correspondent
relationships had grown up between banks, relationships which were
to become a partial substitute for the nationwide branch banking
common in most other countries. Small local banks became customers of larger banks in the nearest city, which in turn became
customers of banks in some metropolitan center, especially New
York. Such correspondent relationships, like branch banking, ful-

filled two purposes: they economized cash reserves and they made possible the collection of out-of-town checks.

Cash was economized because, by depositing part of their cash elsewhere than in their own vaults, out-of-town banks could earn interest on a portion of their reserves, while city banks were furnished with funds to invest—funds which they would not otherwise have possessed. Furthermore, in case of need the country bank could borrow from its city correspondent. The city bank in turn redeposited in New York at least part of the funds it had received from the country bank. To the New York banker these funds appeared to be, but really were not, ideally suited to investment in stock-market call loans. Economizing of cash reserves through pyramiding looked good to the individual banker, but it meant that cash served two or three times over as reserve. As a result the banking system as a whole was not merely fully loaned up, but was—in relation to the available cash—chronically overloaned. A portion of what banks outside New York treated as cash simply was not available in time of crisis, or was available only at the cost of a stock-market collapse. The situation might have been slightly better had the New York banks been able to invest their secondary reserves in commercial paper or short-term governments, but down to World War I and even later the acceptance market was poorly organized and not much short-term public debt existed. But in the absence of sufficient last-resort lending to offset its effects, pyramiding inevitably intensified any crisis that occurred.

Correspondent relationships not only led to the pyramiding of bank reserves: they also facilitated the collection of checks. Suppose the customer of a country bank in Iowa deposited a check drawn on a bank in Louisiana. The Iowa bank would forward the check to its correspondent in Chicago, which in turn would send it to a New York bank, and from there it would travel to a bank in New Orleans, and so to the bank on which it was drawn. If not paid by an actual shipment of currency, the check might be liquidated by the purchase of "exchange," e.g., the New Orleans bank might furnish the country bank on which the check was drawn with a draft on a Chicago bank. Collection charges became an important part of banking revenues.

These correspondent relationships were given legal recognition in the reserve provisions of the National Banking Act. National banks were divided into central reserve city banks (those in New York, Chicago, and St. Louis), reserve city banks (those located in about fifty other cities), and country banks. Those in the first group were required to maintain a reserve of currency in vault of at least 25% of their deposits. The second group also had to maintain a reserve of 25%, but might keep half of it on deposit with the first group. The third group was required to keep reserves of only 15%, three-fifths of which might be kept on deposit with reserve city or central reserve city banks. These requirements conformed more or less to banking practice at the time the National Banking Act was passed. They were intended to set a ceiling on bank expansion and to recognize the fact that a bank will need more cash if some of its deposits are owned by and treated as reserve by other banks, than if its deposits are all owned by the public at large. Unfortunately, since the requirements were legal minima, the banks could not *use* their reserves without breaking the law. Thus the new law destroyed the liquidity of bank reserves without yet making them part and parcel of the mechanism of credit control. Meanwhile it did little or nothing to eliminate the dangers of pyramiding.

While the pyramiding of bank reserves and the resulting intensification of monetary stringencies offered the most dramatic defect of the pre-1914 banking system, there were others. Most notable, perhaps, were losses to depositors through bank failures—a problem not solved until the 1930's. The imposition of charges for collection of checks, and the refusal of many banks to pay checks at par, were tiresome. Finally, the rigid limitation on national bank and Treasury note issues—commonly called "inelasticity"—was often the subject of complaint. The preference of farmers, particularly in the West, for currency rather than checks led to wide seasonal swings in currency needs, as funds moved toward the agricultural sector in the Fall or away from it in the Spring. However, the resulting inconvenience—seasonal tightness in the money market—was an aspect of the absence of adequate facilities for last-resort lending.

But easily the most serious weakness of the American financial system, in the eyes of contemporaries, was its susceptibility to financial panics. The indispensable remedy for panics was a lender of last resort, and to establish such was the primary purpose of the Federal Reserve Act when it came to be passed in 1913. Yet the machinery set up by the Act was only the first step in reform. A long process of institutional development and some further legislation were needed before the management of money could assume the form with which we are today familiar.

Chapter 3

The Federal Reserve System, 1914–1920

> *The primary function [of a central bank]
> is to do these old-fashioned things: protect
> the currency, maintain quality of credit,
> check wild booms, meet emergencies, meet
> seasonal needs, and things like that.*
> —BENJAMIN M. ANDERSON (1935)

> *. . . the Central Bank is the conductor of
> the orchestra and sets the tempo.*
> —KEYNES, A Treatise on Money (1930)

The susceptibility of the American banking system to periodic panics led to increasing pressure for thoroughgoing reform. Treasury maneuvers, clearing-house certificates, and other palliatives were useful in acute crisis, but had not prevented bank failures and widespread bankruptcies of business concerns. The trouble seemed to stem from legal restrictions on the expansibility of currency—i.e., on the supply of liquid funds. Apart from coin (necessarily fixed in amount by forces not susceptible of control), greenbacks were legally fixed in quantity and national banknotes could be issued only against deposit with the Treasury of defined issues of government bonds.

And yet, these very restrictions had been imposed, with all due deliberation, in order to prevent just such an overissue of paper money as had led to depreciation upon so many occasions in the past. The limitations on the issue of national banknotes had been designed to prevent, and had succeeded in preventing, the irredeemability and losses to holders that had plagued the country so long as the notes of state-chartered banks had continued to circulate.

Similarly, the ceiling on the circulation of greenbacks was intended to ensure continued specie payments after resumption in 1879, and this object also had been achieved. Truly the situation was perverse and confusing. Evidently too much elasticity in the currency led to overissue and inconvertibility. Yet too little engendered panic and financial collapse. Was there *no* happy mean?

Obstacles to Reform

The panic of 1907 made reform seem an urgent matter. Yet there scarcely could have been less agreement as to the direction reform should take. Congress was controlled by conservative Republicans, led by Senator Nelson W. Aldrich of Rhode Island, who were firmly committed to the principle of bond-secured currency issued by banks, and believed that the proper way to relieve a crisis was to issue additional bond-secured currency. Accordingly, the Aldrich-Vreeland Act of 1908 provided for the emergency issue of such currency, under stringent conditions somewhat relaxed in 1912. Yet not even its authors could claim that the measure was more than a stopgap: indeed the Act itself implied as much, for it set up a National Monetary Commission to study long-range reform.

Other Congressmen in both parties formed a vocal minority favoring currency issues by the Treasury rather than by banks: these members, especially those from the farm states, were the heirs of the greenback and free-silver movement. Meanwhile, in banking, commercial, and academic circles, sentiment grew in favor of an "asset currency," i.e., a currency to be secured by, and issued in exchange for, commercial assets. The difficulty about this last proposal was that such a currency, if issued by regular commercial banks, promised to return the nation to the chaos of the pre-Civil War period. The logical solution was a central bank to take charge of such issues: yet the establishment of a central bank was so novel an idea, and so far out of line with what were regarded as American traditions, that many persons could not be brought to contemplate such a solution.

The Need for a Central Bank

Within a few years after the panic of 1907, extensive public discussion, stimulated by the investigations of the National Monetary Commission, crystallized opinion with respect to certain matters, although with respect to others controversy remained vigorous and even bitter.

The consensus included the following: First, banking reserves should be centralized in one or more new institutions to be modeled roughly on existing European central banks. Second, this institution (or these institutions) would itself (or themselves) issue currency, and this issue might eventually supersede the national banknote and the greenback. In addition, it (or they) would have the power to discount commercial paper and to buy such paper in the open market, and this paper would serve as collateral for its (or their) notes. There would thus result an "asset currency" which should expand and contract with the supply of commercial paper, just as the supply of commercial paper itself would expand and contract with the "needs of trade." On the one hand, overissue would be prevented by the collateral requirement, and by the further requirement that a gold reserve be maintained for redemption. On the other hand, "elasticity" would be furnished through the expansibility of commercial paper and the fractional character of the gold-reserve requirement. Third, the new institution (or institutions) would not be primarily concerned with maximizing its (or their) earnings, and so would not be and should not be normally or continuously "fully loaned up": emergency lending power would therefore always be available when needed. Fourth, in imitation of the Bank of England and other European central banks, the institution (or institutions) would have the power to vary its (or their) discount rates so as to protect its (or their) reserves. Fifth, it (or they) would be fiscal agent and principal depository for the federal government: thus locking up of currency by the Treasury would cease entirely.

These various elements in a proposed central-banking system, upon which opinion had crystallized by about 1910, were embodied eventually in the Federal Reserve Act of 1913. They varied greatly, as we shall see later, in importance, in soundness, and in relevance to the practical problem that needed solving.

Origins of the Federal Reserve Act

A proposal for a single central bank along these lines was introduced by Senator Aldrich in January 1912, but the Republicans had already lost control of Congress and feared that they might fail to win the approaching Presidential election. Therefore the Aldrich

plan was not pressed. As things turned out, Wilson replaced Taft:
like many other matters, banking reform was up to the Democrats.
After extensive hearings by committees of both House and Senate,
the Glass-Owen bill became the Federal Reserve Act (December 23,
1913). The paternity of the bill was later acrimoniously disputed.[1]
Here I shall merely note the manner in which some of the more
important points of principle were resolved.

Decentralization. The Aldrich bill had called for a single "National Reserve Association" with a head office in Washington and
not less than fifteen branches. The Democratic platform of 1912
explicitly rejected "the Aldrich plan or a [single] central bank."
Had not Jackson, the grand old man of the party, killed that many-
headed monster, the Second Bank? Clearly loyalty to Jackson's
memory demanded opposition to any plan which called for a single
central institution. It was therefore obvious that any plan to be
enacted by the 63rd Congress must provide for several separately-
incorporated regional central banks with suitable provision for coordination of their policies at the national level.

The insistence of the Democrats, led by Carter Glass, chairman
of the House Committee on Banking and Currency, upon separate
regional banks seems to have rested on emotion rather than logic.
Decentralization could not well be defended as a means of promoting
competition among Reserve Banks, for such competition would too
evidently lead straight to the ancient evil of overissue. Indeed by
the terms of the Act member banks were to be confined in their
borrowing to the Reserve Bank of their own district, so that Reserve
Banks were clearly not intended to compete with one another. In
fact, during the debates on the bill decentralization was mostly taken
for granted. The only argument used to justify it which might possibly have had substance was that Wall Street (or Pennsylvania
Avenue) would have more difficulty in "dominating" several banks
than a single bank. The form the domination might take, or the evil
effects it could produce, were conveniently left to the imagination.
With Glass, especially, decentralization seems to have become a
fetish: it was the touchstone distinguishing his bill from the Aldrich

[1] For sharply varying accounts of the origin of the bill, see Carter Glass, *An Adventure
in Constructive Finance* (New York: Doubleday Page, 1927), Chs. I–XIV; Robert L.
Owen, *The Federal Reserve Act* (New York: Century Co., 1919); H. Parker Willis, *The
Federal Reserve System* (New York: Ronald Press, 1923); Paul M. Warburg, *The
Federal Reserve System,* (New York: Macmillan, 1930), Chs. I–VI; J. Lawrence Laugh-
lin, *The Federal Reserve Act* (New York: Macmillan, 1933), Part I.

plan. At one time he seems to have favored a central institution for every reserve city, i.e., as many as fifty regional banks.[2] Robert L. Owen, chairman of the Senate Committee, and outside Congress, Paul M. Warburg, pressed for a smaller and more manageable number, and in final form the Act called for not fewer than eight nor more than twelve.

Composition and powers of the Board. The Aldrich bill had called for a board of 46 directors of whom 39 were to be elected by the branches of the National Reserve Association (i.e., indirectly by the member banks) and seven were to represent the public interest: a governor, two deputy governors, the Secretaries of the Treasury, of Agriculture, and of Commerce and Labor, and the Comptroller of the Currency. However, the Association was in fact to be run by an executive committee of nine: the governor, the two deputy governors, the Comptroller of the Currency, and five directors elected by the 46-man board from among their number. In total contrast to these complex arrangements, Glass' original idea was that all necessary coordination between the regional banks could be obtained by placing them under the Comptroller of the Currency, an arrangement which would have come close to placing central banking inside the Treasury. At one point indeed Secretary McAdoo advanced a proposal, variously attributed to Samuel Untermyer and John Skelton Williams, to establish a central banking institution as a bureau of the Treasury Department.[3] The proposal for an independent board to supervise the system apparently originated with President Wilson.[4]

But if there were to be a board, Glass' ideas of democracy required that the regional banks be accorded at least minority representation, an arrangement which would indirectly have given member banks a say in the board's composition, as under the Aldrich plan. Senator Owen and Mr. Bryan objected to banking representation, and President Wilson supported them with the now famous, if not entirely relevant query: "Which of you gentlemen thinks the railroads should select members of the Interstate Commerce Commission?" The Act provided that the Board should be comprised of the Secretary of the Treasury, the Comptroller of the Currency,

[2] Willis, p. 143.
[3] Glass, pp. 99-111; Willis, pp. 195-96.
[4] Glass, pp. 83-84; Warburg, I, 422.

and five members appointed to staggered ten-year terms by the President.[5]

The note issue. All parties were pledged to do away with the inelasticity of the bond-secured national banknotes and Treasury-issued United States notes (greenbacks). But the notion that the Treasury rather than the banks should issue currency was a prominent part of the Populist tradition. Accordingly, Senator Owen and Mr. Bryan demanded that the new Federal Reserve notes be made an obligation of the Treasury. This was certain to lead to cries of "fiat money" from the conservatives, such as Senator Root, and was agreed to reluctantly by Glass, again at the insistence of President Wilson. Glass defended the compromise:

> To those who advocate government issue, it may be said that we have it here in terms, with discretion in the Reserve Board to issue currency on application or to withhold. To those who contend for bank issues, as I do, we may say that, in the practical operation of the system, you may have it here; because only upon application of a bank can the government issue. To those who affect solicitude for the government's credit, it may be pointed out, as a practical fact, that the security behind the notes is many times more than sufficient to protect the government before the note-holder could reach the Treasury counter. Thus we have yielded to the sentiment for a government issue, but retained the substance of a bank issue.[6]

The manifest absurdity of this particular controversy, which gave rise to so much feeling at the time, lies on the one hand in its complete neglect of bank deposits (which were in no way guaranteed), and on the other in the subsequent need to liberalize drastically the conditions for note issue. Although an obligation of the Treasury from the start (owing to Bryan's insistence), Federal Reserve notes did not become legal tender until 1933.

Some Features of the System

Other provisions of the Act caused less difficulty. National banks were required, and state banks permitted, to become "members" of the System, subscribing 6% of their own capital to furnish capital for the Reserve Banks. In form therefore the System is a cooperative, but dividends on the stock of the Reserve Banks are limited

[5] Glass, pp. 112–16.
[6] Glass, pp. 122–26.

and, although member banks elect directors, their control over policy has always been minimal. Member banks were required to keep their reserves, at first in part and from 1917 (until 1959) entirely, on deposit with the Reserve Banks. The Reserve Banks were to rediscount commercial paper for members, and might also buy such paper in the open market. The ideal of an asset currency was to be achieved by requiring the Reserve Banks to furnish commercial paper as collateral to the full amount (100%) against Federal Reserve notes to be issued to them by the Treasury. In addition they were to keep 40% in gold against notes in circulation and 35% against deposit liabilities.

In fact, neither of these main provisions was well designed. The idea that commercial-paper collateral would furnish exactly the needed degree of elasticity to the note issue was unfounded, as explained in the next section. The Act was soon amended to make gold (still with a 40% minimum) or commercial paper permissible collateral and later (in 1932) to admit Treasury obligations for this purpose. The Act was soon amended also to allow members to borrow on their own note, secured by commercial paper or government obligations, and the rediscounting of "eligible" assets ceased to be important. Moreover, in the open market the System might buy bank acceptances, commercial paper, Treasury obligations of any maturity, and short-term state and local obligations. It was expected that bank acceptances would chiefly be bought, in order to develop the bill market; but after 1928 open-market dealings came to take place almost exclusively in United States securities.

The System was thought of by its founders as a passive agent which would confine itself essentially to husbanding the banking reserves of the country against the need for them in time of emergency. But banking reserves are capable of almost indefinite expansion and contraction, and the System's function came to be to fix their size rather than to husband them. The System's role, in fact, developed in quite different directions from any anticipated by its founders.

Put in other terms, the Reserve Banks were expected to engage in last-resort lending in time of crisis, and to offset seasonal and other autonomous changes in the demand for and supply of currency, such as those caused by Treasury operations. Their primary concern should therefore be, it was thought, to protect their own reserves of gold and legal tender, so as always to be in shape to give assistance when needed. At the time it was founded no suggestion was made that the System should pursue an active policy directed toward stability, in the money market or elsewhere, or that it should be forehanded and attempt to meet trouble half way. Its functions, that is to say, were to be therapeutic rather than prophylactic. Furthermore, it was hoped that elasticity in the note issue would prevent the money market from becoming really tight, and reduce emergency lending to a minimum. Most of these hopes were not to be realized. An automatic character in the central-banking operation was not—and perhaps never can be—achieved. And the System was drawn more and more, at first much against its will, into an active policy of stabilizing the economy.

The Commercial-Loan Theory

Subsequent experience showed that the ideas embodied in the Federal Reserve Act, although pointing in the right direction, were not entirely sound. The reformers were correct in claiming that inadequate elasticity in the supply of currency was a defect of the old system. But we can now see that they placed excessive emphasis on the regulation of *currency* as distinct from checking accounts, and that they were mistaken in thinking that by linking the issue of Federal Reserve notes to commercial paper they could secure *automatically* the desired degree of elasticity.

The notion of an "asset currency," or note issue based on commercial paper, embodied dissatisfaction with the bond-secured national banknotes on the one hand and the fixed issue of fiat money, the greenbacks, on the other. The basic idea was that the money supply should expand and contract in accordance with variations in the volume of production. Thus increased production should require more working capital, more working capital implies a more ample supply of commercial paper, additional commercial paper will be taken by member banks to the Reserve Banks for rediscount, and will in turn be used by the Reserve Banks as collateral for Federal Reserve notes obtained from the Treasury—so that the increased production is matched by additional currency merely by virtue of the fact that currency is based on commercial paper. If production declines, currency will be automatically retired by a simple reversal of the steps indicated.

Such was the theory. Commonly known as the commercial-loan theory of banking,[7] these ideas and the practice which embodied them were faithfully copied from the central banking of the time in Europe, and especially England. The same ideas were used by the directors of the Bank of England in defending themselves against the strictures of Ricardo and others in the early years of the nineteenth century, and they later fortified the Banking School in its opposition to the principles of Peel's Bank Act (1844).[8] In the case of the Federal Reserve System the desire to ensure that the required degree of elasticity would be obtained automatically—i.e., the desire to make the theory work—led to elaborate rules, of statute and interpretation, as to just what constituted paper "eligible" for rediscount at the Reserve Banks and as collateral for Federal Reserve notes. In time, these rules were reluctantly discarded under the pressure of events, but the theory itself is still not entirely discredited in some quarters.

The eligibility doctrine, regarded as an adaptation of the commercial-loan theory to American conditions, falls into two parts. For the doctrine maintains: I. that the money supply should fluctuate in conformity with the volume of production; and II. that arrangements such as those written into the Federal Reserve Act would ensure that this happens.

I. The origin of the first part of the doctrine obviously lies in historical experience with overissue of currency. As the money economy developed, it became clear that, to prevent commodity prices from rising and the currency unit from depreciating in terms of specie, expansion of the money supply should not greatly outrun production. On the other hand, experience with commercial crises seemed to prove that some degree of elasticity was necessary, at least in emergency. Hence the notion that the volume of money should fluctuate—at least roughly—with production. The result to be expected would be—again, roughly speaking—stability in the general level of commodity prices. These are aims that can indeed be

[7] The commercial-loan theory originated in early commercial banking, and maintained that to safeguard its liquidity a bank should hold only "self-liquidating" assets, i.e., commercial paper based on commodities in warehouse or transit and customer loans used exclusively to finance goods in process. This proposition is still maintained by some; the severe qualifications to which it is subject will not be discussed here.

[8] See, e.g., Jacob Viner, *Studies in the Theory of International Trade* (New York: Harper, 1937); also Lloyd W. Mints, *A History of Banking Theory* (Chicago: University of Chicago Press, 1945). Mints uses the term "real-bills doctrine" for what is more generally known as the commercial-loan theory.

criticized from some viewpoints, but they do not appear to be basically unsound. Put forward pragmatically and in an experimental spirit, the objective has undoubted merits. Nevertheless, some difficulties are to be noted. (1) No allowance is made for variations (e.g., seasonal) in the demand for money. (2) No allowance is made for long-run changes in the demand for money due to changes in money-using habits. (3) Compatibility with the international gold standard, to which the United States had been committed by the Act of 1900, is ignored. The gold standard could require upward or downward changes in the volume of money not associated with changes in (domestic) production. (4) No attempt is made to justify stability in the general level of commodity prices on grounds either of efficiency or equity. However, these difficulties might perhaps be circumvented by applying the prescription in a sufficiently undogmatic spirit.

II. That a *currency* based on commercial paper, as contemplated in the Federal Reserve Act, could automatically assure a *money* supply fluctuating with production is a far more dubious proposition. By money, we have said, we mean demand deposits plus currency in circulation. (1) An increase in production normally requires additional working capital, but the amount needed may be large or small, depending upon the type of production which is expanding. (2) Much or little of the increment in working capital may be financed by additional commercial paper, depending upon the type of production and the business habits and banking connections (or lack of connections) of the firms whose output is expanding. (3) The additional commercial paper may or may not be bought by a member bank. (4) If bought by a member bank, customers' deposits, and hence the money supply, are thereby increased. The paper may or may not be taken to a Reserve Bank for rediscount: if it is, it will swell member-bank reserves and become available as collateral for Federal Reserve notes. To this extent the volume of money has risen. (5) Additional Federal Reserve notes may or may not go into circulation. If they do, member-bank reserves and customers' deposits are drawn down once again: the volume of money has increased by the amount of paper discounted, as under (4), but has undergone no further change. (6) If the member-bank reserve is not drawn down through the withdrawal of currency, it becomes available for multiple expansion of bank deposits through member-bank lending.

It will be apparent from this step-by-step analysis that the connection between an increment in production and an increment in the amount of money is extremely tenuous. Considerations (1), (2) and (3) above suggest that the latter will commonly fall short of the former, but consideration (6) leads to the opposite conclusion.

A critical question evidently is the extent to which additions to working capital are financed by banks. This has little to do with the volume of commercial paper, and even less to do with provisions for the issue of currency. Yet the looseness of the links in the above chain are not the whole of the difficulty. Even if banks financed some definite, known fraction of working-capital needs, and if these needs were tightly tied to production, and if banks could expand their lending only by furnishing additional working capital—essentially the assumptions of the commercial-loan theory—regulation still would not be automatic.

The commercial-loan theory, that is to say, is defective in a more fundamental respect: it assumes banks can supply indefinitely large amounts of additional working capital without the occurrence of rising prices and incipient inflation—of what in the old days was known as "overissue." For the truth is that the addition to the money supply occurs before, perhaps a long time before, the increment in production is ready for the market. So long as unused resources exist, no harm may result. But if the new money is used to bid resources away from other uses, factor and commodity prices will rise, and it will soon be apparent that the money supply is increasing faster than production.

In sum, to attain the grand objective, bank expansion must proceed at a certain definite rate and no faster. The volume of funds borrowed may be larger or smaller than this, depending upon the availability of credit, the level of interest rates, and the profitability of using borrowed funds for working capital. And so it turns out that the grand objective—a money supply just keeping pace with production—cannot be achieved by rules governing the eligibility of central-bank assets, or the character of commercial-bank lending. Instead it depends upon other factors—notably upon an appropriate level of interest rates, i.e., upon the central bank's discount policy.

The Personnel of the System

The Federal Reserve Board took the oath of office August 10, 1914, in the Treasury building in Washington, and the twelve Reserve Banks opened for business in rented premises November 16. For a decade and a half two principal forces molded the infant organization: the members of the Board (often leaderless) on the one hand and Benjamin Strong, the capable and articulate governor of the New York Bank on the other.

The Act provided that the Board should consist of five members appointed for staggered terms, together with the Secretary of the Treasury (at first, William Gibbs McAdoo) and the Comptroller of the Currency (John Skelton Williams) ex officio. As we shall see, experience led to doubts about this arrangement, and the two ex officio members were wisely removed from the Board in 1935. In fact, during the twenty years that the two officials were members, other responsibilities normally prevented their attendance at meetings of the Board. Some of them (especially Secretary Mellon) were inclined to defer to the judgment of the appointed members, or at least were unwilling to take a stand in opposition to the latter. Sometimes the Secretary of the Treasury, who presided at meetings when present, would be appealed to as a kind of higher authority in cases where the appointed members were badly split.

By and large, the policies of the Board were shaped by the character and insights, the prejudices and preconceptions, of the five (later six) appointed members. Two of the original members of the Board have left extensive records: Charles S. Hamlin, an inveterate diarist, and W. P. G. Harding (no relation to President Harding), who subsequently published his memoirs under the title *The Formative Period of the Federal Reserve System*.[9] The remaining three original members were Paul M. Warburg, Adolph C. Miller, and Frederick A. Delano.

Mr. Hamlin (Board member, 1914–1936; governor, 1914–1916), a distant relative of Hannibal Hamlin, was a Boston lawyer and Democrat who had been Assistant Secretary of the Treasury under Cleveland and again under Wilson. Fond of detail, painstaking and a trifle pedantic, he had little sense of humor but plenty of good nature. A mild man on the surface, he could be sharp when

[9] (Boston: Houghton Mifflin, 1925).

roused. He was much inclined to let the Reserve Banks go their own way, with no more direction from Washington than seemed absolutely required by statute, for he took literally the Democratic doctrine that the System should consist of twelve regional banks and was in no sense to be a single central bank—a term repugnant to Democratic Party regulars. When appointed in 1914 as the first governor of the Board, he told Secretary McAdoo that the only special ability he claimed was tact in harmonizing conflicting interests. This was fair self-assessment; Parker Willis called him "a diplomat in the best sense."[10] But as governor during the first two years of the Board's existence, he was unfortunate in that his colleagues were bitterly divided over organizational questions, and a firmer direction was needed than he was able to give.

W. P. G. Harding (Board member, 1914–1922; governor, 1916–1922) had risen from a bookkeeper's stool to become president of a commercial bank in Birmingham, Alabama. Considered unbending and somewhat lacking in imagination, he nevertheless proved a capable executive, and the Board's tradition of independence of the Treasury (despite the Secretary's membership) and of the White House owes much to him. In particular, he resisted his namesake President Harding's attempts to use the System to feed the party faithful by political appointments to Reserve Bank directorships. When in 1922 he failed of reappointment to the Board, it was generally believed that this lack of cooperation was the reason.[11] He subsequently became governor of the Reserve Bank of Boston.

Paul M. Warburg (Board member, 1914–1918), formerly a partner in Kuhn Loeb and Company, had been trained in Europe as a banker, principally at the Reichsbank. For this reason if for no other, he often showed his belief that he alone among members of the Board really understood how central banking should be conducted. His failure of reappointment in 1918 was variously attributed to his German descent and to his Wall Street connection.

While Harding and Warburg were bankers by profession, Adolph C. Miller (Board member, 1914–1936) was an economist who had taught at Chicago and Berkeley before coming to Washington as Assistant Secretary of the Interior. How good an economist he was may transpire in what follows. He was not personally popular with his

[10] Hamlin diary, June 12, 1914; Willis, pp. 667–68.
[11] Hamlin diary, January 2, 1923.

colleagues and was generally disliked by his subordinates. Those who worked with him have testified that he found it extremely hard to admit that he was ever in error, or that any idea he did not himself originate could have value. Although an excellent speaker, his manner was didactic and he was prone to lecture the Board. Especially in the later years of his membership, there were complaints that he was lazy and that he took credit for the work of others. It was noted that he frequently changed his position on an issue—apparently for no good reason—between one meeting of the Board and the next, or even during a single session: in consequence he acquired a reputation for lack of principle.[12]

Frederick A. Delano (Board member, 1914–1918) had been a civil engineer and railroad executive. The rather technical work of the Board seems to have been less congenial to him than to other members, and he resigned before his term expired to accept a commission with the United States forces in Europe.

First Concerns of the System

Immediately the Reserve Banks opened for business, the Board established discount rates as by law it was required to do, but large gold inflows kept the market easy and member banks borrowed little during the System's first two years. A need for earnings led the Reserve Banks to acquire assets—particularly municipal warrants—in the open market. But in fact during the first five years of its existence the Board was largely occupied with matters other than credit policy. I shall review briefly a few of the problems that loomed largest.

During 1915, the System's first full year of operation, much of the Board's time was occupied with a controversy over the number and boundaries of Federal Reserve districts. Under the original Act an Organization Committee (Secretary of the Treasury McAdoo, Secretary of Agriculture Houston, and Comptroller of the Currency Williams) had laid out twelve districts and had designated twelve cities for the location of Reserve Banks. Although the Organization Committee had concluded its work, the Board still had power to readjust boundaries. Immediately claims were made that Pittsburgh rather than Cleveland should have the Reserve Bank for the Fourth

---

[12] Hamlin diary; George W. Norris, *Ended Episodes* (Philadelphia: Winston, 1937), pp. 202–3.

District, and Baltimore rather than Richmond the Bank for the Fifth
District. (Richmond owes its Reserve Bank at least in part to the
small-town patriotism of Comptroller Williams.) The entire organization plan now being in the melting pot, Warburg made a proposal
within the Board to reduce the number of Banks from twelve to eight
(the minimum number laid down in the Act), abolishing the Banks
at Kansas City, Minneapolis, Atlanta, and Dallas. Steeped in European central-banking tradition, Warburg believed in as much centralization as the law would allow, and seems therefore to have
favored any move, however incomplete, in the direction of a single
central bank. He was at once seconded by Delano, and appears to
have picked up the support of Miller and Harding. Secretary Mc-
Adoo and Comptroller Williams felt bound to defend the plan of the
Organization Committee— of which they were the authors—and they
therefore joined Governor Hamlin, who as a good Democrat opposed
centralization on principle, in the minority. This awkward schism, in
which the two ex officio members of the Board supported the governor in opposition to the four remaining appointed members, was
fortunately resolved, after months of wrangling, by a ruling of the
Attorney General to the effect that, under the Act, the Board could
neither reduce the number of districts nor alter the location of Reserve Banks. Accordingly, the Board thereafter confined itself to
making boundary adjustments requested by member banks, such as
the transfer of Fairfield County, Connecticut, and several New Jersey
counties, to the Second District.

One may agree with Warburg in desiring centralization in the
management of money without approving his initiative in this matter. His proposal was not only a waste of time; it led to great bitter-
ness within the Board. Unfortunately, he failed to realize that the
key to centralization lay, as history was to show, not in reducing the
number of Reserve Banks, but in a united and determined Board
that would keep the Banks in line.[13]

Another early—and much worthier—concern of the Board was the
establishment of a par collection system. This enterprise proved far
more refractory than had been anticipated. Reserve Banks could of
course insist that member banks remit at par, but many state banks
that had not joined the System, particularly country banks in the

---

[13] For the episode, see Harding, pp. 34–38; Glass, Ch. XVI; Hamlin diary, 1915,
passim; Warburg, Ch. XI.

South and West, firmly resisted the abolition of exchange charges. The System resorted to many expedients to encourage par clearing, such as the payment of transit charges on checks and currency shipments; the refusal to accept checks drawn on banks which did not agree to remit at par; and the collection of checks for banks which did so agree, even though they were not members of the System. Nevertheless the Board found itself engaged in protracted litigation before it succeeded, many years later, in establishing its right to discriminate against banks that continued to impose exchange charges.

The System During World War I

During World War I (as in World War II) the main anxiety of the System was to make elaborately sure that the Treasury should not run short of money. This meant relatively low discount rates and a willingness to acquiesce in credit expansion. Mainly to this end, a group of so-called "war amendments" to the Federal Reserve Act were passed in September 1916 and June 1917.

First, the method of issuing Federal Reserve notes was simplified so that the gold held to redeem them could be included in the collateral lodged with the Federal Reserve Agent to obtain them. This meant that commercial paper need no longer be furnished to the full value of the notes, but only to the extent of that portion of the issue not covered by gold: the gold being at least 40%, commercial paper was now required only for the balance. Second, member banks were now for the first time allowed to borrow, not only by rediscounting commercial paper held by them, but also by giving their own notes secured by commercial paper or (shades of previous wartime inflations!) by Treasury obligations.

It will be recognized that these two amendments further weakened the already loose connection between the size of the note issue and the supply of commercial paper. To this extent their passage implied a partial repudiation of the commercial-loan theory of credit, and was resented by some persons on that account. The final release of the System from the bondage of the commercial-loan doctrine—a doctrine so highly but mistakenly prized by its founders—did not come until 1932. In that year the Glass-Steagall Act for the first time admitted governments as security for Federal Reserve notes.

As shown by its members' speeches and by its annual reports, the Board felt vague premonitions of the inflationary dangers to be expected from American participation in the war in Europe. Partly for this reason it favored a third amendment, also passed in June 1917, whereby member banks were obliged to keep the whole of their required reserves on deposit with their Reserve Banks. On the other hand, required reserves were simultaneously reduced for central reserve city banks (New York, Chicago, and St. Louis), reserve city, and country banks from 18%, 15%, and 12% to 13%, 10%, and 7%, respectively; and on time deposits from 5% to 3%. (The new percentages remained unchanged for almost two decades.) The reduction in reserve requirements was rationalized in this fashion: since bank reserves had been centralized, and arrangements made for their rapid replenishment through borrowing, they could safely be smaller than of yore. Of course the reduction would also make it easier for the banks to help float Treasury securities. Thus the function of bank reserves in controlling credit expansion was not understood, nor were the inflationary implications of the reduction in reserve requirements appreciated.[14]

By the middle of 1917 the Treasury had persuaded the System to establish preferential discount rates on paper secured by government obligations, while both bank and market rates were prevented from rising in the face of heavy Treasury borrowing. Almost identical devices were to be used again in World War II. Member-bank indebtedness, which had been negligible prior to America's entry into the war, increased steadily: at the time of the Armistice in November 1918, borrowings exceeded required reserves, so that "owned reserves" actually were negative.

The policy of the System during World War I was passive, and few if any protests were made against the inflationary measures which the Board was induced to take or in which it acquiesced. In January 1918 the Secretary of the Treasury asked the Board to pass upon proposals for new capital issues, the voluntary arrangements for their control being designed less to prevent inflation than to avoid the diversion of labor and materials to nonessential employments. Warburg, Delano, and Hamlin were delegated to form a Capital Issues Committee. Known as the "money committee," this body took up most of the time of its members for the remaining duration of the war, to judge from the entries in Hamlin's diary. In any case it is

[14] Benjamin H. Beckhart, *Discount Policy of the Federal Reserve System* (New York: Henry Holt, 1924), Ch. VI.

doubtful, politically speaking, if much could have been done by the System to check inflation until the conclusion of hostilities.

The Situation in 1919: Domination by the Treasury

When fighting ceased in November 1918, the general expectation was that the end of war orders would bring a slackening of business and a decline in commodity prices. In fact, wholesale prices did decline through February 1919, but then turned up again and continued to rise until mid-1920. On the one hand, the Treasury did not immediately cease to borrow; on the other, business loans of commercial banks expanded rapidly.

During the first five months of 1919 the System allowed its holdings of open-market assets to decline; but, beginning in June, it made substantial purchases during the remainder of the year, especially of acceptances. We may suppose that these purchases were motivated partly by a desire for earnings, and partly by a wish to help establish the long-promised bill market in New York: but they were not well timed. Since the System also had to support the government-bond market in connection with the Victory Loan flotation in the Spring of 1919, monetary policy as a whole was distinctly inflationary. It is indeed doubtful whether the inflationary effects of open-market purchases were as yet realized. So far as concerns the possibility of exercising restraint through higher interest rates, it is obvious the System must plead that its hands were tied by the Treasury.[15]

Before leaving for Europe in July 1919, Governor Strong of the New York Reserve Bank said he felt the time was about to arrive when rates should be raised. Immediately upon returning to this country at the end of September, on learning that federal receipts and expenditures had at last been brought into balance, he initiated a campaign to persuade the Treasury, under Glass and Leffingwell, to agree to an increase in rates. Since the prohibition on the export of gold had been revoked in June, substantial gold losses had occurred, and the Reserve Banks' own reserve position had become critical. In November the Treasury reluctantly agreed to a moderate rise in discount rates—from 4% to 4¾% in the case of the New York Bank.

[15] Both Governor Harding and Governor Strong subsequently entered this plea: see U.S. Joint Commission of Agricultural Inquiry, Hearings, Vol. 2, 1922, pp. 362, 504.

The stock market responded immediately; stock prices fell, at times in a disorderly manner, and did not again reach their October levels until nearly four years later. Wall Street speculators denounced the Federal Reserve and a few newspaper editors demanded that the System be investigated. Loans to brokers ceased rising and even declined slightly. The rest of the economy was not so responsive. Inflation of commodity prices and wage rates continued, as did commodity speculation and expansions of bank credit and rediscounts at the Reserve Banks. Strong was certain that the situation demanded further rate increases immediately. The other governors agreed that everything except the Treasury's position justified rate increases, but most of them were reluctant to oppose the Treasury. Secretary Glass and Assistant Secretary Leffingwell did not deny the need for restriction but insisted that further rate increases should be postponed until after January 15 [1920], by which time the Treasury would have marketed some new certificates and would be in an improved position. They also worried about the depressed prices of Liberty Bonds. The Federal Reserve Board was disposed to accede to the Treasury's request. Strong was not.[16]

The rise in discount rates was followed by a bitter controversy in which Glass and the Board pressed for credit rationing by the Reserve Banks to prevent overborrowing by member banks and the speculative use of credit (however defined); while Strong, who at the New York Bank would have been saddled with carrying out such a policy, insisted that the proposal was not feasible. (At this period the average member bank owed more than its entire cash reserve.) Strong's and the Board's successors were to debate the same issue all over again in 1928–1929.

Strong then threatened to raise New York's discount rate, if necessary without the Board's approval. This led Glass to seek an opinion from the Attorney General who, on December 9, 1919, declared that the Board had the power to initiate rate changes and to order rates established. This opinion returned to plague Glass when in 1927, as a senator, he criticized the Board for doing just this in the Chicago rate case (see below). Strong argued that, now the war was over, the Treasury should be treated like any other customer, but Leffingwell accused him of having promised higher rates to the Bank of England as an aid in its fight with the British Exchequer.[17]

[16] Lester V. Chandler, *Benjamin Strong, Central Banker* (Washington, D.C.: Brookings Institution, 1958), p. 152. However, the Goldenweiser papers contain a copy of a letter from Leffingwell to Governor Harding, dated December 10, 1919, in which the former reports the successful sale of three-month certificates, and indicates that the Reserve Board may now take any action that it feels desirable: see also Chandler, p. 162.
[17] Hamlin diary, November 26, 1919.

The above occurred in November 1919. By mid-December, or at latest by January 1920, the Treasury's position was greatly eased. Glass and Leffingwell gave the go-ahead, and discount rates were raised with Reserve Board approval—to 6% in the case of the New York Bank.[18] The accord releasing monetary policy from bondage to the Treasury had been reached in little more than a year after the Armistice; after World War II it would take five and a half years for the Reserve to regain its freedom.

[18] Strong later felt that rates should have been raised sometime during the first quarter of 1919: see U.S. Joint Commission of Agricultural Inquiry, Hearings, Vol. 2, 1922, pp. 763–64. In its *Report* the Commission blamed the Reserve System for not having defied the Treasury (Part II, "Credit," p. 44). Seymour Harris also considers that the Treasury was by no means alone to blame (*Twenty Years of Federal Reserve Policy* [Cambridge: Harvard University Press, 1933], p. 72). John R. Commons felt, looking back, that rates should have been raised in March 1919 (House Committee on Banking and Currency, *Stabilization*, Hearings on H.R. 11806, 70th Cong. 1st Sess., 1928, pp. 66, 425).

Chapter 4

The Federal Reserve Feels Its Way, 1920–1929

> *Take short views, hope for the best, and trust in God.*
>
> —SYDNEY SMITH

The expansion of Federal Reserve credit, and particularly of member-bank borrowing, was not halted by the rise in discount rates achieved by the beginning of 1920. Commercial-bank loans continued to expand and commodity prices continued to rise; in February and March still more gold left the country. A special cause for anxiety was the growth in member-bank indebtedness, which now greatly exceeded member-bank reserve balances, so that owned reserves were negative. As a group, that is to say, member banks owed to their respective Reserve Banks, not only the whole of their cash, but also a slice of their earning assets. The Phelan Act had indeed been enacted (April 13, 1920); it allowed the Reserve to penalize excessive borrowing by discount rates graduated according to the amount of indebtedness of individual member banks; but little use was made of it. The tradition against continuous borrowing, which was soon to become so powerful and so useful a convention, had not yet been established. Now, the Reserve could defend itself only by still higher rates: that of the New York Bank went to 7% in June 1920.

Slump, 1920–1921

Member-bank indebtedness continued to increase until October 1920; but by that time prices and output had already turned down, to usher in the sharpest —although not the longest—deflation of credit in our experience. Wholesale prices (on a 1913 base) fell

59

from a peak of 247 in May 1920 to 141 fourteen months later. Industrial production (on a 1923–1925 base; figures were not computed until some years later) fell from a peak of 95 in January-February 1920 to 64 in March-April 1921. Commodity prices did not begin their recovery until the Spring of 1922, but by the Fall of 1921 production had already risen about 10% above its lowest level.

In the face of this collapse of prices and sharp contraction of business, high money rates were maintained for almost a year (Fig. 1). The New York Bank's rediscount rate, for example, was first reduced—from 7% to 6½%—on May 5, 1921. Not until June 1922 was it restored to the 1919 (or precrisis) level of 4%. Meanwhile member-bank indebtedness declined sharply, and the System simultaneously reduced its holdings of purchased paper. Many critics have argued that the contraction in business would have been less severe had the System eased the money market more promptly.[1]

It would have been difficult, although possibly desirable, to ease credit even before the end of 1920. Before the Joint Commission of Agricultural Inquiry, Governor Strong pointed out that credit was freely available at a price throughout the crisis—in the best tradition of nineteenth-century central banking. He further claimed that the System could not have eased credit during the Fall of 1920, even though commodity prices had already fallen sharply, because member-bank credit continued to expand through November, the New York Bank was in debt to other Reserve Banks, and the entire System's reserve position remained tight.[2] This defense may be accepted.

But after the beginning of 1921 the same reasons for a continuation of tight money no longer applied; yet the first rate reduction in New York did not come until May. Indeed in February the minimum terms on which member banks could obtain accommodation from the New York Reserve Bank were actually stiffened, for the preferential rate on paper secured by Treasury Certificates of Indebtedness was abolished; the rate on such paper rose from 5½% to 6%—the rate applicable to paper backed by other Treasury obligations. No doubt

[1] This was the conclusion of a majority of the U.S. Joint Commission of Agricultural Inquiry (*Report*, Part II, "Credit," pp. 86–88), Ogden Mills dissenting. Professor Commons later expressed the view that "the System should have taken action to reduce the rate [of discount] gradually after June, 1920" (House Committee on Banking and Currency, *Stabilization*, Hearings on H.R. 11806, 70th Cong. 1st Sess., 1928, p. 426: in the original "1919" appears as a misprint for "1920").

[2] U.S. Joint Commission of Agricultural Inquiry, Hearings, Vol. 2, 1922, pp. 714–15. The System's reserve ratio, which had been but 45% at the end of 1920, had returned to 71% at the end of 1921.

Strong wished to move toward a single discount rate, but clearly he should have done so by lowering the regular rate, then 7%.

The policy of continued tight money cannot be explained by the System's reserve position, which was improving rapidly. Nor, as was often to happen on later occasions, did any difference of opinion within the System paralyze its power of initiative at this time. Governor Harding is on record as believing, as of January 13, 1921, that "the crisis has been passed," but he did not advocate lower rates.[3] Within a few days Governor Strong returned from a long trip abroad, and it is plain he also felt the time for easier money had not yet arrived. As it turned out, the System was saved from itself by the politicians. On March 29 Andrew Mellon, the incoming Secretary of the Treasury, told Governor Harding he thought the time had come for lower rates. The Governor said he feared a reduction might revive stock-market speculation, but the Secretary replied that a little speculation would do no harm under the circumstances. The Governor asked if Mellon meant he wanted a lower rate for government paper, but Mellon said: No, rates should be uniform. At his first meeting with the Board on April 4, the Secretary expressed the view that Banks with 7% discount rates should lower them to 6%. The Boston Bank at once agreed, and the New York Bank shortly thereafter was forced under protest to follow suit.[4] Yet Strong continued to be unhappy about the move. As late as May 23, 1921, he could write to Assistant Secretary of the Treasury Gilbert:

> I can only repeat what I have previously stated, that in my opinion rate reductions will have no effect of importance in relieving cases of distress, such as now exist in the agricultural sections, unless the reductions are of such a character as to really encourage borrowing from the Reserve Banks. In other words, unless they encourage a period of expansion and inflation with all the accompanying evils of speculation and extravagance. What is [still] needed is a discontinuance of pressure to liquidate, and free extension of credit to institutions that need it. . . . I think I cannot do better than quote Bagehot's golden rule which forty or fifty years ago effected a real revolution in banking thought in London and has since, more or less, determined the Bank of England's policy under conditions similar to the present.[5]

But Bagehot applied his "golden rule," i.e., lend freely but at a high rate, only to the *crisis* phase, during which the central bank's

[3] *Ibid.*, p. 140.
[4] Hamlin diary, March 29 and April 4, 1921.
[5] Lester V. Chandler, *Benjamin Strong, Central Banker* (Washington, D.C.: Brookings Institution, 1958), p. 174.

own reserve ratio was at a dangerously low level. By May 1921, when Strong wrote the above, gold had been flowing in for the past eight months and the monetary gold stock was of record size.

Months earlier the gold situation had returned to normal, and Reserve officials must have been well aware (as Strong shows in the above quotation) that commodity prices had collapsed, and that business was stagnant. Yet all opposed cheaper money. Here is a genuine mystery which at this distance in time can be only partly resolved. In retrospect it appears probable that the reluctance to reduce discount rates, even after the System's own reserve position had eased and it was plain the boom had been broken, was due, at least in part, to a rather doctrinaire belief that "bank rate should exceed market rate," coupled with the fact that open-market rates of interest were slow to decline during 1921–1922.

Bank Rate and Market Rate

With hindsight we can see that the reason market rates of interest did not decline more rapidly during 1921 was that the Reserve was reducing its holdings of purchased paper. The connection between open-market operations and market rates of interest was unfortunately not yet appreciated. Open-market rates for commercial paper, that is to say, are themselves greatly influenced by Reserve policy, and during 1921 that policy was calculated (if unintentionally) to keep them at a high level. The episode deserves further examination, if only for the light it sheds on Reserve thinking at the time.

On July 5, 1921, Governor Strong wrote to Montague Norman:

> Our general policy would ordinarily be to reduce our rates as a consequence of reductions in rates in the market; in other words we would follow rates down. The market rates which would govern our action would be (1) the rate for bankers' bills . . . (2) the rate for Treasury certificates of short maturity . . . (3) the success of the Treasury in its recurrent offerings of three-year notes and the rates paid on such notes . . . (4) the rates for commercial paper in the market. . . . (5) the stock exchange call rate . . .

The Governor continues:

> The only other considerations entering into our policy are (1) general consideration of public policy where, under present conditions, classical methods are not always the wisest, and (2) strictly political considerations brought about by the change of administration. . . . Con-

sideration of general public welfare leads me to believe that the process of deflation has gone dangerously far here and abroad. . . . I firmly believe that the time for all credit pressure passed some months ago, and should we feel that the six per cent rate is causing pressure of a serious character upon borrowers generally, we would not hesitate to reduce it . . . . but I am not yet convinced that such is the case. . . . As to political considerations, those are quite perplexing. Our new Administration is determined to make business good, if means can be found to do so. It is not an easy thing to do; and I am quite out of sympathy with some of our new associates [Mellon?] who think that lower rates will do it.[6]

Speaking a month later, on August 11, the good Governor was sure that his discount rate should follow the market downward, and he did not betray the slightest realization that Reserve policy might be preventing market rates from falling:

The theory upon which we have proceeded in New York . . . is that the same competition should develop to reduce the cost of credit that must likewise develop in order to reduce the cost of goods before it is possible for us to reduce our rates; that is to say, as this process of gradual liquidation takes place and as retail prices come down and new and cheaper things come into the market, the loan accounts of the various borrowing banks come down; they pay us off. As they pay us off they begin to compete to make loans. That is the process of reducing the cost of credit.[7]

Yet even in a competitive market—whether goods or credit be in question—price is dependent on supply, and in 1921 the System was cutting the supply of credit by allowing its portfolio of bills to run off. The degree of competition is therefore irrelevant. Governor Strong claimed[8] that he had struggled to prevent deflation, but we may feel sure that all he meant was that he had lent freely at a high rate, and had refrained from pressing member banks even when they were continuously indebted.

Similarly Governor Harding had this to say about a proposal by John Skelton Williams, then Comptroller of the Currency, to reduce rates in January 1921:

Mr. Williams was undoubtedly sincere in his belief that the discount rates of the Federal Reserve Banks should have been reduced in Janu-

[6] Chandler, p. 176.

[7] U.S. Joint Commission of Agricultural Inquiry, Hearings, Vol. 2, p. 779.

[8] See testimony of Representative James G. Strong, Senate Committee on Banking and Currency, *Restoring and Maintaining the Average Purchasing Power of the Dollar,* Hearings on S. 4429, 72nd Cong. 1st Sess., 1932, p. 24.

ary 1921 without regard to actual conditions in the money market. But other members of the Board, equally sincere, recalling the effect of artificial rates, believed that Reserve Bank rates should be related to [i.e., should rule above] market rates, and that improvement in the position of the banks, increasing confidence in them, and the redepositing of hoarded money, would most speedily and surely result in a general relaxation of interest rates.[9]

Governor Harding is just as oblivious as Governor Strong to the notion that Reserve policy may itself influence open-market rates. Sincerity is a poor substitute for understanding, and one must conclude that in 1921 Reserve officials did not understand the mechanism of the money market.

Adolph Miller later claimed as virtue that it was the Board, and not any of the Reserve Banks (except Boston), which belatedly initiated rate reductions in the Spring of 1921.[10] This is true, although, as we have seen, the initiative in fact came from a single member of the Board, the newly-appointed Secretary of the Treasury, Andrew Mellon. Miller himself opposed Boston's request for a reduction from 7% to 6% (April 12) and came round to Mellon's view only some weeks later.[11] Whether Mellon really understood more about the matter than Strong, Harding, and Miller may be doubted. But he had the right idea, perhaps because he was not committed to the fetish that bank rate should exceed market rate, because he was influenced by the traditional Treasury desire for cheap money, or because he dimly realized the connection between money rates and business activity.

The doctrine that "bank rate should rule above the market" deserves further examination. It was confidently affirmed at the time by such authorities as Beckhart and Miller.[12] Yet it appears to have rested on a mistaken analogy to the London money market.[13] The

[9] W. P. G. Harding, *The Formative Period of the Federal Reserve System* (Boston: Houghton Mifflin, 1925), pp. 211–12.

[10] House Committee on Banking and Currency, *Stabilization*, Hearings on H.R. 7895, 69th Cong. 1st Sess., 1927, p. 648.

[11] Hamlin diary, April 12 and 28, 1921.

[12] Benjamin H. Beckhart, *Discount Policy of the Federal Reserve System* (New York: Henry Holt, 1924), p. 402; Adolph C. Miller, "Federal Reserve Policy," *American Economic Review*, XI (June, 1921), 185. Miller was of course a member of the Federal Reserve Board.

[13] See letter from Governor Harding to the chairman of the Senate Committee on Banking and Currency (December 16, 1920) in U.S. Joint Commission of Agricultural Inquiry, Hearings, Vol. 2, 1922, pp. 381–82.

British bank rate ruled above the market rate for eligible paper, because the market did not normally take eligible paper to the Bank. Bank of England credit consisted of assets other than eligible paper—mainly Treasury obligations. To the (restricted) extent that this situation obtained in the United States, the same could be said of the Federal Reserve System. The American analog was the bank acceptance. If the Reserve Bank buying rate for acceptances was above the market rate, bank acceptances would not be offered to the Reserve. If the buying rate was equal to the market rate, the Reserve might find itself buying substantial quantities of acceptances. For the buying rate to be below the market rate—unless the Reserve were to refuse paper offered—was a manifest impossibility. Hence the buying rate must be equal to or greater than the market rate. The analogy with London holds.

So much for the acceptance-buying rate. With the discount rate matters stood otherwise. For the Reserve System's discount rates applied then (as they do today), not to paper offered by Tom, Dick, or Harry, but to paper discounted by member banks. And for such paper there *was* no market: (1) eligible paper discounted by a member bank was seldom sold, and no regular market existed for such paper, i.e., trade or bank acceptances carrying a member bank's endorsement; (2) no market whatever existed for a member bank's own note, which was then becoming the usual method of obtaining access to Reserve credit. Hence the notion that the discount rate should bear some stated relation to the market rate *for the particular class of paper in question* breaks down because no such market rate existed, and no analogy with the London money market was possible. Comparison between the discount rate and open-market rates on paper not eligible for rediscount—a comparison popular with writers of the period—is seen to have been irrelevant.

Both Governor Harding and Governor Strong defended the doctrine before the Joint Commission of Agricultural Inquiry. Their opinion that bank rate should rule above market rate was endorsed by the Commission:

> The discount rates of the Federal Reserve Banks . . . should normally be slightly above the rates carried by the class of paper to which they apply, in order that the lending power of the Federal Reserve Banks

may be preserved for times of financial stringency and crisis, and in
order that this lending power shall not be depleted by member banks
borrowing from them for purposes of profit only.[14]

As explained, the doctrine can suitably be applied to the acceptance-
buying rate, in case more acceptances are outstanding than the System
wishes to hold. But so far as discount rates are concerned, it is in
error at two points. First, there are no open-market rates for "the
class of paper to which [the discount rates] apply," so that the comparison suggested in the quotation cannot be made. Clearly comparison with rates on open-market paper which is ineligible, or if
eligible does not carry a member bank's endorsement, is irrelevant.
Second, to render member-bank borrowing unprofitable, much higher
rates might be needed.

To summarize: the Reserve need not have feared to reduce its
discount rates below market rates on commercial paper. Moreover,
by reducing open-market holdings during the first half of 1921,
the Reserve by its own action (if unwittingly) maintained open-
market rates. Not until December did it reverse this policy, and
start to rebuild its holdings of open-market paper. I conclude that
the discount rate should have been reduced several months earlier,
and that paper should have been bought in order to maintain or
increase Reserve holdings, instead of being allowed to run off.[15]

The Personnel of the System

During the crisis of 1920–1921, W. P. G. Harding was governor
of the Board. An able professional banker, first appointed to the
Board in 1914, he had served as governor since 1916. Other original members of the Board were Miller and Hamlin, sketches of
whom have been given in the preceding chapter. When his term
expired (August 9, 1922), Harding became governor of the Boston
Reserve Bank. It was commonly believed that he had failed of reappointment to the Board owing to his unwillingness to cooperate
with the White House in matters to which President Harding attached importance. To be specific: within a few days of assuming

[14] Hearings, Vol. 2, 1922, p. 313; *Report*, Part II, "Credit," 1922, p. 11.
[15] Others who have criticized the System for its deflationary policy in 1921–1922 are:
Gustav Cassel, *Money and Foreign Exchange after 1914* (London: Constable and Co.,
1922), pp. 218–26; Walter W. Stewart, House Banking and Currency Committee, *Stabilization*, Hearings on H.R. 7895, 69th Cong. 1st Sess., 1927, pp. 785–86.

office, the President had asked that the System's insurance business (which concerned, e.g., currency shipments) be turned over to a relative. More recently President Harding had tried on at least two occasions to have the Board appoint political friends as Federal Reserve Agents. These moves, which some felt were designed to convert the System into a political machine, were resisted. Certain it is that Governor Harding wished to be, but was not, reappointed.[16]

During a nine-month interregnum, Vice-Governor Edmund Platt (originally appointed June 8, 1920, at that time a Congressman from New York and chairman of the House Committee on Banking and Currency) was Acting Governor. Finally the governorship was filled (May 1, 1923) by D. R. Crissinger of Marion, Ohio, a life-long friend of the President. Crissinger, who had been Comptroller of the Currency since 1921, already had some acquaintance with Reserve problems. He was and remained extremely sensitive about the obviously political nature of his appointment: perhaps on this account, he proved himself a conscientious administrator and a hard worker. Somewhat indecisive and perhaps too easily swayed, he yet turned in a far better record than might have been expected. Later he resigned (September 15, 1927) to engage in an ill-starred enterprise in private business. He was succeeded in the governor-ship by Roy A. Young, a banker by profession.

Also appointed about this time (May 14, 1923) were George R. James and (to represent agriculture) E. H. Cunningham. James was a Memphis storekeeper of parochial views but much common sense: Cunningham was an Iowa farmer without background who seems to have contributed little. These men—Crissinger followed by Young, and Platt, Hamlin, Miller, James, and Cunningham—were the appointed members of the Board during most of the 1920's. Secretary Mellon and Comptroller MacIntosh, followed in 1928 by Comptroller Pole, were the ex officio members.

The other important seat of power within the System was the Federal Reserve Bank of New York. At the New York Bank—until his untimely illness and death in 1928—only one name need be mentioned: Governor Benjamin Strong.[17] After his death Strong was

---

[16] Hamlin diary; Paul M. Warburg, *The Federal Reserve System* (New York: Mac-millan, 1930), I, 446; H. Parker Willis, *The Federal Reserve System* (New York: Ronald Press, 1923), pp. 1488–91.

[17] See Chandler, *op. cit.*

succeeded by George L. Harrison, a man who had spent much of his working life in the service of the New York Bank.[18]

Business Revival, 1922–1923: The Discovery of Open-Market Operations

During 1921 large amounts of gold came from abroad. The gold imports were occasioned less by relatively higher rates of interest in the United States than by Europe's need to finance its substantial past and present import surplus. In fact, the monetary gold stock increased without interruption from late in 1920 almost to the end of 1924. This enabled member banks to repay their debts to the System; it also placed the Reserve Banks themselves in a highly liquid state, giving them a freedom of action they never previously possessed. During the first half of 1922 the System made substantial open-market purchases, and these still further reduced member-bank indebtedness. The consequent decline in rates for open-market paper allowed the New York Bank to reduce its discount rate from 4½% to 4% in June without feeling that it violated the spirit of the injunction to keep bank rate above market rate.

The additions to open-market holdings during the first half of 1922 were made "to offset the reduction in discounts,"[19] and the implication is plain that their purpose was to prevent a decline in the earnings of the System.[20] As early as November 21, 1921, the Federal Advisory Council had pointed out that the System was not operated for profit, and had recommended against the purchase of investments with a view to bolstering earnings.[21] But the value of

[18] Herbert Hoover, who was a personal friend of Adolph Miller and took his part, both while Secretary of Commerce and later as President, had this to say about the System's personnel late in 1925: "Crissinger was a political appointee from Marion, Ohio, utterly devoid of global economic or banking sense. The other members of the Board, except Adolph Miller, were mediocrities, and Governor Strong was a mental annex to Europe" (*Memoirs* [New York: Macmillan, 1952], III, 9). It is not clear whether Mellon and MacIntosh were included in this condemnation.

[19] *Annual Report of the Federal Reserve Board for 1922*, p. 4.

[20] ". . . with so little experience of banking of this character, it is quite impossible to ask nine active, intelligent, progressive business men, three of them bankers, to serve as directors of a reserve bank, and at once, before they learn a little of the philosophy of reserve banking, not to assume that one of their responsibilities is to earn enough money to pay dividends on the stock . . . many directors, or many of the reserve banks, strongly held the feeling that a part of their duty was to earn enough to pay expenses. Any business man of experience would feel that way, not possibly realizing, as was the fact, that there were times when it would not be desirable to earn the expenses and dividends." Benjamin Strong before the House Committee on Banking and Currency, *Stabilization*, Hearings on H.R. 7895, 69th Cong. 1st Sess., 1927, p. 309.

[21] *Annual Report of the Federal Reserve Board for 1921*, pp. 691–92.

open-market operations as a means of influencing the money market was only slowly appreciated. The sharp reduction in discounts that followed the investment purchases made early in 1922 was possibly the crucial lesson: Reserve Bank credit might hold steady, open-market holdings replacing discounts, but once member banks were out of debt they were more apt to lend, and rates declined as a result. At any rate, on April 25, 1922, six months after its previous comment, the Federal Advisory Council stated quite explicitly its belief that purchases and sales in the open market could and should be used to tighten or relax the market as occasion demanded.[22]

The purchases made in 1922, for the first time mainly of short-term government paper rather than of acceptances, were carried out more or less independently by each Reserve Bank. The Treasury, under Mellon and Gilbert, became unhappy about possible consequences. In particular, fluctuations resulting from these uncoordinated purchases made it difficult to gauge the market, and on at least one occasion led the Treasury to fix too low a rate on its current offering, so that the issue was a failure. Treasury officials took the matter up with Governor Strong of the New York Bank, and at a meeting on May 2, 1922, Strong persuaded the Governors' Conference to set up an open-market committee, comprised of governors from Boston, New York, Philadelphia, Chicago, and later Cleveland, to handle such purchases. At its September meeting the Federal Advisory Council reiterated its earlier recommendations and expressed its satisfaction that a "committee of governors" had been set up to unify open-market policy.[23] The Council, composed of commercial bankers, seems from the start to have had a clearer view of the possible significance of open-market operations for credit policy than either the Board or the Reserve Bank Governors. Except for Strong, the latter were so preoccupied with the need for earnings at this period that they found it hard to realize the wider implications of their actions.

The new body, known officially as "The Committee of Governors on Centralized Execution of Purchases and Sales of Government Securities by Federal Reserve Banks," was originally to be concerned with technique rather than policy, but soon came to make

[22] *Annual Report of the Federal Reserve Board for 1922*, pp. 409–11.
[23] *Ibid.*, p. 413.

recommendations to the individual banks as to whether they should buy or sell. Early in 1923 the Reserve Board, and especially Miller, woke up to the fact that important policy decisions were being made by a committee of governors without the Board's participation. A stormy meeting took place between a not entirely unanimous Board, led by Miller, and a Governors' Conference for whom W. P. G. Harding was the principal spokesman. Harding, now Governor of the Boston Reserve Bank, seems to have taken pleasure in turning on his old colleagues. The Board successfully established its authority over open-market policy, although Hamlin doubted its legal powers in the matter. In view of its undoubted responsibility for discount policy, for it to renounce control over open-market operations would have been sheer abdication. The governors' open-market committee was reorganized as the Open Market Investment Committee, with the same membership as before, but now strictly under the jurisdiction of the Board. Strong was furious that his fellow governors had surrendered to the Board; but from Colorado, where he was recuperating from tuberculosis, he could do little.[24]

The controversy between the Board and the Banks was bedeviled by a side issue: there were many, among whom Hamlin and Warburg were prominent and Glass was probably included, who regarded acceptances as the preferred open-market assets for the Reserve Banks to hold. According to this view, the proceeds of acceptance purchases are likely to be used primarily for "legitimate" business purposes, and money used to buy governments is likely to be used primarily for "speculative" purposes. This doctrine, a corollary of the commercial-loan theory of credit,[25] is without substantial merit. But it strengthened opposition to the Reserve Banks' plans to buy governments at this time. The same doctrine was to cloud Reserve policy toward the stock-market boom in 1928 and 1929.

Meanwhile, an additional weapon—open-market policy—had been discovered in the underbrush and was now added to the arsenal. Moreover, ultimate responsibility for its use, as with discount policy, had been assumed by the Board. But the question as to what guideposts should be used in determining policy was no nearer resolution. During the war the Treasury had caused the System to keep

[24] The account given here is based chiefly upon Chandler, Ch. VI.
[25] See above, Ch. 3.

the market easy—at the cost of a great inflation; in 1920 the reserve position of the Banks had joined with a desire to halt inflation in forcing credit restriction; in 1921 the inflow of gold, relaxing the System's reserve position and lowering open-market rates, had eventually prompted a reduction of discount rates. But the flood of gold had continued. During 1922 the money market was allowed to remain easy, despite some anxiety concerning the heavy and prolonged indebtedness of member banks. The System had not as yet adequately cultivated the tradition against continuous borrowing, and had somewhat exaggerated ideas as to the profitability to member banks of adding to their indebtedness.

By the beginning of 1923 member-bank credit was expanding rather rapidly as a result of the gold inflow. Wholesale prices (on a 1913 base) had recovered from a low of 138 in January 1922 to 155 in July, but remained rather stable during the second half of 1922. In February 1923 the System decided to slow down the credit expansion. The New York discount rate was raised from 4% to 4½%, and during the first six months of 1923 substantial quantities of securities were sold—the first use of open-market operations with a deliberate view to influencing credit conditions (Fig. 1). This mild credit restriction obviously was not induced by the reserve position of the System, for the gold stock had now become almost embarrassingly large. The policy amounted, in fact, to gold sterilization. Evidently fear of a renewed rise in prices was a dominating consideration, although little change had occurred in the BLS wholesale index since mid-1922.[26] The two criteria—the reserve position on the one hand and the desire to curb credit expansion and a fear of rising prices on the other—in 1920 had both worked toward restriction. Now, in 1923, they pushed in opposite directions: in any event, the reserve position was disregarded, and mild respect was paid instead to the dangers of inflation.

The dilemma which the System faced at this time was described, in a memorandum written in April 1923 by Benjamin Strong as follows:

[26] See testimony of Adolph C. Miller, House Committee on Banking and Currency, *Stabilization*, Hearings on H.R. 7895, 69th Cong. 1st Sess., 1927, pp. 700, 708; also discussion in Harold L. Reed, *Federal Reserve Policy* (New York: McGraw-Hill, 1930), pp. 40–41. Miller later testified that, looking back, the mild credit restriction of 1923 "might have been dispensed with": he refrained from adding that, in such case, the recession of 1924 might never have occurred! (See House Committee on Banking and Currency, *Stabilization*, Hearings on H.R. 11806, 70th Cong. 1st Sess., 1928, p. 295).

Before the war one of the chief guides and influences in moving the banks of issue to raise and lower their discount rates was the state of their gold reserves—whether they were a large or small percentage of their note issues and deposits. Here are we with a mass of gold in the Reserve Banks so vast that it amounts to 75 per cent of all the deposits and outstanding notes of the twelve Reserve Banks. The notes could be wholly paid off in gold and still leave enough to serve as about 42 per cent reserve for the deposits of the Reserve Banks; a reserve percentage even then larger than they had for both notes and deposits at the peak of expansion in 1920. . . . If the Reserve Banks expanded their loans to a point where the reserves stood at 40 per cent—about the legal minimum—instead of 75 per cent as at present, we would lend three and three-quarters billions in excess of what we are now loaning, and this addition to banking reserves of all the banks of the country would enable them in turn to expand loans and deposits by something like fifteen or sixteen billions.[27]

This—the "classical" or "orthodox" policy in the circumstances—would lead, the Governor is convinced, to a dangerous inflation. He continues:

So the reserve percentage is a bad and dangerous guide to a lending policy. But it will then be asked, "What shall be the guide if not the reserve percentage?" and a chorus of answers will come back—"Prices," or "An index number," and we again get around to the point where, for the moment, some people think that prices should be *the* guide. . . .

Strong's own answer to the question was far from simple:

Just as credit is *one* of the influences upon the price level, so the price level should be *one* of the influences in guiding a credit policy. There are other influences which affect prices, and so must there be other influences which affect a credit policy. Here are a few briefly suggested:

Is labor fully employed?
Are stocks of goods increasing or decreasing?
Is production up to the country's capacity?
Are transportation facilities fully taxed?
Is speculation creeping into productive and distributive processes?
Are orders and repeat orders being booked much ahead?
Are bills being promptly paid?
Are people spending wastefully?
Is credit expanding?
Are market rates above or below Reserve Bank rates?

[27] Benjamin Strong, *Interpretations of Federal Reserve Policy* (ed. W. Randolph Burgess) (New York: Harper, 1930), pp. 232–34.

Most of the criteria proposed by the Governor relate more or less directly to the level of business activity. Indeed the references to full employment and the utilization of productive capacity as guideposts for monetary policy anticipate the Keynesian arguments of a later era. However, the references to speculation and the prompt payment of bills suggest a continued concern with the uses or quality of credit which harks back to the commercial-loan theory. When he asks, "Is credit expanding?" it is hard to know what is in the Governor's mind. Finally, he is not yet emancipated from the notion that bank rates should be adjusted to market rates, instead of the other way around.

We may say in summary that the Governor believed there were five guideposts to credit policy:

(1) the reserve (i.e., gold) position of the Reserve Banks;
(2) the behavior of the commodity-price level;
(3) the level of business activity;
(4) the quality of credit, or uses to which it is put;
(5) the relation of the Bank's discount rate to open-market rates.

To anticipate the results of four decades of discussion since that time, one could dogmatize that to pay attention to (1) would be a regrettable necessity; that (4) and (5) are not appropriate criteria for credit policy; and that (2) and (3) probably are the proper objectives.

The Governor offered no guidance as to what should be done if his criteria conflicted, except that as of the time of writing (April 1923) the reserve situation was a dangerous guide and should be subordinated to other criteria. In Strong's mind the practical prescription for the time seems to have been that member-bank reserve balances should be kept roughly constant, securities being sold to offset the (otherwise inflationary) effects of gold imports. The conflict between this position and the classical "rules of the gold-standard game"—which would have called for internal credit expansion to check the gold movement—did not apparently bother Strong at this time, although it was to do so later when (after the return to convertibility in Europe) the international gold standard became, temporarily, a reality once more. Strong therefore confined himself, in 1923, to resisting pressure from Miller, through the Board, for the opposite policy—the liquidation of such governments as the System then held. Miller's attitude toward open-market policy, then as later, was ambiguous. In principle the purchase of governments made him unhappy because it did not jibe with the commercial-loan theory; in practice he disliked open-market policy because it was difficult for the Board to control. Later he was to be very critical of the use Strong made of open-market policy, and even to argue that open-market purchases were an "interference" that should be kept for "emergencies."[28]

Early in 1924, in its *Annual Report for 1923*, the Board staged a partial retreat from the pristine dogmatism of its view that bank rate should rule above market rate. Partly because of the very great dispersion of customer-loan rates, regionally and by size of borrower and community, the Board no longer felt that rates prevailing in the open market could be decisive in fixing discount rates. The "loose analogy with the London market" was repudiated.[29] But there was still no sign that the Board realized that its own policies helped to determine market rates, and that to use them as a basis for fixing the discount rate—except in the most proximate sense—involved circular reasoning.[30] Strong's guidepost (5) still had some life in it. Meanwhile, for the first time the Board had something to say about guidepost (3)—the state of business:

> When production reaches the limits imposed by the available supplies of labor, plant capacity, and transportation facilities—in fact, whenever the productive energies and resources of the country are employed at full capacity—output cannot be enlarged by an increased use of credit and by further increases in prices.[31]

Yet this passing reference, which has such a modern ring, was not pursued. Instead, the Board retreats into vagueness:

> When production, trade, and employment are in good volume and the credit resources of the commercial banks of the country are approxi-

---

[28] For the events of 1923, see Chandler, Ch. VI. Miller's later views are to be found in House Committee on Banking and Currency, *Stabilization*, Hearings on H.R. 11806, 70th Cong. 1st Sess., 1928, pp. 187–93.

[29] *Loc. cit.*, p. 8.

[30] More than two years later, in 1926, W. Randolph Burgess, then Assistant Federal Reserve Agent of the New York Bank, continued to give open-market rates as the prime criterion for fixing the discount rate. In a lengthy statement he asserted that the discount rate should be fixed at a point below the open-market rate on commercial paper, but above that on bank acceptances, yet (as of that date) he betrayed no realization that the open-market rates in question are powerfully influenced by the System's own open-market policy, and that the reasoning is in large measure circular (House Committee on Banking and Currency, *Stabilization*, Hearings on H.R. 7895, 69th Cong. 1st Sess., 1926, pp. 964–70). Even as late as 1931, the New York Reserve Bank continued to exhibit the same blind spot (see below).

[31] *Annual Report of the Federal Reserve Board for 1923*, p. 5.

mately all employed and there are signs neither of speculative business expansion nor of business reaction, Federal Reserve Bank rates should be neither so low as to invite the use of credit for speculative purposes nor so high as to discourage its use for meeting legitimate productive needs of the business community. It seems clear that if business is undergoing a rapid expansion and is in danger of developing an unhealthy or speculative boom, it should not be assisted by too easy credit conditions. . . . It seems equally obvious that if industry or trade are in process of recovery after a period of reaction, they should be given the support and encouragement of cheaper credit. . . .[32]

These attitudes on the part of Governor Strong and the Board represent a high-water mark of openmindedness and good sense. Renewed rational discussion of these matters was to be postponed many years, first by bitter controversy as to the proper attitude toward the stock market, and then by the apparent impotence of policy in the face of business collapse. Not until the regime of Chairman Eccles in the late 1930's was further progress possible in the intellectual attack upon the System's problems.

The Recession of 1924

Having climbed almost without interruption since April 1921, industrial production (on a 1923–1925 base) reached a peak of 106 in April through June 1923, and then fell intermittently to a low point of 84 in July 1924. Thus the downturn followed, with a 3- to 4-month lag, the gentle restraints imposed on credit early in 1923. The System's response was reasonably prompt. The New York discount rate was reduced from 4½% to 3% in steps between May and August 1924. On May 29 the Open Market Committee voted purchases, and a substantial amount of governments was bought during the last seven months of the year: together with continued gold imports, they assured easier money. The policy was clearly intended to revive business, but a desire to discourage the import of gold and to revive European currencies were also given as reasons.[33] Yet the latter reasons had been applicable for the past two years at least, and can hardly have been decisive at this juncture.

The discount rate was still thought of, at least in Washington, as something you adjusted to a market rate whose level was not under your control:

[32] *Ibid.,* p. 10.
[33] Memorandum by Strong, December 1924: see Strong, pp. 256–61; also Hamlin diary.

Discount rates . . . were reduced [during 1924]. . . . These reductions were made at a time of a recession in industrial activity, decreasing factory employment, slackened demand for commodities, and unusual ease in the money market. Money rates by the middle of the year, as the result of the less active demand for credit, and the abundance of funds arising out of the inflow of currency and of gold, had declined to the lowest levels in a decade, and discount rates at the Reserve Banks were adjusted to prevailing credit and business conditions.[34]

What, it may be reasonably asked in the light of this statement, would the System have done about discount rates, had not "the less active demand for credit" and "the inflow of gold" lowered open-market rates? Would it have recognized its responsibility to influence open-market rates through security purchases, would it have lowered discount rates without waiting for open-market rates to fall, or would it have maintained discount rates despite the evident decline in business activity?

Business Revival, 1925–1926

Business revived rapidly, perhaps in response to the easy-money policy, and by the early months of 1925 had returned to its best levels of 1923. The System could feel reasonably well satisfied with its handling of the situation. During the first quarter of 1925 there occurred the first substantial exports of gold in more than four years (Fig. 1), but the decline in the monetary gold stock was not great enough to reimpose the reserve ratio as a criterion of credit policy. In fact during this entire period—from the end of 1920 until late in 1931—the System was able to neglect external factors in reaching its decisions. The gold export soon slackened, and from April 1925 until the end of 1926 neither gold movements nor open-market operations were of much consequence. Gentle restraint was imposed between November 1925 and January 1926, the discount rate being increased to 4% at banks (including New York) with a 3½% rate. This move was undoubtedly connected with a desire to keep credit out of the stock market, but it divided the System. It furnished a preview, in fact, of the battle royal that was to be fought out in 1928 and 1929.[35]

[34] *Annual Report of the Federal Reserve Board for 1924*, p. 10.
[35] See Adolph C. Miller in House Committee on Banking and Currency, *Stabilization*, Hearings on H.R. 7895, 69th Cong. 1st Sess., 1927, pp. 641–42; also Hamlin diary.

Since mid-1924 equity prices had been rising steadily and brokers' loans increasing, although commodity prices were on the whole declining. Concern to keep credit out of the stock market seems to have been general—a concern that was to mount during the next three years. The movement for higher rates seems to have been led by Platt and Miller: Strong went along reluctantly, being concerned about the possible effect in Europe. Secretary Mellon, Governor Crissinger, and Cunningham appear to have had no strong opinion; James represented the agrarian desire for cheap money, and Hamlin proposed "direct action," a term that is said to have been invented by Leffingwell. In substance, this meant Reserve credit would be denied to member banks that lent to the stock market. The matter was thrashed out at a meeting of the Open Market Committee (November 27, 1925) at which Governors Harding and Strong for the Boston and New York Banks exposed the obstacles to direct action. The objections, valid enough but repeated *ad nauseam* over the next several years, were: the Reserve Banks can control only those member banks in debt to them; not only call loans to brokers, but also other security and real-estate loans feed speculation; the policy, if pressed, would lead to credit rationing and create a panic. One's sympathies certainly are with the Banks, which would have had to enforce an unpopular, arbitrary, and administratively complicated procedure, and one cannot help feeling that Hamlin, and other Board members who subsequently espoused his proposal, were somewhat lighthearted in their freedom from operational responsibility.

During March 1926 the stock market underwent a short but sharp reaction, occasioned perhaps not so much by the mild credit restriction as by the publication for the first time of figures for brokers' loans, which revealed the considerable dependence of the stock market on borrowed money. In April the New York discount rate was reduced to 3½% and in August—when equity prices again showed a rising tendency—it was raised to 4%. This slight easing of credit, for which there is no firm explanation, has been attributed to a desire to stem the decline in the stock market,[36] but it is more plausible to suppose the decline checked the growth of brokers' loans and that the System therefore felt less concern on this account.

[36] Charles O. Hardy, *Credit Policies of the Federal Reserve System* (Washington, D.C.: Brookings Institution, 1932), pp. 122–23.

The Stabilization Bills[37]

As the practical men at the Federal Reserve picked their way among conflicting objectives, a movement developed to substitute one broad and simple criterion for all others. This was to be no less than the stabilization of the general level of commodity prices, to be prescribed by law as the over-riding—or at least the primary —purpose of Reserve policy. In fact the original draft of the Federal Reserve Act of 1913 would have provided that discount rates should be fixed "with a view to accommodating the commerce of the country, *and promoting a stable price level.*" The phrase in italics was inserted in the bill by Senator Owen at the suggestion of George H. Shibley, a long-time bimetallist, but was not enacted. After World War I, numerous bills were introduced to amend the Federal Reserve Act in this sense, and extensive hearings were held before the banking committees of Senate and House in 1922–1923, 1926–1927, 1928, 1932, and 1934.[38]

Our present interest in the debate, which extended over more than a decade, stems from the information it yields about the thinking of Federal Reserve officials and from its effect upon public attitudes toward the System.

The first Goldsborough bill, introduced in 1922, embodied the Fisher plan for a compensated dollar. The gold content of the dollar was to be made to vary inversely with the purchasing power of gold. The hearings on the bill before the House Committee on Banking and Currency were devoted largely to exposition of the proposal by Irving Fisher, James Harvey Rogers, Willford King, and George H. Shibley. The novel and ambitious nature of the plan must have startled the Committee, and it had no difficulty in deciding to shelve the bill without calling on Treasury or Federal Reserve officials for their opinions.

[37] The history of these legislative attempts is well summarized in Irving Fisher, *Stable Money: A History of the Movement* (New York: Adelphi Co., 1934).

[38] House Committee on Banking and Currency, *Stabilization of Purchasing Power of Money*, Hearings on H.R. 11788 (first Goldsborough bill), 66th Cong. 4th Sess., 1923; *Stabilization*, Hearings on H.R. 7895 (first Strong bill), 69th Cong. 1st Sess., 1927; *Stabilization*, Hearings on H.R. 11806 (second Strong bill), 70th Cong., 1st Sess., 1928; *Stabilization of Commodity Prices*, Hearings on H.R. 10517 (second Goldsborough bill), 72nd Cong. 1st Sess., 1932; Senate Committee on Banking and Currency, *Restoring and Maintaining the Average Purchasing Power of the Dollar*, Hearings on S. 4429 (Fletcher bill), 72nd Cong. 1st Sess., 1932; House Committee on Banking and Currency. *To Establish the Federal Monetary Authority*, Hearings on H.R. 7157 and H.R. 8780 (third Goldsborough bill), 73rd Cong. 2nd Sess., 1934.

Much the most interesting debate arose over the two Strong bills of 1926 and 1928. They were introduced by Representative James G. Strong, no relation to Governor Benjamin Strong. The proposal they embodied was much less sensational than the Fisher plan and left far more discretion to whomever should administer the law. The first bill (H.R. 7895, 69th Congress) would have provided that rates of discount should be established

> with a view to accommodating commerce and promoting a stable price level for commodities in general. All of the powers of the Federal Reserve System shall be used for promoting stability in the price level.

Irving Fisher felt the bill did not go far enough, and pointed out particularly the difficulty that would arise if deflation should occur in the rest of the gold-standard world. But the objections of Reserve Board officials were of a practical nature. Governor Strong was diplomatic: he sympathized with the aims of the bill, but felt it would be misinterpreted—farmers would think it promised the stabilization of individual product prices. He claimed that since 1921 Federal Reserve policies had been as nearly directed toward stabilization of the price level as human wisdom would allow. His fundamental objection to writing price stabilization into the law was that, while the System could always influence the volume and cost of credit, the volume and cost of credit might not always influence the price level, and that therefore passage of the bill might lead the public to expect too much.

Miller's position in opposition to the proposal was somewhat more extreme, and also less well defined. He went so far as to claim that the restoration of the international gold standard, then in progress, would secure a greater degree of stability in the purchasing power of money than could any managed-currency proposal. In another part of his testimony he asserted that, if only credit could be kept out of speculative channels, stabilization of the commodity-price level would be automatically achieved! When pressed for his reasons for the latter statement, he revived the commercial-loan theory:

> Whenever credit is extended . . . to facilitate current productive operations, that credit washes itself out. It liquidates itself; because, at the moment credit goes forth, there are goods going forth, and they move in parallel lines, and as the goods come to market they extinguish the credit. Broadly speaking, you cannot have excessive credit without speculation. You cannot have an excess of credit where credit is re-

stricted to the financing of current operations in industry, trade, and agriculture in the making and marketing of goods.[39]

In 1926 the commercial-loan theory was by no means dead—perhaps is still alive today—yet it seems unlikely that Miller really held it in this simple form. Rather, any stick was good enough with which to beat the stabilization proposals: if pressed, Miller surely would have taken refuge in his qualification, "broadly speaking."

The common denominator of the official opposition to the Strong bill rested on an avowed depreciation of the powers of the System and of monetary policy at large. This opposition is epitomized in what W. P. G. Harding, then Governor of the Boston Bank, said to the Stable Money Association in New York on May 3, 1926:

> In my opinion most of the criticism which has been directed against the System . . . is based upon misapprehension of the powers granted to the Federal Reserve Board by the Federal Reserve Act, or rather an exaggerated idea of what those powers are. . . . When a banking system is proclaimed as a cure-all . . . failure to relieve any adverse conditions brings it into disrepute. Should Representative Strong's bill become law, I apprehend that a large part of the public, at least, would assume that the Federal Reserve Board had power not only to promote a stable price level for commodities in general but to correct any maladjustment in the price level [of individual commodities]. . . . Believers in the almighty power to swing trade and prices of the discount rates of central banks lay great stress on the psychological effect produced by their movements . . . the price of money is a factor undoubtedly, but it is not the only factor. . . . Do not understand me as being out of sympathy with the objects of the bill which Representative Strong has introduced in the House. I have merely attempted to give some of my reasons for believing that the object desired cannot be accomplished by the means proposed.[40]

Early in 1927 Representative Strong withdrew H.R. 7895, partly in consequence of a promise by Governor Strong to help him revise the bill. This promise was honored in the course of several conferences between the Congressman and the banker during the winter of 1927–28. The revised version was introduced as H.R. 11806 in March 1928. This, the second Strong bill, made direct reference to the gold standard and was far less dogmatic about stabilization:

[39] Hearings on H.R. 7895, pp. 853–54.
[40] Ibid., pp. 1038–42.

> The Federal Reserve System shall use all the powers and authority now
> or hereafter possessed by it to maintain a stable gold standard; to pro-
> mote the stability of commerce, industry, agriculture, and employment;
> and a more stable purchasing power of the dollar, so far as such pur-
> poses may be accomplished by monetary and credit policy.

Governor Strong did not testify at the hearings on this bill, for he
had left for Europe to recuperate from a bad attack of shingles:
indeed he had only a few more months to live. Probably we shall
never know how far he would have been willing to go in support of
the new bill which he undoubtedly had helped to write. For the
Board, Miller testified at enormous length, and Governor Young
very briefly: both opposed the bill, denying the System had power to
control the price level. Yet, reading the testimony, one feels the substantial reason for their opposition was that they hated, as adminis-
trators, to see their discretion limited. As Miller put it, the bill
"awakens expectations as to a general improvement in the operation
of our whole social and economic system that will be pressed home
upon the Federal Reserve Board for attainment."[41]

Irving Fisher has suggested that the virulence of Miller's attack
upon the bill, a virulence that so bewildered Representative Strong,
may have been due to the fact that Miller knew that Governor Strong
had had a hand in drafting it.[42]

A third member of the Board, Hamlin, who was seldom found to
share any opinion with Miller, testified that, with some minor
changes, the bill was acceptable to him. He expressed the interesting
belief that prices should be allowed to fall with increasing productivity, and to this Representative Strong made no objection. Hamlin's
reason was, not that price stabilization could lead to profit inflation
under such circumstances, but that exports might be checked if
prices outside the United States were allowed to fall. Commons, on
the other hand, argued that stabilization of the price level is desirable even in the face of rapidly increasing productivity, on the
dubious ground that falling prices depress business whatever the
cause of the fall.

Commons and Sprague, economists sympathetic to the bill, pointed
out the impossibility of stabilizing commodity prices in the United

[41] Hearings on H.R. 11806, p. 109.
[42] Fisher, p. 180; this opinion is supported by some passages in the testimony (see
Hearings on H.R. 11806, pp. 189–90, 213).

States, under the gold standard, in the event the international price level should prove unstable. For this reason they advocated de facto stabilization of the commodity value of gold through international action, and instanced recent cooperation between central banks as evidence of its feasibility.

Many years later Miller had this to say:

> In my judgment, the persistent propaganda that went on in the twenties to try to amend the Federal Reserve Act so as to write into it a price commodity index formula did more than anything else to divert the attention of the mind of the Federal Reserve System from its true function. There was enough of flirtation with that theory in the Federal Reserve System that some of the leading minds of the System were pretty thoroughly infected with the price stabilization philosophy, and I think they were led into believing that so long as the price commodity index was all right, everything was all right.[43]

Miller did not say what he considered the System's "true function," from which it had been seduced, but he probably meant keeping money out of the stock market. Others, who think commodity-price tendencies during the 1920's were inflationary, may feel that the "propaganda" prevented the System from allowing commodity prices to decline in face of increasing productivity.

The Recession of 1927

The year opened with gold imports and hesitant business. The gold imports eased the money market only slightly, for they were accompanied by open-market sales of securities (Fig. 1). After two years of almost continuous business expansion, industrial production (on a 1923–1925 base) declined from 111 in September–October 1926 to 101 in November 1927. The recession was milder than that of 1924, but international considerations reinforced domestic concerns in causing the System to lower discount rates and, beginning in August, to make large open-market purchases. The gold flow soon turned outward, but the expansion of Reserve credit was—until the end of the year—more than sufficient to prevent any decline in member-bank reserves. As the Reserve Board later reported:

> . . . a policy of easing the credit situation was adopted by the System in consideration of the recession in business in the United States . . . During [1927] it also became evident that there was a serious credit

---

[43] Senate Committee on Banking and Currency, *Banking Act of 1935*, Hearings on S. 1715, 74th Cong. 1st Sess., 1935, pp. 719–20.

stringency in European countries generally, and it was felt that easy money in this country would help foreign countries to meet their autumn demand for credit and exchange without unduly depressing their exchanges or of increasing the cost of credit to trade and industry.[44]

But behind this bland account lay events that shook the System to its foundations.

The policy of easy money during the second half of 1927 was undoubtedly initiated by the New York Reserve Bank under Governor Strong. This was perhaps natural, for international considerations played a role, and the New York bank was in closer touch with foreign money markets than were other parts of the System. Early in July, Montague Norman, Governor of the Bank of England, Hjalmar Schacht, President of the Reichsbank, and Charles Rist, Deputy Governor of the Bank of France, had several conferences with Strong in New York and spent most of a day (July 7, 1927) with the Board in Washington. It is evident that the visit to Washington was almost wholly social, and the content of negotiations (if any) with Strong in New York has never been revealed.[45] On July 27 at a meeting of the Open Market Committee, Strong announced that Great Britain would not be able to maintain convertibility unless either she raised her rates or we lowered ours; that if the British raised their rates it would mean they could buy less cotton and wheat; that New York would like to reduce its discount rate, but wished to make the policy of ease a System matter. Governor MacDougal promptly said that Chicago would not cooperate. All agreed the only possible reason against such a policy lay in the risk of encouraging stock-market speculation, but most thought this problem should be handled by direct action. Probably Strong himself was somewhat concerned about the effect of cheaper money on the stock market, the more so since he did not believe in direct action:[46] evidently the business recession and the desire to help Europe overcame any doubts he may have had on this score. As for the opposition of Chicago, Strong advised against *ordering* rate reductions, denying that the Board had the power to give such orders.

Strong's ideas were sympathetically received by the Board and

---

[44] *Annual Report of the Federal Reserve Board for 1927*, p. 10.
[45] See Adolph C. Miller in House Committee on Banking and Currency, *Stabilization*, Hearings on H.R. 11806, 70th Cong. 1st Sess., 1928, pp. 216–20. See also Hamlin diary.
[46] Benjamin H. Beckhart, *The New York Money Market* (New York: Columbia University Press, 1932), IV, 66.

most of the other governors. Although gold imports since 1924 had been moderate, there seemed to exist a rather persistent tendency for gold to gravitate here. Complaints were frequent, especially from those European countries that had recently resumed convertibility, to the effect that the United States had sterilized a large part of the world's gold and so caused a shortage elsewhere. In view of our then generally accepted interest in the further restoration and maintenance of an international gold standard, the System undoubtedly was sensitive to these complaints. No doubt they were gently pressed home by the three European visitors.

It soon became evident that the Chicago Bank was firmly wedded to other ideas. On September 6, Cunningham moved that the Board put in a 3½% rate at that Bank. Governor Crissinger, Comptroller MacIntosh, and James supported him; Hamlin, Miller, and Platt voted against the proposal. Only Platt thought the Board lacked authority: others relied upon the opinion that Glass had obtained from Attorney General Palmer (December 9, 1919; see Ch. 3). Hamlin and Miller wanted postponement in the hope that Chicago would shortly give way of its own accord. Secretary Mellon was away from Washington. Chicago seems to have been motivated partly by jealousy of New York, partly by disapproval of a policy of cheap money to help Europe, and partly by fears of its Class A directors that lower rates might damage member-bank earnings.[47]

The repercussions were immediate. Partly because it was soon revealed that the action had been taken by a bare majority of the Board, a vehement protest arose, led by Senator Glass, against what was described as usurpation of authority by the Board. In self-defense the Board published the Attorney General's ruling, and re-

[47] See Hamlin diary. See also Adolph C. Miller, "Responsibility for Federal Reserve Policies: 1927–1929," *American Economic Review*, XXV (September 1935), p. 442; Hearings on H.R. 11806, pp. 165, 223; and Senate Committee on Banking and Currency, *Operation of the National and Federal Reserve Banking Systems*, Hearings on S.R. 71, 71st Cong. 3rd Sess., 1931, p. 134, where Miller characterized easy money in 1927 as "one of the most costly errors committed by [the Federal Reserve] or any other banking system in the last 75 years." Apparently persuaded by Miller that the Board's policies were inflationary, Herbert Hoover, then Secretary of Commerce, tried to interfere in the early Fall of 1927, but Crissinger and James reproached him for his "parochical view of world affairs . . . I urged President Coolidge, as I had done eighteen months before, to send for Crissinger and express alarm at the situation. Mr. Coolidge, a strict legalist, again insisted that the Reserve Board had been created by the Congress entirely independent of the Executive and that he could not interfere. The Secretary of the Treasury, Mr. Mellon, also declined and seemed to think that my anxiety was alarmist and my interference unwarranted" (*Memoirs*, III, 11). See also William Allen White, *A Puritan in Babylon* (New York: Macmillan, 1958), pp. 367–370.

vealed that the ruling had been asked for by Glass himself when Secretary of the Treasury, and that when requesting it Glass had claimed for the Board the very powers that he was now describing as a usurpation. Others can afford to be inconsistent, but not politicians. If the sting was taken from the protest, the locus of authority within the System was not finally settled.

A few days later (September 15, 1927) Governor Crissinger announced his resignation from the Board. It was generally thought that Secretary Mellon had demanded his resignation: the presumptive ground was that the Governor should not have forced the Board to take action in the Secretary's absence on a matter which could well have awaited the Secretary's return to Washington within a day or so.[48] On October 4, Roy A. Young was appointed Governor of the Board. In January 1928 the Chicago Bank asked for a 4% rate, and this was approved, only Cunningham voting in opposition. Peace reigned once more with the return of the status quo.[49]

The Stock Market Boom, 1928–1929

By the end of 1927 the level of common-stock prices and the volume of brokers' loans had each roughly doubled since the middle of 1924. Rates on call loans had risen to a high level, and thereby substantial amounts of money had been attracted from the interior to the New York market. There is no doubt that, ever since 1925, these developments had worried Reserve officials. Miller, and perhaps other members of the Board, had disliked the easy-money policy of 1927, regarding it as an encouragement to stock-market lending: they welcomed a somewhat tighter money market in 1928. Whether Strong, who had initiated credit relaxation in 1924 and again in 1927, himself felt that a mistake had been made, probably we shall never know. On August 18, 1927, shortly after he had successfully sold the easy-money policy to the Reserve Board, he wrote:

> . . . if the Federal Reserve System is to be run solely with a view to regulating stock speculation instead of being devoted to the interests of the industry and commerce of the country, then its policy will degenerate simply to regulating the affairs of gamblers. I have no hesitation in expressing my impatience with such a view of our role.[50]

[48] Hamlin diary, September 15, 1927.
[49] On the Chicago incident, see William O. Weyforth, *The Federal Reserve Board* (Baltimore: Johns Hopkins Press, 1933), pp. 74–81.
[50] Chandler, p. 444.

But on May 25, 1928, only a few months before his death, he made this wry comment:

> [We are] now paying the penalty for the decision which was reached early in 1924 to help the rest of the world back to a sound financial and monetary basis [by easing credit in the United States].[51]

As early as January 10, 1928, the Board discussed the probable need for higher rates on account of the stock market. On the following day it was decided to reverse the open-market policy, selling instead of buying securities. Soon rates were raised, the New York discount rate going in steps from 3½% to 5% by midyear. During the first six months of the year gold continued to leave the country—in fact, until finally checked by higher money rates. The gold loss was accompanied by large open-market sales of governments (Fig. 1). Member-bank reserve balances declined slightly—for the first time since 1921—and member-bank borrowing rose sharply, so that the higher rates were quickly made effective. However, these measures did not prevent member-bank credit from expanding and brokers' loans from increasing, although the tightening of credit did have the effect of raising call-money rates from around 4% in January to around 6% in June.

During the second half of 1928, the stock market continued to rise, brokers' loans increased further, and call-money rates rose to around 9%. Open-market acceptance rates rose, and by January 1929, when acceptance-buying rates finally were raised, two-thirds of all outstanding acceptances were held by the System. Miller later claimed that the System had "drifted in the midst of a perilous situation" at this time, while the Board waited for proposals or action by the Banks. "It is abundantly clear," he said in retrospect,

> that acceptance by the Board of aggressive easing action proposed by the New York Federal Reserve Bank in 1927 and of complete abandonment of restraining action in the second half of 1928 proves that the Board, under the established tradition, was first too quick to fall in with a daring and dangerous proposal and later too slow to assume the leadership which was needed and was lacking at a most critical time . . . in the second half of 1928 the Board looked to the Federal Reserve Banks for the initiation of further measures of restraint and the Banks, in turn, depended on the leadership of the Federal Reserve Bank of New York. And New York's leadership proved to be unequal to the situation.

[51] *Ibid.*, p. 281.

The "daring and dangerous proposal," which Miller had fought at the time, was of course initiated by Strong. "Brilliant of mind, engaging of personality, fertile of resource, strong of will, ambitious of spirit, [Strong] had extraordinary skill in impressing his views and purposes on his associates" in the System. But by the summer of 1928 Benjamin Strong was a very sick man, and in November he died. The "drifting" to which Miller refers was perhaps due to the Governor's illness. But Miller was soon to renew his struggle even more bitterly with Strong's successors at the New York Bank.[52]

Yet the indecisiveness of Reserve policy during the second half of 1928 is due more to differences of viewpoint within the System than Miller was later willing to admit. In fact the differences of viewpoint became ever sharper, and the indecisiveness ever more acute, until the stock market collapsed in the Fall of the following year. During the first half of 1928 the System was able to agree upon a reversal of the cheap-money policy of 1927. Higher rates, although they seemed to have no effect on the stock market, were not called for by the business situation, and they threatened to drain gold from Europe at a time when the gold standard had only recently been re-established there.[53]

At the Board, sentiment revived for direct action. Cunningham proposed (May 28, 1928) to direct the Reserve Banks to report the names of all borrowing member banks with call loans outstanding. He was supported by Miller and James, but other members of the Board felt the problem should be left to individual Reserve Banks to handle, or that call loans should not be singled out from other speculative loans. In August the Open Market Committee decided, over the opposition of Miller and James, to ease the autumn strain through purchases, principally of acceptances. In September, Acting Governor Harrison of the New York Bank favors easing the market, but is in conflict with his own directors. Later (January 4, 1929) when the autumn strain is presumably over, the New York acceptance-buying rate is increased and open-market purchases are brought to a halt.[54]

As the stock market rose and brokers' loans expanded, the opinion

---

[52] Quotations are from Adolph C. Miller, "Responsibility for Federal Reserve Policies: 1927–1929," *American Economic Review*, XXV (September 1935), 442–58.
[53] Seymour Harris, *Twenty Years of Federal Reserve Policy* (Cambridge: Harvard University Press, 1933), pp. 476–80.
[54] Hamlin diary.

became more definite that the use of member-bank credit, itself perhaps indirectly furnished by the Reserve Banks, for stock-market
purposes was contrary to the spirit, if not to the letter, of the Federal
Reserve Act. Section 4 of the Act charged the System with "the accommodation of commerce, industry, and agriculture," and the use
of funds—or at any rate the increased use of funds—for loans to
brokers was not considered to fall within this category. Miller was
among those who felt this most strongly. Indeed, he pursued his aim
of keeping credit out of the stock market with a single-mindedness
one cannot but admire, albeit worthy of a better cause. In April
1926 he had said:

> I have always taken the view that, though it is not categorically ex-
> pressed in the Federal Reserve Act, the whole intent and implication of
> the Act is that credit of the Federal Reserve System is to be restricted
> to productive uses in commerce, agriculture, trade and industry. But I
> think possibly there are some who take a different view. Perhaps they
> do not take it very positively, but nevertheless feel that there is doubt;
> while they might at times perhaps regret that there is evidence of some
> seepage of Federal Reserve credit into speculative channels, neverthe-
> less, they feel that it is not their responsibility to try, by all means,
> direct and indirect, to stop it. I think perhaps I am an extremist on
> this point. To me the most simple formula of operating the Federal
> Reserve System to give the country stability . . . is to stop and abso-
> lutely foreclose the diversion of any Federal Reserve credit to specu-
> lative purposes.[55]

At that time Miller had expressed a belief in the use of the discount
rate to curb stock-market credit, but now he felt other methods were
called for. Accordingly, with missionary-like zeal, he set out to persuade his colleagues on the Board to instruct the Reserve Banks to
force member banks to reduce their call or other security loans. The
new policy of "direct pressure" (or "moral suasion" as it was also
called) was approved by the Board early in 1929. The policy was
announced in a long statement of which the kernel read: "a member
bank is not within its reasonable claims for rediscount . . . when
it borrows . . . for the purpose of making speculative loans."[56]
The Reserve Banks were urged by the Board to deny credit to
member banks that made security loans. The reaction was immedi-

---

[55] House Committee on Banking and Currency, *Stabilization*, Hearings on H.R. 7895,
69th Cong. 1st Sess., 1927, p. 671.
[56] Circular of February 2, 1929. See *Federal Reserve Bulletin*, February 1929, p. 94.

ate. On February 4 Governor Harding says direct pressure can achieve nothing and asks for a 6% rate for Boston. On the following day Governor Harrison, who has now succeeded Strong, comes before the Board to plead for a 6% rate in New York; his Bank, he says, has done all it can to admonish those member banks which are out of line; he admits that 6% would not be good for trade, and suggests even higher rates may yet be necessary. For these and similar increases asked by other Banks, the Board refuses to give permission.

Unfortunately for the Board, not being an operating agency, it could enforce direct pressure, if at all, only with the active cooperation of the Reserve Banks, and particularly of the New York Bank. And the New York Bank refused to cooperate. Apart from the real difficulties of the policy, administrative and otherwise, if rationing and gross inequities were to be avoided, we may recall that three of the nine directors were member bankers, and could scarcely be enthusiastic about the proposed policy. The attitude of the New York directors may have been influenced, too, by knowledge that the Board's initiative resulted from a split decision, the Secretary of the Treasury, Governor, and Vice-Governor being in the minority.[57] There undoubtedly was an element of personal animosity and suspicion involved. Harrison was thought to be under Norman's influence, although the notion that the Bank of England wanted higher rates is a manifest absurdity. On February 14, 1929, Hamlin records in his diary: "I feel that [the] N[ew] Y[ork] directors . . . thought they could bluff the Board into a favorable decision. The Board however called their bluff and taught them a lesson they never will forget." On March 3, Hamlin gleefully reports that "the N[ew] Y[ork] directors are in a blue funk. They seem to have utterly lost their heads!" The opinions the New York (and Boston) directors held of the Board are not on record, but can well be imagined.

The dispute was aired before a Senate subcommittee in January 1931, nearly two years later, when tempers had had time to cool.

[57] Adolph C. Miller, "Responsibility for Federal Reserve Policies: 1927–1929," *American Economic Review*, XXV (September 1935), p. 456. The majority of the Board, supporting "direct pressure," was led by Miller and included Hamlin, Comptroller Pole, Cunningham, and James. The minority which was lukewarm about direct pressure and would have allowed the Banks to raise discount rates, was comprised of Secretary Mellon, Governor Young, and Vice-Governor Platt. Subsequently in committee hearings the following year, however, Governor Young refrained from explicitly dissociating himself from the Board's position (House Committee on Banking and Currency, *Branch, Chain and Group Banking*, Hearings, 1930, pp. 647–48).

Senator Glass, chairman of the subcommittee, took the part of the Board and desired Governor Harrison to explain why he had not followed the policy laid down from Washington, admonishing the member banks in his district, and if necessary refusing them credit. Was it not against the spirit of the Federal Reserve Act itself, Glass asked, to allow Reserve credit to be used for speculative purposes?

Governor Harrison at first replied that borrowing by a member bank, to meet a shortage of cash at the end of a day's business, could not be linked to the making of any specific loan or loans by the member bank. This is in general a sound position and is in line with that taken by most Reserve Board officials, including W. P. G. Harding, as Governor of the Board, as far back as 1921. Glass then wanted to know why Harrison had not denied accommodation to those member banks whose security loans were visibly increasing at any given time. Harrison's reply was that he could not supervise the day-to-day operations of his 900 member banks, and that in any case call loans of New York member banks did not appreciably increase during the year 1929. So far as concerned time loans on securities, the Governor pointed out that many commercial and industrial loans were secured by stock or bond collateral, and that an increase in such loans by member banks could by no means be equated with an increase in "speculative" lending. Furthermore

> our directors felt from the beginning the proper method of breaking [the expansion of brokers' loans], if it occurred, was through the rate rather than through a particular admonition to particular banks.

The Governor gave his opinion that such admonitions should be confined to cases of excessive or continuous borrowing.[58]

The great increase in brokers' loans during the Spring and Summer of 1929 came predominantly from nonbanking lenders, and Miller used this fact to claim success for the Board's policy of direct pressure.[59] Despite the refusal of the Reserve Bank of New York to apply pressure, publicity given to the Board's policy, and fear of its application, may of course have influenced member banks. More significantly, the ability of the stock market to finance itself from

[58] Senate Committee on Banking and Currency, *Operation of the National and Federal Reserve Banking Systems*, Hearings on S.R. 71, 71st Cong. 3rd Sess., 1931, pp. 50–60.

[59] Adolph C. Miller, "Responsibility for Federal Reserve Policies: 1927–1929," *American Economic Review*, XXV (September 1935), p. 456.

nonbanking sources may be interpreted as a justification of Governor Harrison's views:

> I do not think it is possible, through any action on the part of the Reserve System or any other central banking authority, to make money cheap for business and expensive for speculation. The credit pool is too big and fluid a pool for any group of men, whoever they may be, to dictate the rates for funds that are to be put to different purposes.

With call rates at 10%, 15%, and even 20%, it was profitable, for instance, for a businessman to pledge his inventories and other physical assets for a bank loan at 6%, 7% or 8% and lend the proceeds to a broker. While not regretting the cheap money of 1927, Harrison felt, as he looked back, that the New York rate should have been raised sooner and more courageously, perhaps 1% in December 1927 instead of ½% in January 1928. This is one of the very few points upon which Miller and Harrison agreed. Miller, in his appearance before the subcommittee, said he would have voted for a 6% rate in 1928, had it been proposed, although he voted against the proposal when it actually was made in February 1929.[60]

But to resume our story. Having denied the feasibility of the "direct pressure" desired by the Board, the New York directors continued to press for higher rates. Their position seems to have been that the cost of business borrowing had already risen, and would only return to normal once the boom had collapsed, and the stock market had ceased to be a major borrower.[61] Higher rates, particularly in New York, might help to restrain the stock market. Accordingly, the application by the New York Bank for a 6% rate, first made in February, was renewed in March 1929 and was promptly voted down 7 to 1 by the Board. Secretary Mellon and Governor Young, although they thought an increase would eventually be necessary, apparently felt "direct pressure" should be given a trial and therefore voted with the majority: only Platt was recorded in favor of the increase. Late in March call-money rates reached 15% and 20%, and equity prices receded some 10%. It was at this point that Charles E. Mitchell, chairman of the National City Bank and a director of the New York Reserve Bank, publicly offered call money

<hr>

[60] Senate Committee on Banking and Currency, *Operations of the National and Federal Reserve Banking Systems*, Hearings on S.R. 71, 71st Cong. 3rd Sess., 1931, pp. 59, 66, 141.

[61] Goldenweiser papers, George L. Harrison to Roy A. Young, April 10, 1929.

to those who needed it in consequence of the current liquidation. Mitchell was promptly lambasted by Senator Glass for sabotaging the Reserve System's efforts to keep money out of the stock market. Mitchell's motives may not have been as public-spirited as he claimed, but it is hard to see how he was bound, as a commercial banker, by a directive without legal force which he had had no part in framing. The incident reflects the tensions of the time, and suggests a question as to whether commercial bankers make good directors for a central bank.

During April the beginnings of a change in the Board's attitude may be observed. On the 19th the Federal Advisory Council meets with the Board, and explains at enormous length from the bankers' viewpoint the obstacles to enforcing "direct pressure." On the 25th still another New York application for a rate increase is disapproved, but now Secretary Mellon joins Platt in the minority and Governor Young and Comptroller Pole are not recorded. On May 4, a rise in the rate at Kansas City is approved, on grounds of its reserve ratio, only James voting in the negative. On May 16 yet another New York application is disapproved by a 5-to-3 vote, Mellon, Young, and Platt being in the minority.[62]

The rise in equity prices had been resumed, but in late May or early June the Board retreated from its position and quietly suspended "direct pressure." The reasons for the abandonment of the policy at this juncture are obscure, although arguments advanced by the New York Bank seem to have been a factor. Hamlin later claimed that the policy was abandoned because it had achieved its objective:[63] we can disbelieve this explanation without believing in the total ineffectiveness of the policy. It seems more likely that time brought each side to realize the weakness of its own position. Finally on August 9 the Board approved the long-standing request of the New York Bank for permission to raise its discount rate from 5% to 6%, and in return the Bank lowered its acceptance-buying rate to 5⅛%.

On October 23 the stock market reached its peak. Within a week the System began to replenish its holdings of governments, and on

[62] Hamlin diary.

[63] Senate Committee on Banking and Currency, *Operation of the National and Federal Reserve Banking Systems*, Hearings on S.R. 71, 71st Cong. 3rd Sess., 1931, pp. 164–65.

November 1 the discount rate at the New York Bank was cut to 5%. The great boom was over.

The Federal Reserve and the Stock Market

There is every sign that the Reserve Board and the New York Bank were in agreement that the use of Federal Reserve credit in the stock market was contrary to the spirit, if not indeed the letter, of the Federal Reserve Act. But they differed, particularly in the Spring of 1929, as to how to prevent this use. As early as April 1926, the articulate, yet somewhat cantankerous Adolph Miller, told the House Committee on Banking and Currency:

> I want to say a thing that perhaps cannot be repeated too often. I think it is true that the Federal Reserve System as a whole, and I think it is true of my own situation. I am not concerned with speculation. That does not interest me. What interests me is what becomes of the credit withdrawn from the Federal Reserve Banks. I take that view because it is my opinion that the intent of the Federal Reserve Act, as I read it, is that Federal Reserve credit is not to be used for speculative purposes. I think that is a sound position, and the only position that will safeguard both the Federal Reserve System and the country against serious shocks and occasionally serious disasters. I think we have got to try . . . to insure that credit that gets out of the Federal Reserve goes to the manufacture, distribution, and marketing of goods.[64]

This position needs comment.

The substance of the charge against the stock market was that the use of bank credit to hold stocks on margin raised its cost to other borrowers. The implication is that a given business situation justifies (or requires) a given volume of credit, and that, to the extent that the stock market absorbs credit, less is available for other users. The Reserve System and its apologists did not argue that instability in the level of equity prices would adversely affect business, but only that the absorption of credit (itself of course a by-product of the boom in equities) would do so. Was this argument sound?

A prolonged and somewhat acrimonious debate took place in the late 1920's and early 1930's as to whether absorption of credit by the stock market can occur. The matter has theoretical interest, and also has some bearing upon the justification for subsequent regulation of security credit by the Securities and Exchange Act of 1934.

[64] *Stabilization*, Hearings on H.R. 7895, 69th Cong. 1st Sess., 1927, p. 661.

The proponents of the view that absorption occurred, at least during the equity boom that culminated in 1929, were the Federal Reserve Board, and especially its most articulate member, Adolph Miller.[65] A large number of critics, especially university economists, have attacked the view that any significant absorption of credit can occur.[66] I shall try to summarize the outcome of the debate.

The rising level of brokers' loans, statistics for which first became available in 1925, showed that large sums were lent, by banks and others, to brokers for the use of their clients. Clearly the money was used by bulls to purchase stocks. If the bears, who sold the stocks to the bulls, kept the proceeds in the shape of idle balances, then indeed would funds be absorbed: the funds would be needed to satisfy the bears' demands for cash.[67] But in fact bears can equally well be satisfied with a money claim: and with call rates at a high level, there is no doubt that most sellers of securities lent out the cash they received, instead of holding idle balances. This reasoning makes it plain that the volume of transactions in a market can increase, the price level rise, and the bull and bear positions both expand, without any addition to idle cash balances. The bears borrow stock from the bulls, and the bulls buy it from the bears with money borrowed from the bears. No doubt some of the brokers' loans reported as obtained from nonbank sources record such loans from the bears to the bulls: such funds are lent by the market to the market and do not represent an inflow from outside, although they serve of course to swell the recorded total of "brokers' loans." Yet much of the money from nonbank sources came from elsewhere. Some small amounts of additional cash may indeed have been needed by the market for additions to working balances as the volume of transactions rose, but no such large amounts as were in fact contributed from outside. What then became of the vast volume of brokers' loans poured into the market from outside?

The answer is of course that the outflow of funds from the market

---

[65] See *Annual Reports of the Federal Reserve Board* and Miller's testimony before the House Banking and Currency Committee in the *Stabilization* hearings. Benjamin M. Anderson also took this viewpoint: see *Chase Economic Bulletin*, 1929, *passim*.

[66] Fritz Machlup, *The Stock Market, Credit and Capital Formation* (Edinburgh: Hodge, 1940); Harold L. Reed, *Federal Reserve Policy* (New York: McGraw-Hill, 1930); James H. Rogers, *Stock Speculation and the Money Market*, (Columbia, Mo.: Lucas, 1927).

[67] This is the (unreal) situation envisaged by Keynes in his classic treatment of the subject (*Treatise on Money* [London: Macmillan, 1930], I, 249–53).

was furnished by the sale of new issues. New issues of common stock could be more and more readily floated as the boom progressed. Paradoxically, the rise in short rates, resulting from the bulls' demand for call loans, made short-term financing more expensive, while the bulls' demand for stock made long-term financing a great deal easier. And the growth of brokers' loans can readily be correlated with the growth of new issues. Thus the expansion of bank credit served the capital needs of industry indirectly, by way of brokers' loans and the new-issue market. Meanwhile some of the money obtained from new issues, instead of being used right away for capital expenditure, was lent right back to the stock market, appearing as loans from "others." Thus vast extensions of the bull and bear positions could occur with very little expansion of bank credit.

A survey of the literature shows that the analysis summarized here stands up well and was not seriously controverted. I conclude that the charge that the stock market absorbed an appreciable volume of funds, or substantially raised the over-all cost of industrial capital, during the boom which culminated in 1929 cannot be justified.

The policy of trying to keep credit out of the stock market, i.e., trying to reduce the volume of brokers' loans, cannot be justified on the grounds principally advanced by the Reserve System. However, other lines of defense are open. It might be argued, for instance, that a stock-market boom should be checked because it makes long-term capital too easily accessible, thus encouraging too high a level of investment spending; or because a stock-market boom will be overdone and lead to a reaction, and that a reaction in stock prices may cut consumer expenditures, and so depress business; or because a stock-market boom promotes speculative activity, which is contrary to sound morals. Except possibly in the Spring of 1926, there is no suggestion that the Reserve System interested itself in the level of stock prices as such, although its efforts to reduce brokers' loans, had they been successful, might perhaps have kept the price of stocks at more moderate levels. Certainly the System never justified its anxiety about the scale of brokers' loans by appeal to any of the arguments just listed, and we shall not discuss them further at this point.[68]

[68] See, however, Charles O. Hardy, *Credit Policies of the Federal Reserve System* (Washington, D.C.: Brookings Institution, 1932), pp. 173–77.

Despite the indifference of the New York Reserve Bank, success was claimed for the Reserve Board's policy of "direct pressure" or "moral suasion," as it was applied from February to May 1929, on the ground that its immediate objective was achieved. Loans by member banks to brokers were kept stable or slightly reduced over the months indicated. In this narrow sense the success of the policy may be admitted. But that bank credit, viewed more broadly, was kept out of the stock market may be doubted. For commercial borrowers lent their own resources to the market, and some speculators no doubt borrowed directly from the banks instead of doing so through their brokers. The money market can be compartmentalized, but the compartments are not watertight. We shall return to the problem when we come to consider the legislation which gave the Reserve Board control of margin requirements.

Chapter 5

The Federal Reserve and the Great Depression, 1929–1939

> *The Governor was strong upon*
> *The Regulations Act:*
> *The Doctor said that Death was but*
> *A scientific fact:*
> *And twice a day the Chaplain called*
> *And left a little tract.*
>
> —OSCAR WILDE,
> The Ballad of Reading Gaol

Toward the end of October 1929 the New York Bank had resumed the purchase of governments without specific authorization from the Open Market Committee. Since the Bank could reasonably claim the purchases were of an emergency nature, it is doubtful whether such authorization was necessary. On October 31 the Board unanimously approved a reduction in the New York discount rate from 6% to 5% on the understanding no further purchases of governments would be made without the approval of the Board. Early in 1930 the Open Market Committee was reorganized as the Open Market Policy Conference as part of a move by the Board to tighten control over open-market operations in governments.

Cheap Money, 1930–1931

As the recession in business took hold, considerable disagreement developed within the System as to the usefulness of cheap money in stemming the decline. In general, the New York Bank under Harrison pressed for cheaper money, and the Board rather reluctantly went along. Miller, Cunningham, and James were most hesitant, Miller being especially distrustful of open-market purchases. In the

Spring of 1930 the stock market again became active with rising prices, causing doubts as to the wisdom of cheaper money.[1] Despite these reasons for hesitation, the System's reaction to declining business was to cheapen money, and the cheapening, as measured by rediscount rates, was considerable. The New York Bank's rate, for instance, declined from 6% in October 1929 to 2½% in June 1930 and 1½% in May 1931 (Fig. 1).

That the money market was made easier is not in doubt; but an inspection of Reserve Bank discount rates gives an exaggerated idea of the degree of ease which was in fact achieved. Between October 1929 and May 1931, customer-loan rates in the North and East declined from 5.99% to 4.19%, while the yield of Aaa bonds fell from 4.77% to 4.37% between the two dates. During the year and a half that followed the stock-market crash, therefore, the cost of commercial borrowing at short term was cut moderately, and the cost of long-term borrowing only slightly. Member-bank indebtedness was reduced sharply between October 1929 and April 1930, partly by the large-scale open-market purchases made during the last three months of 1929 and partly by the gold inflow that occurred during the first few months of 1930. After April 1930, additional gold imports were just about sufficient to offset the hoarding of currency, open-market operations were inconsequential, and both member-bank reserve balances and indebtedness remained roughly stationary —until the new crisis developed in the Summer of 1931. During this period no attempt was made through open-market policy to make effective the handsome reduction in discount rates.

Contemporary Standards of Credit Policy

As to standards that should be used in determining credit policy, it is perhaps too much to expect the System to speak with a single voice. We have already seen that a booming stock market and high rates for call money led to differences of viewpoint as to the appropriate policy to be followed. It is not to be expected that the evolution of ideas within the System will follow a single consistent line.

In 1931 the Federal Reserve Bank of New York prepared a

[1] Senate Committee on Banking and Currency, *Restoring and Maintaining the Average Purchasing Power of the Dollar*, Hearings on H.R. 11499 and S. 4429, 72nd Cong. 1st Sess., 1932, p. 9.

Figure 1. PRODUCTION, PRICES, AND MONEY-MARKET DATA, 1919–1941

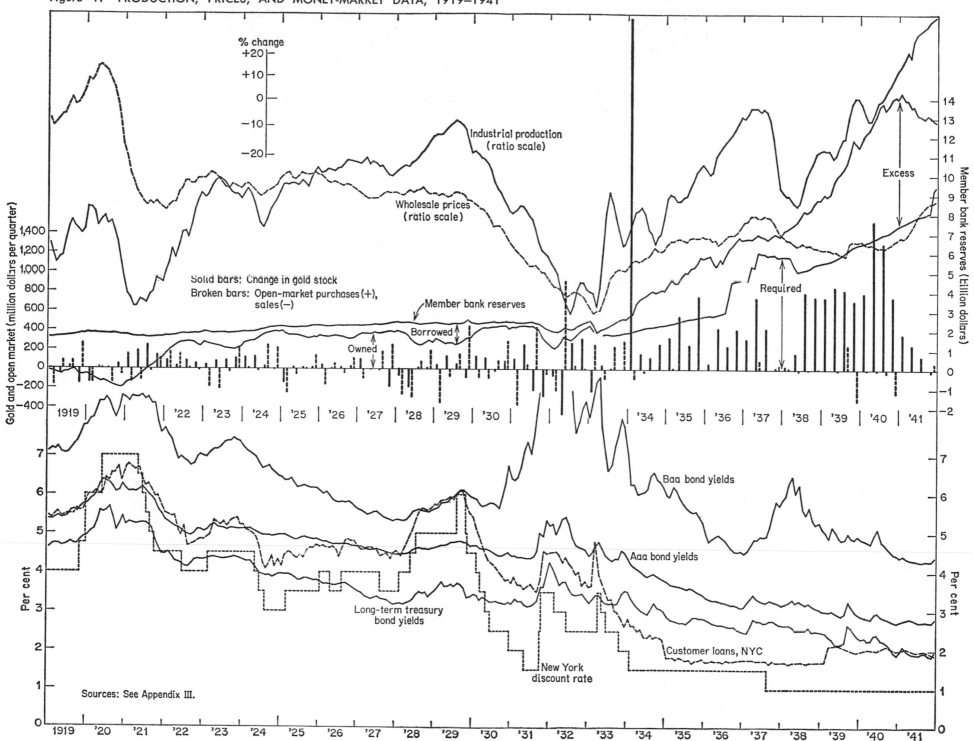

% change
+20
+10
0
-10
-20

Industrial production (ratio scale)

Wholesale prices (ratio scale)

Solid bars: Change in gold stock
Broken bars: Open-market purchases (+), sales (−)

Member bank reserves

Borrowed

Owned

Excess

Required

Gold and open market (million dollars per quarter)
1,400
1,200
1,000
800
600
400
200
0
-200
-400

Member bank reserves (billion dollars)
14
13
12
11
10
9
8
7
6
5
4
3
2
1
0
-1
-2

1919 | '22 | '23 | '24 | '25 | '26 | '27 | '28 | '29 | '30 | | | '34 | '35 | '36 | '37 | '38 | '39 | '40 | '41

Baa bond yields

Aaa bond yields

Long-term treasury bond yields

Customer loans, NYC

New York discount rate

Per cent
7
6
5
4
3
2
1
0

Per cent
7
6
5
4
3
2
1
0

Sources: See Appendix III.

1919 '20 '21 '22 '23 '24 '25 '26 '27 '28 '29 '30 '31 '32 '33 '34 '35 '36 '37 '38 '39 '40 '41

memorandum for the benefit of the Senate Committee on Banking and Currency, which began:

> The traditional guides to bank of issue policy have been of little help since 1921. In the past banks of issue of necessity determined discount policy largely in relation to changes in their gold reserves or in relation to the foreign exchanges, anticipating gold movements. Since the end of 1921 the gold reserves of the Federal Reserve System have been so large and the reserve ratio so high that no discount rate increase has been forced by the depletion of reserves.

What other criteria were available?

> There has been . . . one semiautomatic guide to policy having historical precedent which has proved serviceable. To some extent discount rate adjustments have been directly in response to changes in the market price for money.

It is a little sad to see the Bank still refusing to recognize, after eight years of experience with open-market policy, that it itself determines open-market rates. Perhaps the Bank is less than candid, and is here a victim of the administrator's temptation to minimize his freedom of action. Yet the memorandum admits that

> a rate in perfect technical adjustment with other money rates may at one time be stimulating and at another time depressing. . . . The economic life of this country moves in a constantly changing current from depression to prosperity and back again . . . it has been the policy of this Bank to exercise its influence toward restraint at times when business and speculative activity appeared to be excessive, and to remove credit restraints at times of business depression in the hope that this policy might aid in avoiding the extremes of business expansion and contraction and encourage greater business stability.

This ranks as the first official admission that the Reserve System has the power to influence business activity, and the first declaration that it felt a responsibility to stabilize business. The Bank goes on to express the belief that credit should be allowed to expand

> at a rate proportionate with the long-time growth of business . . . if the growth [of credit] is at a rate greater than that at which experience has shown the country's business can grow on a sound and secure basis, the Federal Reserve authorities have the responsibility, however unpopular, of lending their efforts, either through open-market operations or discount rates or both, toward restraint. Conversely, in a

period of credit contraction or of less than the normal rate of growth, whether caused by business recession, declining prices, wages and employment, or any other cause, Federal Reserve policy, in our opinion, should be to lend its efforts toward making money and credit plentiful and cheap.

These doctrines were soon to be put to the test.

Echoing its controversy with the Reserve Board two years previously, the Bank rejects the qualitative control of credit:

> It is our belief that it is in this direction that the Federal Reserve System can most effectively exert an influence to prevent excessive speculation and to mollify business depression rather than in any attempt to control directly the use to which Federal Reserve credit is put. Efforts by the Reserve System to control the particular uses of credit are, we believe, impracticable and ineffectual, whereas the System does have a considerable influence over changes in the total volume of credit and its cost.

The memorandum by the New York Bank concludes with a discussion of the dilemma presented by the gold standard. It had been difficult to drive away the gold which, sucked from Europe, would have caused inflation here unless sterilized. The Bank enters an implicit defense of the cheap money it had promoted in 1927, but offers no long-term solution of the dilemma—a dilemma which was to continue to plague the System for another decade.[2]

The Gold Crisis in the Fall of 1931

In the Summer of 1931, bank failures in Europe led to suddenly increased demands for liquidity there. These demands were met in part by large-scale withdrawals of gold from the United States. Simultaneously, bank failures here increased currency hoarding sharply. The gold losses and currency withdrawals would have cut member-bank reserves by more than a billion, or roughly in half, between August and December had not Reserve credit been expanded to fill the gap. During August and September the System met the crisis by open-market purchases designed to offset the gold and currency outflow, to keep money cheap, and to maintain bank reserves without the need for increased member-bank borrowing.

[2] Senate Committee on Banking and Currency, *Operation of National and Federal Reserve Banking Systems*, Hearings on S.R. 71, 71st Cong. 3rd Sess., 1931, pp. 760–63.

Commodity prices were still declining and production falling: the domestic situation perhaps called for still cheaper, but certainly not for dearer money.

In October the System suddenly reversed its policy, raising the New York discount rate from 1½% to 3½%. From November 1931 through February 1932 governments were sold by the System in roughly the amount they had been purchased during August, September, and early October. As a result, member banks were forced to borrow on a large scale. Despite such borrowing, member-bank reserves declined by about one-fifth during the space of six months (Fig. 1).

The reversal of policy had catastrophic effects, particularly in the long-term market. Yields on the longest-dated governments rose from 3.3% in September 1931 to 4.5% in January 1932, and declined thereafter only slowly. Yields of Aaa bonds, which had fallen below 4.4% during the summer of 1931, rose to around 5.3% by the end of the year, higher than in a decade: such yields did not again decline below 5% until mid-1932, nor below 4½% till mid-1933. Industrial production during the second half of 1931 had halted its decline at around 75% of the 1923–1925 average: but now it took a fresh nosedive from which it did not recover decisively for another three years.

A credit restriction during the progress of a serious business depression would seem to be the very last policy called for. It is plausible to suppose that the monetary policy initiated in October 1931 measurably intensified the depression and delayed recovery. The motives and justification for the credit restriction of October 1931 must therefore be investigated with especial care.

The immediate reason for the rise in discount rates and sale of governments clearly was the decline in the monetary gold stock. On many previous occasions adequate gold reserves had enabled the System to regard gold exports with indifference. For the first time in more than a decade a shortage of "free gold" was threatened. Throughout the previous history of the Reserve System, the appropriate measure of "free gold" had been the excess gold held over and above legal minimum requirements (at that time 40% against Federal Reserve notes, 35% against deposits). Unfortunately the Federal Reserve Act contained a further requirement, i.e., that against Federal Reserve notes there should be held as to 100%

either gold *or* eligible paper. If eligible paper fell short of 60% of the note circulation, gold had to be used to make up the shortage: governments, collateral notes of member banks, or other ineligible assets could not be used for the purpose. Now holdings of free gold were sharply cut by the need to substitute the metal for eligible paper at a time when the circulation of Federal Reserve notes was expanding rapidly owing to hoarding. Had governments, as a substitute for acceptances, been eligible in the allowable 60% fiduciary backing for the note circulation, no difficulty would have arisen. No wonder Governor Harrison later described the shortage of free gold at this period as "due to a technicality in the Act."[3]

The situation was remedied by the passage on February 27, 1932 of the Glass-Steagall Act, which allowed governments to be used as collateral for Federal Reserve notes. The question at issue is whether or not this "technicality" was an insuperable obstacle to the continuation of cheap money from October 1931 through the following February. Certainly we may grant that, short of abandoning the convertibility of the dollar, tighter money was the way to check gold exports; and if "free gold" could not be increased, gold exports had to be checked. The problem is to determine whether the System did all it could—short of credit restriction—to maintain the margin of free gold within the law as it stood prior to the passage of the Glass-Steagall Act. In other words, could the System have held more eligible paper, as a substitute for gold, than it did in fact, during these months?

Eligible paper consisted of two kinds: bills rediscounted by member banks and bank acceptances bought in the open market. The System could only induce member banks to discount additional bills by making money tight. The question therefore turns upon whether the Reserve Banks could have bought more bills in the open market. The custom was for the System to buy all bank acceptances offered to it at its published buying rates. Could it have purchased more acceptances than it did, by lowering its buying rates, without losing so much gold in consequence that the policy would have been self-defeating? The matter has been carefully examined by Villard.[4] At no time during 1931 and 1932 did the System hold more than

[3] House Committee on Banking and Currency, *Stabilization of Commodity Prices,* Hearings on H.R. 10517, 72nd Cong. 1st Sess., 1932, p. 467.
[4] Henry H. Villard, "The Federal Reserve System's Monetary Policy in 1931 and 1932," *Journal of Political Economy,* 45 (December, 1937), 721–39.

about two-thirds of all acceptances outstanding, and Villard gives reasons for believing that the supply to the Reserve Banks was by no means inelastic, i.e., that a moderate decline in acceptance-buying rates relative to other short-term rates of interest would have pulled much of the remaining volume of acceptances into the Reserve Banks. Insofar as this happened, the amount of free gold would have risen dollar for dollar, except to the extent that increased gold exports resulted. Villard gives reasons for doubting that additional gold exports would have vitiated the proposed policy. A partial recognition of Villard's thesis was furnished by Goldenweiser:

> In 1931 . . . the Federal Reserve System, in order to protect itself [against gold losses] followed the orthodox practice of raising its rates, and holding them at a higher level. It seems, in retrospect, that those rates were kept high longer than was desirable, *and that is particularly true of the bill rates,* which were held above the market rates for three or four months, during which time there was a rapid run-off of bills.[5]

There appear to have been still other ways in which—within existing law—the "technicality" might have been circumvented. For the System held at the time substantial quantities of acceptances— 10% or more of the amount outstanding—for the account of foreign correspondents, chiefly the Bank of France. Some of these correspondents might have been persuaded to turn their acceptances over to the System—in exchange for repurchase agreements, or for short-dated obligations of the United States. Villard suggests that the Bank of France, then committed to a policy of deflation *à outrance,* would probably have proved unhelpful: yet we note that, even had it refused to part with its acceptances in exchange for anything but gold, the paper sold would have been available for releasing the gold required.

Villard confines himself to the possibility that the Board could have increased the volume of bank acceptances that it held. But the search for collateral might well have been extended to trade acceptances. Under Sec. 14 of the Federal Reserve Act, Reserve Banks were empowered to buy trade acceptances, from member banks or others, although in order to qualify as collateral for Federal Reserve notes, under Sec. 16, such bills had to be endorsed by a mem-

---

[5] House Committee on Banking and Currency, *Banking Act of 1935,* Hearings on H.R. 5357, 74th Cong. 1st Sess., 1935, pp. 440–41. Italics supplied.

ber bank. True, purchase of such paper was not customary, but emergencies call for novel policies to meet them. If necessary, the large New York banks should have been pressed, as a patriotic duty, to turn in their commercial paper to the Reserve Bank. Indeed on January 19, 1932, the Board actually discussed such a plan, in connection with a proposal to ask the Bank of France to withdraw its deposits. Governor Meyer opined it would not be difficult to persuade fifty or more member banks to agree to turn sufficient commercial paper over to the System to repay the French with gold. The proposal was ostensibly to reduce the supposed influence of the Bank of France over conditions in the New York money market. Nothing came of it, partly because the Board suspected the real purpose of the proposal was to apply political pressure to Paris.[6] But if the plan to enlist the cooperation of member banks was feasible for this purpose in January, it must have been equally feasible as a means of obviating the credit restriction in October.

Even if no such plans had worked, there still remained the possibility of suspending the reserve requirement of 35% in gold to be held against deposits, as permitted by Sec. 11(c) of the Federal Reserve Act. No provisions existed at that time for the issue of emergency currency in quantities to satisfy hoarders: the Aldrich-Vreeland Act had long since expired, and the Banking Act of March 1933 lay in the future. But if in October 1931 the Board, instead of restricting credit, had announced its intention to suspend reserve requirements if necessary, it seems possible that Congress would have been galvanized into passing the Glass-Steagall Act somewhat sooner. The Act removed the "technicality" on February 27, 1932, almost six months after the crisis developed and after great damage had been done. In April Representative Goldsborough was to assert that Congress would gladly have given the Board this legislation a year earlier, had the Board asked for it.[7] But that, perhaps, was demanding a superhuman degree of foresight.

The truth seems to be that the wisdom—or at least the necessity— of the credit restriction of October 1931 went unquestioned until, months later, its serious effects upon the economy had become apparent. The requests of the New York Bank for higher discount rates

[6] Hamlin diary.
[7] House Committee on Banking and Currency, *Stabilization of Commodity Prices*, Hearings on H.R. 10517, 72nd Cong. 1st Sess., 1932, p. 488.

were approved by the Board unanimously and—so far as the Hamlin diary reveals—without discussion. Reserve officials seem to have felt that, so long as discount rates were not over, say, 4%, it did not much matter whether they were 1½% or 3½%. Although it was realized clearly enough that restriction, as a method of coping with the crisis, could work only through rediscounting, the effect upon credit availability of putting the banks in debt to the System was overlooked. Above all there was complete neglect of the disastrous effect of the policy on the state of the bond market.

The Futility of Open-Market Operations, 1932

Early in 1932 officials of the System began to realize, at least dimly, what harm had been caused by the reversal in October 1931 of the cheap-money policy. For the first time the minutes of the Open Market Committee (or Policy Conference as it was then called) contain comments upon the deflation of bank credit. In fact, deflationary pressure, as measured by the fraction of member-bank reserves that were owed, was greater than at any time since 1921. During the first few months of 1932 the production index fell to fresh low levels. Large open-market purchases obviously were called for, in order that member-bank indebtedness might be cut and open-market rates reduced. Yet, granted the unimaginative acceptance policy of preceding months, there was little the System could do, until after the passage of the Glass-Steagall Act on February 27, that would not risk the elimination of the "free gold." Buying of governments began slowly in March; really large purchases were not made until April; not until May were governments actually used as collateral for Federal Reserve notes as permitted by the new legislation. Even in June member-bank reserves were still below their level at the beginning of the year, and member-bank borrowing, though much reduced, had not yet been eliminated. In July, purchases ceased, partly owing to the unwillingness of the Boston and Chicago Banks to cooperate.[8] Between the end of February and the end of July the System bought just over $1 billion of governments, mostly with maturities of less than a year (see Appendix III). Although small by modern standards, the purchases were large for the time, more than doubling System holdings of Treasury obligations. However, owing to the decline in member-bank indebtedness and in

[8] Hamlin diary, July 5, 1932.

holdings of purchased bills, total Reserve Bank credit rose by only about $700 million.

During the second half of 1932 gold imports were sufficient to raise member-bank reserves to the level of mid-1931, and at the same time to eliminate the net indebtedness of member banks, despite a continued and ominous growth in the note circulation. For the first time in the history of the System excess reserves appeared in significant volume, and by the end of the year, as just indicated, exceeded borrowings of member banks still in debt (Fig. 1).

In sum, the banking situation improved in a statistical sense during the year 1932, for member banks were more liquid than they had ever been before, and their reserve balances reached a record level. But at year's end things were not really as happy as these facts might suggest. Bank failures had not been stemmed, and during the Fall lack of confidence in banks had spread to some of the larger business centers which had hitherto appeared immune to such troubles. Also, the very liquidity of the banks was in part achieved through an unwillingness to lend, an unwillingness that gave rise to widespread complaint. Customer-loan rates in New York City had indeed fallen to low levels, but the South and West experienced no similar decline. Moreover, the open-market purchases made during the Spring had consisted almost entirely of very short-dated Treasury obligations, and long-term rates of interest were still above the by no means very low levels to which they had fallen by mid-1931, before the onset of the gold crisis. The benefits which might have accrued from a decline in bond yields were not appreciated, or were neglected.

Country banks, especially, held Treasury bonds, and the depreciation of their portfolios during the winter of 1931–1932 had contributed to bank failures that might otherwise have been avoided.[9] Besides, a substantial decline in long-term interest rates probably was a necessary condition for the revival of investment spending. At a meeting of the Federal Advisory Council (May 24, 1932), Melvin A. Traylor, a Chicago banker, proposed that the System buy long-term governments, but he made no impression on his colleagues. Governor Meyer and Mr. Miller for the Board said that such a

[9] See testimony of Bernard Ostrolenk, economist for *Business Week*, House Committee on Banking and Currency, *To Establish the Federal Monetary Authority*, Hearings on H.R. 7157 and 8780, 73rd Cong. 2nd Sess., 1934, pp. 99–101.

policy would "tie up the System," and that if the obligations ever had to be sold the result might be to break the bond market.[10] To which the proper reply obviously is that there never would be any point in selling them, unless policy at some future time called for lower bond prices and higher long-term interest rates! As late as 1938 Chairman Eccles doubted the wisdom of buying bonds, chiefly because he saw the System buying them high and selling them low, and so losing money.[11] But this should not be considered an obstacle if bond purchases are desirable for other reasons.

Even after the passage of the Glass-Steagall Act, open-market policy still was inhibited by fear of withdrawal of funds by foreigners and a feeling that (in the words of Governor Harrison) it was dangerous for the System to "dissipate its credit."[12] One suspects that many Reserve officials shared the opinion of Governor MacDougal of the Chicago Bank, who told a Governors' Conference "that he thought it was the duty of the Federal Reserve Banks to be liquid, in order to meet the steady withdrawal of deposits from member banks."[13] We may feel the Governor's remark reveals a pathetic misunderstanding of the nature and sources of central-bank liquidity. But it is only on the basis of some such false analogy between central banking and commercial banking that the opposition to bond purchases, and indeed in some instances to any open-market operations at all, is to be explained.

So far as fighting the depression was concerned, by the end of 1932 the Reserve System, pervaded by an atmosphere of gloom and frustration, was about ready to retire from the fray. Its restriction of credit in the Fall of 1931 had plunged the economy into an even worse state of collapse. Its open-market purchases in 1932, such as they were, had indeed lowered short-term interest rates, but had failed to salvage the bond market and had proved fruitless so far as business recovery was concerned. It had become increasingly criti-

---

[10] Hamlin diary. Miller later said: "I am far from being convinced that liquidity is an old-fashioned virtue in banking, any more than I believe that chastity is an old-fashioned virtue in womanhood" (Senate Banking Committee, *Banking Act of 1935*, Hearings on S. 1715, 74th Cong. 1st Sess., 1935, p. 722): we may assume that Miller intended "banking" to include central banking.

[11] House Committee on Banking and Currency, *Government Ownership of the Twelve Federal Reserve Banks*, Hearings on H.R. 7230, 75th Cong. 3rd Sess., 1938, p. 453.

[12] House Committee on Banking and Currency, *Stabilization of Commodity Prices*, Hearings on H.R. 10517, 72nd Cong. 1st Sess., 1932, pp. 471, 480, 517; see also Frank A. Vanderlip, same, *To Establish the Federal Monetary Authority*, pp. 469, 473.

[13] Hamlin diary, January 11, 1932.

cized in Congress and elsewhere. For the next three years the center of the stage would be occupied by the Treasury. The System was not to emerge from its eclipse until after a substantial legislative reorganization.

In the interim, novel fiscal policies were to be given a trial, but before this could happen the nation was to experience a total collapse of the banking system. Before proceeding with our story we must turn briefly to the renewed efforts to enact legislation to stabilize the level of commodity prices.

The Stabilization Bills Once More

The connection between falling commodity prices and business depression was not perhaps well understood: yet it was obvious that a connection existed. It was scarcely surprising, therefore, that the years of depression should see a revival of the movement to give legislative direction to the Federal Reserve System to require it to base its policy upon the level of commodity prices. The new proposals were not simply to stabilize commodity prices at their current depressed level, but to reflate them to some pre-depression level, and then stabilize them. In 1931 and 1932 numerous bills were introduced, especially by Congressmen from agricultural districts. Three of them (the second Goldsborough bill, the Fletcher bill, and the so-called "monetary authority" or third Goldsborough bill) reached the stage of extended committee hearings. For our story the interest of these bills, like those of the former series discussed in a previous section, lies in the ideas they embodied, in their effect in revealing the opinions of Reserve officials, and in their indirect influence upon Reserve policy.[14]

Under the second Goldsborough bill, hearings on which were held during March and April 1932, the System would have been

> authorized and directed to take all available steps to raise the present deflated wholesale commodity level of prices as speedily as possible to the level existing before the present deflation, and afterwards to use all available means to maintain such wholesale commodity level of prices.

In addition the bill would have empowered the System, if short of gold, to raise the price of gold; and, if short of assets to sell, to

[14] For detailed provisions of the various bills, see Irving Fisher, *Stable Money: A History of the Movement* (New York: Adelphi Co., 1934), pp. 183–215.

issue debentures in order to withdraw money from the market. (In fact the price of gold was to be raised by Treasury action after the change of administration the following year.) That the Reserve Banks should be empowered to sell debentures was an interesting suggestion which was never followed up. Had it been enacted, it might have proved a useful method of sterilizing gold during 1936 and 1937 and have made it unnecessary for the System to be beholden to the Treasury.[15]

The hearings on the bill, conducted by Representative Goldsborough's subcommittee of the House Banking Committee, were notable for extensive supporting testimony by Irving Fisher. He argued for higher prices from a desire not so much to encourage business revival as to secure justice for debtors. There followed a lengthy, ingenious, but somewhat pointless discussion as to the average age of existing debt contracts. More important for our purpose, the bill evoked opposition from Governors Harrison and Meyer. Both officials repudiated the suggestion that the Reserve System had anything like complete control over the level of commodity prices, but nevertheless claimed to be pursuing the policy envisaged by the bill (i.e., reflation of the price level):

> GOVERNOR HARRISON: I do not think we would act any differently from the way we are acting today, even if you had this bill law. . . . I do not see what we could or should be doing differently from what we are doing today, even if you should pass this bill.
>
> . . . .
>
> GOVERNOR MEYER: I think the Federal Reserve System has always endeavored to do just exactly what we are talking about, within the limits of possibility.[16]

Both officials vigorously opposed the bill on the ground that to instruct the System to follow a particular price-level policy would give rise to expectations that might be disappointed. Their attitude, in fact, echoed that of Governor Strong upon an earlier occasion: we may guess it was chiefly prompted by the familiar anxiety of the administrator not to have his hands tied. In addition, Governor Meyer put in a strong plea for the federal chartering of all banks and for basing member-bank reserve requirements partly upon the activity of

[15] House Committee on Banking and Currency, *Stabilization of Commodity Prices*, Hearings on H.R. 10517, 72nd Cong. 1st Sess., 1932.
[16] *Ibid.*, pp. 487, 498, 552.

deposits. He strongly implied that the dual banking system and the inelasticity of current reserve requirements were two reasons why the System could not carry out the mandate in the proposed bill. The dual banking system is still with us, despite repeated attempts at reform since then. The activity-reserve proposal—a fashion of the time —later gave way to other ideas for the modification of member-bank reserve requirements.

The interesting proposal to authorize the Reserve Banks to sell debentures was not discussed during the hearings. The bill was amended in committee to make the average level of prices during the years 1921 to 1929 the target, and the power to issue debentures and to change the price of gold were deleted: in this form the bill passed the House, but died in the Senate.

The Fletcher bill was identical with the second Goldsborough bill as passed by the House, except that in addition it sought to make permanent the one-year authority contained in the Glass-Steagall Act to use Treasury obligations as collateral for Federal Reserve notes. Governor Meyer repeated his testimony before the House Committee and also implied that the Senators were meddling in matters they did not understand:

> Gentlemen, I think you have entered here into a field of highly technical financial operations . . . credit is like some drugs. If handled by people who are experienced and competent in its use, it may have a very helpful and healing effect. But if used by people who do not understand it, it may become very dangerous and perhaps disastrous.

Adolph Miller, the only professionally-trained economist on the Board, echoed the Governor:

> I would say exercise a little patience, a little forbearance. Have a little more faith in our recovery from this through normal processes. . . . Nature is doing her work. She must be our main reliance. . . . You can interfere and meddle, but in my judgment with very little good result.

Like other officials of the System, Miller thought it politic to minimize the effectiveness of monetary policy, but he also put his finger on a serious weakness in the Goldsborough-Fletcher proposals:

> A stable price level in a progressive society may frequently result in a profit inflation. Progress in technical organization, more efficient production methods, and so forth, such as we usually have, all mean that

costs of production keep going down. . . . Unless wage payments increase enough to absorb all of the savings made possible by more efficient methods, the proceeds of the sale of goods [at] stable prices are
going to go somewhere else. Where do they go? Into profits. And what
do profits do? When conditions favor a profit inflation, the stage is set
for a speculative boom. And most of the stabilizationists in this country,
I believe . . . are really unconscious inflationists. What they want is
rising profits insured by a stable price level. I would say that in the
long run a piece of legislation of this kind might be expected to insure
that the country from time to time will have profit inflation, speculative
booms and speculative collapses.

This serious criticism was not met, probably because of the almost
offensive way in which Miller had referred to his audience as
"meddlers," and had characterized the price level as "merely a
metaphysical concept . . . a figment of the mind."[17]

The Goldsborough and Fletcher bills were opposed, not only by
the Reserve System, but by Ogden Mills, Secretary of the Treasury,
and by Senator Glass. The Senate Committee reported neither of
them.

The third Goldsborough bill, upon which hearings were held between January and March 1934, also asked for a return to a former
price level—that of 1926. But it was more radical than previous
bills in seeking to supersede (although not to abolish) the Reserve
System by setting up a Federal Monetary Authority of five members,
and allowing this body to buy and sell both gold and silver at such
prices as it chose. The case for reflating and then stabilizing the
price level was made by Irving Fisher and others before the House
Banking Committee along much the same lines as in previous hearings. Father Coughlin enlivened the proceedings by making an elo-
quent if confused plea for silver on the ground that it had been used
in biblical times. The opposition was led by Secretary Morgenthau
and Governor Black. Secretary Morgenthau, fresh from his experiment with gold-buying and the devaluation of the dollar, was con-
ciliatory and pleaded for time to see how steps already taken might
work out. Governor Black, evidently feeling that the whole proposal
amounted to a frontal attack upon the Reserve System, was not con-
ciliatory, and his appearance before the Committee contributed little

[17] Senate Committee on Banking and Currency, *Restoring and Maintaining the Average
Purchasing Power of the Dollar*, Hearings on H.R. 11499 and S. 4429, 72nd Cong. 1st
Sess., 1932, pp. 215, 217, 225, 227, 251.

light and some heat. The House Committee ended by taking no action on the bill.[18]

The stabilization hearings of 1932 and 1934 produced fewer side-lights on the actual operation of the Reserve System than did the previous hearings in 1926–1928, but they are more interesting for the development of economic doctrine. Not only the eventual stabilization of some price level was in question, but the raising of the existing level. The ineffectiveness of the open-market purchases of 1932 and of the gold buying of 1933 as price-raising measures led to long discussion and many expressions of frustration. Already some reformers cast an eye in the direction of fiscal policy as a possible way out, and the (fortunately ineffectual) efforts at budget balancing were praised by some but seriously questioned by others. There were occasional criticisms, by the committees or by witnesses, of the credit restriction of 1931, but the damage done to the economy by this episode does not seem to have been adequately recognized. Nor, despite numerous comments upon the connection between the state of the bond market and bank failures, was there any realization of the importance of lowering long-term interest rates. The one measure which—at that time—might have achieved significant results, i.e., large-scale buying of bonds by the Reserve, was neither proposed by System officials, nor pressed upon the System by committee members or other witnesses.

Since the problem of "reflation" was so much more immediate, the matter of eventual stabilization of the price level received less thorough attention than it had at previous hearings. The collapse in prices during the early 1930's, following hard upon the apparently successful stabilization of wholesale prices during the 1920's, merited an explanation which it did not receive. Here and there hints may be found of a shift of interest away from the stabilization of prices toward the stabilization of the level of business activity. From time to time both Congressmen and witnesses seem to be groping for the broader but less well-defined policies later to be embodied in the Employment Act of 1946.

Collapse of the Banking System, 1933

During 1931 and 1932 about 3,600 banks closed their doors. Deposit banking, as commonly conducted, is of such a nature that fail-

---

[18] House Committee on Banking and Currency, *To Establish the Federal Monetary Authority*, Hearings on H.R. 7157 and 8780, 73rd Cong. 2nd Sess., 1934.

ure of even a few unsound banks leads to distrust of many sound banks and widespread hoarding of currency. Both branch banking and deposit insurance had been suggested as remedies, but neither had received nationwide acceptance. In 1931 the public's conversion of deposits into currency had helped to induce an unwanted credit restriction which, I have argued above, might have been prevented by a more imaginative acceptance policy on the part of the Reserve System. Now, in 1933, the public's distrust, even of sound banks, became so great that the entire banking system had to be put on holiday while an emergency currency could be manufactured and legalized. In this case different Reserve policies during the preceding two and a half years might probably have prevented the deflation of which these difficulties were the outcome. But by the beginning of 1933 no conceivable measures on the part of the System, within existing legal constraints, could have prevented the collapse— and the further dose of deflation which resulted therefrom.

Hoarding of currency mounted rapidly during the last few months of 1932. A twelve-day bank holiday proclaimed by the governor of Nevada at the end of October was followed by legislation or executive orders in many states allowing banks to restrict their payments to depositors, usually to a given percentage of each customer's deposit. The dramatic events of January, February, and March 1933 have often been described and will not be detailed here.[19] In February, Michigan ordered a bank holiday, and other states soon followed. By March 1, thirty states had restrictions of one kind or another on the convertibility of bank deposits into currency. Plainly a nationwide bank holiday was imminent. The immediate occasion for it was the demand by the New York banks, frightened by heavy currency withdrawals to the interior, for a moratorium early on Saturday, March 4. Over the weekend the incoming President proclaimed a four-day bank holiday to begin Monday, March 6.

The breathing space thus obtained allowed the new Congress time to pass the Emergency Banking Act of March 9, 1933. The bank holiday was legalized retroactively, and provision was made for the issue of additional Federal Reserve banknotes without gold backing, the reorganization of banks by "conservators," and the issue of preferred stock. Meanwhile the new Administration took hurried measures looking toward the reopening of the banks at the earliest

[19] See, e.g., H. Parker Willis and John M. Chapman, *The Banking Situation* (New York: Columbia University Press, 1934), Chs. I and II.

possible date. The nation's banks were divided into four classes. (1) From 9,000 to 10,000 banks, including nearly all the large metropolitan institutions, were allowed to reopen without restriction. (2) About 5,000 were reopened, but with restrictions on the amounts depositors might withdraw. (3) Between 3,000 and 4,000 were placed in the hands of conservators who might or might not liquidate them. (4) About 1,000 were definitely and finally closed.

The deflationary effects of these events were considerable, and may be measured in various ways. Of the $40 billion of deposits, demand and time, available to the public without restriction a few months previously, about $30 billion were similarly available after the banks reopened. Of the remaining $10 billion, perhaps $4 billion were still available subject to restrictions on withdrawal; about $6 billion had disappeared, temporarily or permanently, in banks that did not reopen after the holiday. Member-bank reserve balances were cut rather sharply, but were restored within a few months to their previous level through open-market operations and the return of currency from circulation. The gradual decline of interest rates since the gold crisis of eighteen months earlier was checked, but resumed within a few months. The production index, which had begun a hesitant recovery late in 1932, fell back to its mid-1932 level, but no lower.

Whether the credit contraction of the Winter of 1931–1932 or the total collapse in the Spring of 1933 did more damage to business activity is perhaps an academic question. But from the policy standpoint the most striking difference between the two crises surely is that the onset of the first (1931) might probably have been avoided by a different Federal Reserve policy, whereas the onset of the second (1933) was beyond the power of the System to prevent.

When the banks reopened, Reserve policy was directed, but only after some delay, toward undoing the deflationary damage caused by the collapse. Not until the end of May did the New York discount rate, which had been raised to 3½% at the time of the collapse, return to the 2½% level of the previous year. Only in June were open-market purchases resumed. But during the last six months of 1933 large purchases were made and real ease in the money market achieved. Early in 1934 the New York discount rate was reduced to 1½%, the all-time low previously reached only briefly in 1931. More significantly, customer-loan rates resumed their decline, and Aaa bond yields fell again to their 1931 levels (between 4¼% and

4½%). Thus interest rates were brought down once more to levels which obtained prior to the two mid-depression credit restrictions. Yet real ease in the bond market had never yet been achieved and still lay in the future. Finally we may note that by the end of 1933 member-bank reserve balances were at predepression heights and member-bank indebtedness (gross) had been virtually eliminated (Fig. 1).

It has been the fashion to argue that experience during the early 1930's casts doubt upon the effectiveness of monetary policy in fighting depression. The low short-term interest rates of 1931 and the massive open-market operations of 1932—not to speak of the Treasury's devaluation of the dollar in 1933—failed to revive investment spending. Yet it may be doubted whether these experiments were as crucial as they are sometimes represented. On the one hand the three years (1931 to 1933) in question, the three years which cover the pit of the depression, were punctuated by two violent deflationary shocks. The first of these shocks, which struck the economy in September-October 1931, was the consequence of legal restrictions on the note issue which were later removed. The second, in February–March 1933, resulted from defects in the structure of the commercial banking system, which we hope have now been remedied—through deposit insurance. It is of course true that these institutional shortcomings were not appreciated by the men of that time, and that other institutional weaknesses may still exist of which we ourselves are unaware—weaknesses of a kind to produce similar shocks at critical moments in the future. Yet a fair test of the effectiveness of monetary policy cannot be conducted in a situation where it is hamstrung by legal and institutional obstacles. On the other hand Federal Reserve policy—when not dominated by these obstacles—was deliberately confined to easing the short-term market and (prior to 1936) any influence it may have had upon long-term interest rates was indirect and seems to have been quite minor. The bond market was left to its own devices. This fact also, in my opinion, prevents the experience of these years from furnishing a valid test of the effectiveness of monetary policy during a period of severe depression.

Legislation in 1933 and 1934

The Emergency Banking Act of March 9, 1933, passed during the bank holiday, was strictly an ad hoc measure to deal with the crisis, and had no permanent influence upon our banking code. The Banking Act of June 16, 1933, passed with breakneck speed after three years of painful deliberation, combined emergency and permanent features.

In July 1930, at the instance of Senator Glass, the Senate passed the celebrated Resolution 71 calling for a full-dress investigation of the nation's banking by the Senate Committee on Banking and Currency with subpoena powers. The hearings which resulted afford by far the most interesting single source of information about the Reserve System and Reserve policies which appeared during the period between the two wars.[20] But no legislation resulted. In January 1932, some time after the hearings were concluded, Senator Glass did indeed introduce a bill to keep credit out of the stock market, to base reserve requirements of member banks upon deposit turnover, to hasten the liquidation of closed banks, to divorce security affiliates from commercial banks, and to provide for a limited extension of branch banking. Further extensive hearings followed,[21] but no action: some of the provisions were distasteful to the American Bankers Association, others were declared by Federal Reserve officials to be unworkable. Further discussion of Senator Glass' bill had been indefinitely postponed, when the collapse of March 1933 suddenly changed the Congressional climate. The bill was hastily abstracted from the pigeonhole in which it reposed, dusted off, and radically revised. The reserve-requirement gimmick was dropped, deposit insurance was reluctantly substituted for the liquidation provisions, and a definitive divorce decreed between deposit and investment banking. The Federal Open Market Committee was given statutory recognition. The extension of branch banking—a highly controversial topic—was not so much as mentioned. Interest on demand deposits was prohibited, and on time deposits regulated. Such were the main provisions of the Banking Act of 1933 enacted June 16.[22]

For a thoroughgoing solution the more complex problem of stock-market credit had to await the Securities and Exchange Act of 1934. The 1933 Act proposed to keep credit out of the stock market by

[20] Senate Committee on Banking and Currency, *Operation of the National and Federal Reserve Banking Systems,* Hearings pursuant to S.R. 71, 71st Cong. 1st Sess., 1931.

[21] Senate Committee on Banking and Currency, *Operation of the National and Federal Reserve Banking Systems,* Hearings on S. 4115, 72nd Cong. 1st Sess., 1932.

[22] For the legislative history of the Banking Act of 1933, see Willis and Chapman, Chs. IV–VIII.

allowing the Reserve Board to limit the amount which individual member banks might lend on stock or bond collateral as measured by a percentage of their individual capital and surplus. The importance and even the desirability of this type of qualitative regulation of credit has been much questioned. Yet even if the desirability of regulating stock-market credit is granted, the weakness of this particular form of regulation is obvious. The New York Reserve Bank at once protested the difficulty of enforcement. In any case the Act did not touch loans to brokers by nonmember banks and by nonbank lenders. In 1928 and 1929 nonbank lenders had obtained funds from the stock market itself (via new issues) and from the banking system (via loans not secured by stock or bond collateral) and had lent such funds to brokers. Since credit comes from so many sources, but is received by a single group—the brokers—it was apparent that the most effective way to regulate stock-market credit must be through a limitation of demand rather than of supply. But brokers had hitherto been wholly unregulated.

An opportunity for a fresh approach to the problem, through the borrower rather than through the lender, came in 1934 with the drafting of the Securities and Exchange Act. The main provisions of this act are of no concern to us, since they do not relate to banking—least of all central banking. But the decision to license security brokers, whether trading on a regular exchange or in the over-the-counter market, made it possible to control their use of credit on behalf of their customers. Brokers henceforth were prohibited from borrowing except from member banks. In addition, the margin to be required of their customers was to be regulated by the Reserve Board.

These rather elaborate provisions were no doubt politically inevitable in the light of the financial history of the preceding years. Yet they prompt several questions. First, is such qualitative control of credit in any case desirable? Second, if we admit that, even if undesirable, it does little harm, why not prohibit stock-market credit altogether and place all stock trading on a cash basis? Are margin transactions really necessary in order that a securities market shall function efficiently? No doubt professional dealers need credit, as do any other businessmen. But is the ability of the customer to obtain credit in fact a necessary condition for liquid and smoothly functioning markets? Certainly the power to regulate margin requirements, placed in the hands of the Reserve Board, has the appearance of giving the Board a concern with the level of equity prices. This concern the Board has understandably repudiated on numerous occasions; yet the possession of the power may one day conceivably prove an embarrassment.

Marriner Eccles and the Banking Act of 1935

Two governors of the Reserve Board served during the worst years of the depression—Eugene Meyer from September 1930 to May 1933, and Eugene R. Black from May 1933 to August 1934. Each found the office an unhappy and frustrating experience. Plainly disappointed by the ineffectiveness of open-market operations during 1932, Governor Meyer turned away from the Board and threw ever more of his energies into the Reconstruction Finance Corporation, of which he was chairman, as the best hope of ameliorating the situation. In the Spring of 1933 he resigned, partly in order to give the incoming President a chance to select his own man. Roosevelt's first choice was not a happy one. Black, an ultra-conservative banker, had been governor of the Federal Reserve Bank of Atlanta. He was opposed to the gold-buying policy and the devaluation of the dollar, and fought and lost a major battle with the Treasury Department over the substitution of gold certificates for gold among the assets of the Reserve Banks. This issue, which in the light of history could hardly seem more highly academic, was fought out largely in the field of abstract ethics and—perhaps for that reason—raised feelings to fever pitch. Defeated by Secretary Morgenthau, Governor Black retired, a bitter and a disillusioned man.

It was evident that the President would have to think again, and this time he was more fortunate. Marriner Stoddard Eccles was a commercial banker from Utah who had ideas about social policy in general, and money and banking in particular, which for those days were advanced or even radical. When approached he expressed his willingness to become governor of the Board, but only on condition that the Administration sponsor legislation which would (1) give permanent shape to some of the emergency measures of the preceding three years, and (2) reduce the division of authority within the System by increasing the power of the Board. The result was the

Banking Act of 1935, a major revision of the code. The Act consists of three parts: Title I, making deposit insurance permanent; Title II, amending the Federal Reserve Act; and Title III, containing technical amendments of a noncontroversial nature. We shall be concerned here only with Title II, which Eccles began to draft as soon as he became Governor in November 1934.

(1) The temporary provisions of the Glass-Steagall Act of 1932, which allowed governments to be used as security for Federal Reserve notes and permitted the Reserve Banks to lend upon any collateral they considered sound, were made permanent. The commercial-loan theory, embodied in the provisions of the 1913 Act, had been seriously weakened by the 1916 amendment enabling member banks to borrow on their own notes secured by governments; it had been given a mortal blow by the Glass-Steagall Act; now it was decently interred.

Further, the emergency provision contained in the Thomas amendment to the Agricultural Relief Act of 1933, whereby the Board might vary the reserve requirements of member banks, was made permanent. The emergency provision had required the affirmative vote of five members of the Board and the approval of the President. By the 1935 amendment, the change in reserve requirements (not below current levels nor above twice current levels) could be made simply by regulation of the Board. This valuable instrument of control, first suggested by Secretary Shaw in 1906,[23] was now confided to the System in large measure because Glass and other conservative Senators feared inflation.

(2) The Reserve Board itself was reorganized in the following manner. Instead of six appointed and two ex officio members, it was in future to consist (as it still does) of seven members appointed for 14-year overlapping terms. Senator Glass seems to have been impressed by the power he was able to exercise over the Board as its chairman when he was Secretary of the Treasury, and (perhaps distrusting Mr. Morgenthau) he exacted the removal of this ex officio member from the Board's membership as his price for swallowing the demise of eligibility. But Secretary Morgenthau was incensed at the notion that a subordinate should keep his seat while the Secre-

---

[23] *Annual Report of the Secretary of the Treasury for 1905–06*, p. 48.

tary's own membership was eliminated: so the Comptroller of the Currency was also removed from the Board.[24]

The name was changed from Federal Reserve Board to Board of Governors of the Federal Reserve System; and the title of its chief executive officer, to be designated by the President from among the members for a four-year term, was changed from "governor" to "chairman." These amendments should have bolstered the position of the Board: yet, as we shall see, the degree of its independence from the Treasury after World War II was no greater than, if as great as, it had been after World War I.

The offices of Reserve Bank governor, hitherto elected by the Bank's directors, and chairman and federal reserve agent, at that time designated by the Board, were to be combined. The new executive officer was to be known as president of the Reserve Bank, and be elected by its directors subject to confirmation by the Reserve Board. The intention was to end such disputes as had occurred between the Board and the New York Bank.

Open-market operations as an instrument of credit policy were not contemplated in the Federal Reserve Act. Their management, as we have seen, was the subject of dispute upon numerous occasions between the Board and the Banks, and the resulting compromises had been less than satisfactory. Not inaccurately, Governor Eccles described the existing situation to the House Committee as follows:

> Under existing law open-market operations must be initiated by a committee consisting of representatives of the twelve Federal Reserve Banks, that is, by persons representing primarily local interests. They must be submitted for approval or disapproval to the Federal Reserve Board, and after they have been approved by the Federal Reserve Board, the boards of directors of the Federal Reserve Banks have the power to decide whether or not they wish to participate in the operations. We have, therefore, on this vital matter a set-up by which the body which initiates the policies is not in a position to ratify them; and the body which ratifies them is not in a position to initiate them or to insist on their being carried out after they are ratified; and still a third group has the power to nullify policies that have been initiated and ratified by the other two bodies. In this matter, therefore, which requires prompt and immediate action and the responsibility for which should be centralized so as to be inescapable, the existing law requires the participation of 12 governors, 8 members of the Federal Reserve Board,

[24] Marriner S. Eccles, *Beckoning Frontiers* (New York: Knopf, 1951), p. 222. Eccles comments: "This is one case where the public result of Morgenthau's fragile feelings was highly beneficial."

and 108 directors scattered all over the country before a policy can be put into operation.[25]

Eccles somewhat overstated the matter, since effective open-market operations could be (and were) successfully undertaken even though individual Reserve Banks declined to participate. This was possible because it had wisely been provided that the Board could require any Reserve Bank to rediscount for any other Reserve Bank. Yet the substantial criticism was valid: decentralization was excessive, and the power of veto lodged in entirely too many persons. We have seen that the Board and the New York Bank frequently failed to agree, and undoubtedly policy decisions had sometimes been much delayed by the need to secure agreement. To remedy these defects, the new Act placed the conduct of open-market operations in the hands of the entire Board, together with five Reserve Bank presidents, of whom the New York president would always be one. All Reserve Banks were required henceforth to participate ratably in its operations.

Lastly, much to the delight of authors such as myself, the Act provided that in future the Board should publish in its annual report a record of policy decisions during the year with the reasons therefor. On the other hand a proposal to require the Board "to promote . . . business stability and to mitigate by its influence unstabilizing fluctuations in the general level of production, trade, prices, and employment, so far as may be possible within the scope of monetary action and credit administration" was not enacted. But a decade later the government as a whole became committed to a similar objective through the passage of the Employment Act of 1946.

The Banking Act of 1935 became law August 23: the commissions of the members of the old Board were to expire and the new Board was to be appointed February 1, 1936. Of the outgoing members, apart from Eccles himself, only M. S. Szymczak was reappointed. The President was persuaded to drop the remaining four members, the youngest of whom was 66, on account of age. Two of them—Charles S. Hamlin and Adolph C. Miller—were close personal friends of Mr. Roosevelt. The President, says Eccles,

> could seethe at the thought of old men blocking New Deal policies; he could talk a great deal about setting sixty years as the maximum age at which a federal judge could be appointed; but when old men were his

[25] House Committee on Banking and Currency, *Banking Act of 1935*, Hearings on H.R. 5357, 74th Cong. 1st Sess., 1935, pp. 181–82.

friends and held governmental posts, the act of dislodging them was an ordeal he delayed facing as long as possible.[26]

But if it was hard for Roosevelt not to reappoint old and now aged friends, it was sometimes impossible for him to refrain from paying political debts. Back in 1933, J. J. Thomas, chairman of the Democratic State Committee of Nebraska, had been appointed to the Board at the insistence of Arthur Mullen, floor manager of the 1932 convention, and had created something of a scandal by refusing to resign his state chairmanship even after he became an active Board member. However, in 1936 Roosevelt did not reappoint Thomas; he admitted to Hamlin that Thomas should never have been appointed in the first place, and gave as one reason for not reappointing Hamlin (age 74) his wish to exclude Thomas (age 66) on grounds of age.[27] Yet to please Vice-President Garner he appointed one Ralph W. Morrison to the new Board, who shortly thereafter left suddenly for Mexico amid unpleasant rumors about his business affairs.[28]

Credit Expansion, 1933 to 1937

The year 1933 brought a highly unorthodox monetary measure—the celebrated gold-buying policy. The dollar was deliberately—one might almost say forcibly—devalued by about 40%. As a price-raising measure undertaken by the Treasury on the advice of George F. Warren, Cornell professor and extreme exponent of the most mechanistic version of the quantity theory of money, the policy was disappointing to its sponsors. From the standpoint of Federal Reserve policy its interest is only indirect: it gave the initial impetus

[26] Eccles, p. 238. Roosevelt and Hamlin had known each other since childhood. In this connection a touching passage may be quoted from an unpublished paper, "Some memories of Franklin Delano Roosevelt," written in May 1945 by Mrs. Hamlin, in which she describes a visit by the Roosevelts to the Hamlin summer home at Mattapoisett, Massachusetts: "The summer of 1926—the Roosevelts took a house in North Marion called 'Willow Bud Farm'. . . . They came over to Mattapoisett quite often and sometimes the children went swimming. . . . One evening he and Eleanor came over to dinner—he was carried into a seat at the dining-room table. He told the men not to return until 9:30. We wondered how he would spend the evening—probably staying in the dining room. But when dinner was over, Franklin pushed back his chair and said: 'See me get into the next room.' He dropped down on to the floor and went on his hands and knees and got up into a chair himself. My husband was so overcome by such courage, and seeing that superb young fellow so pleased by being able to do this, that—on the plea of hearing the telephone—he went into his den for a while before joining us again. It seems that Dr. McDonald taught his patients this way of helping themselves so that they would have a feeling of freedom to move if necessary—or for reasons of safety." The original is among the Charles S. Hamlin papers, Library of Congress.
[27] Hamlin diary, June 14 and 29, 1933; March 7, 28, and 30, 1934; January 23, 1936.
[28] Eccles, pp. 245–46.

to the golden avalanche which threatened to engulf the System—or at the very least greatly complicated monetary control—during the later 1930's. By 1936 member-bank reserve balances had doubled: by 1940 they had doubled once again.

Open-market purchases during the second half of 1933 had finally wiped out member-bank indebtedness and had furnished the banks with substantial excess reserves. The golden tide began to flow toward these shores as soon as gold had been definitely revalued at $35.00 an ounce in January 1934. Open-market operations were abandoned. Monetary ease at the short end of the market was soon so great that further relaxation seemed neither desirable nor possible. Rates on Treasury bills fell virtually to zero. However, the continued unwillingness of the System to hold longer-dated obligations meant that the gap between short and long rates of interest was enhanced, and long-term rates declined only slowly in response to a continuation of extreme ease at the short end of the market. Aaa bond yields, for instance, which fell below 4¼% for the first time in 1934, were still well above 3% at the end of 1936.

During 1934 and 1935 gold imports lifted member-bank reserves to a level of about twice required reserves. Despite the fact that industrial production was still well below the level of the 1920's and unemployment was still severe, the System began—with or without justification—to worry about the inflationary possibilities of such large excess reserves. I shall first describe the manner in which the System faced and resolved this dilemma between mid-1935 and mid-1937. I shall then discuss whether this was a true dilemma—i.e., whether its fears of inflation were justified—and shall consider what alternative policies may have been open to it.

As a result of the Banking Act of 1935 we begin for the first time to be furnished, from the fall of 1935, with a systematic record of Reserve opinion and policy decisions. The Federal Open Market Committee met October 22 to 24, 1935, and unanimously resolved

that there is nothing in the business or credit situation which at this time necessitates the adoption of any policy designed to retard credit expansion. But the Committee cannot fail to recognize that the rapid growth of bank deposits and bank reserves in the past year and a half is building up a credit base which may be very difficult to control if undue credit expansion should become evident . . . the Committee is of the opinion that steps should be taken by the Reserve System as promptly as may be possible to absorb at least some of these excess reserves, not with a view to checking some further expansion of credit, but rather to put the System in a better position to act effectively in the event that credit expansion should go too far.

Two methods of absorbing excess reserves have been discussed by the Committee: (a) the sale of short-term government securities by the Federal Reserve System, and (b) the raising of reserve requirements [the power to take such action had been conferred on the Board by the legislation enacted just two months previously].

While the Committee feels that method (a), if employed, would have the dual effect of absorbing excess reserves and improving the position of the Reserve Banks, nevertheless, there are two risks in the method, first, that it may be a shock to the bond market, inducing sales of securities by banks all over the country; second, that however it may be explained publicly, it may be misconstrued by the public as a major reversal of credit policy, since this method has never been employed except as a means of restraint, which is not desired at this time. A majority of the Committee is opposed to the sale of government securities at this time, believing that its advantages do not now justify the risks involved in this method of dealing with the subject.

There are also risks incident to method (b)—raising reserve requirements. This method of control is new and untried and may possibly prove at this time to be an undue and restraining influence on the desirable further extension of bank credit. The Committee feels, therefore, that before this method of dealing with the problem of excess reserves is employed, it would be wise for the Board of Governors of the Federal Reserve System to make a thorough study, through the 12 Reserve Banks, of the amount and location of excess reserves by districts and by classes of banks, in order thus to determine whether, or to what extent if at all, an increase in reserve requirements might interfere with the extension of loans and investments of member banks.

For the next two years—until business ebbed away decisively in the Fall of 1937—policy was dominated by the dilemma set forth in the above quotation. At a meeting on November 8, 1935, the Reserve Board decided that the time for action had not yet arrived. In December the Federal Open Market Committee, which was still composed of all twelve Reserve Bank governors, decided by a majority to urge specific action on the Board:

Some of the members of the Committee would prefer the employment of method (a) and others would prefer method (b). Those members of the Committee who prefer method (a), that is, the reduction of holdings of short-term government securities by the System, are so strongly of the opinion that some early action should be taken that they join with those members favoring method (*b*), an increase in reserve requirements, in a recommendation that the Board of Governors of the Federal Reserve System should consider some early and substantial increase in the present reserve requirements of member banks. . . .

On December 18 the Committee met with the Board and endeavored to persuade it to take action, but the Board again decided that the time had not yet arrived. On January 21, 1936, indeed, Eccles told the Committee that further credit expansion in the mortgage and capital-goods fields was still desirable.[29]

On February 1, 1936, the Board of Governors was reconstituted under the Banking Act of 1935, as noted above, without the Secretary of the Treasury and the Comptroller of the Currency. Marriner S. Eccles was chairman and M. S. Szymczak was the only other holdover. On March 1, 1936, the twelve-man Federal Open Market Committee was in turn transformed and became the seven members of the new Board plus the governors—now called "presidents"— of five of the Banks. The Federal Advisory Council alone survived the 1935 legislation unchanged: it had favored and continued to recommend an increase in reserve requirements.

Action came soon. On July 14, 1936, the Board voted 4 to 2 to increase member-bank reserve requirements by 50%, effective August 15. In a press release the Board said:

> Thorough surveys made by the Board show that the reserves are so well distributed that practically all member banks are in a position to meet the increased requirements either by utilizing their excess balances with the Reserve Banks or by drawing upon their excess balances with correspondent banks.
>
> In the light of recent experience and in view of the fact that after the increase in requirements goes into effect member banks will still have approximately $1,900 million of excess reserves, the Board is convinced that this action will not affect easy money conditions now prevailing. It does not constitute a reversal of the easy money policy which has been pursued by the System since the beginning of the depression.

One at least of the two members on record against the increase (Mr. McKee) seems to have objected, not on the ground that excess reserves should be maintained at the existing level, but because of

[29] *Annual Report of the Board of Governors for 1935*, pp. 205, 223–25, 231–34. George L. Harrison papers, "Federal Open Market Committee," Vol. III.

his belief that the reduction should be effected through open-market sales.[30]

Reserve requirements were now half-way between the minima and maxima established by the 1935 Act. In the case, for instance, of central reserve cities (New York and Chicago), actual requirements were 19½%, the permissible limits of variation being 13% and 26% respectively. The increase had in fact been achieved virtually without disturbance to the money market. The announcement, after the close of business on July 14, 1936, brought a fall of about half a point in government bonds. The System bought about $100 million, presumably of maturities in the 5- to 10-year range which commercial banks might be expected to sell, and disposed of a corresponding volume of shorts. The operation dwarfed previous small-scale bond purchases in November 1929 and March–June 1932. The purpose of the intervention was to slow the decline, any attempt to peg the market being clearly disavowed.[31]

Excess reserves were still very large. Aid soon was brought to the embattled System by the Treasury, which announced December 21, 1936, that it would sterilize future gold imports in an inactive gold account. This works as follows. The imported gold ordinarily would swell member-bank reserves. To prevent this, the Treasury moves a corresponding volume of funds from its balances with member banks to the Reserve Banks. But the possibilities of this method are limited by the size of Treasury balances and the operating needs of the Treasury. A further device is for the Treasury to borrow in the market to pay for the new gold. This costs the Treasury interest. The whole procedure has the further disadvantage of making the Reserve beholden to the Treasury. Nevertheless during 1936 and 1937 the Treasury sterilized over $1 billion of gold.

[30] *Annual Report of the Board of Governors for 1936*, pp. 216–218, 229.

[31] George L. Harrison papers, "Conversations," Vol. III, memorandum of July 15, 1936. The figure of $100 million may be estimated from the following: on January 15, 1936, the System account held $2,029 million of Treasury bills, certificates, and notes (i.e., all less than 5 years), $121 million of Treasury bonds maturing in 10 years or less, and $73 million maturing in more than 10 years (these were Libertys bought in 1932 and converted in 1934: Harrison papers, "Open Market Committee," Vol. III). In July 1936 the first date for which published data are available (*Federal Reserve Bulletin*), the System held $2,105 million of governments maturing in 5 years or less, and $325 million maturing in more than 5 years. (The published maturity distribution does not segregate "10 years and over" until October 1950.) The difference of $131 million in bond holdings between the two dates, however, includes any bonds among the $223 million of governments which were transferred from individual Reserve Banks to the System account June 30, 1936. See Appendix III.

But the Board was not satisfied that the inflation danger was yet out of the way. On January 30, 1937, it voted 5 to 1 to increase requirements to the maxima the law allowed for each class of bank, the increase to be effected in equal steps on March 1 and May 1. The member of the Board recorded in the negative was again Mr. McKee, and presumably for the same reason as before. The press release read:

> The Board estimates that, after the full increase has gone into effect, member banks will have excess reserves of approximately $500 million, an amount ample to finance further recovery and to maintain easy money conditions. At the same time the Federal Reserve System will be placed in a position where such reduction or expansion of member bank reserves as may be in the public interest may be effected through open-market operations, a more flexible instrument, better adapted for keeping the reserve position of member banks currently in close adjustment to credit needs. . . . The excess reserves of about $1,500 million eliminated as a base for further credit expansion by this action could support an increase in the supply of money, in the form of bank credit, which beyond any doubt would constitute an injurious credit expansion.
>
> The present is an opportune time for action because, as was the case when the Board announced its prior action last July, excess reserves are widely distributed among member banks, and balances with correspondent banks are twice as large as they have generally been in the past. All but a small number of member banks have more than sufficient excess reserves and surplus balances with other banks to meet [the present] increase in reserve requirements. As of January 13, the Board's survey indicates that only 197 of the 6,367 member banks lacked sufficient funds to meet such an increase in reserve requirements by utilizing their present excess balances with the Reserve Banks and *not more than one-half of their balances with correspondent banks. On this basis* these 197 banks, in order to meet the full requirements, would have needed an additional $123 million, of which $110 million would have been needed by banks in central reserve cities. . . .
>
> It is the Board's expectation that, with approximately $500 million of excess reserves remaining with the banks, credit conditions will continue to be easy. . . . The Board's action does not reduce the large volume of existing funds available for investment by depositors, and should not, therefore, occasion an advance in long-term interest rates or a restrictive policy on the part of institutional and other investors in meeting the needs for sound business, industrial and agricultural credit.
>
> In view of all these considerations, the Board believes that the action taken at this time will operate to prevent an injurious credit expansion and at the same time gives assurance for continued progress toward full recovery.[32]

[32] *Annual Report of the Board of Governors for 1937*, pp. 195–98. Italics supplied.

I have followed the genesis of the dilemma, and its solution by the Board over a period of eighteen months, at some length because the hopes of the Board were not realized, and its actions were later blamed for the violent reaction in business which occurred between the Summer of 1937 and the Spring of 1938. First, was the dilemma a real one? Second, if so, was the policy chosen by the Board the best method of resolving it?

The inflationary potentialities of very large excess reserves are not to be denied. Yet the Reserve System seems to me to have exaggerated the danger, at least in the circumstances of 1936–1937. Was not the System itself perhaps infected in mild degree by the truly nonsensical inflation scares propagated at that period by opponents of the gold-buying policy, of the Thomas Amendment, and of numerous more or less crackpot schemes for monetary reform? Whether or not this was the case, the Board seems to have believed that the well-established decline in the velocity of bank deposits since the 1920's was strictly temporary and abnormal, and that a sharp rise in deposit velocity might be expected at any time. This illusion no doubt contributed to the prevailing nervousness. Moreover, instead of welcoming a further fall in long-term interest rates as a stimulus to investment, Chairman Eccles, at least, seems to have feared such a trend, on the ground that levels lower than those then prevailing could not be maintained, or anyhow that institutional investors would not believe in their continuance. This would mean, the Chairman believed, that money which should have been available for bonds and mortgages would be used for "speculative . . . buying" of stocks and commodities, and that such a development would be inflationary.[33] In any case President Harrison of the New York Reserve Bank argued that the existence of large excess reserves rendered monetary control ineffective, and that in order to prevent inflation the System should get back to a situation in which member banks were forced to borrow.[34] At this point the critic finds himself asking whether it were not better to recognize that "recovery" must *inevitably* be in some sense "inflationary."

[33] House Committee on Banking and Currency, *To Extend the Period During Which Direct Obligations of the United States May Be Used as Collateral Security for Federal Reserve Notes*, Hearings on S. 417, 75th Cong. 1st Sess., 1937, pp. 35–36.
[34] George L. Harrison papers, "Conversations," Vol. III, August 27, 1937.

Yet if the Board exaggerated the danger, we may yet sympathize with its belief that it ought to have been possible to remove the excess reserves without disturbing the money market. For unless a startling change had occurred in the psychology of the commercial banker, it was safe to assume that his excess reserves meant little to him; should he lose even a substantial part of them, he was hardly likely to alter his behavior. Of course it could not be assumed that excess reserves would be uniformly distributed among member banks. The problem evidently was, as the Board realized, to cut A's excess reserves without driving B into a tight spot.

As we have seen, the first increase in reserve requirements, in the Summer of 1936, was achieved without untoward effects. The second increase, in two steps in the Spring of 1937, had slight effect on short-term rates, at least as measured by the commonly available quotations, nor does any lessened availability of bank credit seem to have resulted. But the Board's action was followed by a wave of bond sales by member banks during March. As a consequence of Secretary Morgenthau's protests at a stormy meeting in the White House one Sunday afternoon, the New York Reserve Bank was instructed to check the fall in governments. As a result there occurred the first substantial open-market purchases in more than three years. This was Treasury interference in monetary policy with a vengeance: but the circumstances were unusual. On the one hand, Chairman Eccles sympathized wholeheartedly with the Treasury's dislike of falling bond prices, for he feared the effect on business: the line-up really was Eccles (supported by Morgenthau) versus Harrison and Sinclair (of the New York and Philadelphia Banks), with other members of the Open Market Committee on the sidelines. On the other hand, the Treasury possessed an unusual (and no doubt unwelcome) weapon in the shape of power to desterilize $1 billion or so of gold.[35] At any rate the purchases were made, but they did not prevent the yield on Aaa bonds, which had declined steadily during 1936, from rising from 3.10% in January 1937 to 3.42% in April: not until late in 1938 did it decline again to the former level.

To the Board these consequences of its second increase in reserve requirements, announced January 30, 1937, must have been un-

[35] Eccles, pp. 291–93. George L. Harrison papers, "Conversations," Vol. III, two memoranda by J. H. Williams, April 14, 1937.

welcome and were certainly unexpected. The implication of its statement (quoted above) that 197 banks in all would need a mere $123 million of additional reserves was too optimistic. In fact, between January and June 1937, member banks sold on balance $856 million of governments and $330 million of other investments, or well over $1 billion in all. Chairman Eccles later claimed that these sales were primarily speculative, and occurred because the banks now foresaw the end of the bull market in governments.[36] But this cannot have been the entire explanation, and—even if partly true—it merely serves to underscore the error in policy.

The mistake made by the Board obviously was that it based its calculation on the assumption that member banks could use up to "one-half of their balances with correspondent banks" without incommoding their correspondents. The bulk of the bond sales were in fact made by New York and Chicago banks, and were obviously occasioned by the need to replenish reserves depleted by the loss of deposits owed to out-of-town banks.[37]

How, it may be asked, was the Board to know that member banks would react in this fashion? Why should not New York and Chicago banks, upon which the shortage of reserves was concentrated, have borrowed from their respective Reserve Banks or have purchased federal funds? Presumably because they felt that either of these remedies would prove temporary, whereas the increase in reserve requirements announced by the Board had every air of permanence. Indeed, that they would not resort to these remedies, but instead would sell investments, might have been apparent from the way they reacted to the first increase in reserve requirements in August 1936. Between the June and December call dates in that year, investments of New York City member banks declined by $603 million in response to the withdrawal of balances by banks in the in-

[36] House Committee on Banking and Currency, *Government Ownership of the Twelve Federal Reserve Banks*, Hearings on H.R. 7230, 75th Cong. 3rd Sess., 1938, pp. 469-70, 476.

[37] I have here followed the excellent account to be found in Kenneth D. Roose, *The Economics of Recession and Revival: An Interpretation of 1937-38* (New Haven: Yale University Press, 1954), Ch. 7. See also testimony by Chairman Eccles, February 16, 1937 in House Committee on Banking and Currency, *To Extend the Period During Which Direct Obligations of the United States May Be Used as Collateral Security for Federal Reserve Notes*, Hearings on S. 417, 75th Cong. 1st Sess., 1937, pp. 15-16.

terior: but meanwhile (other) out-of-town banks purchased $526 million, so that investments held by all member banks declined by only $77 million, an inconsequential amount. The Board should have realized that the higher required reserves were pushed, the larger the number of banks that would be forced to draw down their balances with correspondents and the smaller the number that would continue to purchase investments.

Various reflections are suggested by this experience. The original dilemma—the accumulation of vast excess reserves in time of semi-depression—was provoked, in part at least, by an error in public policy for which the Reserve was in no way responsible: the rise in the buying price of gold. Once it was faced by the dilemma, the System seems to me to have been unduly nervous about the risk of inflationary consequences caused by the existence of excess reserves. It should have contented itself with the 50% increase in reserve requirements imposed in 1936, and should not have proceeded with the further increase in 1937.

Even were it desired to reduce excess reserves to a few hundred million dollars, other means of doing this were open to the System. Certainly the sale of securities in the open market, advocated at the time by some within the System, could not have proved an effective alternative. The impact of such sales would not have been confined to the banks where the excess was located, any more than was the impact of the increase in reserve requirements. However, open-market sales, having less of an air of finality than a change in reserve requirements, might perhaps have been met by member banks by borrowing or purchase of federal funds, rather than by sale of investments.

Still better might it have been to prevent such vast excess reserves from accumulating in the first place. This could have been done by persuading the Treasury to help out by sterilizing gold at a much earlier stage. Yet it is embarrassing for an ostensibly independent monetary authority to have to depend on the Treasury for such assistance. Another plan might have been to sell securities as and when gold was imported: to this it may be objected that the System would eventually have been entirely denuded of securities. The answer is possibly that, if the Treasury can borrow to sterilize gold, why cannot the Federal Reserve? Federal Reserve debentures would be an admirable novelty, but would of course require legislative approval.

There remains the question whether interest rates could have declined—as they in fact did—during 1935 and 1936 had excess reserves been prevented from accumulating in the first place. A categorical answer cannot be given. The argument for the belief that interest rates still would have fallen is as follows. When gold imports are sterilized on arrival, by Federal Reserve security sales or by Treasury borrowing, reserves are increased and immediately reduced again. Gold is mostly imported through New York, and the transactions required to sterilize it also take place in the New York market. Hence the reserves that are increased and those that are reduced, if not reserves of identical member banks, are at least reserves of member banks in the same Reserve District, so that things are left substantially as they were before gold was imported. However, if excess reserves accumulate, in time they spread across the country, affecting the liquidity of banks and classes of banks quite unevenly. When that has happened, there is no longer any way of reducing the reserves of those member banks, or even of those Reserve Districts, where the excess is located, and leaving others unaffected. The most that can be said is that, if the elimination of excess reserves that have existed for some time raises interest rates, it by no means follows that the avoidance of such excess reserves through gold sterilization would have a like effect.

The Recession of 1937–1938

The business setback that began in the Fall of 1937 was more severe even than that of 1920–1921. Industrial production (on a 1923–1925 base) fell from 117 in August 1937 to 76 in May 1938. The recession was especially disheartening since it began at a level by most tests well below that of 1929. Was Reserve policy—and particularly the second increase in member-bank reserve requirements in the Spring of 1937—to blame?

The origins and course of the recession have been well analyzed by Roose. As he points out, other relevant factors in the situation were the sudden disappearance of the federal deficit (when calculated upon a cash basis) and the sharp rise in labor costs. His conclusions as to the causes of the decline are worth quoting in full:

In broad outline, the causation may be reduced to a relatively few important elements. In an economy which was still excessively depression conscious and in which business expectations were extremely uncertain (in part because of the serious political conflict between the New Deal and business), net government contribution to income was drastically reduced in January 1937. Consequently, the responsibility for sustaining and increasing national income and production was shifted to private investment and enterprise.

However, at the same time that net government contribution ceased, the Federal Reserve action on excess reserves caused short-term governments to weaken and set up thereby a chain of reactions which resulted in increased costs of capital and the weakening of the securities markets to which business expectations are very sensitive, especially in the United States. The operation of the undistributed profits tax, in addition to its effects on business expectations, also reduced the cash position of even the large companies. The imperfect supply of capital funds and their increased cost made it more difficult for borrowers to obtain capital.

Most important of all, however, was the reduced profitability of investment, beginning in the first quarter of 1937. This resulted from the increased costs in which labor costs played a prominent part. Given a situation in which business men were most unwilling to initiate long-term investment projects which alone could raise income and production to higher levels, the immediate decline in profit ratio, accompanied by the prospect of sharp declines in future profits, is adequate reason for the occurrence and timing of the recession. . . .

In no sense can it be concluded that any one factor caused the downturn of 1937. . . .[38]

It would thus be unfair to charge the Reserve System with sole, or even major, responsibility for the recession. Bad luck allowed three, or perhaps four, deflationary influences to appear on the scene simultaneously. Yet, if judged by the high standards which Governor Eccles had himself proposed, the policies of the System fell short. As laid down by Congress, the original and continuing purpose of the System is "to furnish an elastic currency, to afford a means of rediscounting commercial paper, to establish a more effective supervision of banking . . . [and] to accommodate commerce and business."[39] For this vague and, indeed, outdated mandate numerous substitutes were at different times proposed. Although other parts of the Act were amended beyond recognition, these definitions of purpose remain unchanged to this day. Among the

[38] Roose, pp. 238–39.
[39] Federal Reserve Act, Preamble and Sec. 14 (d).

substitutes proposed, but not enacted, was the following by Governor Eccles:

> It shall be the duty of the Federal Reserve Board to exercise such powers as it possesses to promote conditions making for business stability and *to mitigate by its influence unstabilizing fluctuations* in the general level of production, trade, prices, and employment, so far as may be possible within the scope of monetary action.[40]

The complaint against the Board is that its policy in the Spring of 1937 failed to "promote conditions making for business stability," but instead acted in a manner which reinforced other destabilizing influences by inadvertently tightening money in a situation in which such action was not called for. How far could the System have been expected to detect other destabilizing factors so as to "mitigate them by its influence"? The sharp reduction in the federal cash deficit, although not recognized until too late, could readily have been detected at the time by a study of Treasury figures, or even from a contemplation of the probable effects of the old-age provisions of the Social Security Act. The rising costs and reduced profits might have been noticed in general terms, but would have been difficult or impossible to document statistically until after the event. As for the undistributed profits tax, its responsibility is equivocal; indeed, Eccles later expressed the opinion that the tax had nothing whatever to do with the recession.[41]

In a spirited defense of the Board's policy, made ten years after the event, Chairman Eccles rightly laid main emphasis on the deflationary fiscal situation.[42] He pointed out that the gentle restraint upon credit resulting from the increases in member-bank reserve requirements was scarcely in itself an adequate explanation of the decline in business. But it still could be true that—in the light of Eccles' own prescription—the fiscal situation called for an *easing* of credit during the first months of 1937. We may conclude that the proper criticism to be made of the Board in this context is that it did not detect in time, or if it did so, did not give sufficient weight to, the sudden change in the relation between cash receipts and disbursements of the Treasury which occurred about the end of 1936.

[40] House Committee on Banking and Currency, *Banking Act of 1935*, Hearings on H.R. 5357, 74th Cong. 1st Sess., 1935, p. 251. Italics supplied.
[41] Eccles, p. 301.
[42] Senate Committee on Banking and Currency, *To Provide for the Regulation of Consumer Credit for a Temporary Period*, Hearings on S.J.R. 157, 80th Cong. 1st Sess., 1947, pp. 164–65.

How did the Board react to the recession once it materialized? On August 27, 1937, the New York Bank reduced its rediscount rate from 1½% to the record low of 1%. An academic manifesto of continued monetary ease, this action occurred too early to have constituted a response to incipient decline in business activity. It was more probably a belated recognition of the need for greater monetary ease in the light of the developing fiscal situation. Desterilization of gold by the Treasury, requested by the Board September 12, was considered to have no more than seasonal significance.[43] In fact the Board's first formal response to the decline of business activity seems to have occurred April 15, 1938, when it somewhat reduced reserve requirements (from 26%, 20%, and 14% of demand deposits for the three classes of member bank to 22¾%, 17½%, and 12%, respectively). This measure was taken in conjunction with a new program of public spending announced by President Roosevelt as an anti-recession measure. The rapid conversion thereafter of the federal cash surplus into a cash deficit was probably the chief factor in promoting the sudden business revival which began in June 1938.

The Last of the Stabilization Bills

The recession of 1937–1938 gave rise to much disappointment with the results of the New Deal recovery program and in many quarters a feeling of disillusionment. Partly for this reason, hearings were held in the Spring of 1938 on the last of the bills to promote stabilization of commodity prices—the Patman bill.[44] Like the third Goldsborough bill, it coupled stabilization with a reorganization of the agencies of monetary control. The bill proposed Treasury purchase of the stock of the Reserve Banks, and the appointment of all of their directors by a reconstituted Reserve Board of 15 members—one from each Federal Reserve district, plus the Secretary of the Treasury, the Comptroller of the Currency, and the chairman of the Federal Deposit Insurance Corporation. The Federal Advisory Council and the Open Market Committee were to be abolished, and the functions of the latter transferred to the Board. A fresh mandate was offered to the Board: it was to be instructed to

[43] *Annual Report of the Board of Governors for 1937*, pp. 203–6.
[44] House Committee on Banking and Currency, *Government Ownership of the Twelve Federal Reserve Banks*, Hearings on H.R. 7230, 75th Cong. 3rd Sess., 1938.

raise the level of commodity prices "until full employment of all persons able and willing to work shall have been achieved," and until the 1926 price level was restored. To sew matters up, Congress was to have the power to remove Board members, although they would continue to be appointed by the President.

Representative Patman apparently intended his mandate to require the attainment of a price level that would secure full employment, or the 1926 level, whichever proved higher, but the language of the bill is not free from ambiguity. The bill was the expression of a simple-minded belief in a close correlation between the level of prices and the volume of employment. No provision was made in the bill for possible incompatibility between long-run stable prices and full employment. However, the proposal that the level of employment should become an explicit criterion for public policy offers an interesting anticipation of the Employment Act of 1946. To be sure, the later Act offers a generalized declaration of Congressional intent rather than a policy mandate to any individual agency.

For obvious reasons the bill was resisted in testimony by Chairman Eccles and Vice-Chairman Ransom, but Eccles had to admit that he favored the abolition of the Open Market Committee and that he had no objection to the elimination of the Federal Advisory Council. He did not even quarrel with the 1926 price level, provided it were approached gradually, but—like every Reserve official who had testified during the past ten years—he denied the System's power to control prices and objected to the mandatory character of the bill.

The hearings were notable for an argument by Chester A. Phillips, Dean of the State University of Iowa, in support of the view that the comparative price stability of the 1920's had had inflationary results because of the decline in costs. The argument echoed, but was more closely reasoned than, that made by Adolph Miller against the Fletcher bill six years earlier. It did not impress the Committee. An attack on the bill by Walter E. Spahr was even less well received. But Professor Spahr, like other members of the Economists' National Committee on Monetary Policy, mostly offered the Committee dogmatic assertion in place of argument.

The Patman bill was introduced at a time of waning confidence in the effectiveness of monetary policy. Such an ambitious reorganization of the monetary authority had no chance of enactment, especially since a major revision of the Federal Reserve Act had been undertaken just three years previously. Yet the proposal to make employment a policy objective anticipated—and perhaps eased the enactment of—the Murray Act of 1946.

Chapter 6

The Treasury Takes Over, 1939–1951

Inter arma silent leges.
—ANON.

As the year 1939 advanced, the steady rise in the level of business activity convinced the authorities that the recession of the previous year was now safely in the past. All that seemed necessary for the complete recovery of business was a continuation of low interest rates and easily available credit. Therefore, when war clouds gathered in Europe during the Summer of 1939, the Reserve System became much preoccupied with the current and prospective behavior of the government-bond market. A crisis in the bond market as a result of events abroad might react upon short-term rates, threaten the regime of easy money, and mar the prospects for further recovery of business. Moreover, apart altogether from the *level* of bond prices, the System had developed, since the Spring of 1937, under pressure from the Treasury, a feeling of responsibility for their *stability*. Thus arose the concept—never too well defined—of the "orderly market" as the appropriate objective for Reserve operations.

From the Invasion of Poland to Pearl Harbor[1]

Unquestionably the outbreak of war in Europe placed these objectives—for whatever they were worth—in dire peril. The longest-term bond then extant, the partially tax-exempt 2¾'s of 1960–1965, declined from 108-3/4 on June 6 to 106-3/32 on August 31, 1939 —not a sensational fall. The German invasion of Poland on Septem-

[1] See, especially, George L. Harrison papers, "Conversations," Vol. IV.

ber 1 brought a further sharp retreat, however, and the System was at once faced with the question in what manner and to what extent to intervene. The executive committee of the Open Market Committee had no difficulty in deciding to bail out the security dealers by offering to take over their floating supplies of governments during the crisis. How to handle the market itself was more difficult. The open-market account had been authorized to buy up to $500 million—a large amount for those days. How should it be used?

Ever since April 1937, because of its dissatisfaction with the manner in which the New York Bank had handled the government-security market at that time, Washington had insisted on keeping a tight rein over open-market operations. The Board's majorities on the Open Market Committee and its executive committee had seen to it that the discretion accorded the manager of the open-market account (at this time Allan Sproul) was kept to a minimum. This entailed frequent meetings of the executive committee. During a crisis such as that of September 1939, the necessary membership (Chairman Eccles and two other members of the Board of Governors, President Harrison of the New York Bank and one other Reserve Bank president) would confer daily by telephone before 10 a.m., at which hour the market opened. It is hardly surprising that New York officials were apt to become restive under the need to refer decisions to Washington daily or even oftener.

The prevailing method of market support consisted at that time of placing bids at the opening of the market ¼ or ⅛ below the preceding close. In a falling market such bids might turn out to be well above the level at which the market opened. Therefore more discretion was needed, which Harrison extracted from Washington only with difficulty. On September 5, the Tuesday following Labor Day, it was clear that the war in Europe was spreading; but the executive committee took so long in reaching agreement that the market almost went without support. Broadly speaking, Chairman Eccles and the Board of Governors wanted to drop the market sharply, allowing longs to fall by two or three points, and then come in with massive support. By contrast, Harrison and the other Reserve Bank presidents were skeptical of their ability to peg the market at any definite level and fearful of the speed with which even so large an authorization as $500 million might be exhausted. They favored following the market down, buying only at such times as selling seemed likely to dry up once support was offered. On this issue the Treasury sided with the Reserve Bank presidents and urged that bonds be allowed to find their "natural" level—a striking contrast to its attitude a few years later.

On September 11 the executive committee met with Secretary Morgenthau in Washington, who urged that bonds be allowed to fall faster with less money put into the market: but it was decided to attempt to peg the 2¾'s of 1960–1965 at 101. By this time the shorter maturities were recovering, but long-term governments continued weak and fell to a low of 99-14/32 on September 22, when somewhat over $400 million had been bought, of which less than $100 million was in longs. By November the market was strong and controversy developed as to which maturities should now be sold. Eccles wanted to sell bills, feeling that the longs were still underpriced and were also valuable as a source of earnings: the New York view was that bills were the only proper open-market instrument, and proposed to sell the longs, feeling that they had only been acquired as the result of misfortune. Fifteen years later New York and Washington were to have precisely exchanged their positions on this issue.

Perhaps partly as a result of lack of agreement as to what to sell, and partly from a desire to consolidate business recovery, the open-market account declined only slightly during 1940. Meanwhile, as a consequence of gold imports, excess reserves continued to increase. Bond prices rose rather steadily, and by the end of 1940 and during 1941 yields were at an all-time low: partially tax-exempt long-term governments returned less than 2%. Treasury bills, yielded virtually nothing, or even sold on a negative-yield basis on account of the exchange rights accorded to their holders.

The negligible yield of short-term governments, the System's principal asset, led to anxiety over earnings, anxiety such as had not existed since the early 1920's. In the later 1920's substantial earning assets had been held at high yields; after 1929 yields had indeed declined, but the great increase in the volume of earning assets had compensated for the decline in yields. Now yields on short-term assets approached the zero level. As a consequence, anxiety for the System's earnings won over to bond purchases even those who most disliked them.

Holdings of bonds with more than 10 years to mature, acquired for the first time by the System account in 1934 through conversion, probably still were negligible. On the other hand bonds over 5 years from maturity, which after the purchases of March and April 1937 had amounted to 27% of the System account, had gradually risen (through substitution for shorter maturities) to 34% just prior to the invasion of Poland. The operations of September 1939, described above, raised the ratio to 42%. During the year 1940 short-term governments were deliberately allowed to run off without replacement, but bond holdings remained steady: the latter constituted 58% of the portfolio at the time of Pearl Harbor (see Fig. 2).[2]

By the end of 1940, business had recovered from a mild recession earlier in the year, and the rise in commodity prices, combined as it was with extreme ease in the money market, gave cause for concern. Accordingly, in a special report to Congress, endorsed by the Board of Governors, the Reserve Bank presidents, and the Federal Advisory Council, the System asked for additional powers to control the excess reserves of member banks, at that time amounting to some $7 billion.[3] Authority was asked to double reserve requirements and to make them apply to all commercial banks. Increased reserves for member banks only, it was realized, would drive state-chartered banks from the System and perhaps cause national banks to give up their federal charters. However, federal regulation under the commerce clause of state nonmember banks was now thought to be feasible. Yet Congress did not act. Instead, when war came a year later the American banking system was quite extraordinarily liquid—an advantage or a disadvantage according to one's point of view.

To the Treasury this liquidity seemed an advantage. By the time of Pearl Harbor, the cessation of gold inflow following the enactment of lend-lease, the raising of reserve requirements to the legal limit, together with commercial bank expansion, had reduced excess

[2] All Reserve Bank holdings of Treasury obligations were transferred to System account as of June 30, 1936, prior to which date transactions for System account give an incomplete picture of Reserve open-market operations as a whole. Maturity distribution of System account holdings has been published regularly since September 30, 1936, but maturities in excess of 10 years were not reported separately from those between 5 and 10 years until October 1950. The maturity of Treasury obligations refers to first-call date through April 15, 1953; since then final-maturity date has been used as the basis for classification. In the discussion in the text, published tabulations have been supplemented by data from the George L. Harrison papers, especially "Open Market Committee," Vols. II and III. See Appendix III.

[3] *Annual Report of the Board of Governors for 1940,* pp. 68–70.

reserves to around $4 billion. The Treasury's position from then on was that large excess reserves were a condition for the success of government financing. Indeed the Treasury was critical of the System's measures to reduce their level even as low as $4 billion.[4]

Pearl Harbor and Beyond

Despite the fact that excess reserves, although still large, had fallen somewhat since their peak, the Japanese attack was not followed by any such crisis in the bond market as had occurred after war broke out in Europe in 1939. After Pearl Harbor the 2½'s of 1967–1972 declined only from 101½ to par, and quite small purchases by the Reserve proved sufficient to keep them there. An explanation of this contrast must be sought in the events of the two preceding years. Sentiment was encouraged by the large supplies of governments that had recently been absorbed at rising prices, by the announced intention of the Treasury to finance the war without a rise in interest rates, and perhaps by the experience of Britain, where interest rates had declined after war had come.

With relief, Reserve officials turned from the market to discussions with the Treasury as to the handling of the large amount of government borrowing then in prospect. As early as December 18, 1941, less than two weeks after Pearl Harbor, the Reserve and the Treasury had no difficulty in agreeing that yields on government securities of different maturities should henceforth be maintained at prescribed levels. These levels, it was further agreed, should roughly accord with the existing gradation from short to long. Although the Reserve made no issue with the Treasury on the main question, a number of minor details continued to be a subject of controversy during 1942. While it was agreed that some rise in the abnormally low bill rate (then around ¼%) was desirable, the Treasury suggested ⅜%, and the Reserve ½% to ¾%: the Reserve yielded. As for the 2½% long-term rate, here also minor differences arose. Eccles and Sproul would have liked to allow the 1967–1972 maturities to fall as low as 98, reserving support at par for a somewhat shorter 2½% issue; they also proposed that support should be discretionary, in order that some degree of market fluctuation might be preserved and bonds be prevented from becoming in effect

[4] Henry C. Murphy, *National Debt in War and Transition* (New York: McGraw-Hill, 1950), pp. 28–29.

a demand obligation. On these points also the Treasury had its way, insisting that the 1967–1972 2½'s be supported at par indefinitely. It appears that there were even extremists in the Treasury who desired that a public announcement be made of the latter decision, but this proposal was wisely—and successfully—resisted.[5]

Various attempts were made, then and later, to rationalize these decisions. Thus for instance Murphy, who as a Treasury official had a good deal to do with the matter, suggests that the establishment of a 3% wartime yield on British Consols was regarded as a model, the notion being that the "credit of the United States" (a vague enough term) must for some unspecified reason be at least ½% better than Britain's. He also suggests that 2½% was in line with the "needs" of the life insurance companies, which at that time computed reserves on a 3% basis, but systematically underestimated mortality, so in effect relying on a 2½% yield. It seems clear however that this particular pattern of rates was mainly chosen because the simplest plan was to perpetuate the situation existing at the time the United States became a belligerent.

Before the year 1942 was out, things had been made still easier for banks and others interested in the short end of the market. In April the System announced a "posted buying-rate for Treasury bills," whereby the Reserve Banks would purchase all bills offered at ⅜%: the arrangement was analogous to the acceptance-buying rate which had earlier been intended to encourage the acceptance market. In August the Open Market Committee announced its willingness to resell to the original owner, at ⅜%, any bills previously bought at the posted rate. The Treasury bill had now become a demand obligation bearing interest, and banks' holdings of bills were excess reserves in all but name. In October a preferential discount rate of ½% was established for loans secured by governments maturing within 12 months: this assured ultra-cheap reserve money even for small interior banks that might own no bills. A further proposal, to make bills automatically renewable on maturity, provoked President Sproul of the New York Bank to the following protest:

> . . . the whole operation is in a fair way to become ridiculous. We are already selling good dollar bills for ninety nine and nine-o-six cents. To mask this essentially simple transaction, we ask the buyer to do a

[5] *Ibid.*, Ch. 8.

little elementary arithmetic, and to make a bid, so that he will still think he is in a competitive market. But now it is proposed to do away with this, for those who are too lazy to bid. Hereafter the bargain-counter dollar bills will be wrapped as gifts and delivered to the buyer's door. Hocus pocus carried to this extreme destroys illusions rather than supports them.[6]

The task of preserving the "pattern" was to prove more difficult than had been anticipated, and eventually became a serious embarrassment to the Reserve if not to the Treasury. The reason is not far to seek. In the past, long-term yields on governments had commonly (but not always) been higher than short-term in accordance with the market's valuation of the greater risk that long-term bonds might fall in price. This risk had now been sharply diminished, if not removed, and so therefore had the reason underlying the differentiation in yields according to maturity. That is to say, at the rates established by the authorities, longs looked a much better buy than shorts. In consequence, the Reserve was before long the only buyer of Treasury bills: by 1944 the substantial portfolio of bonds held by the System in 1940 and 1941 had all but vanished. The scramble for long-term bonds in the market was mitigated only because, unless callable within 10 years, they were not eligible for commercial banks to hold.

Market conditions, as established by the Treasury and Federal Reserve, made it profitable to "play the pattern of rates" by "rolling down the curve" of yields. A 5-year obligation would yield more to maturity than investment and reinvestment in five successive 1-year obligations, without greater risk. In addition, the 5-year security would appreciate as a reflection of reduced yield to maturity as maturity approached: therefore, by buying securities with many years to run and selling them at a premium on the steepest part of the yield curve, yields considerably in excess of the coupon could be obtained. Especially was this true where bank-ineligible bonds were bought, and sold again shortly after becoming eligible.

Reserve officials already saw this problem, at least dimly, in 1942, and became tireless advocates of higher short-term rates. The Treasury felt differently. According to Murphy:

> The sluggishness of the long-term market in responding to the large volume of excess reserves and its readiness—demonstrated in 1937— to respond rather promptly to a tightening of short-term money rates

[6] Eccles papers, Sproul to Eccles, November 6, 1942.

had left a deep impression on the minds of Treasury officials. While, as a group, they were not in favor of extremely low short-term interest rates *as such*, they knew of no other sure way of guaranteeing the continuance of the 2½% long-term rate except by continuing the short-term rates that had brought it about.[7]

Yet the known or supposed reluctance of the Reserve at the time to buy long-term bonds may well have been a main reason for the "sluggishness" of the bond market to which Murphy refers. In view of the regime of bond support then in prospect, the Treasury's position lost cogency. As confidence grew in the liquidity of long-term governments, the reason for the differential in yields melted away. It soon became clear that the problem was not to prevent bonds from falling, but to keep them from rising.

Of course bond prices would not be stabilized forever. Moreover, for some investors the idea of regarding a bond as a demand obligation involved too great a break with convention to be accepted. Yet on the market's estimation, anything like equal net advantages would have required far smaller differentials between short and long yields than actually obtained. This prompts the question as to which alternative—higher short-term or lower long-term rates—would have been preferable as a solution to the difficulty. So long as private investment was determined by the allocation of materials rather than by the cost of raising capital, little difference to the actual conduct of the war could have resulted whichever alternative were chosen. It seems that the question should be resolved rather on grounds of equity. Consideration of the earnings of life insurance companies (see above) and other institutions would argue for higher short-term rates. The general interest would however appear to be better represented by the Treasury's concern for the cost of the debt, and those who claim that the war could have been fought with lower long-term rates would seem to have the better of the argument. On the other hand, lower rates during the war might have made the situation even more difficult to unfreeze after the war, when the interest cost of private capital would again become important.

Certainly, so long as the war lasted, interest rates had little or no bearing on the inflation problem. That is to say, the degree of wartime (as distinct from postwar) inflation was determined almost entirely by fiscal policy, and we must conclude that even much higher

[7] *Loc. cit.*, p. 96.

rates would have had almost no effect in cutting down the supply of money or the volume of spending. Private investment was small and quite insensitive to the rate of interest; consumer credit had almost disappeared; and the interest elasticity of saving cannot have been large. It therefore seems to follow that—apart from questions of equity—the level of interest rates during the war was a matter of indifference, except for its effect upon the postwar situation.

If monetary measures were blunted during the war, they could again be used for fighting inflation once the war was over. As it happened, the main obstacle to their use, once the guns were silenced, was not the level of interest rates with which we emerged from the war, but the fact that the Treasury remained in the saddle.

The Wartime Pattern Prolonged: July 1945 to July 1947

Owing to the large number of investors (bank and nonbank) who had come to consider bonds practically as liquid as bills, the low level of short-term rates inevitably produced—by simple arbitrage —a powerful downward pressure on long rates. During 1944 the yield on long-term governments was only slightly less than $2\frac{1}{2}\%$: September had the lowest monthly average with 2.47%. So long as large additional supplies of Treasury bonds were still to be expected, their yields might not indeed fall far. But the prospective end of the war presumably meant that fresh sales would be confined to funding operations. Hence the upward pressure on bond prices increased during 1945 with the end of fighting, and by December long-term governments were selling on a 2.33% yield basis. With the flotation of the Victory Loan just before Christmas, the prospect of further net borrowing by the Treasury was virtually at an end. The continued anchoring of short-term rates was now free to exert its full effect on the long-term market. A boom in long-term governments resulted which pushed their yields down to a record low of 2.08% (monthly average) for April 1946. On April 6 the Victory $2\frac{1}{2}$'s 1967–1972, which had been floated at par in December, sold up to $106^{15}\!/_{32}$. Bonds were far from needing a peg to maintain their prices at par!

The boom evidently resulted from a growing belief that money would become cheaper rather than dearer. This belief was encouraged, first, by widespread predictions of a reconversion slump; and, second, by the knowledge that the Treasury must engage in much refunding, coupled with rumors that such refunding would be undertaken at progressively lower rates. The Treasury might be delighted by the buoyancy of its obligations, but the Reserve System was obviously embarrassed. Yet so long as the "pattern" was maintained at the short end, the System was powerless. As matters turned out, the boom was short-lived.

The long rate now was so far below the agreed 2½% level that the Treasury apparently felt some concession had to be made. It happened that the Victory Loan had raised war loan accounts at commercial banks much above the working minima. Accordingly the Treasury could and did assist the Reserve System in limiting bank reserves during the first few months of 1946 by repaying maturing debt. Insofar as such debt was held outside the banks, this action tightened credit, for reserves had to be held against customers' deposits, but did not need to be held against the Treasury's war loan deposits. The repayment of bank-held debt had no effect upon bank reserves, but the fact that the Victory Loan had far exceeded the current federal cash deficit implied a restraining influence, even apart from any effect on the banks' reserve position. During 1946 the revival of demand for bank loans consequent on industrial reconversion also led to some tightening of the reserve position of the banks. Yet too much should not be made of this, for reserves still could be replenished at negligible cost.

The first small hesitant step toward restraint was taken April 24, 1946, when the ½% preferential discount rate on loans secured by bills and certificates was abolished, leaving 1% as the cost of credit at the Reserve. The System had threatened to take this step as early as July 1945, but the Treasury had objected. Now, ten months later, in the middle of the boom in governments, the patience of the Reserve was exhausted, and it decided at last to defy the Treasury. Since member banks could turn in ⅜% bills to the Treasury at any time, little use was in fact being made of collateral loans: only banks that had no bills (small western banks) would need to borrow at the discount rate. Substantially, therefore, Reserve money was as cheap as ever. Yet the move had psychological importance, for it created some mild uncertainty as to the durability of the "pattern" and so may have helped to break the boom in bonds.

Meanwhile, with the end of rationing and price control, commodity prices started upward sharply in July 1946. The money market became slightly less easy as the year advanced, for higher commodity prices and rapidly expanding peacetime production increased the pressure on the banks for loans. Simultaneously the authorities' ability to control the situation diminished. By the beginning of 1947 the Treasury "hoard" of war-loan balances, accumulated during the Victory bond drive, was about exhausted, so that further debt repayment had to await a budget surplus. At the same time a flood of new gold from abroad began to expand member-bank reserve balances. Once again it looked as if money would remain cheap indefinitely, and the consequence was a fresh boom in long-term governments. Some slight relief was obtained by the sale of bonds from trust accounts, but the situation had clearly become so desperate that the wartime "pattern" would have to go. A new Undersecretary, Lee Wiggins, seems to have persuaded the Treasury that it dare not risk responsibility for further inflation on the present scale: wholesale prices had risen 25% within twelve months. Early in July 1947, with the concurrence of the Treasury, the Reserve abolished the ⅜% buying rate for Treasury bills, but it continued to purchase 9- to 12-month certificates, and announced that the yield on the longest-term governments would still be kept down to 2½% (to this point no bond purchases had of course been needed). Treasury bills were now free to find their own level, and they promptly did so at around ¾%, or only slightly below the (still pegged) rate on certificates (Fig. 3).

Shortly thereafter, in the Fall of 1947, the Reserve gradually raised its buying rate for certificates to around 1%. To this the Treasury apparently made no objection, and indeed relations between the two agencies seem to have been more amicable at this period than previously or subsequently. Perhaps the Treasury was relieved to find, despite the rapid expansion of bank lending and rise in commodity prices, that the Reserve was satisfied with this limited freedom at the short end of the market, and that it showed continued willingness to monetize one-year certificates and to peg 2½'s at par (should this prove necessary). The latter measure was not necessary—as yet—for, with the one-year rate still anchored, long-term bonds remained buoyant.

Mr. Eccles' "Special-Reserves" Plan[8]

The System may well have savored the small amount of elbow room it had recaptured with so much difficulty by the Summer of

[8] Joint Committee on the Economic Report, *Anti-Inflation Program*, Hearings, 80th Cong. 1st Sess., 1948, especially pp. 143–44, 623–33, 636–39.

1947 after five years in a straitjacket. The prospects for still greater liberty—and especially for a further rise in short- and medium-term rates—seemed dim in the face of Treasury opposition. Yet inflationary pressures continued to mount. A complete break with the Treasury, with of course the risk of total defeat through White House or Congressional action in the Treasury's favor, does not seem to have been seriously contemplated at this stage. In any case the idea of such a break was inhibited by doubts among Reserve officials as to whether higher interest rates could in fact be used to check inflation without at the same time producing a panic. The emphasis in Reserve thinking was upon the need to regain control over member-bank reserves, and higher interest rates were not thought of—at any rate at this period—as the indispensable means to this objective, or even as the inevitable result of its attainment. Certainly the System desired higher interest rates—although still only at the short end of the market—but its desire was motivated rather by a wish to end pattern-playing and to revive the 3-month Treasury bill as a market instrument.

It was perhaps natural, therefore, that much thought should be given to more direct methods of controlling bank reserves. Proposals for additional reserve requirements of one kind or another for commercial banks had already been adumbrated in the Board's *Annual Reports* to Congress for 1945 and 1946. In the Fall of 1947 President Truman's decision to send a special message to Congress recommending anti-inflation measures furnished an ideal—perhaps a fatal—opportunity for Chairman Eccles to ask for what he wanted. The bulk of Mr. Truman's requests were for the reimposition of price, wage, and commodity controls that had been dropped the previous year. The program as a whole was so obviously unpalatable to the Republican-controlled 80th Congress, and had such small prospect of enactment, that it was commonly regarded as primarily a piece of electioneering on the part of the White House. Yet the proposed new powers to control bank reserves had undoubtedly received long and earnest consideration by the Board, and were put forward by Eccles—if not by President Truman—with every hope that they would be enacted.

The plan left existing reserve requirements of member banks unchanged, but empowered the Federal Open Market Committee to require the holding of large new secondary reserves by all commercial banks, member and nonmember. These reserves, of up to

25% against demand and 10% against time deposits, were to consist of government securities with original maturities of not more than two years or other cash assets—balances with Reserve Banks or correspondents, items in course of collection, or vault cash. These other cash assets were, however, only to be eligible to the extent that they exceeded 20% of demand and 6% of time deposits—a provision necessary to prevent nonmember from obtaining an advantage over member banks. The new requirements were to be introduced gradually, and power to enforce them was to run initially for three years. Clearly the proposal would freeze substantial amounts of short-term governments in the commercial banks, and would force the banks to absorb additional amounts as and when their deposit liabilities expanded. But the claim that it would insulate the market for government securities from the market for private credit goes much too far.

It was calculated that, with an initial special-reserve requirement of 10% against demand and 4% against time deposits, all banks would have adequate reserves in the existing situation. On the other hand, with the full requirement of 25% and 10%, substantial deficiencies would occur, particularly among the larger banks. These deficiencies would have to be met in the short run largely by resort to the Reserve Banks, and especially by sale of Treasury bonds to, and purchases of certificates and notes from, the System. In a somewhat longer run the volume of customers' deposits, and ultimately of the banks' commercial loans, could be restrained by the amount of short-term governments that the Treasury chose to make available. Evidently the multiple expansion made possible under existing arrangements by a given increase in primary reserves would have largely disappeared.

What would the plan have achieved? By creating a highly inelastic demand for short-term governments, it would have enabled the Treasury, by restricting their supply, to drive their yields down to very low levels without expanding bank lending or bank deposits. (At very low yields there might of course be a tendency to substitute "other cash assets.") In this sense bank holdings—now practically the only holdings—of short-term governments would indeed have been sterilized or frozen, at a saving in interest cost to the Treasury and without furthering inflation.

So much the plan clearly could have achieved. But what of the medium- and long-term market? Nothing would have happened to prevent the banks—or nonbank holders, for that matter, such as insurance companies—from selling Treasury notes or bonds in order to lend more to business, buy corporate obligations, or acquire mortgages. Victory bonds still were to be kept at par (or above) with the expansion of bank cash as a possible consequence. Such cash could be used partly for primary, partly for secondary reserves, although (as noted) the element of multiple expansion would have been greatly reduced. However the advantage of this reduction is largely illusory, for the ability of the banks to buy governments when they received additional cash would have been correspondingly reduced. The Reserve Banks would therefore find that they had to buy more bonds to keep them at par in given circumstances, and so give the banks more cash, than had the plan not been in effect. This would roughly offset the advantage of the reduced element of multiple expansion.

The principal effect of the plan would therefore be to cut somewhat the interest charge on the public debt at the expense of the earnings of commercial banks. It would resemble a tax on the gross income of the latter. Or rather, this would be the principal effect so long as the System remained able to keep short-term governments scarce by manipulating the requirements for special reserves in the light of the outstanding volume of such short-term governments, and of "other assets." However, should the special requirements reach their legal maxima, and should the Treasury choose to "unfund," e.g., by converting maturing bonds into one-year certificates, the game would be up. Unless the System sold longs and bought shorts to counter the Treasury, short-term obligations would again become plentiful and their yields rise. The banks would once again have ample reserves, both primary and secondary. And the cost of carrying the debt would again be what it was before.

In sum, the plan might have had advantages for the Treasury, so long as it kept bills and certificates scarce. But so long as bond support was continued, its effect in restraining bank credit would seem to have been extremely slight. And if bond support had been ended, ample opportunity to restrain credit by more usual methods would have become available. But Eccles made it plain that he had no thought of ending bond support.[9]

The plan was a proposal by the Board of Governors, although,

[9] *Ibid.*, p. 141.

since it was recommended to Congress in the President's message, it might be assumed to have Administration support. Eccles knew from the start that, as so often was the case, he must reckon with the opposition of commercial bankers. More serious for prospects in Congress, the plan lacked the support of the Reserve Banks. But the most unexpected and quite fatal blow to the plan was dealt by Secretary Snyder, who indicated he did not particularly care whether it was enacted or not. Paradoxically, Chairman Eccles was advocating a plan whose chief, or perhaps whose only benefit would accrue to the Treasury, a plan which for its part the Treasury spurned.

The instinct of commercial bankers naturally was to resist a novel and apparently drastic form of control. Speaking through a unanimous Federal Advisory Council, they opposed the plan, but did not base their objections on opposition to control as such. Instead they played down the growth of bank loans and bank deposits as an inflationary factor, and pointed to the activities of FHA and RFC in expanding housing credit, to agricultural subsidies, to foreign aid, and to the high level of federal spending in general. They asked for a revival of discount-rate and open-market policy, but did not face the question whether bond support should be ended.

For the Reserve Banks, President Sproul of the New York Bank expressed the view that the plan would not only cause "grave market disturbances" while going into effect, but would fail to achieve its objective. He played down the role of credit expansion in pushing up prices, and indeed adopted a rather helpless attitude toward the solution of the problem:

> I believe both logic and facts will support the view that the current expansion of bank credit is more a result than a cause of advancing prices. . . . We have been able to arrange with the Treasury for withdrawals of funds from the market, and the use of the proceeds to retire government securities held by the Federal Reserve Banks. . . . We have created enough uncertainty in the market to obliterate bank appetite for long-term government securities, and to restrain their lending at long term. We have made some progress in narrowing the spread between short and long-term rates of interest which, combined with the uncertainty thus created, has lessened the urge on the part of the banks to reach out for longer-term government securities or to make undesirable loans and investments, in order to maintain earnings. . . . We

are doing all that I think can or should be done in the field of monetary and credit action, which I think is a minor part of the problem.[10]

Sproul's position at this time was that any credit restriction severe enough to check inflation must cause the banks to unload securities, that this would risk a "violent upset in the government securities market" and higher interest rates, and that higher interest rates would lead to a contraction of production and income. "I do not think that can be the right policy now," he added. We may note that he makes no distinction between bringing the expansion to an end and starting a contraction: one is left to assume that, in the circumstances of 1947–1948, he believed the two policies to be equivalent. At any rate Sproul thought of himself as engaged in a holding action, extracting concessions from the Treasury piece by piece. I would say that his testimony implies too modest a view as to what can be achieved through monetary controls, which scarcely resemble a "meat-axe." Indeed, three years later, in the midst of the credit expansion resulting from the Korean War, Sproul had modified his views. But that is a different issue. Meanwhile, his opposition to the special-reserves plan revealed an unfortunate lack of unanimity within the System which could not but confuse Congress.[11]

The final nail was driven into the coffin by Secretary Snyder, who told the Joint Economic Committee that he had discussed the proposal with Eccles on a number of occasions, but that—like Sproul—he did not believe that it would accomplish its objective. Eccles later denied that he had ever discussed the details of the program with Snyder, and pleaded ignorance of the Secretary's position. On the record Snyder's stand is indeed far less clear than Sproul's but seems to have been analogous: any restriction of credit sufficient to check the inflation then in progress must jeopardize "the continued confidence of the public in government obligations," for which read "lead to a rise in interest rates." In this Snyder was probably correct. Unlike Sproul, he did not explore the further consequences of a rise in interest rates, or claim that it must lead to panic conditions in the money market or a recession in business:

[10] Senate Committee on Banking and Currency, *To Provide for the Regulation of Consumer Credit for a Temporary Period*, Hearings on S.J.R. 157, 80th Cong. 1st Sess., 1947, pp. 228, 230, 241.
[11] *Ibid.*, pp. 235, 240.

it was sufficient for Snyder that he foresaw a rise in the cost of carrying the debt. Inflation could be fought only by a budget surplus and debt retirement. Snyder paid no attention to the probability that, even if ineffective for controlling credit, the plan might enable him to levy a tax on the commercial banks by restricting the supply of short-term securities. Probably he felt that, whatever Eccles said, the desire on Constitution Avenue was to tighten credit, and the eventual outcome would be a more expensive public debt.[12]

Secretary Snyder's testimony ended any prospect that the plan could be enacted. One has every sympathy with Senator Tobey, Chairman of the Senate Banking Committee during the 80th Congress. After Sproul had given a fair and sympathetic account of the special-reserves proposal, the following passage occurs:

> MR. SPROUL: . . . If I were convinced that the remedy suggested would accomplish what is claimed for it, I would support it. I am not convinced.
>
> SENATOR TOBEY: You are not convinced? Here is a committee of Senators who are not experts in the banking field, but realize what a delicate subject this matter of credit control is and want to be very wise before we make any move at all. Yet here we sit. We have Mr. Eccles with all his personal charm and sincerity, make the statement before us, which you have summed up very well, and we find that it is backed by the unanimous vote of the Board; we find the Secretary of the Treasury in strong disagreement on the plan suggested by Mr. Eccles; and then we see the Federal Advisory Council, whose members are a unit on the other side of the picture. We sit here trying to uncover and separate the wheat from the chaff, and to act wisely. You can see the dilemma we are in.
>
> MR. SPROUL: Yes, sir.
>
> SENATOR TOBEY: It is an amazing situation, is it not?
>
> MR. SPROUL: Yes, it is.[13]

Why then was the plan put forward? The opposition of the commercial bankers was known in advance. One must assume that the criticisms launched by Sproul and Snyder came as a surprise, unless, indeed, the whole proposal was merely intended by the Board of Governors as an academic protest or a means of salving its collective conscience. The complex nature of the plan must have concealed its probable ineffectiveness in controlling credit without a rise in interest rates. Its original appeal was rather clearly de-

---

[12] *Anti-Inflation Program*, pp. 245–46; *Consumer Credit*, p. 189.
[13] *Ibid.*, p. 232.

rived from the Board's preoccupation with the control of bank reserves to the exclusion of interest rates—with the quantity of money as distinct from its price. For the plan, when reduced to essentials, represents the mistaken belief that quantity can be appreciably restricted without a rise in price. The preoccupation with bank reserves is illustrated by Eccles' statement that he considered the plan a substitute for an outright increase in primary reserve requirements.[14] But such an increase also would be ineffective unless money became more expensive.

As bond support continued, as and when necessary to keep the Victory 2½'s at par, for three more years, the illusory nature of the special-reserves and similar plans for controlling credit became more and more generally recognized. Thinking moved in some quarters toward proposals even less likely of adoption involving drastic surgery upon the public debt. *Marketability* came to be regarded as the cardinal sin, and plans emerged for converting all except very short-term debt into nonmarketable obligations redeemable before maturity only at stiff discounts. Alternatively, if insurance companies and other institutions insisted on bonds being marketable—who knows?—it might be necessary to subject their investments to public control. Thus continued support of government bonds led to ever more drastic proposals for neutralizing its inflationary effects.[15]

The End of the Postwar Inflation and the Recession of 1949

As the year 1947 drew to a close, an emerging budget surplus for the first time made debt retirement possible by means other than the mere drawing down of Treasury balances. The surplus was used chiefly to repay Treasury bills. Since outstanding bills were held almost entirely by the Reserve Banks (for reasons explained above), this welcome development would have reduced member-bank reserves sharply but for a continued increase in the monetary gold stock (Fig. 3).

In the last months of 1947 a marked change occurred in the financial outlook. The debt repayment made the market realize that gold imports, even though they continued, could no longer

[14] *Anti-Inflation Program*, p. 602.
[15] See, e.g., Marriner S. Eccles, "The Defense of the Dollar," *Fortune* (November 1950), 78–81, 198.

be counted on to expand bank reserves. More important, the end of the wartime rate pattern for the first time created genuine uncertainty as to future interest rates. The three-month rate had been unpegged; and the authorities continued to raise the one-year rate. Eleven-month certificates were sold at 1% in November and 13-month notes at 1⅛% in December. Then, too, the revival of a demand for mortgage and other long-term credit prompted sales of long-term governments by insurance companies and others. Yields on long-term Treasury issues rose from a monthly average of 2.24% in September to 2.39% in December. Buoyancy in the bond market was no longer the problem: the boot was on the other foot.

Whatever rates might be prescribed or permitted at the short end of the market, the announced policy still was to maintain existing issues—of whatever maturity—at par. Yet, if the "pattern" could so readily be consigned to the ashcan, was par after all as sacrosanct as the authorities insisted? Large amounts of medium- and long-term governments were held as liquid assets by commercial banks and others to whom doubts on this score were anathema. The sudden and surprising discovery that you are not in fact nearly as liquid as you thought you were is the progenitor of panic. To some holders' fears of illiquidity were joined the speculative calculations of others, for the days of handsome premiums were clearly over. The bandwagon began to roll: "par" was now to be put to the test.

To this point substantially the whole of the System's portfolio had consisted of securities payable in one year or less, for the System had bought almost no bonds since Pearl Harbor (Fig. 2). During November 1947, weakness in the long-term market caused the System to begin buying bonds, and the 2½'s were stabilized at approximately 101⅞ (the September average had been around 104). By December the Reserve found itself acquiring bonds at a rapid rate, although it was able to unload bills, which the commercial banks now acquired. To insert a tentative peg almost two points above par was perhaps a mistake, for it was well understood in the market that par itself had been selected as the last ditch for a final stand. The effect was (1) to encourage holders to sell so long as a premium, no matter how small, was still obtainable; and (2) to lead some persons to the conclusion that, after all, the System had protested too much, and perhaps in the last resort might even abandon par. Either because small premiums over par could still be realized (though by now many sellers must have taken a loss), or because of a growing distrust in par itself, over $1 billion of medium- and long-term Treasury obligations were sold to the System during the final week of 1947 at prices (for the Victory 2½'s) between 100 and 100½.

Early in 1948 both the Reserve and the Treasury took some further small steps to limit monetary ease, insofar as such steps were available to them within the orbit of the new bond-support program. Twelve-month certificates were sold on January 1 for 1⅛% and the New York discount rate was raised to 1¼%—the first change since 1937, and the first upward movement since 1933. On January 23 the Board announced that reserve requirements in New York and Chicago would go from 20% to 22% on March 1; in June they were raised again to 24% (legal maximum 26%). Meanwhile the Treasury continued to repay bills (held mostly by the Reserve), and allowed its deposits with the Reserve Banks to increase, thus countering the expansion of member-bank reserves which would otherwise have resulted from continued gold imports and from the bond-support program. The Treasury also agreed to build up its "tax and loan accounts" (successors to the "war loan accounts") in commercial banks, and henceforth to require reserves against these deposits.

These very mild measures of restraint at the short end of the market were accompanied by continued acquisition of bonds by the Reserve. During the first few months of 1948, total Reserve credit declined, for the reasons just indicated; but the inflationary implications of the bond-support program induced an air of pessimism at the Board. Sales of bonds by banks were not the worst of it, for the banks bought shorts instead, which the Reserve supplied, so that member-bank reserves remained unchanged. More serious, the increasing spread between Treasury and corporate yields must tempt insurance companies and others to switch; and when the System bought the Treasuries the institutions sold (which it would have to do to maintain the peg), member-bank reserves would be expanded correspondingly. It was evident that the inflationary consequences of bond buying could be avoided only if the System was able to sell shorts at the same time that it bought longs. But for the System to sell shorts—perhaps even for it not to have to buy them—a further rise in short-term rates seemed indispensable. Against this proposal the Treasury was adamant. The gloom on Constitution Avenue was enhanced by Congressional rejection of the special-reserves plan and the prospective disappearance of the budget surplus.

To be sure, the inflation that had already occurred during the three years since the end of the war was substantial, however you measured it. Yet acute pessimism concerning the immediate future was not in fact warranted. In a few months more the postwar inflation would have run its course; a mild recession was to take its place. Existing rates of interest were soon to approximate those needed for business stabilization. But before this happened, some further mild measures of restraint were undertaken. In August 1948 the Treasury was at last persuaded to allow the one-year rate to go to $1\frac{1}{4}\%$ and the New York discount rate was raised to $1\frac{1}{2}\%$. Perhaps in repentance for its total rejection of Eccles' special-reserves plan, Congress now granted the Board, under McCabe, who had succeeded Eccles as chairman, a small increase in maximum legal reserve requirements, and restored controls over consumer credit, both provisions to expire after twelve months.

The end of the postwar inflation was heralded, not only by declining wholesale prices (they reached a peak in August 1948), but by a rise in long-term governments above par. Support was no longer needed: indeed the System began to sell bonds as yields declined. The boom in the bond market seems to have been precipitated by the unexpected re-election of Mr. Truman: in those days the Democrats were far more clearly identified with soft money than were—or are—the Republicans. Had not a presumably nonpartisan Reserve Board been battling a succession of Democratic Secretaries of the Treasury for higher interest rates for more than three years with very little success? The incipient boom in governments was soon fortified by bank and insurance purchases, resulting from lessened demand—in the one case for commercial accommodation, and in the other for mortgages and industrial capital.

By February 1949—six months after the turn in wholesale prices —the Board gave thought to easing credit. Since general controls never had been tightened appreciably, the obvious course was to relax selective controls on credit. Accordingly, in March the consumer-credit regulations were eased and margin requirements for stock trading were reduced. In April consumer credit was relaxed again and member-bank reserve requirements were also lowered. On July 1 consumer-credit control lapsed by law. By midyear prices had flattened out. Production, which declined about 15% between November 1948 and July 1949, then began to rise again (Fig. 3).

The mildness and brief duration of the recession of 1949 must be attributed in large part to the fortuitous and politically-motivated tax cut which became effective July 1, 1948: immediately thereafter the federal cash surplus declined rapidly from the combined influence of built-in stabilizers and of the tax cut. The Administration seems nonetheless to have regretted the tax cut and, as the budget headed toward deficit, fresh tax proposals were sent to and considered by Congress, but not acted upon. Secretary Snyder was particularly uneasy about the lack of fiscal responsibility that a peacetime deficit might imply, even though recession-induced.[16]

Until the Fall of 1949 the Reserve System was concerned to keep money easy. On June 30 the Federal Open Market Committee issued the following statement:

> The Federal Open Market Committee, after consultation with the Treasury, announced today that with a view to increasing the supply of funds available in the market to meet the needs of commerce, business, and agriculture it will be the policy of the Committee to direct purchases, sales, and exchanges of government securities by the Federal Reserve Banks with primary regard to the general credit situation. The policy of maintaining orderly conditions in the government security market, and the confidence of investors in government bonds, will be continued. Under present conditions the maintenance of a relatively fixed pattern of rates has the undesirable effect of absorbing reserves from the market at a time when the availability of credit should be increased.[17]

This manifesto amounted to a declaration of independence by the System *vis-à-vis* the Treasury—but a declaration of a decidedly left-handed character. In effect it said that, if necessary "to meet the needs of commerce, business and agriculture," it would push rates *down*, below the pegged level. To flexibility in this direction the Treasury was unlikely to object. Obviously the Open Market Committee hoped that, if the System could establish its independ-

[16] Wilfred Lewis, Jr., *Federal Fiscal Policy in the Postwar Recessions* (Washington, D.C.: Brookings Institution, 1962), Ch. IV.
[17] *Annual Report of the Board of Governors for 1949*, p. 8.

ence in a period of recession, it might be able to retain this independence should inflationary pressures again develop. But this would mean flexibility in an upward direction, to which the attitude of the Treasury might be far less friendly. The question remained whether, in that case, the System would feel able to *raise* rates, above the pegged level—that is to say, to allow Treasury obligations, at least of some maturities, to fall below par.

Later in the year (December 3, 1949) Chairman McCabe was closely questioned by Senator Douglas about the System's intentions and its relations with the Treasury:

MR. McCABE: . . . [The] announcement . . . was submitted to the Treasury.

SENATOR DOUGLAS: And it was acceptable to them?

MR. McCABE: It was acceptable to them.

. . . .

SENATOR DOUGLAS: Did not [the] announcement . . . mean that at the time it was issued—namely, one of recession or inventory adjustment—that securities would not be sold; and did it not, therefore, tend to keep down or to depress interest rates, and, therefore, of course, would it not be acceptable to the Treasury? But does it follow that, because the Treasury agreed at this time that the Treasury will go along with primary regard to the general business and credit situation in other periods?

If we were in a period of inflation and were to carry out this policy, it might mean—it would mean to the degree that the Federal Reserve Board exercised its powers—the sale of securities, a rise in interest rate, and a fall in the prices of government securities.

In other words, the instance of cooperation which you chose was one which was very happy from the Treasury point of view, when there was no conflict between the two purposes in a period of depression. But would this cooperation necessarily continue in a period of [renewed] inflation?

MR. McCABE: The acid test of relationships and even of partnerships, Senator, comes when you have to meet a critical situation in the future. I am going on the assumption that this was an agreement made by men of understanding and goodwill and that it means what it says . . . To the Federal Reserve, it means flexibility.

SENATOR DOUGLAS: That in periods of inflation the interest rate will be increased and, if necessary, the price of government securities depressed?

MR. McCABE: That the open-market operations will be flexible—

SENATOR DOUGLAS: Flexible both ways?

MR. McCABE: And that we will conform to the economic situation with which we are confronted.

SENATOR DOUGLAS: You will have flexibility both ways?

MR. McCABE: Both ways.

SENATOR DOUGLAS: Do you think the Treasury so understands it?

MR. McCABE: That is my understanding. . . .[18]

Within less than a year the Treasury's attitude would be put to the test.

The Korean Inflation and the Accord of 1951[19]

Industrial production reached a low point in July 1949, but wholesale prices continued to decline slowly until the end of the year. By early 1950 recovery was in full swing. Yet renewed inflationary pressures at first developed slowly. By mid-1950 System holdings of governments were substantially less, and the yields on government maturities of all maturities virtually the same, as a year earlier. But Korea changed all this. It was soon obvious that higher rates would be needed if a rapid expansion of credit were to be avoided.

On August 18, 1950, nearly two months after fighting began in Korea, the System made the following announcement:

> Within the past six weeks loans and holdings of corporate and municipal securities have expanded by 1.5 billion dollars at banks in leading cities alone. Such an expansion under present conditions is clearly excessive. In view of this development and to support the Government's decision to rely in major degree for the immediate future upon fiscal and credit measures to curb inflation, the Board of Governors of the Federal Reserve System and the Federal Open Market Committee are prepared to use all the means at their command to restrain further expansion of bank credit consistent with the policy of maintaining orderly conditions in the government securities market. . . .[20]

"Flexibility both ways" was to be put to the test. As a sign that the System meant business, discount rates were raised at all Reserve Banks from 1½% to 1¾%.

[18] Joint Committee on the Economic Report, *Monetary, Credit and Fiscal Policies,* Hearings, 81st Cong. 1st Sess., 1950, pp. 493–94.

[19] See Joint Committee on the Economic Report, *Monetary Policy and the Management of the Public Debt,* Hearings, 82nd Cong. 2nd Sess., 1952, pp. 32–39, 519–23, 942–66; Replies to Questions, Part I, pp. 65–76, 346, 351, 361–63. Marriner S. Eccles, *Beckoning Frontiers* (New York: Knopf, 1951), pp. 479–99. Details have been filled in from the Eccles papers.

[20] *Annual Report of the Board of Governors for 1950,* p. 2.

The Treasury was not consulted in advance about these moves, and Secretary Snyder later complained that the announcement of August 18 constituted an ultimatum. To this Chairman McCabe and President Sproul replied that they had been trying unsuccessfully for more than a year to induce the Secretary to take the monetary problem seriously. The Treasury replied almost immediately by announcing the terms of its $13 billion September–October refunding as a 13-month note at 1¼%—terms that a month before had been, but no longer were, in line with the market. The System dutifully bought most of the issue.

No doubt with confidence born of victory the Treasury next announced a 5-year 1¾% note to replace bonds and certificates maturing during the last two weeks of the year. The Reserve loyally supported the new issue until the books were closed, but allowed a moderate fall to occur in outstanding issues. Although no single obligation fell below par, the Treasury complained.

On January 17, 1951, apparently at Secretary Snyder's request, President Truman met with the Secretary and Chairman McCabe. At this meeting, according to Snyder, McCabe "assured the President that he need not be concerned about the 2½% long-term rate on government securities." There probably was a misunderstanding. Chairman McCabe, who had no authority to commit the Federal Open Market Committee, may have meant to indicate that there was no present intention of allowing outstanding long-term issues to decline below par, but it seems unlikely that he gave any assurance about future financing. On the following day, January 18, perhaps trying to bluff the Board and certainly without having given McCabe any inkling of what he was about to do, Secretary Snyder unwisely said in the course of an address in New York:

> In the firm belief, after long consideration, that the 2½% long-term rate is fair and equitable to the investor, and that market stability is essential, the Treasury Department has concluded, after joint conferences with President Truman and Chairman McCabe of the Federal Reserve Board, that the refunding of new money issues will be held within the pattern of that rate.

Several members of the Federal Open Market Committee immediately indicated they would not go along with this plan.

On January 31 President Truman, obviously at Secretary Snyder's suggestion, invited the entire Committee to confer with him.

During a friendly discussion no commitment was asked for or given. Secretary Snyder was not present, but on the following day, in order to sew the thing up, he had a "Treasury spokesman" declare that as a result of the meeting "the market for government securities will be established at present levels" and that "these levels will be maintained during the present emergency." And to clinch the matter, the White House released a letter from President Truman to Chairman McCabe which said: "As I understand it, I have your assurance that the market on government securities will be stabilized and maintained at present levels. . . ." At this point Governor Eccles released a memorandum to the press describing the meeting of the Open Market Committee with the President, which showed that no such assurance had been asked for or given. It is impossible to resist the conclusion that Secretary Snyder was attempting to use the authority of the President to overawe the Committee, but that he failed adequately to brief the President on the assurance desired. Still less did the Secretary bring Mr. Truman to an understanding of the issues involved.

In Chapter 11 I take the position that ultimate authority for monetary as for any other policy must rest with the President. But in this instance the issues never were brought to the President's attention; no one made clear to him what the Treasury was asking the Reserve to do, or the nature of the Reserve's objections to doing it. If Secretary Snyder did not choose to brief the President adequately, some blame must also attach to Chairman McCabe for not bringing the issue into the open, either in a private conference with Mr. Truman or at the White House meeting. It would seem, too, that the Council of Economic Advisers might have been helpful in avoiding the obvious embarrassment to which the President was subjected, but so far as one can discover the Council played no role whatever.[21]

---

[21] President Truman's surprise and his lack of understanding of the issues both are illustrated by the following quotation: "I invited the members of the Federal Reserve Board [sic!] to visit with me. . . . When they left I firmly believed that I had their agreement to co-operate in our financing program. I was taken by surprise when subsequently they failed to support the program. Eventually an agreement was reached, but not until the differences of opinion between the Treasury and the Board had caused considerable worry to the President and much added expense to the taxpayers. . . . My approach to all these financial questions always was that it was my duty to keep the financial capital of the United States in Washington. This is where it belongs—but to keep it there is not always an easy task" (Harry S Truman, *Memoirs* [Garden City, N.Y.: Doubleday, 1956], II, 44–45).

By now it had become obvious that the Secretary would have to settle for something less than indefinite "stabilization at present levels." On February 6 to 8 the Federal Open Market Committee met, reviewed the situation at length, and authorized its executive committee to drop governments to par (Victory Loan was currently held at $100^{22}/_{32}$). Meanwhile on February 7 Chairman McCabe sent Secretary Snyder an olive branch:

> We should like to discuss with you . . . a program along the following lines:
>
> (1) The Federal Reserve, for the present, would purchase the longest-dated restricted Treasury bonds now outstanding in amounts necessary to prevent them from falling below par.
>
> (2) If substantial Federal Reserve support of the longest-term restricted bond is required, you would be prepared to announce that at an appropriate time the Treasury would offer a longer-term bond with a coupon sufficiently attractive so that the bond would be accepted and held by investors. . . .
>
> (3) For the purpose of restricting the creation of bank reserves through sales of short-term securities to the Federal Reserve, particularly by banks, the [Federal Open Market] Committee would keep its purchases of such securities to the minimum amounts needed to maintain an orderly market. . . .

As a result of this invitation, there followed staff-level conferences between the two agencies (February 20 to 24). Among the representatives of the Treasury was William McC. Martin, Jr. (later Chairman of the Reserve Board), and for the Reserve, Winfield W. Riefler. Now for the first time the Reserve was able to insist that short-term governments should find their own level in the market in relation to the discount rate (then $1\frac{3}{4}\%$). A promise not to raise the discount rate before the end of 1951 was eventually made. The Treasury persuaded the Reserve that support should still be given to the long-term $2\frac{1}{2}$'s, but the Reserve demanded that a limit be placed on the amount of resources it would be expected to commit for this purpose. It was apparently during these conferences that Riefler suggested the Victory $2\frac{1}{2}$'s be made convertible into a nonmarketable $2\frac{3}{4}\%$ bond: this gimmick had the signal virtue, from the Reserve's standpoint, of doing away with the fetish of "$2\frac{1}{2}\%$," and simultaneously furnishing the Treasury—now in full retreat—with the face-saving opportunity to claim that Secretary Snyder's reference to the 2½% rate in his speech of January 18 still held good, since he was talking only of *marketable* issues.

The Treasury staff men reported back to the Secretary, but Snyder was not yet ready to give up. On February 26 President Truman announced the appointment of Secretary Snyder, Chairman McCabe, the Director of Defense Mobilization (Charles E. Wilson), and the Chairman of the Council of Economic Advisers (Leon Keyserling) as a committee "to study ways and means to provide the necessary restraint on private credit expansion and at the same time to make it possible to maintain stability in the market for government securities." Wilson was to be in the chair. This led to proposals for a mandatory ceiling on credit volume. There were lengthy discussions at the staff level as to whether an executive order would suffice or whether fresh legislation would be necessary; the plan was to apply to insurance companies and other nonbanking institutions as well as to commercial banks. But long before a report could be drafted, this final attempt to salvage the Treasury's position had been overtaken by events.

During February extensive newspaper discussion indicated considerable public sentiment for the Reserve. In addition, Congressional criticism of the Treasury's inflexibility was growing. On the afternoon of February 28, Secretary Snyder decided to capitulate, and authorized Martin to convey to the Reserve his agreement to the terms worked out between the staffs of the two agencies. No doubt Martin had told the Secretary this was the best that could be obtained. The Federal Open Market Committee met March 1 and 2. The Accord was announced March 3:

> The Treasury and the Federal Reserve System have reached full accord with respect to debt-management and monetary policies to be pursued in furthering their common purpose to assure the successful financing of the Government's requirements and, at the same time, to minimize monetization of the public debt.

The terms of the Accord, if they were reduced to writing, have never been made public. In exchange for the 2½'s of 1967–1972 the Treasury offered a new 29-year nonmarketable 2¾% bond redeemable before maturity only by conversion into a 5-year Treasury note. Meanwhile the Reserve agreed to continue to support long-term bonds, but was not to be required to put more than $400 million into the market. The Treasury itself was able to furnish an additional $500 million from Postal Savings, and may have thought that these considerable resources would prove sufficient to keep the 2½'s at par: but it was to be disappointed.

Immediately following the Accord all governments fell sharply except the long-term 2½'s. The latter were pegged at 100²²⁄₃₂ till March 8, and at par from then till March 13, on which day they were allowed to fall to 99, funds for their support being exhausted. On this Tuesday they were worth less than par for the first time since original issue in 1945.

> It is understood that support purchases during the balance of the week—that is, Wednesday through Friday—have amounted to virtually nothing. Instead, the market has been stabilized without much official support at just above 99. Developments seem to have discredited those prophets of doom who believed that chaotic conditions would result from any break through par on 2½'s, and by the same token have given encouragement and support to those that believed a flexible anti-inflationary open-market policy still possible and desirable despite the size of the public debt.[22]

The long-heralded panic had failed to materialize, although by the end of the year long-term marketable governments were selling on a 2¾% basis. But by that time Chairman McCabe had resigned and had been replaced by Mr. Martin. There were even those who felt that McCabe's resignation was forced by the Treasury as the price of the Accord.[23]

The Federal Reserve and the Treasury, 1945–1951

During the Second World War, as during the First, the Federal Reserve System did not—probably could not—offer effective resistance to the inflation of credit through Treasury borrowing. After World War I monetary policy was dominated until January 1920 by the Treasury's continuing desire to borrow cheaply: within fourteen months of the end of fighting the Reserve had regained its freedom of action. After World War II, by contrast, emancipation from the Treasury did not come until March 1951, more than five years after hostilities had ceased. To be sure I have argued that in 1920 the System used its new-found freedom of action much too drastically in restraining credit. But from 1945 to 1951 the manufacture

---

[22] *Goldsmith Washington Service*, No. 365, March 17, 1951.

[23] Joint Committee on the Economic Report, *January 1956 Economic Report of the President*, Hearings, 84th Cong. 2nd Sess., 1956, p. 303.

of purchasing power was inhibited mainly by the willingness of the Treasury to use surpluses for debt retirement. During this period monetary policy was in the hands of the Treasury and was for the most part quite inflationary.

By what steps was the dominance of the Treasury undermined? Should the Reserve System have fought earlier and harder to recover its freedom? How, if at all, can the Treasury's attitude be defended?

At the Reserve the task of recapturing the initiative in matters of monetary policy rested mainly on Marriner Eccles and Allan Sproul. Sproul was President of the New York Reserve Bank during the entire period: Eccles was Chairman of the System's Board of Governors until February 1948, and continued on the Board as its most articulate member until after the Accord of March 1951. In his autobiography Eccles has described his difficulties with successive Secretaries of the Treasury.[24]

Secretary Morgenthau had resigned at the end of the war, and was succeeded in July 1945 by Secretary Vinson and in 1947 by Secretary Snyder. In the postwar period, says Eccles in retrospect, "it was the continued domination of Treasury policy by a Morgenthau staff, with its chronic bias for cheap money in all seasons, that lay at the source of [our] difficulties."

The positions taken by the Reserve and the Treasury respectively, and the reasons used to support them, shifted somewhat with the development of events. These shifts are worth tracing.

In November 1945, for the Treasury, Undersecretary Bell and Secretary Vinson defended the continuation of cheap money, not only on grounds of the cost of the public debt, but as a means of preventing the much-awaited reconversion slump.[25] Despite pessimistic predictions by business analysts, the stock market was booming at this period, and the Reserve raised margin requirements to 100%, putting all stock trading on a cash basis. This was almost the only measure of credit restraint within the power of the System to which the Treasury could not well object. It was accompanied by a statement by Eccles on January 17, 1946, in which he urged primary dependence on fiscal measures for fighting inflation, but also raised tentatively the need for higher short-term interest rates.[26]

[24] Eccles, especially pp. 421–25.
[25] *Annual Report of the Secretary of the Treasury for 1945–46.*
[26] *Federal Reserve Bulletin*, 32 (February 1946), p. 121.

Meanwhile, as early as July 1945—in fact, a few days before Secretary Morgenthau resigned—the System asked Treasury approval of elimination of the preferential discount rate of ½% on loans secured by government securities due or callable within one year. To this the Treasury refused to agree. In conferences with Secretary Vinson and his staff during the Winter of 1945–1946 the Reserve pressed the point. It also pressed for an increase in the rate on three-months Treasury bills from ⅜% toward the ⅞% rate on one-year certificates. The System based the latter proposal on the need to prevent pattern-playing. Out of consideration for the susceptibilities of the Treasury, it even went so far as to argue that a rise in the bill rate would not raise, and might actually lower, the cost to the Treasury of servicing the public debt. This unlikely result was to be brought about through the commercial banks holding more bills and fewer certificates (the gap in yield between the two having narrowed), and the System more certificates and fewer bills. True, the nominal cost of the debt would have risen (owing to the higher bill rate), but so would the amount of interest paid to the Reserve Banks—eventually in large measure to be recaptured by the Treasury.

But the Treasury was not satisfied with these assurances, and instead carried the war into the enemy's camp. In staff conferences with the Reserve, Henry C. Murphy argued not merely against higher rates, but in favor of still lower rates. At a staff conference in January 1946

> Mr. Murphy made a strong case for lower interest rates and indicated his belief that long-term rates should go lower than they are now. He thought long-term rates might in the near future reach 2% and later might approach zero. His case for low interest rates is that they not only reduce the cost of carrying the public debt, but also that they encourage consumption and investment and result in a more equitable distribution of income. Although admitting the desirability of discouraging spending during a period of inflation, he preferred to use other methods and not permit interest rates to rise, because that would delay the desirable long-run downward adjustment of rates.[27]

We should remember that postwar investment opportunity was at that time much underestimated, partly as a consequence of the doctrine of secular stagnation popular in the late 1930's, and it was

[27] Eccles papers, memorandum of January 28, 1946.

expected that the maintenance of adequate levels of private investment in the postwar period might prove difficult. Also one must
grant the Treasury's willingness to use such other methods as lay
within its power: budget surpluses, to the extent that these occurred,
were used to repay bank-held debt, and trust fund and other balances were also for the most part disposed in the least inflationary
manner. Further, the prospective equilibrium level of long-term
rates of interest was plainly a matter upon which more than one
view might reasonably be held. Yet, once the sensitiveness of investment expenditures to interest rate levels was assumed, it did
not make much sense in 1946 to reject higher rates as a measure
against inflation.

Led by Murphy, the Treasury staff persuaded Secretary Vinson
that the elimination of the preferential discount rate, and more
important, any increase in the Treasury bill rate, would be interpreted by the market as the forerunner of a general rise in yields
of government obligations. In reply the System, perhaps unwisely,
denied that it desired or would allow increases in yields of any
governments except 3-month bills. Replying to Secretary Vinson's
refusal to agree to the elimination of the preferential discount rate,
Chairman Eccles wrote, April 19, 1946:

> There is nothing in the record to justify the statement in your letter
> that the proposal to eliminate the preferential discount rate is "really
> part of a program to increase short-term interest rates." That is not
> its purpose. The purpose is to avoid giving impetus to the inflationary
> forces which now exist in our economy, among which must be included
> the supply of money in the hands of the public. . . . We refuse there-
> fore to be ranged on the side of the advocates of a higher interest rate
> policy. . . . We wish to emphasize with all the force we can command
> that our purpose and policy are based not on a desire for a higher
> level of interest rates, and hence increased costs of carrying the public
> debt, but entirely on grounds of discouraging further needless monetiza-
> tion of the debt through a wartime mechanism. . . . The only official
> recommendation the System has made at any time for any higher rate
> related exclusively to the bill rate.[28]

Both Eccles and Sproul maintained at this period that further monetization of the debt could be prevented without raising interest rates.
In retrospect it may be doubted whether they were wise to adopt such
an uncompromising position, for they failed to convince the Treas-

[28] *Ibid.*, Eccles to Vinson, April 19, 1946.

ury, and gradually over the next five years were forced by events to admit an increasing role for interest-rate policy. Especially under the influence of continued pattern-playing, the System came to argue for higher short- and medium-term rates, so as to diminish the gap between them and the 2½% long-term rate. Consistently, however, right down to the controversy immediately preceding the Accord of 1951, System officials disclaimed any desire to see the long-term rate on governments rise above 2½%.

By 1947 some slight easing of the Treasury's attitude is apparent. The preferential discount rate had been abolished in the face of Treasury disapproval. The Reserve had hesitated to force higher bill rates by unilateral action. However, early in 1947 as noted above, after Lee Wiggins became Undersecretary, the Treasury was induced to agree to the elimination of the posted buying-rate of ⅜% for 3-month bills. The bill rate rose promptly to about ¾%, or just below the rate on 1-year certificates. Yet this change was not sufficient to prevent pattern-playing and the ready access by member banks to reserve credit through the sale of certificates. By November 1947, Eccles was advocating a rise in the certificate rate as a means of diminishing the relative attractiveness to the banks of longer-term governments and of commercial loans and investments. But by this time Washington had espoused the "special-reserves" proposal as a means to control the situation without having to fight a pitched battle with the Treasury, while Sproul in New York had temporarily lost faith in monetary control as such.

Early in 1948 it became clear that, partly through lack of support from the Treasury, "special reserves" could not be enacted. In circumstances of mounting inflationary pressures and an atmosphere of continued frustration, there was nothing to do but fight for higher rates on all maturities, except the longest term for which the 2½% yield still was not questioned on Constitution Avenue. At hearings in April 1948 the System took positions which were not substantially modified until early 1951, immediately prior to the Accord. Eccles said:

> The people in the Reserve System, not only the Board, but the Reserve Bank people, as well as the Board people, are unanimous, I think, in feeling that, taking the matter on balance—with the public debt the size it is, so much larger than the entire private debt, in fact equal to about 60% of all the debt—we must maintain the stability of the gov-

ernment securities market and confidence in it. The public have taken quite a drubbing already on the decrease in the purchasing power of the dollar that they put in bonds, and now, to make them take a further decrease, by letting the bonds drop below par, would be a very serious step.

I want to make another matter clear: We have never made the statement that we should support all government securities at par. What we have said is that we should maintain the 2½% rate on long-term bonds. That should be the basic long-term rate.

. . . that is something to which we are committed for the foreseeable future. Nobody wants to say for ever, but certainly so far as the Federal Reserve people can see things at the present time, we have an unavoidable responsibility to the support of the 2½% rate. . . .

The short-term rate should be permitted to fluctuate to the extent that it can be useful. And if the short rate should go up, certainly the very short securities may drop below par. And they have.[29]

At the same hearings Eccles gave his views on cooperation with the Treasury:

. . . at no time have we tried to force a rate on the Treasury that they were unwilling to accept. I do not think it would be practical to do so. I think the central bank has certainly got to recognize the responsibility of the Treasury and to advise and work with Treasury officials in that regard; and I will say this, that in that connection the Treasury and the Federal Reserve have cooperated pretty fully in connection with the management of the public debt.[30]

Thus Eccles criticizes the Treasury only for its views about short-term rates: he admits no desire to remove the long-term peg. Moreover, in the last resort the Federal Reserve submitted to the will of the Treasury, and not vice versa. The picture Eccles painted in 1948 was to dissolve completely in 1951. In the infighting which preceded the Accord, he was to figure as the champion who forced the Treasury to accept not only higher short rates but total unpegging of the long-term market. Perhaps his views had changed. Perhaps the times were more propitious.

In May 1948 Sproul takes a similar position, showing no disposition as yet to quarrel with the Treasury on the point of principle:

Why should we support the government securities market, and to that extent circumscribe our powers and our actions to control the volume

[29] Joint Committee on the Economic Report, *Credit Policies*, Hearings, 80th Cong. 2nd Sess., 1948, pp. 16–17, 45.
[30] *Ibid.*, p. 32.

of credit? . . . I justify the policy we have followed, not on the basis
of cheap money or low interest rates so far as the government debt is
concerned, although that has its important aspects, but because I question what good could have been accomplished by a vigorous aggressive
policy of over-all credit contraction—such sales of government securities
from our portfolio as might have broken the market. . . . Such action
would probably be effective in checking the further expansion of bank
credit, but at a cost in fiscal and financial disorder, and in terms of
reduced production and employment which no one would want to contemplate now.[31]

He proceeded to paint a picture of near-panic in case the peg should
be removed:

A decline in prices of long-term Treasury bonds more than frac-
tionally below par, under existing conditions, would throw the whole
market for long-term securities—corporate and municipal, as well as
federal—into confusion. . . . An attempt to reestablish stability in the
market, for example at a level only moderately below par, would en-
counter serious difficulties . . . flotations of long-term securities would
be made very difficult if not impossible, until the market became
stabilized at a new level, and even then could proceed only on a limited
scale until confidence developed in the new level. There is no telling
how long that would take.[32]

One feels that Sproul protests too much. Nobody in a responsible
position was urging deflation: all the critics wished to do was to
limit the possibilities of further expansion.

The dilemma of System officials at this period is suggested by a
letter written by Eccles to Senator Brien McMahon in which he
speaks of "the difficulty of writing the case for support of the government bond market . . . without putting myself in Snyder's camp,
where I do not belong and where I do not want to be."[33] But in an
address before the Iowa Bankers Association a few days later Eccles
still opposed higher yields on long-term bonds:

Any moderate rise in long-term interest rates would not, in itself,
reduce significantly the demand for money. Investing institutions, which
are now switching from long-term government bonds to private credit
forms, would still be motivated to do so by a continuing margin of
return between the two kinds of investment.

Thus, under the "flexible" policy, the Federal Reserve System would
still be called upon to support the bond market and would thereby con-

[31] *Ibid.*, pp. 94–95.
[32] *Ibid.*, p. 101.
[33] Eccles papers, Eccles to McMahon, November 13, 1948.

tinue to create bank reserves. It is possible that the amount of support required under these conditions would be much greater than is now the case. Investors generally would lose confidence in the market and would rush to sell their securities before prices declined further.[34]

This position, which seems to have been shared by other System officials, amounts to saying: (1) private borrowers will not be deterred by a moderate increase, i.e., long-term investment is interest inelastic; (2) anyhow, a moderate rise in rates is unthinkable, because panic would ensue.

During 1949 the struggle for higher short-term rates continued, despite the recession in business which for the moment made credit restraint less urgent. On February 4 President Sproul wrote from the New York Bank to Secretary Snyder:

> Since there is to be continued support of the 2½% long-term rate, it is essential that there be permitted a greater degree of flexibility in short-term rates. It is not possible to exercise a flexible monetary policy with two pegs—one at the short end and one at the long end—as far apart as at present.[35]

It is difficult to think of a more moderate statement!

By December 1949, Eccles appears for the first time to have had doubts about the wisdom of maintaining the 2½% long-term rate: "This policy of rigid support of Government securities should not be continued indefinitely. The circumstances that made it necessary are no longer compelling."[36]
Almost fourteen months later, in January 1951, Eccles had had enough:

> SENATOR O'MAHONEY: Do I understand you are against pegged prices?
> MR. ECCLES: That's right.
> SENATOR O'MAHONEY: Therefore, you want the prices of government securities to seek their own level in the open market?
> MR. ECCLES: That is right.

[34] This address was delivered November 27, 1948, and much of the text may be found in the *American Banker*, March 7, 1951. The passage quoted was endorsed a year later by Eccles in Congressional testimony November 22, 1949 (Joint Committee on the Economic Report, *Money, Credit and Fiscal Policies*, Hearings, 81st Cong. 1st Sess., 1949, pp. 229–30).

[35] Eccles papers, Sproul to Snyder, February 4, 1949.

[36] Joint Committee on the Economic Report, *Monetary, Credit and Fiscal Policies*, Hearings, 81st Cong. 1st Sess., 1950, p. 223.

Figure 2. SYSTEM HOLDINGS OF U.S. TREASURY OBLIGATIONS, 1932–1963

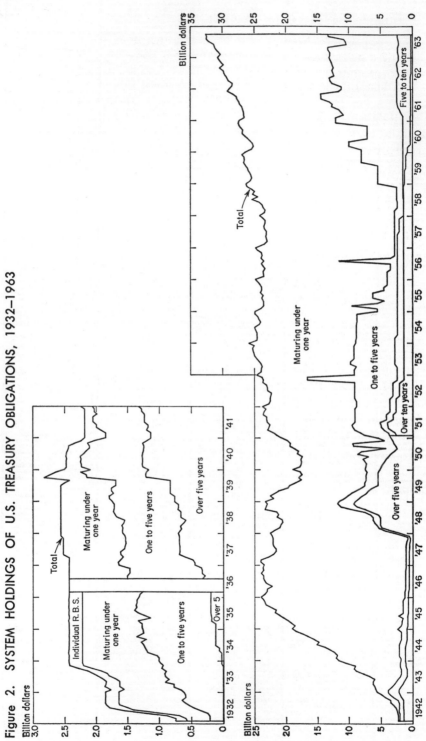

Nor would a panic ensue:

> SENATOR O'MAHONEY: If we abandon support of federal securities in the open market, and allow interest rates to increase, isn't it inevitable that the price of those securities would fall?
>
> MR. ECCLES: I am not sure that they would fall. They may temporarily go down, but I do not think they would fall far.[37]

The metamorphosis was complete. Rates not merely on bills, or certificates, or even 5-year notes, were to be unpegged, but rates on all maturities, even the longest, before the Reserve would be satisfied. Secretary Vinson and Mr. Murphy had been right after all. The elimination of the preferential discount rate, threatened in 1945 and effected in 1946, was indeed the forerunner of a general rise in yields of government securities, however vigorously Chairman Eccles and President Sproul may have denied at the time that this could be so. But doggedness and persistence paid off in the end. In 1951 the Reserve was able to win a pitched battle with the Treasury which it might have lost had it chosen to fight some years earlier. Who can say?

[37] Joint Committee on the Economic Report, *January 1951 Economic Report of the President*, Hearings, 82nd Cong. 1st Sess., 1951, pp. 181, 182.

Chapter 7

The Federal Reserve Comes into Its Own, 1951–1963

> *'Twixt failure and success the point's so
> fine*
> *Men sometimes know not when they touch
> the line.*
> —HENRY AUSTIN

> *I am not trying to shirk responsibility. I
> have made many mistakes.*
> —Chairman MARTIN

The two years following the Accord of March 1951 tell a story of very active business, slowly rising commodity prices, and gradually increasing money rates. Being decidedly less liquid now that they were unpegged, government bonds lost their popularity with commercial banks. Bank lending continued to expand, but less rapidly than prior to the Accord. Member-bank indebtedness increased steadily, now that short-term governments could no longer conveniently be monetized; after the middle of 1952 borrowings exceeded excess reserves, so that free reserves became negative (Fig. 3). The revival of the discount window was hailed as a return to traditional central banking.

After the Accord

For more than a year after the Accord the System, although not supporting existing issues of Treasury obligations, continued to purchase rights in connection with the refunding of Treasury certificates.

In November 1952, for the first time since the war, the Treasury sold an issue of 12-month certificates entirely without support from the Reserve. This event, which occurred shortly before the end of Secretary Snyder's term of office, may be said to mark the final emancipation of monetary policy after the war, bringing to an end the transition period which followed the Accord.

By this time the business situation again had a decidedly inflationary aspect. The Reserve Board later summed it up like this:

> Beginning in the Spring of 1952 the rate of increase in defense spending slackened, but there was a renewed expansion of private expenditures, and private credit demands became more vigorous. Around the middle of the year direct regulation of consumer installment and real-estate credit and the voluntary credit-restraint programs were discontinued. These actions increased the dependence on general credit measures for restraining excessive credit and monetary expansion. . . . By late 1952 the economy generally was operating on an overtime basis. . . . Bank loans to businesses, reflecting inventory accumulation, expanded very sharply in late 1952 and failed to show the usual seasonal decline in early 1953.[1]

The picture in January 1953 was subsequently described by Chairman Martin as "a bubble on top of a boom":[2] the peak was to come, as matters turned out, about midyear. Table 1 shows changes in components of national product since the preceding cyclical trough (fourth quarter of 1949) and since the Accord (first quarter of 1951). (The figures are in current dollars: prices rose, especially between 1949 and 1951, but the use of constant-dollar data, which are available, would have slight advantage for the present purpose.) It is evident that the "boom" and "bubble" to which the Chairman referred were chiefly a consequence of the growth of federal purchases of goods and services—especially in connection with the war in Korea. The expansion was not primarily a capital-goods boom: in fact, expenditure on fixed investment did no more than keep pace with consumer and government outlays. On the other hand, net additions to business inventories during 1950, 1951, and 1952 averaged over $6 billion a year, or 2% of gross national product—a wholly unprecedented rate of accumulation. The expansion may therefore be classed as a military-expenditure and inventory boom.

[1] Joint Committee on the Economic Report, *United States Monetary Policy*, Hearings, 83rd Cong. 2nd Sess., 1954, p. 7.
[2] *Ibid.*, p. 246. The phrase was originally coined by Sproul.

TABLE 1

CHANGES IN NATIONAL PRODUCT FROM TROUGH TO PEAK, 1949–1953[a]
$ billion; seasonally adjusted quarterly data at annual rates

Components of national product	1949 4th quarter	1951 1st quarter	1953 2nd quarter	Change 1949.IV to 1953.II	Change 1951.I to 1953.II
Consumer expenditures	184.0	211.5	233.3	49.3	21.8
Residential construction	10.9	14.1	14.0	3.1	—.1
Other construction	9.0	11.6	13.8	4.8	2.2
Equipment	16.0	20.7	22.0	6.0	1.3
Inventory change	—5.3	10.5	3.1	8.4	—7.4
Net exports	2.1	—.2	—.7	—2.8	—.5
Federal purchases	21.6	28.7	58.9	37.3	30.2
State and local purchases	18.7	20.9	24.3	5.6	3.4
Gross national product	257.0	317.8	368.8	111.8	51.0

[a] Data are from *Survey of Current Business* and supplements. Rounding may prevent agreement between totals and detail.

About the beginning of 1953, while business was still expanding, the System seems to have decided on a further tightening of credit. On January 16 the New York discount rate was raised from 1¾% to 2%—the highest level in almost two decades. More significantly, open-market sales of governments combined with gold losses to push interest rates up at a more rapid pace than the very slow advance during the preceding year and a half. The yield of long-term governments, which had been under 2½% at the time of the Accord, fluctuated around 2¾% during 1952, but rose above 3% during the first months of 1953.

Despite the circumstance of rising interest rates, the new team at the Treasury—Secretary Humphrey and Mr. Burgess—determined on an effort to lengthen the maturity of the debt. Early in April 1953 the Treasury announced the issue May 1 of a bond repayable 1978–1983 bearing a 3¼% coupon. The when-issued securities at first sold at a comfortable premium, but by May 1 had fallen to a discount: the succeeding weeks brought a sharp upward revision of yields throughout the capital market. For the maturity in question the coupon was about ¼% above the yield curve at the time the terms were announced. Although oversubscribed, the new issue was followed within a few weeks by a slump in the bond market. This was the first issue by the Treasury of long-term marketable bonds since the war. Its practical failure has been variously ascribed to the unwillingness of the market to believe the Reserve would not support the bonds close to par; to inadequate notice, so that institutional investors did not have time to plan subscriptions; and to too large an allotment to individuals, who were looking for a "free ride."

Yet it is hard to see what harm the incident did, or to criticize the authorities for their conduct of the financing. If the fall in bonds did not fit in with the Reserve's view of what monetary policy should be at the time, the Reserve could and should have supported the market —not out of kindness to the Treasury, but because of its view of what monetary policy required. Indeed this seems to be just what the System now decided. Production was still expanding, but commodity prices were stable, and it seemed obvious that the inflation touched off by the Korean War had at long last been brought under control. The slump in bonds was therefore unwelcome. Accordingly, following a meeting of the executive committee of the Open Market Committee May 6, 1953, the System bought about $1 billion of short-term securities (but not bonds), and in July released another $1 billion to the market by reducing member-bank reserve requirements. By June interest rates had passed their peak. Excess reserves remained rather steady, but member-bank borrowing was cut sharply by these and subsequent steps to ease the market. As a result by July, when business began to slide, free reserves were again positive.

Thus the easing of monetary policy occurred on this occasion practically simultaneously with the end of the business expansion. However, the excellence of timing was due less to efficient forecasting than to prior miscalculation. The System recognized that it had allowed interest rates to rise too sharply and Chairman Martin later admitted that in the early months of 1953 "we jammed on the brakes . . . a little bit too tight."[3] The easing of the market was nonetheless opportune.

Meanwhile a drastic reappraisal of central-banking doctrine was in progress.

"Bills Only"

After an intensive re-examination by an ad hoc committee, the Reserve System decided in the Spring of 1953 on the following princi-

[3] Joint Committee on the Economic Report, *January 1954 Economic Report of the President,* Hearings, 83rd Cong. 2nd Sess., 1954, pp. 125, 667–69; *United States Monetary Policy,* Hearings, 83rd Cong. 2nd Sess., 1954, pp. 179, 234.

ples for governing open-market operations. (1) Instead of maintaining orderly conditions, it would in future merely correct "disorderly situations" in the money market. (2) It would discontinue operations to support the market during Treasury refinancing. (3) It would confine its operations to the short end of the market. These guiding principles were issued by the Federal Open Market Committee as directives to its executive committee. The first two represent minor reaffirmations of the Accord of two years earlier and call for mild applause but no other comment. The third directive, which became known as the doctrine of "bills only," must be considered at some length.[4]

From the narrow viewpoint of influencing bank reserves, the choice of assets to be bought or sold by the System is of course a matter of indifference. What matters is the payment by a Reserve Bank to someone who banks with a member bank—or vice versa—and such a payment will influence member-bank reserves whether the Reserve Bank buys a 90-day bill, a 20-year bond, a share of common stock, a bushel of wheat, or the services of a cleaning woman.

Yet the fixing of bank reserves at an appropriate level—it is to be assumed—is merely an intermediate and qualified objective. The ultimate objective of Reserve policy, at least in recent years, has been to influence the course of business activity or the level of commodity prices. And from this broader and more interesting standpoint, it makes a great deal of difference just what the system does decide to buy and sell. Because the System decides to operate in one market rather than in another, it cannot help but disturb relative prices and incomes. The prices of the assets it buys and sells will rise or fall by amounts which depend upon the elasticities of supply and demand in the market for them. The prices of other assets may change too, by amounts which hinge upon the substitutability of these other assets for those which the System is buying or selling. These principles are very general but their application to the matter in hand is plain. If the System wishes to produce the quickest and largest effect with a given volume of purchases or sales, it should choose the right kind of assets to buy and sell.

As an illustration, suppose that the objective is to raise com-

[4] *Ibid.*, pp. 15–26. "Bills" should be taken to include certificates, and "only" sometimes was interpreted as "preferably."

modity prices: clearly the System should buy those commodities whose supply is least elastic. If the purpose is to stimulate business activity, it should buy the output of those industries where the repercussions will be largest—in technical language, where the combined multiplier and acceleration effects are most considerable. Other things equal, of course. And other things may not be equal: the reactions of the commercial banks, of other financial institutions, and of business in general to Reserve policy will vary. If possible, policies should be chosen which are reinforced by these reactions, rather than policies which evoke no response, or the reactions to which render them nugatory. For a great variety of reasons, legal, traditional, and practical, commodities or current output are not serious subjects for central-bank open-market operations. Yet even within the range of more conventional types of assets, whether commercial or Treasury obligations, the choice will not be indifferent.

When a central bank deals in debt instruments, it chooses a certain maturity and the obligations of a certain class of borrower. Its initial effect, therefore, is to change the terms on which money is available to specific borrowers at given maturities—to commercial borrowers at short term, perhaps, or to the U.S. Treasury at long term. The effect will fan out to other borrowers—and also to other maturities—by means of arbitrage, to the extent to which substitution on either side of the market is possible. Of course, if there is perfect substitution, it makes no difference what assets are bought and sold, but this is ordinarily very far from being the case. The question to be answered is: By dealing in what type of assets will the System most readily secure its objectives? The elements of an answer to this question can now be seen. A given change in bank reserves may have much or little effect upon the terms upon which money is available to a given class of borrowers, depending upon the assets dealt in. A given change in the terms on which money is available may have much or little effect upon business activity, or upon commodity prices, depending upon the class of borrowers and the maturity to which the change in terms applies.

Let me illustrate by an extreme example. Suppose long-term investment cannot be financed by short-term funds, nor short-term investment by long-term funds. Suppose long-term rates of interest are insensitive to changes in the short-term market, and vice versa. Suppose further that investment spending is interest elastic for long-term capital assets (plant, equipment, residential construction) and interest inelastic for short-term assets (inventories and other working capital). In these circumstances changes in System holdings of short-term securities will have little or no effect upon business activity or commodity prices, despite substantial changes in the volume of bank reserves. Changes in System holdings of long-term securities, on the other hand, having precisely the same effect on bank reserves, will have marked effects upon the level of business activity and upon commodity prices.

A policy of operating exclusively in the short end of the market—to conform to the "bills only" doctrine—will be effective if the System's only concern is with the level of bank reserves. If, however, it desires to influence business activity or commodity prices, the effectiveness of Reserve policy *may* be greatly reduced by such a policy of self-abnegation. In fact the System could be operating with one hand tied behind its back.

The above theoretical considerations suggest that for maximum effectiveness the System should buy and sell both long and short. It should be willing to deal in longs because the long-term rate is believed to have the most influence upon investment spending: it should deal in shorts because the flexible control of bank reserves may be unnecessarily disturbing to the long-term market, should it deal only in longs. But it does not have to deal in all maturities: rates for some maturities may well be left to be settled by normal arbitrage within the market.

What then was the case for the abdication of powers implied in the "bills only" doctrine? The defense offered by the Board of Governors, and especially by Chairman Martin, was a technical one. It was said that any intervention in the market increases the risks dealers must run, encourages jobbers to convert themselves into brokers, checks arbitrage, and leads to "thin" markets in which a small addition to or subtraction from the floating supply induces disproportionately large price changes. The claim was made that these disadvantages of intervention are more pronounced when the Reserve operates at the long than at the short end of the market—a claim which, so far as it goes, is obviously accurate. The fact that so important a policy was based on so restricted a foundation certainly calls for explanation.

The System's own description of the genesis of the "bills only"

doctrine is contained in the report of a subcommittee of the Federal
Open Market Committee, organized in 1952 and consisting of Chair-
man Martin, Governor Abbot L. Mills, Jr., and Malcolm Bryan,
President of the Atlanta Reserve Bank.[5]

The advent of the doctrine obviously reflects in large measure a
revulsion against the pre-1951 policy of pegging long-term governments. The speculative movements that developed in these bonds
from time to time, based on confidence in the durability of the peg,
and the large-scale intervention in the market undertaken in order to
check such movements, plainly had the undesirable results listed
above. Indeed, Robert H. Craft, a New York commercial banker who
acted as consultant to the subcommittee, went so far as to claim for
Treasury bills, as a medium for Reserve operations, the virtue that,
unlike other short-term governments, they can never be exchanged
but are always redeemed in cash. By holding only Treasury bills,
therefore, the System is automatically relieved of pressure from the
Treasury to convert rather than to take cash, when the obligations
mature. This argument turns "bills only" into one more device to
buttress the System's independence of the Treasury. It seems doubtful that Chairman Martin would lay stress on this argument, however, for he is on record as anxious to confine operations to the short
end of the market, but not exclusively to Treasury bills.[6] Nevertheless the doctrine may, I think, fairly be described in its origin as a
reaction against pegging. Revulsion against pre-1951 policies may
excuse, but can hardly justify, "bills only."

Obviously the doctrine was also inspired by "respect for the traditional Anglo-American central banking practice of operating exclusively in 'the nearest thing to money.' "[7] In this sense the tradition
owes its origins, if not its continued existence, to the notion that a
central bank—like any other bank—should hold earning assets that
are liquid. In fact a central bank is the one institution that never needs
to worry, and may cause havoc by worrying, about its own liquidity.
As for respect for central-banking tradition, Chairman Martin might
reflect upon the damage caused in the past by such respect. As we

[5] Ibid., pp. 257–307.

[6] Ibid., pp. 301–2, and 230.

[7] Comment by Rudolf Smutny, ibid., p. 78; see also p. 267. Mr. Smutny, a dealer in
government bonds, while in no way defending the pegging of long-term Treasury obligations, denied the Board's contention that an exclusive concentration of open-market
operations on bills was beneficial to dealers in the market.

saw in Chapter 3, the tradition that bank rate should rule above market rate—rigidly adhered to—was mainly responsible for the business collapse of 1921 (see above, pp. 60–66). And without doubt it was central-banking tradition that prevented a more imaginative acceptance policy in the Fall of 1931, and led to a disastrous credit restriction in the very middle of the Depression (pp. 100–5 above).

The "bills only" doctrine advocated by the subcommittee was vigorously criticized by the Federal Reserve Bank of New York under Allan Sproul:

> It is quite likely that in most circumstances the System will be able to attain its policy objectives by operating only in the market for Treasury bills and other short-term securities. It is at least possible, however, that on some occasions the System might better be able to effectuate its policies by operating in other sectors of the market—even the longest maturities—depending on the economic conditions then prevailing, investor and market psychology and expectations, the structure of the public debt, etc. In most circumstances, when intervention in the long-term market by the System was considered appropriate or necessary, restriction of operations to short-term securities would probably either make the System's intervention ineffective or require larger-scale intervention to achieve its objectives.

The Bank then cites its efforts to mitigate the fall in long-term governments which occurred on the outbreak of war in 1939—efforts which it thinks could not have succeeded had purchases been confined to bills. A better example, perhaps, is the ineffectiveness of massive purchases of shorts in 1932 to raise the price of longs. The Bank continues:

> . . . there is serious question whether the facilities for market "arbitrage" are so highly developed, or could be, as to assure a smooth flow of reactions from any System action in the short-term area throughout the longer sectors of the market in all circumstances. The subcommittee refers to operations in the short-term market as traditional central banking policy, but one of the major questions raised concerning traditional central banking policy concerns its ability to achieve the general restraint or ease intended solely through action in the short-term market.

The Bank then quotes Keynes and Riefler, writing in the early 1930's, as skeptical of the effectiveness of arbitrage in transmitting ease or tightness from the short-term to the long-term market.[8]

---

[8] *Ibid.*, pp. 307–31; the quotations are from pp. 310–11. See J. M. Keynes, *A Treatise on Money* (London: Macmillan, 1930), II, pp. 362–63; W. W. Riefler, *Money Rates and Money Markets* (New York: Harper, 1930), p. 218.

Keynes was no longer living, and Riefler, now assistant to Chairman Martin, had shifted his opinion. In a paper written in 1958, Riefler takes a far more favorable view of what arbitrage can achieve than he did previously and lays particular stress on the reactions of commercial banks, although he admits that the time required by the latter to adjust their portfolios "sometimes accounts for what may seem to be a sluggish response in the long-term markets to changes in the availability of funds in the short-term markets." He defends the "bills only" doctrine mainly because of his belief in the greater danger of creating false expectations when the Reserve buys and sells longs rather than shorts:

> Not infrequently, the professionals overshoot the mark in trying to estimate either supply or demand even apart from the effects of System policy or the direction of that policy. There is always the possibility that they may assume that a given purchase or sale by the System foreshadows larger changes in bank reserve positions than in fact develop. In such cases, they may take positions and establish, for a period, an unsustainable level of prices or yields that is inconsistent with the actual supply-demand situation. . . .
>
> The possibility that an unsustainable level of prices or yields will prevail temporarily because market expectations are not borne out is a major reason for the System's policy of nonintervention in the intermediate- and long-term sectors of the market. Its operations in longer-term securities would be much more subject to comment and possible misinterpretation by market professionals than are its operations in Treasury bills. This would probably be the case even if the market were accustomed to frequent System operations in these sectors. The very fact that the System took the initiative in buying or selling long-term securities, where the market is almost always thin as compared with the bill sector, would indicate a feeling on the part of Federal Reserve authorities that existing prices and yields on long-term securities were out of line. Market professionals perforce would have to try to assess this implication in their subsequent trades. Bill operations can also give rise to false or misleading expectations, but they are much less likely to do so.[9]

So the professionals are apt to jump overboard and may even burn their fingers! Yet this is just the feature most likely to intensify the results and enhance the effectiveness of Reserve policy: to produce large effects from small measures. Where small effects only are desired, for day-to-day operations, Riefler may be right that "bills

[9] Winfield W. Riefler, "Open Market Operations in Long-Term Securities," *Federal Reserve Bulletin*, 44 (November 1958), 1260–74. The quotations are from p. 1264.

only" will allow more delicate control. But if and when the ability of monetary policy to achieve the desired result is in question, effectiveness rather than delicacy is needed and what to Riefler are vices must be rated virtues.

To be sure, the volume of operations needed to control bank reserves is such that they could not all be conveniently conducted in medium- or long-term securities. This is especially true of purchases and sales around tax and other payment dates. But at times when it is desired not only to control bank reserves but to influence long-term rates of interest, we may agree with the New York Reserve Bank that it is better to operate directly in the long-term market than to await the results that Martin and Riefler so hopefully expect from arbitrage. Nevertheless the subcommittee's views prevailed, and transactions outside the short end of the market were abandoned. A year and a half later, in December 1954, President Sproul did not even concede that concentration of System operations in short maturities had in fact improved the "depth, breadth and resiliency" of the government securities market as a whole. According to him, even these advantages claimed for the "bills only" policy had proved illusory.[10]

Chairman Martin replied as follows:

> I think the process of arbitrage . . . which Mr. Sproul thinks has more of a lag than I think it has, takes place very quickly in the market for government securities.
>
> I believe that when we inject funds via the closest equivalent to money that there is . . . the injection of those funds will quite rapidly permeate to the other areas of the market and will be reflected by the forces of the market in changes in interest rates throughout the market.
>
> Now, if we should operate directly in all maturities, we could, perhaps, be wise enough to know just what the relationships between the prices of different securities ought to be at all times. . . . While I respect Mr. Sproul's judgment, I think that that is a step toward pegging which he deprecates just as much as I do.[11]

Three comments may be made upon this defense of the System's abdication. First, the speed with which arbitrage occurs may well be a function of the market situation. The very large spread between short-term and long-term rates which developed so disastrously dur-

---

[10] *United States Monetary Policy*, pp. 223–28.
[11] *Ibid.*, p. 230.

ing the 1930's, a period when operations were confined to the short end of the market, suggests a complete breakdown of arbitrage at that time. Second, it is not necessary to operate in all maturities, and the precise shape of the yield curve can be left for the market to determine, once the levels of its two ends have been settled by Reserve policy. Or if, for technical or other reasons, not more than one "anchor" is desired, let it be at the long-term end: then the entire yield curve, including the bill rate, will be settled through arbitrage in the market, even though the Reserve continues to operate in bills for reasons given earlier. Third, to influence the long-term rate—to push it up or down as required—should not be confused with pegging as that term was understood in the dreadful days before the Accord.

I do not wish to argue that damage was done or that opportunities were missed as a result of the "bills only" policy during the years it was in effect. They were years of relatively great sensitiveness of business to Reserve policy, and the advantages that could have accrued to operations in the long-term market may not have been great. Late in 1960 a desire to keep New York attractive to foreign-owned short-term balances led to a partial abandonment of "bills only," and in December 1961 the Open Market Committee voted to rescind the 1953 policy statement. Yet this action seemed to owe more to Congressional criticism than to any belief that "bills only" is unsound.[12]

The Recession of 1953–1954

To resume our story: production reached peaks in May and July 1953 and then ebbed away. As already noted, the System began to release bank reserves in May, and soon after the end of the year the discount rate was cut to 1½%. As 1954 advanced, open-market rates reflected monetary ease still more strongly, and the yield on long-term governments fell once again to the 2½% basis which had prevailed prior to the Accord.

The character of the reaction in business can best be shown with the help of the components of income and product detailed in Table 2. Gross national product reached a peak in the second quarter of 1953 and the subsequent trough occurred in the second quarter of 1954. Between these dates GNP fell by $10 billion

[12] See below, pp. 208–12.

Table 2

CHANGES IN INCOME AND PRODUCT FROM PEAK TO TROUGH, 1953–1954[a]
$ billion; seasonally adjusted quarterly data at annual rates

Components of income and product	1953 2nd quarter	1954 2nd quarter	Change
Consumer expenditures	233.3	236.5	3.2
Residential construction	14.0	14.7	.7
Other construction	13.8	14.2	.4
Equipment	22.0	20.9	−1.1
Inventory change	3.1	−2.7	−5.8
Net exports	−.7	.8	1.5
Federal purchases	58.9	47.1	−11.8
State and local purchases	24.3	27.3	3.0
Gross national product	368.8	358.9	−9.9
Capital consumption, etc.[b]	29.5	29.0	−.5
Business taxes less subsidies	30.5	30.5	0
Social security taxes	8.9	9.6	.7
Compensation of employees[c]	200.8	197.0	−3.8
Proprietors' income	40.7	39.6	−1.1
Rents and interest (exc. govt.)	18.6	19.9	1.3
Corporate profits before tax	39.8	33.3	−6.5
Gross national income	368.8	358.9	−9.9
Consumer expenditures	233.3	236.5	3.2
Personal taxes	35.9	32.8	−3.1
Personal saving	19.6	18.3	−1.3
Personal outgo	288.7	287.6	−1.1
Compensation of employees[c]	200.8	197.0	−3.8
Proprietors' income	40.7	39.6	−1.1
Dividends	9.4	9.5	.1
Rent and interest (inc. govt.)	23.7	25.3	1.6
Transfer payments	14.1	16.1	2.0
Personal income	288.7	287.6	−1.1

[a] Data are from *Survey of Current Business* and supplements. Rounding may prevent agreement between totals and detail.
[b] Capital consumption allowances plus statistical discrepancy plus excess wage accruals plus business transfers.
[c] After social security contributions but before personal taxes.

(annual rate), or slightly less than 3%. This drop is more than accounted for by the drop in federal purchases consequent upon the end of the Korean War, and the switch from accumulation to decumulation of inventories. These two elements of contraction were partly offset by continued growth of consumer expenditures and of state and local purchases. Most notable is the buoyancy of consumption. How may the latter be explained?

The lower portion of the table reveals that personal income fell by only $1 billion, a much smaller decline than occurred in GNP. This satisfactory outcome reflected (1) the maintenance of dividends despite the decline in corporate profits, and (2) increased rent, interest, and transfer payments. No doubt the $2 billion increase in transfer payments mainly took the form of unemployment compensation. Inspection of the figures shows that consumer expenditures could still increase, despite the cut in consumer income, because less was paid in taxes and less was saved. Roughly, what was no longer paid in taxes was spent, and consumers made the cut in income good by saving less.

Despite the large decline in federal purchases, the net influence of government (federal, state, and local) was not deflationary (as in Table 2, figures are seasonally adjusted annual rates):

Change from peak to trough in:	$ billion
Federal purchases	—11.8
State and local purchases	3.0
Transfer payments (govt. only)	2.1
Government interest	.3
Total change, expenditures	—6.4
Corporate income taxes	—5.0
Business taxes less subsidies	0
Social security taxes	.7
Personal taxes	—3.1
Total change, receipts	—7.4

The government's contribution to the income stream therefore increased by about $1 billion, net, between the second quarter of 1953 and the second quarter of 1954. Although not enough to offset the reversal of the inventory movement, the "built-in" fiscal stabilizers, fortuitously aided by a tax cut (January 1, 1954), more than neutralized the reduction in public spending which followed the Korean armistice. And they made a small contribution to stemming the decline in private spending.

The slump in private investment was in fact largely confined to adjustment of inventories. Equipment expenditures declined, but construction continued to advance, and private *fixed* investment as a whole was unchanged. Inventory disinvestment no more than matched the extraordinary investment in inventories during 1950–1952 noted in a preceding section. Like the cycles of the 1920's, and with perhaps even better justification, the movement that culminated in 1953 may be called an "inventory cycle." The production index (1947–1949 = 100) declined from 137 in July 1953 to 123 a year later, or roughly the level of mid-1952. The cycle differed from previous examples in that commodity prices remained remarkably stable (Fig. 3).

The Expansion of 1954–1957

Mainly stimulated by buoyant consumer expenditures, industrial production turned up in the Summer of 1954, and before long pressed once again against available resources. Commodity prices, which had been steady or declining since 1951, began to edge upward once more. For the next three years member-bank reserve balances were kept rather steady; but such stabilization was achieved only at the cost of a decided upward movement of interest rates. The New York Reserve Bank's discount rate was raised from 1½% in April 1955 to 3½% in August 1957. By the latter date long-term governments were selling to yield slightly under, Aaa bonds slightly over 4%. That is to say, interest rates, short and long, rose to levels not seen since 1933.

Some held that the "tight money" of the 1950's represented a return to something nearer the long-run or "natural" level of interest rates, as measured by the "real" demand and supply for capital in our economy. According to this view, the low levels that obtained during the twenty years from 1934 to 1954 were the results of the Great Depression of the 1930's, and thereafter of decisions which implied that World War II would be fought on a basis of cheap money even at the cost of inflation. An eventual postwar return to more normal conditions in the capital market, according to this view, would see the longest-term Treasury bonds yielding (say) 3½%, Aaa corporate bonds around 4%, and so forth. The difficulty with this analysis is that serious inflation in the United

States came to an end in 1948. The relative mildness of the Korean inflation does not suggest a level of interest rates in the early 1950's seriously out of line with long-run equilibrium. And between 1948 and 1955, before yields rose to their present levels, the return on long-term governments averaged under 3% (Fig. 3).

An alternative explanation of the rise in interest rates since 1955 would suggest that a succession of misadventures may have kept rates above their equilibrium level. Beginning in 1954, it may be argued, the Reserve System let the economy run away. According to this view, rising interest rates did not catch up with the optimism of businessmen—induced by the cheap money of 1954—until three years later. A fresh wave of optimism was induced by monetary— and especially fiscal—policy in 1958–1959. By 1960 the deficit in international payments prevented the decline in rates which ordinarily would have accompanied recession. This explanation is awkward, too, for the expansion of 1961–1964 could scarcely have occurred if interest rates still were above their long-run equilibrium level. It would seem necessary to conclude that, as the 1950's advanced, investment opportunity threatened to outrun the supply of saving, thus raising the equilibrium level of interest rates.

Certainly the recovery during the last months of 1954 and during 1955 was extraordinarily rapid. Industrial production (1947–1949 = 100) rose from 123 in August 1954 to 132 in January and 144 in December 1955, eventually reaching 147 in December 1956— which compares with the previous peak (May and July 1953) of 137. The growth of GNP between the trough in the second quarter of 1954 and the peak in the third quarter of 1957 is summarized in Table 3. This 3¼-year expansion may be compared with the 3½-year expansion which culminated in 1953 (Table 1). The earlier expansion of GNP is greater: $112 billion, or 44%, compared with $89 billion, or 25%. But the difference is largely accounted for by the substantial rise in prices during the earlier period. Most notable is the large dependence of the 1949–1953 boom on federal spending (Korean War): during 1954–1957 federal purchases grew only slightly. On the other hand, the 1957 expansion was more of a capital-goods boom: nonresidential construction and equipment expenditures grew by $13.1 billion ($10.8 billion in the 1953 expansion) and state and local purchases, much of it for construction,

TABLE 3

CHANGES IN NATIONAL PRODUCT FROM TROUGH TO PEAK, 1954–1957[a]
$ billion; seasonally adjusted quarterly data at annual rates

Components of national product	1954 2nd quarter	1957 3rd quarter	Change
Consumer expenditures	236.5	288.7	52.2
Residential construction	14.7	17.0	2.3
Other construction	14.2	19.3	5.1
Equipment	20.9	28.9	8.0
Inventory change	−2.7	2.5	5.2
Net exports	.8	5.1	4.3
Federal purchases	47.1	50.0	2.9
State and local purchases	27.3	36.9	9.6
Gross national product	358.9	448.3	89.4

[a] Data are from *Survey of Current Business* and supplements. Rounding may prevent agreement between detail and totals.

by $9.6 billion ($5.6 billion in the earlier expansion). Inventory accumulation also occurred, but on a smaller scale than in the earlier boom.

Federal Reserve policy reacted slowly to the recovery in late 1954. Open-market sales of securities in January and February 1955 were no more than seasonal: the New York discount rate was not increased until April 15, and then only from 1½% to 1¾%. Evidently the Reserve was in no hurry to abandon the easy-money regime established early in 1954. In February 1955 the Treasury sold an issue of 40-year 3% bonds, but the Reserve seems to have been less concerned with the success of this financing than with a desire not to halt recovery.

The gradual—in hindsight perhaps too gradual—change in the System's thinking can be followed in reports of meetings of the Open Market Committee.[13] On January 11, 1955, it appeared to the Committee that

> easy credit was no longer needed to foster recovery. . . . While the Committee did not believe that it was yet fighting inflation, it took the position that [a] shift in emphasis was desirable to avoid credit conditions that might encourage the development of an inflationary situation. This would contemplate a gradual contraction in the volume of

[13] *Annual Report of the Board of Governors for 1955*, pp. 89–111.

free reserve funds of banks from the level that had prevailed, and some increase in the cost and decrease in the ready availability of credit. On the other hand [there was no] call for pursuit at this stage of a program of credit restraint or of firmness in the money market.

Free reserves (excess reserves minus member-bank indebtedness) did indeed decline and in August became negative, less through open-market policy than through the growth of commercial-bank lending. On March 2 the Committee noted that

> unemployment was still relatively high, notwithstanding the degree of recovery that the country had experienced. Concern was indicated with respect to the relaxation of terms for and the volume of expansion in mortgage and consumer credit, and there were some fears that in a few industries, including building, activity was reaching levels that could not be sustained.
>
> This situation did not appear to call for a generally restrictive credit policy. . . . Monetary policy had been taking some of the slack out of the money market since the turn of the year and money rates had risen. Thus, while policy had not become restrictive, it had recently resulted in some restraint on the rate of credit expansion.

On May 10, 1955—after the first small increase in discount rates —the words "to encourage recovery" were at last deleted from the Committee's directive to those managing the open-market account, and the objective left simply "to avoid the development of unsustainable expansion." It was reported that

> a number of industries were operating at or close to capacity. Supply shortages had appeared in some industrial materials and prices of metals had advanced, although price averages were still generally steady. Business, financial and consumer confidence was extraordinarily high. On the other hand . . . a substantial amount of unemployment still existed in some areas. . . . There had been no seasonal contraction of business loans, and rapid expansion of real estate and consumer loans had continued.

On June 22 the May directive was left unchanged: the Committee was still concerned about unemployment. On July 12 the Committee was discouraged from intensifying the degree of restraint by the stability of general price indexes and the prospect of further Treasury financing. Finally on August 2 the Committee switched its position and prescribed "restraining inflationary developments" as the main objective. Almost simultaneously the New York discount rate was increased from 1¾% to 2%.

In subsequent months the new policy of restraint was reaffirmed, but the System chiefly relied on burgeoning demands for credit to tighten the market, and can hardly be said to have itself actively exercised restraint. On November 30, 1955, matters were confused by a contradictory decision to help the Treasury by buying up to $400 million of certificates of indebtedness to be issued the next day, in violation of the policy adopted in 1953 against buying when-issued Treasury obligations.

On January 24, 1956, the managers of the System account were instructed, not only to "restrain inflationary developments" (as laid down the previous August), but to take "into account any deflationary tendencies in the economy."[14] The Committee

> noted the currently reduced levels of farm prices and uncertainties in the housing and automobile markets; and it gave consideration to the view that the domestic economy after a year and a half of expansion might be nearing a cyclical peak and that a reaction might be in prospect before long. . . .
> The net of the Committee's review was that there had been a slight —perhaps almost imperceptible—change in the state of the economy in recent weeks, which might make some relaxation of restraint appropriate in the near future.

The production index did in fact decline from a peak of 144 in December 1955 to 136 in July 1956 (the month of the steel strike), but an easing of credit would certainly have been premature. On March 27 the Committee decided correctly that the boom was by no means over, and deleted the instruction, made in January, to take "into account any deflationary tendencies in the economy," leaving as the single policy objective the "restraint of inflationary developments." Among the reasons it gave were

> the much greater than expected plans of business concerns in all major lines for plant and equipment expenditures, the widespread optimism of consumers as to the economic outlook and their own financial position and income prospects, and evidence of an exceptionally heavy demand for bank credit. . . . The Committee also noted that common stock prices had risen sharply further. Growing pressures for increases in prices and wages were evident, and there was danger that if supported by further credit expansion pressures would engender an inflationary spiral.

[14] Reports of meetings of the Open Market Committee during 1956 will be found in *Annual Report of the Board of Governors for 1956*, pp. 17–47.

The Committee discussed the extent to which monetary policy might be used to combat an inflationary cost-price spiral and the risk of incurring temporary unemployment on the one hand, as against the risk of undermining the basis of sustained employment on the other. It was suggested that while monetary policy could not be expected to achieve all of the task of combating inflationary pressures, the System would be derelict in its duty if it did not exercise additional restraint in this situation.

Yet additional restraint was scarcely exercised. Between April and August discount rates were raised from 2½% to 3% in two steps, but free reserves (though negative) were not as tight during the second half of the year as during the first.[15]

Vacillation is reflected in the reports of the debates of the Open Market Committee. On April 17, 1956, it was agreed that

there should be no relaxation of pressures. However, the restrictive policy should not be pressed too strongly pending more opportunity to observe reactions to the mid-April increase in discount rates, increased pressure on bank reserve positions [shortly to be eased!], and clarification of the economic outlook.

On May 9 the Committee felt that "no change either toward increased pressure or toward relaxation would be justified at this time." On May 23 the Committee again instructed the managers of the open-market account to look out for "deflationary tendencies," and on June 26 declared that "doubts should be resolved on the side of ease during the next few weeks, rather than on the side of actions that might be construed as additional restraint, even though there was the possibility that the System would find it desirable to move toward substantially greater restraint in the Fall." On July 17,

continuation of firm restraint seemed necessary not only because most current indicators were tending upward but also because it was felt that whatever settlement of the steel strike was arrived at would create additional inflationary pressures. The Committee did not believe, however, that this was the time for clearly increased restraint. It recognized that if a settlement of the steel strike was delayed for a considerable period, action of an easing nature might become necessary.

Arguments can always be found on both sides of the question if a sufficient search is made!

[15] George Humphrey, Secretary of the Treasury, and Arthur F. Burns, Council Chairman, thought that the April discount rate increases were at least premature (Joint Economic Committee, *Conflicting Official Views on Monetary Policy: April 1956*, Hearing, June 12, 1956, 84th Cong. 2nd Sess., 1956, *passim*).

On August 7, 1956, the steel strike had been settled and commodity prices were rising. The System again veered toward further restraint, and the instruction to the managers in New York to look out for "deflationary tendencies" was once more deleted. On September 11 they were told that "doubts should be resolved on the side of tightness rather than of ease." Yet one wonders whether the managers were listening, for the free-reserve position became easier month by month. More than ample funds were supplied to the market to tide it over the year end, and in January 1957 excess reserves briefly exceeded member-bank indebtedness for the first time in nearly two years. On January 28 the Committee

> recognized that the current relative ease was unintended, since it reflected a larger than expected decline in loans and return flow of currency, as well as the relative immobility imposed on the System by the Treasury financing operation. It was believed that operations now should be designed toward restoring approximately the degree of restraint of the late November-early December period. . . .[16]

Accordingly, net free reserves were restored to a level of about minus half a billion dollars (Fig. 3).

The open-market directive remained substantially unchanged, and no other significant policy change occurred, until August 1957. Meanwhile commodity prices continued to edge upward, and interest rates, which had eased slightly during the early months of the year, resumed their advance. In August discount rates were raised from 3% to 3½% at all Reserve Banks, at a time when production was on a plateau just short of its all-time peak (but actually about to slide into a trough!). The reason for the increase—the first since 1933 of as much as ½% at one time—can best be reconstructed from reports of meetings of the Open Market Committee. On July 9

> considerable feeling was expressed that an increase in the degree of pressure was called for, particularly since the Federal Reserve System would have to supply reserves during the remainder of 1957 to take care of seasonal borrowings and Treasury needs. One of the possibilities discussed was that of putting additional reserves into the market through the System account and at the same time increasing the discount rates of the Federal Reserve Banks as a signal that the System felt that credit policy should be tighter than it had been.

---

[16] Reports of meetings of the Open Market Committee during 1957 will be found in *Annual Report of the Board of Governors for 1957*, pp. 33–62.

This proposal, which may be described as an attempt to have your cake and eat it too, resembled the tactic used on a celebrated former occasion in August 1929. But for the moment the Treasury was in the market, and nothing could be done. Three weeks later, on July 30,

> it was observed during the Committee discussion that the discount rates of the Federal Reserve Banks at 3% were already lagging behind the rate structure generally and that if other rates continued to rise the directors of some of the Reserve Banks could be expected to give consideration to raising their discount rates. . . .

And on August 20:

> The increase of one-half percentage point in discount rates generally was regarded as primarily a technical move made at a time when market interest rates were considerably above discount rates.

August proved to be a peak in output, for the production index fell steadily month by month from 145 to a low of 126 in April 1958. Wholesale prices, which had risen month by month for the past year, continued upward for another eight months: but the third postwar recession had arrived nevertheless.

How shall we assess the manner in which the System handled the business expansion which began in the Summer of 1954 and ended in the Summer of 1957? The above review of Reserve policy during these three years certainly suggests that the System acted too slowly, that it let the economy run away—that in fact it had a bear by the tail which it could not control. In 1954–1955, monetary ease was continued too long after recovery was already under way. Reserve officials have frankly admitted that they would do it differently if they had to do it again. Chairman Martin, for example, is on record as follows (February 5, 1957): "If we had the whole period to go through again, I think I would be inclined toward having a little bit more restriction in monetary policy from the latter part of 1954 to date."[17] Similarly the Reserve Bank presidents, in a joint report to Congress, raised the question

> whether the System moved fast enough in exercising restraint in the early and intermediate stages of the boom. Granted that a somewhat

[17] Joint Economic Committee, *January 1957 Economic Report of the President,* Hearings, 85th Cong. 1st Sess., 1957, p. 606. See also similar testimony by Martin, Senate Committee on Finance, *Investigation of the Financial Condition of the United States,* Hearings, 85th Cong. 1st Sess., 1957, pp. 1304–6.

less easy policy in 1954 would have reduced commercial-bank purchases of securities at that time, even the excessive liquidity existing
at the beginning of 1955 might have been absorbed more quickly, and
credit expansion thereby restrained further, had policy been tightened
faster in 1955. . . . During 1955 and 1956, a more restrictive credit
policy might have curtailed the shift from bank investments to loans
and restrained total spending.[18]

Such frank admissions disarm the critic. Yet the record provokes
a number of comments.

(1) As late as June 1955, at a moment when the upward march
of commodity prices was about to be resumed, unemployment was
a factor inhibiting credit restraint. The latent conflict between price-
level stability and full employment was very near the surface. The
System is perhaps not to be blamed for the way it resolved the
dilemma.

(2) The wisdom of frequent small upward changes in the discount rate may be questioned. Over a period of eighteen months
six successive increases were required to go from 1½% to 3%. In
cases like the present where there was no substantial change in the
economic outlook between one increase and the next, the need to
make the second increase implies an error of judgment, i.e., that
the first increase was not large enough. Furthermore, if the claim
is correct that the chief effect of discount rate changes is psychological, an air of greater single-mindedness and determination might
be achieved by increments of ½% or 1% in place of ¼%. As a
consequence of its differences with the Treasury in the days before
the Accord of 1951, the Reserve was forced into an exaggeration
of the virtues of small changes in short-term rates—since small
changes were the most it could hope for—as part of its effort to
recapture control of bank reserves. To my mind the doctrine has
outlived whatever usefulness it may have had.

(3) The boom of 1954–1957 was characterized by large construction and equipment expenditures. Not until late in 1956 does
there seem to have been any difficulty in financing these expenditures. Between mid-1954 and mid-1956, rates for prime commercial
paper rose from 1½% to 3¼%, but yields of Aaa bonds rose only
from just under 3% to 3¼%: the contrast in behavior between

[18] Senate Committee on Finance, *Investigation of the Financial Condition of the United
States*, Joint and Supplemental Comments of the Presidents of the Federal Reserve
Banks, 85th Cong. 2nd Sess., 1958, pp. 44–45.

short- and long-term governments was similar. Evidently the tightening of short-term rates had only limited effect on the bond market during the first two years of the boom: only during the last year of the boom, after mid-1956, did bond yields rise appreciably. This was of course a consequence of the "bills only" policy. Not until late in the boom does the fall in bond prices seem to have been sufficient to discourage financial intermediaries from selling bonds in order to furnish business and mortgage loans, or to postpone plans for corporate and municipal bond issues. Some advantage might have been derived from open-market sales of long-term in place of short-term governments by the System in 1955 and 1956. (At that time the System owned only about $2½ billion with maturities in excess of five years; but under a different policy it would have built up its bond portfolio, which it could have done with advantage early in 1954.)

(4) Did the Treasury influence the Reserve against raising interest rates? Apparently not. It is plain that the System frequently delayed measures of restraint for periods of a few weeks in order to facilitate Treasury refinancing. In the Spring of 1956 the Treasury seems to have objected to discount rates going above 2½% and a somewhat longer delay occurred.[19] But the indications are that on the main issues the Reserve called the tune, and that it could have established higher long-term rates, or higher rates in general, during the early phases of the boom without encountering insuperable objections from the Treasury. Yet if the Reserve should continue to consult the Treasury's convenience in matters of timing, it would make it much easier for the System if the Treasury could arrange its major financing at longer intervals.

(5) During the period under consideration the System had no power to control consumer-installment or residential-mortgage credit. Would such power have been helpful? Certainly the expansion of these two types of credit was very rapid during 1955 and 1956. Nor is it probable that a more restrictive policy in general would have slowed the expansion of consumer credit. Also the automobile industry was one of the earliest to run up against shortages during the revival. The power to set terms for consumer-installment contracts might have helped. On the other hand, higher long-term rates

[19] Testimony of Chairman Martin, Senate Committee on Finance, *Investigation of the Financial Condition of the United States*, Hearings, 85th Cong. 1st Sess., 1957, pp. 1362–63.

of interest, which the System could have induced through open-market policy, would surely have checked the growth of mortgage credit. The usefulness of this type of selective control is therefore more doubtful.

The Recession of 1957–1958

As late as October 22, 1957, the Open Market Committee unanimously reaffirmed its policy directive of March 5 which looked toward "restraining inflationary developments." However, "in renewing the directive without change, the Committee agreed that although general policy was not to be changed appreciably, it should tend on the easier side from where it had been in recent weeks."[20] Business sentiment was now far less optimistic, but the recession was not yet clearly reflected in statistical indicators. To this point the System could scarcely be blamed for hesitating to shift from brakes to accelerator.

By the time the Committee held its next meeting, November 12, 1957, data for October confirmed the slight declines already registered in September. In the Committee's view, "there no longer was much doubt that at least a mild downturn in business activity was under way, and there was widespread belief that it would probably continue well into 1958." By a majority the Committee changed the policy directive to "fostering sustainable growth in the economy without inflation, by moderating the pressures on bank reserves." Governor Robertson still thought pressure against inflation should be maintained, and voted against the change.

At its meeting on December 17, 1957, the Committee learned that November production (1947–1949 = 100) was down to 139 from 145 in August. The decline in plant and equipment expenditures, the liquidation of business inventories, and unemployment at the highest rate since late 1954, pointed to a "general recession" and "a faster and a greater downward adjustment than had been indicated earlier." A fresh policy directive now asked for "cushioning adjustments and mitigating recessionary tendencies in the economy."

[20] On the basis of this phraseology Chairman Martin later claimed that "the meeting of October 22 clearly tended toward easier money," despite the renewal of the directive without change, i.e., that the reversal of monetary policy began in October rather than in November. See Senate Committee on Finance, *Investigation of the Financial Condition of the United States*, Hearings, 85th Cong. 2nd Sess., pp. 1916–17.

The System was rather slow in putting the new policy into effect, perhaps because each succeeding month through March 1958 showed higher wholesale prices. The discount rate had been reduced to 3% in November, but the next cut did not come until January, and it fell as low as 1¾% only in April. Nor did the Open Market Committee speak with a single voice: Governor Robertson voted against the January rate reductions on the ground that "the country having passed only recently through a period of strong inflationary pressures which resulted in a substantial increase in wholesale and consumer prices from which there had as yet been no general downward readjustment, a move to ease too rapidly might place a floor under existing price levels."[21] Perhaps because of divided opinion, the open-market account reacted slowly. Funds were supplied to the market over the year end, making free reserves positive in January, but the latter did not reach the half billion mark until March. Had the System taken its December directive seriously, it surely might have acted faster.

On March 4, 1958, "indications of deepening recession" induced the Open Market Committee to change the December objective of "cushioning adjustments and mitigating recessionary tendencies" to "contributing further by monetary ease to resumption of stable growth of the economy." By now Governor Robertson, too, was convinced.

It later turned out that a rather rapid recovery was to set in starting in April; in fact the first quarter of 1958 represents the low point of the recession. Changes in product and income between the peak in the third quarter of 1957 and the trough two quarters later are summarized in Table 4. Although short-lived—the decline lasted only two quarters instead of four—the recession was sharper than that of 1953–1954. GNP fell by $15 billion (compared with $10 billion: see Table 2) and consumer expenditures actually fell (no such decline occurred in 1953–1954). The chief components of the drop in GNP were a large cut in equipment expenditures and a violent swing from accumulation to decumulation of inventories. The decline in fixed investment might have been expected, in view of the character of the preceding expansion: the large cut in

[21] Reports of meetings of the Open Market Committee during 1958 will be found in the *Annual Report of the Board of Governors for 1958*, pp. 32–71. The January 21 meeting of the Board of Governors, at which rates were lowered to 2¾%, is reported on pp. 73–75.

TABLE 4

CHANGES IN INCOME AND PRODUCT FROM PEAK TO TROUGH, 1957–1958[a]
$ billion; seasonally adjusted quarterly data at annual rates

Components of income and product	1957 3rd quarter	1958 1st quarter	Change
Consumer expenditures	288.7	287.4	−1.3
Residential construction	17.0	17.1	.1
Other construction	19.3	18.2	−1.1
Equipment	28.9	24.1	−4.8
Inventory change	2.5	−5.5	−8.0
Net exports	5.1	1.7	−3.4
Federal purchases	50.0	50.6	.6
State and local purchases	36.9	39.2	2.3
Gross national product	448.3	432.9	−15.4
Capital consumption, etc.[b]	39.0	38.7	−.3
Business taxes less subsidies	37.6	37.4	−.2
Social security taxes	14.7	14.6	−.1
Compensation of employees[c]	243.4	237.3	−6.1
Proprietors' income	45.2	45.9	.7
Rent and interest (exc. govt.)	25.8	26.4	.6
Corporate profits before tax	42.5	32.5	−10.0
Gross national income	448.3	432.9	−15.4
Consumer expenditures	288.7	287.4	−1.3
Personal taxes	43.0	41.7	−1.3
Personal saving	24.0	23.9	−.1
Personal outgo	355.6	353.1	−2.5
Compensation of employees[c]	243.4	237.3	−6.1
Proprietors' income	45.2	45.9	.7
Dividends	12.9	12.6	−.3
Rent and interest (inc. govt.)	32.1	32.5	.4
Transfer payments	22.0	24.6	2.6
Personal income	355.6	353.1	−2.5

[a] Data are from *Survey of Current Business*, July 1962. Rounding may prevent agreement between detail and totals.
[b] Capital consumption allowances plus statistical discrepancy plus excess wage accruals plus business transfers.
[c] After social security contributions but before personal taxes.

inventories was more surprising, especially in view of the continued firmness of commodity prices. As on former occasions, the drop in personal income was much smaller than in GNP: dividends fell far less than corporate profits, and transfer payments actually increased.

Both federal and state and local purchases continued to rise, and the net influence of government was strongly antideflationary (as in Table 4, figures are seasonally adjusted annual rates):

Change from peak to trough in:	$ billion
Federal purchases	0.6
State and local purchases	2.3
Transfer payments (govt. only)	2.6
Government interest	—0.2
Total change, expenditures	5.3
Corporate income taxes	—4.9
Business taxes less subsidies	—0.2
Social security taxes	—0.1
Personal taxes	—1.3
Total change, receipts	—6.5

From peak to trough the swing in the fiscal picture was thus almost $12 billion from surplus toward deficit (annual rate, including state and local units). By contrast, from the 1953 peak to the 1954 trough the swing was a mere $1 billion. On the former occasion a drastic decline in federal purchases was occasioned by the armistice in Korea: on the present occasion federal purchases scarcely changed. Other changes—the increase in state and local purchases and in transfer payments, and the decline in corporate and personal taxes—were about the same as on the former occasion. To be sure, the swing in the fiscal picture was not entirely the consequence of the so-called automatic stabilizers, for the increased expenditures partly reflected highway contracts and liberalization of the Social Security Act effective January 1, 1958. From our viewpoint these measures were of course fortuitous.

Certainly the large change in the fiscal picture, in no way due to measures taken to combat the recession, must have done much to stem the decline in business. There now followed other fiscal measures taken in response to the recession, none of which had any impact until recovery had already begun in April 1958: a speed-up of expenditures in the housing and highway areas and a temporary unemployment compensation bill (enacted June 4). Taxes on freight transportation were repealed as of August 1.[22] Unfortunately these measures of a discretionary nature, deliberately taken against the recession, came late and contributed to a further swing in the fiscal situation such that by the end of the year a sizable federal deficit had emerged. Even so, actual expenditures lagged well behind larger contract authorizations for defense, following the launching by the Russians of the first sputnik. By late 1958 the fiscal situation began to look quite inflationary, yet production was barely back to 1957 levels and unemployment remained around 7% of the labor force.

The Abortive Recovery, 1958–1960

By June 17, 1958, the Open Market Committee had decided that the recession was "bottoming out," but some differences of opinion within the Committee become apparent from the record. We read that one minority desired a further release of reserves through reduction of reserve requirements, while a second minority felt that the market was now dangerously liquid and feared a speculative rise in government securities. In fact, beginning in late June, governments moved down rather than up, and in two telephone conferences July 18 the Open Market Committee authorized unlimited intervention to deal with a "disorderly market." The sharp reversal of sentiment in the bond market was due to a sudden conviction that business revival was on the way—and with it higher interest rates. Some traders burnt their fingers through carrying governments on borrowed money. The incident was later used as a stick with which to beat the Federal Reserve and the Treasury, but it is hard to see what harm it did or to feel that emergency purchases in the amount of more than $1 billion by the Reserve really were necessary.

The market had correctly anticipated Reserve policy, which was to be reversed within a few weeks. On August 15, 1958, the Board approved a rate increase by the San Francisco Bank from 1¾% to 2%, and on August 19 the Open Market Committee changed its basic objective from "contributing further by monetary ease to resumption of stable growth" (adopted March 4) to "fostering conditions in the money market conducive to balanced economic recovery." That the new language should be intended to imply less

[22] Wilfred Lewis, Jr., *Federal Fiscal Policy in the Postwar Recessions* (Washington, D.C.: Brookings Institution, 1962), Ch. VI.

ease than the old may seem odd, but such was the case. The expressed purpose of the Committee now was to allow seasonal demands for cash to reduce or eliminate free reserves. Easy money was to be brought to an end. As a reason the Committee cites the inflationary implications of the growing federal deficit and "the emergence of an inflationary psychology in the stock market and other financial markets that could easily spill over into commodity and real estate markets." The System evidently was determined not to repeat the much-criticized tardiness with which it tightened money in 1955 and 1956. In fact net free reserves fell to less than $100 million in September and by December were eliminated completely. In late October and early November discount rates were raised to 2½%.

It is evident that System officials were not entirely happy with these decisions. The policy dilemma seems first to have been discussed explicitly at the meeting of the Open Market Committee November 10, 1958. Here it was reported that productivity increases "were being reflected in corporate profits and not in lowered industrial prices," and complaint was made of "persistent upward pressures on industrial prices notwithstanding the existence of unused resources." However, the Committee seems to have had no difficulty in resolving the dilemma on the side of restraint, although the existing policy directive was left unchanged for the time being. The Committee expressed disbelief "that such restraint would retard sound recovery and growth in the economy," but its confidence may have been misplaced.

On December 16, 1958, another turn was given to the screw. The Committee deleted the reference to "recovery" and substituted "sustainable economic growth and stability" as its objective. By this alteration further restraint was implied, the argument being that too rapid an advance might not be sustainable. President Hayes of the New York Bank, who had gone along up to this point, voted against the change, arguing that further restraint was premature.

During 1959 production reached and exceeded 1957 levels—and the rise in interest rates was pushed further. In March, at the end of May, and again in September, successive ½% increases in discount rates lifted their level from 2½% to 4%; money rates rose to heights not seen since 1930. In the minds of Reserve officials justification for this restraint was furnished by the edging up of commodity prices, the rapid rise of output and the inflationary implications of the continued federal deficit (Fig. 3). Although substantial amounts of gold had been lost since early 1958, the adverse balance of payments does not yet appear as a significant factor in policy making.

The Open Market Committee's directive remained unchanged until May 26, 1959, when the objective of "fostering conditions in the money market conducive to sustainable economic growth and stability" was altered to "restraining inflationary credit expansion in order to foster sustainable economic growth and expanding employment opportunities."[23] Governor Mills voted against this further restriction, although he went along two days later in approving the rise in discount rates to 3½%. The sudden introduction at this juncture of a reference to expanding employment opportunities is puzzling; perhaps it was a way of recognizing the continued high level of unemployment and the System's concern therefor (the seasonally adjusted percentage did not fall below 5 until May). As the new policy was implemented, free reserves moved from zero at the beginning of the year to minus $300 million in May and minus $500 million in June and later months.

The published record of the Open Market Committee fails to recognize the rapid swing of the federal budget toward surplus during the second half of 1959. But the practical cessation of growth in the money stock after midyear and the sharp rise in interest rates led some members of the Committee to feel that the restriction was excessive. Moreover it was far from clear how the steel strike which began in July should be interpreted, or whether a settlement would lead to increased inflationary pressures. In November, with Treasury bill rates approaching 5%, Governor Mills proposed a revised directive calling for diminished restraint, but no one joined him.

It is evident from the record of the Open Market Committee that between November 1959 and March 1960 a gradual shift in sentiment occurred toward lessened restraint.[24] The settlement of the steel strike in January failed to provoke the upsurge that had been feared. In the early months of 1960 industrial production and the money stock were no higher than a year previously, and the stock market was weak. On March 1, in a move toward monetary ease, the

[23] Reports of meetings of the Open Market Committee during 1959 will be found in *Annual Report of the Board of Governors for 1959*, pp. 31–65.
[24] For the record of policy actions during 1960, see *Annual Report of the Board of Governors for 1960*, pp. 34–88. See also Joint Economic Committee, *Review of Annual Report of the Federal Reserve System for the Year 1960*, Hearings, 87th Cong. 1st Sess., 1961, especially pp. 147–61.

objective of "restraining inflationary credit expansion in order to foster sustainable economic growth and expanding employment opportunities" was changed to "fostering sustainable growth in economic activity and employment while guarding against excessive credit expansion." Net free reserves became steadily less negative and exceeded zero by early summer as the new policy went into effect.

The cyclical peak occurred in May 1960. The expansion is reviewed in Table 5 and is seen to be typical, except for the very large swing in inventories—larger than in either of the two preceding, and much longer upswings. Lasting but 25 months, and leaving the economy operating well below capacity, the expansion of 1958–1960 has been called "abortive," and the peak "submerged." This characterization is not unfair.

The federal deficit, which gradually disappeared during 1959 (mainly through the operation of built-in stabilizers), was suddenly converted into a surplus of $6 billion (national income basis, seasonally adjusted annual rate) in the first quarter of 1960 (Fig. 3). This was the effect partly of higher OASI and gas taxes which came into force January 1, 1960, and partly of a slowdown in expenditure prompted by an economy wave in reaction to what had undoubtedly

TABLE 5

CHANGES IN NATIONAL PRODUCT FROM TROUGH TO PEAK, 1958–1960[a]
$ billion; seasonally adjusted quarterly data at annual rates

Components of national product	1958 1st quarter	1960 2nd quarter	Change
Consumer expenditures	287.4	329.9	42.5
Residential construction	17.1	21.2	4.1
Other construction	18.2	19.5	1.3
Equipment	24.1	28.4	4.3
Inventory change	−5.5	4.4	9.9
Net exports	1.7	2.4	.7
Federal purchases	50.6	53.1	2.5
State and local purchases	39.2	45.9	6.7
Gross national product	432.9	504.8	71.9

[a] Data are from *Survey of Current Business*, July 1962. Rounding may prevent agreement between detail and totals.

been an unnecessarily large deficit for the fiscal year 1959.[25] Fiscal restriction was accompanied by tight money, as noted above; the expansion might have been able to survive one or the other, but not both.

The Joint Committee versus Chairman Martin

During 1959 and 1960 the Democratic majority of the Joint Economic Committee, under the leadership of Senator Douglas and Representatives Patman and Reuss, made a concerted effort to persuade Chairman Martin to agree to abandon both "bills only" and the practice of reducing reserve requirements as a means of expanding the money supply.[26] To quote from the Committee's 1960 Report:

> In summary, our major recommendations are [that] the Federal Reserve should:
> (a) abandon its discredited "bills only" policy,
> (b) agree to build up its portfolio of long-term bonds, and
> (c) use open-market operations rather than lowering [sic!] reserve requirements as the means of bringing about the secular expansion of credit which the Federal Reserve and the banks [sic!] desire.[27]

By and large these recommendations have the approval of economists. Since Martin was totally unimpressed and the Committee got nowhere, the episode affords an interesting illustration of the difficulty a Congressional committee faces if it tries to make policy, even in the broadest sense, in this area. Ironically, a year later Martin had to yield to the balance of payments crisis what he would not yield to the Committee, when the Reserve did in fact partially (and it would seem unwillingly) abandon "bills only."

Clearly, provision for the secular growth of the money supply can be made either by open-market purchases or by a reduction of reserve requirements. In the former case part of the addition to the earning assets of the banking system will accrue to the Reserve Banks, part to the commercial banks; in the latter case all of the

---

[25] Lewis, Ch. VII.

[26] See, especially, Joint Economic Committee, *Employment, Growth and Price Levels,* Hearings, 86th Cong. 1st Sess., 1959, pp. 1241–1332, 1455–1500; same, *January 1960 Economic Report,* Hearings, 86th Cong. 2nd Sess., 1960, pp. 171–74, 185–88; same, *1960 Joint Economic Report,* S.R. 1152, 86th Cong. 2nd Sess., 1960; same, *January 1961 Economic Report,* Hearings, 87th Cong. 1st Sess., 1961, pp. 478, 487–88. See also House Committee on Banking and Currency, Subcommittee No. 2, *Member Bank Reserve Requirements,* Hearings on H.R. 5237, 86th Cong. 1st Sess., 1959, pp. 283–319.

[27] *1960 Joint Economic Report,* p. 16.

additional assets will be held by the commercial banks. The Committee could not see why the Reserve System should sacrifice its share, or give up earnings that it might otherwise eventually have the opportunity of turning over to the Treasury.

The flavor of the controversy may be gleaned from the following:

REPRESENTATIVE REUSS: . . . let us just take a situation where, for good and sufficient reasons, the Federal Reserve determines that it wants to increase bank reserves by $1 billion, picking that figure out of the air. Whether it does that by reducing bank reserve requirements in an amount equal to $1 billion of new reserves or whether it does it by purchasing $1 billion worth of U.S. securities is equal, from the standpoint of monetary policy, is it not?

. . . .

MR. MARTIN: In the ultimate effect on the reserves, yes.

. . . .

REPRESENTATIVE REUSS: You would not call a fellow an engineer of inflation or a funny-money fellow or a printing-press money man if, where you were prepared to increase the total money supply $1 billion by the lowering of bank reserve requirements, he, while agreeing that the total money supply ought to be increased to the very nickel, as you suggested, and not one nickel more, nevertheless suggested doing it by purchase of U.S. securities? There is no printing press involved there, is there?

MR. MARTIN: No. No printing press except in the atmosphere in which you are operating . . . what we are dealing with at the moment is . . . a very serious inflation atmosphere. . . .

A palpable red herring, this!

REPRESENTATIVE REUSS: I know all that, and I do not yield to you, Mr. Chairman, in my detestation of inflation.

MR. MARTIN: I know you do not.

REPRESENTATIVE REUSS: . . . I take it that you and I are agreed that a billion dollars is a billion dollars, and that one method of adding it to the money supply is no more inflationary and no less inflationary than adding it by another method. Is that correct?

MR. MARTIN: I think in mathematical terms, yes, but I want to reemphasize that the flexibility of monetary policy [sic!] revolves around how it is interpreted as well as what actually is achieved by it . . . you do not think that your method is inflationary, and I think that under present conditions it would be.

REPRESENTATIVE REUSS: That is right; and all I ask is that you give me some reasons. . . .[28]

[28] Joint Economic Committee, *Employment, Growth and Price Levels,* Hearings, 86th Cong. 1st Sess., 1959, pp. 1242–43.

But no reasons were forthcoming.

Senator Douglas was not much more successful:

> SENATOR DOUGLAS: . . . Why is it inflationary to increase the lend-
> ing capacity of banks through open-market operations, but not inflation-
> ary to increase the lending capacity of banks by lowering reserve
> ratios? . . .
>
> MR. MARTIN: Senator, I can only answer that by saying that both will
> have the same end result.
>
> . . . .
>
> SENATOR DOUGLAS: . . . If the two methods give the same ultimate
> result, which you admit, but one of them in the process yields a gain
> to the Federal Reserve and to the government of an average of $500 mil-
> lion a year, and added interest earnings which accumulate as additional
> amounts, why not take the method which, giving the same ultimate
> result, yields large capital gains and large increases in net revenue to
> the government?
>
> MR. MARTIN: Because, Senator, we are not dealing with ultimate re-
> sults. We are not dealing with a mathematical equation that comes out
> at a certain point. We are dealing with a flow of money of a continuous
> nature. It just is not, in my judgment, an easy matter, nor is it correct
> to say that you can regulate that flow just as effectively by something
> that will come out with an end result in terms of benefit to the Treasury
> or benefit to the banks.
>
> SENATOR DOUGLAS: . . . If both methods give the same ultimate re-
> sults so far as expansion of credit is concerned, but one yields capital
> gains to the government probably of around $500 million a year, on the
> average, and cumulative interest, why not adopt the open-market sys-
> tem? What are its disadvantages?
>
> MR. MARTIN: The disadvantages are in the current flow of money
> and credit. . . .

Chairman Martin later submitted a statement for the record, the
relevant parts of which read as follows:

> For the most effective performance of its statutory duties, it is es-
> sential that the Federal Reserve System should not be influenced by
> extraneous considerations having to do with the profits that result from
> its operations as long as the public interest benefits. One fundamental
> factor that denotes the special characteristics of the Federal Reserve
> Banks is that their residual profits ultimately flow to the account of the
> Treasury.
>
> It follows from this position that member-bank reserve requirements
> should not be used as a means to influence Treasury revenues. . . .
>
> These fundamental propositions should not be read to imply in any
> sense whatever that the private banks should not carry their fair propor-

tion of the nation's expenses. The Congress has the power to tax and if it should ever feel that commercial-bank profits from the performance of their operations are excessive, it can preempt a larger share of those profits to the public Treasury through increased taxes on all commercial banks, nonmembers as well as members. This would be preferable to a request or directive to the Federal Reserve System to so operate its policy instruments as to affect member-bank earnings, actual or potential, for any reason other than the requirements of a sound monetary policy.[29]

Martin's reference to the desirability of banks carrying "their fair proportion of the nation's expenses" suggests that he does not understand the essential nature of the point at issue. The manufacture of means of payment is a profitable activity; and if the money stock needs to expand with the size of the economy, the question is, who gets the resulting profits? Perhaps banks should be specially taxed in order to recapture these profits. Certain it is that the successive reductions in reserve requirements during Martin's chairmanship have handed these profits to the banks. This is one issue on which Representative Patman's sense of outrage is understandable.

A final attempt to pin Chairman Martin down, and his successful evasion of the issue, may be quoted:

> REPRESENTATIVE REUSS: . . . If the open-market method by and large is the method that is good for the taxpayers, because it results in the Federal Reserve getting the income from those bonds which is then channeled through the Treasury, if that is true of open-market purchases, should we not then adopt a working principle of using open-market purchases as the royal road in this day and age [to furnish needed increments in the money stock] except where there are countervailing considerations? . . .
>
> MR. MARTIN: . . . Now, you can carry this thing to the extreme of using the Federal Reserve to make money for the taxpayer and you will gradually work yourself into a position where . . . you are defeating the general public interest, and as a minimum are certainly undermining our private enterprise system. I am not saying we are in any danger of that in the foreseeable future, but the ultimate is that you will have the entire banking system being run to make profits for the government and run by the government.[30]

[29] *Ibid.*, pp. 1328–29, 1459–61. Senator Douglas' "$500 million" was the increment in Federal Reserve credit corresponding (with given reserve requirements) to an assumed average annual increase in member-bank credit of $3 billion.

[30] Joint Economic Committee, *January 1960 Economic Report*, Hearings, 86th Cong. 2nd Sess., 1960, p. 187.

Admittedly this is not Martin at his best; but his reluctance to "make money for the taxpayer" lends color to Patman's unlikely charge that the Federal Reserve has come to show "more and more solicitude for the profits of the vested interests."[31] Perhaps the critics would have done better to claim that the banks are subsidized by the public, especially since they are prohibited from paying interest on demand deposits.

Martin's desire for lower reserve requirements apparently stems from his view that banks should have more capital, and that larger earnings will encourage them to increase equity investment in banking, although this viewpoint fails to come out in his oral testimony. I return to the question of optimum reserve requirements in Chapter 13.

The Recession of 1960–1961

The System responded with remarkable promptness to the renewed weakening of business activity that began in May 1960. On May 24 the Open Market Committee deleted its reference to "guarding against excessive credit expansion" and substituted the aim of "providing reserves needed for moderate bank credit expansion." On June 2 the Board of Governors approved discount rate reductions from 4% to 3½%. May was the peak month according to National Bureau chronology—which of course could not be known at the time; but durable goods output was already declining and the Treasury surplus continued to mount (Fig. 3). In August, on the basis of business hesitancy rather than any actually observed decline, discount rates were reduced from 3½% to 3%, and the open-market directive was changed by majority vote of the Committee to "encouraging monetary expansion for the purpose of fostering sustainable growth in economic activity and employment." Treasury bill rates fell to a 2¼–2½% level and net free reserves became positive, reaching $400 million in September.

Gold outflow resumed in July 1960, and the balance of payments now became a factor in Reserve policy—for the first time since the 1930's. This was recognized October 25 when the Open Market Committee added the phrase "while taking into consideration current international developments" to its directive. The gold outflow did not reflect any further deterioration in the United States balance of pay-

[31] House Committee Hearings on H.R. 5237, p. 296.

ments but rather the reduction of money rates in New York in comparison with rates in European centers. The Board of Governors by actions in August and October supplied about $2 billion of additional bank reserves through amendments to Regulation D: these allowed banks to count all vault cash as reserve (under legislation passed in 1959) and reduced reserve requirements for banks in central reserve cities to the level for banks in reserve cities—16½% (see Appendix III).

The System had paid slight attention to the gold losses of 1958 and 1959, but the run up in the London gold price in October 1960 and the half-billion dollar gold loss in November seem to have provoked extended discussion in the Open Market Committee. Interest rates—and particularly short-term interest rates—might have little or no immediate bearing upon the size of the basic payments deficit, but they might be expected to have a rather direct influence upon the manner in which that deficit was financed, whether by gold export or by the import of short-term capital. Easy money, desirable as a means of stemming the incipient recession, would tend to turn the balance of short-term lending against the United States and encourage the outflow of gold. These considerations were canvassed at the December 1960 and January 1961 meetings of the Committee, and the record for January 24 recognizes for the first time that a "dilemma" for monetary policy had come to exist.[32] In the interests of business recovery the Committee would attempt to maintain free reserves around $500 million; but it would also, with a view to keeping foreign short money here, seek to prevent the Treasury bill rate from falling during the present decline in business below a level of about 2¼% (in the 1958 recession it had been allowed to fall below 1%).

It was obvious that this potentially contradictory policy would be facilitated if "bills only" were abandoned. Were the System to supply reserves to the banks through the purchase of medium- and long-term securities, instead of Treasury bills, downward pressure on the bill rate would be avoided. More generally, the sale of short-term and the purchase of long-term securities could alter the relative supply of different maturities available in the market and might, for a time at least, be expected to tilt the yield curve, raising it at the short

[32] The record of the Open Market Committee for 1961 will be found in *Annual Report of the Board of Governors for 1961*, pp. 33–99.

end and lowering it at the long. The whole idea of course rested upon the assumption that short rates have more influence than long upon the international balance of short-term lending; and that long rates have at least as much influence as short upon the level of business activity. Implying a kind of reverse arbitrage in the domestic money market, it was thought that the policy might allow the United States to finance its balance of payments deficit by importing short-term capital instead of by selling gold: but it could scarcely remove the deficit itself.

In accordance with this thinking the Open Market Committee on February 7, 1961, authorized the New York Bank

> to acquire for the System Open Market Account intermediate- and/or longer-term U.S. government securities having maturities up to ten years, or to change the holdings of such maturities, in an amount not to exceed $500 million.

While this meant a reversal of the eight-year-old "bills only" policy, it was to be a reversal on a rather modest scale: less than 2% of the portfolio might be placed in maturities that were not to exceed 10 years. Perhaps appropriately, in view of its modesty, the new policy came to be known as Operation Nudge. The Committee preserved a suitably experimental attitude and hoped that "the procedure might throw some light on the possibility of influencing longer-term rates while maintaining the short-term rate level."

Governor Robertson voted against the new policy. He claimed that "in deviating from its established policies the Committee was in effect asserting, without reason, that it had made a critically incorrect judgment [in adopting "bills only"] eight years ago and had pursued incorrect operating practices since." He felt the Committee was running a serious risk of "undermining domestic and foreign confidence in the System's integrity and judgment." These harsh words jibe oddly with Robertson's simultaneous desire for a greater degree of ease, on the curious ground that, as a result of the ensuing upward movement of the economy, "interest rates would rise and the current outflow of capital . . . would be reversed." On March 7, when the Committee reaffirmed the abandonment of "bills only," Governor Robertson's minority position was also embraced by President Allen of the Chicago Bank, a new member of the Committee.

On March 28, 1961, the fact was not yet clear that business activity had turned up, but the gold outflow had ceased for the time being. Governor Robertson was now joined by Governor Balderston and President Swan of the San Francisco Bank in desiring an easier policy, but the majority decided not to modify the existing directive or its implementation. At this meeting the Committee lifted the restriction on the purchase of bonds to those with a maturity of 10 years or less, giving the manager of the account complete freedom as to maturity within his existing $500 million limitation on medium- and long-term purchases.

The recession of 1960–1961 was extremely mild (Table 6). At annual rates from the peak quarter to the trough, GNP fell by $4 billion (compared with $15 billion in 1957–1958 and $10 billion in 1953–1954). Monthly industrial production fell by 7%. The change in the fiscal situation from peak to trough—from the second quarter of 1960 to the first quarter of 1961—was as follows (seasonally adjusted annual rates):

Change from peak to trough in:	$ billion
Federal purchases	2.3
State and local purchases	3.5
Transfer payments (govt. only)	3.6
Government interest	—0.2
Total change, expenditures	9.2
Corporate income taxes	— 3.5
Business taxes less subsidies	—0.7
Social security taxes	0.5
Personal taxes	—0.9
Total change, receipts	—4.6

At nearly $14 billion the swing in combined governmental budgets was thus even larger than the similar shift toward deficit that occurred in 1957–1958. In view of the much slighter easing of the credit situation in 1960–1961, the mildness of the fourth postwar recession evidently owed much to this larger change in the fiscal picture. About two-thirds of the fiscal shift was due to automatic stabilizers and the remainder to increased governmental purchases of goods and services. Of the increase in federal purchases, most went for defense; the increase in state and local purchases mainly

Table 6

CHANGES IN INCOME AND PRODUCT FROM PEAK TO TROUGH, 1960–1961[a]
$ billion; seasonally adjusted quarterly data at annual rates

Components of income and product	1960 2nd quarter	1961 1st quarter	Change
Consumer expenditures	329.9	330.5	.6
Residential construction	21.2	19.0	−2.2
Other construction	19.5	20.3	.8
Equipment	28.4	24.4	−4.0
Inventory change	4.4	−3.6	−8.0
Net exports	2.4	5.3	2.9
Federal purchases	53.1	55.4	2.3
State and local purchases	45.9	49.4	3.5
Gross national product	504.8	500.8	−4.0
Capital consumption, etc.[b]	41.0	43.1	2.1
Business taxes less subsidies	46.6	45.9	−.7
Social security taxes	20.6	21.1	.5
Compensation of employees[c]	274.0	273.0	−1.0
Proprietors' income	46.9	46.5	−.4
Rent and interest (exc. govt.)	29.6	31.1	1.5
Corporate profits before tax	46.2	40.1	−6.1
Gross national income	504.8	500.8	−4.0
Consumer expenditures	329.9	330.5	.6
Personal taxes	51.9	51.0	−.9
Personal saving	19.7	23.8	4.1
Personal outgo	401.4	405.4	4.0
Compensation of employees[c]	274.0	273.0	−1.0
Proprietors' income	46.9	46.5	−.4
Dividends	14.2	14.7	.5
Rent and interest (inc. govt.)	37.4	38.7	1.3
Transfer payments	28.9	32.5	3.6
Personal income	401.4	405.4	4.0

[a] Data are from *Survey of Current Business*, July 1962. Rounding may prevent agreement between detail and totals.
[b] Capital consumption allowances plus statistical discrepancy plus excess wage accruals plus business transfers.
[c] After social security contributions but before personal taxes.

reflected their steady upward trend, amounting recently to about $3 billion a year.

Yet if the recession was mild, this may also be partly explained by the fact that it followed an abortive recovery. In 1960 unemployment scarcely fell below 5% and the peak of that year can fairly be described as "submerged."

Recovery, 1961–1963

Discretionary fiscal measures to promote recovery were practically confined to a special National Service Life Insurance dividend in March 1961 and extended unemployment compensation payments beginning in April under legislation enacted March 24.[33] Meanwhile the Open Market Committee evidently felt it had done what it could to ease monetary policy and from March to October, as business revival proceeded, its intention was to maintain the general credit situation unchanged: its success is shown by the steadiness of the Treasury bill rate and of the level of free reserves. Beginning in August, and following a rise to 7% in the British bank rate and the announcement in Washington of increased defense expenditures on account of the Berlin crisis, a minority of the Committee under Governor Mills' leadership pressed for a gradual tightening of the market. At the October 24 meeting the Committee yielded to the extent of saying that, although a continuation of existing monetary policy "would be appropriate from the standpoint of domestic conditions," nevertheless "doubts arising in the conduct of open-market operations" should henceforth be resolved "on the side of less ease." Certainly the Treasury bill rate rose in November and December from below 2½% toward 2¾% (discount rates were still 3%). On November 14 Governor Mills was joined by President Hayes of the New York Bank in pressing for a higher Treasury bill rate as a means of improving the balance of payments.

On December 19, 1961, a majority of the Committee still rated "fuller utilization of the economy's resources" as its main concern, but called for "a somewhat slower rate of increase in total reserves than during recent months." This satisfied President Hayes, but Governor Mills continued to call for greater restraint, while Governors King and Mitchell dissented on the ground that the time had not yet arrived for moving toward less ease.

The December 19 meeting of the Committee was notable for its action in rescinding, by a majority, the three policy statements adopted eight years previously, in 1953, to implement the "bills only" doctrine. This curious episode deserves comment.

[33] Lewis, Ch. VII.

The "bills only" resolutions of 1953 (1) rejected support of "any pattern of prices and yields" for governments; (2) called for open-market operations to "be confined to short-term securities (except in correction of disorderly markets)"; and (3) required that such operations "be entered into solely for the purpose of providing or absorbing reserves" and not "for the purpose of altering the maturity pattern of the System's portfolio."[34] These resolutions, modified (however ineffectively) since February 1961 by Operation Nudge, had since February been subject to review by an ad hoc subcommittee of the Open Market Committee. Formal rescinding of the resolutions at the December meeting may have resulted from failure to agree upon a revised text: we do not know. All that can be reported is that in the published record three reasons, none of them convincing, are given for repeal: (1) Greater latitude in future operations might be required than had been the case since 1953. (But latitude had been obtained—and not used—for Operation Nudge.) (2) A major purpose of "bills only" had been to repudiate bond pegging, a danger now no longer significant. (3) More detailed guidance had been needed when the Open Market Committee met but four times a year than was now the case with more frequent meetings. The minutes conclude lamely:

> The decision to discontinue the statements of operating policies related solely to the desirability of continuing to have such statements; it was not a decision to change the basic position of the System in relation to the Treasury or the market. The action was taken with the recognition that the bulk of open market operations would, in the nature of the case, continue to be in short-term securities; with the understanding that decisions about operations in securities of all maturities would continue to be made by the Committee in light of prevailing circumstances; and with the understanding that the Committee had no intention of pegging government security prices, or of creating artificial market conditions at times of new security offerings by the Treasury.

The reference to pegging, more than a decade after the Accord, suggests an almost obsessive fear of Treasury pressure.

The most that can be said for Federal Reserve policy during 1961 is that the System succeeded in maintaining a substantial volume of free reserves even though it did not allow money to become really cheap, and that it helped to discourage gold exports without com-

[34] See above, pp. 179–187.

pletely preventing business recovery. As for Operation Nudge, it was never put to the test. Figures for a year before, just before, and a year after the "new policy" of February 7, 1961, are shown in Table 7.

TABLE 7

MATURITY DISTRIBUTION OF SYSTEM HOLDINGS OF U.S. GOVERNMENT SECURITIES, 1960–1962
$ billion

Maturing	End of month		
	Jan. 1960	Jan. 1961	Jan. 1962
Within 90 days	6.7	5.4	6.9
91 days to 1 year	10.7	9.1	10.4
1 to 5 years	6.5	10.7	8.8
5 to 10 years	.7	1.2	2.2
Over 10 years	.8	.3	.3
	25.5	26.6	28.5

Source: *Federal Reserve Bulletin.*

Evidently the shift in the maturity distribution during the year following the change in the directive was inappreciable and total holdings of securities maturing in excess of one year actually declined. The Treasury meanwhile was engaged in lengthening the debt: during 1961 substantial amounts of long-term bonds were offered in exchange for maturing debt, and securities in the hands of the public with more than ten years to run rose by about $2 billion. Between January 1961 and January 1962 the market yield of 3-month Treasury bills rose from 2.24% to 2.72%, i.e., by 48 basis points; over the same interval the yield on long-term Treasury bonds also rose—from 3.89% to 4.08%, i.e., by 19 basis points. The yield curve was raised, but it can scarcely be claimed that it was tilted in the desired direction.

In view of repeated doubts expressed by members of the Open Market Committee, the half-hearted manner in which the experiment was adumbrated, and the large volume of transactions that would have been needed merely to offset debt lengthening by the Treasury, it is perhaps not surprising that Operation Nudge was stillborn. The episode throws no light upon the possibility of tilting the yield curve by a different open-market policy—or by large-scale Treasury "unfunding."[35]

In 1962 the System became increasingly concerned with foreign operations—as it had not been since the early 1930's. Apparently the Treasury had started in March 1961 to acquire a mass of maneuver in the shape of foreign currencies purchased through the Stabilization Fund, but the resources of the latter were limited and it seemed desirable for the System to supplement them by purchases on its own account.[36] Accordingly, at its meeting January 23, 1962, the Open Market Committee adopted a resolution "favoring in principle the initiation on an experimental basis of a program of System foreign currency operations," and calling upon the System to explore with the Treasury "needed guidelines for actual operations, drawing on the experience of the Treasury Stabilization Fund" and to make plans for working relations with the Treasury.[37] The Committee adopted the resolution over the negative votes of Governors Mitchell and Robertson. Governor Mitchell wanted more discussion before making such an innovation; Governor Robertson doubted the legality of regular foreign operations by the System, pointed out that swap transactions could not increase net U.S. monetary reserves, and felt that in any case exchange stabilization should be left to the Treasury.

The new policy and subsequent foreign exchange operations by the System for its own account (and not merely as agent of the Treasury) obviously were inspired by Robert V. Roosa, formerly vice-president of the New York Reserve Bank, who had become Undersecretary of the Treasury for Monetary Affairs; they form a tribute to the close cooperation between the System and the Treasury at this period.

At successive meetings of the Open Market Committee during the early months of 1962 the impossibility, in view of the foreign situation, of easing credit as much as the domestic situation required be-

[35] That a relatively large operation would be required appreciably to tilt the yield curve seems clear. For example, in the refinancing of early 1958 the Treasury shifted $3½ billion of very short securities into the intermediate range and $1½ billion into long-term bonds—amounts together equal in size to about a fifth of the Reserve's entire portfolio—but the effect on the yield curve was slight. This episode is discussed by Riefler, *Federal Reserve Bulletin*, 44 (November 1958), 1271–72.

[36] Joint Economic Committee, *January 1962 Economic Report*, Hearings, 87th Cong. 2nd Sess., 1962, pp. 174–75 (testimony of Chairman Martin).

[37] The record of the Open Market Committee for 1962 will be found in *Annual Report of the Board of Governors for 1962*, pp. 45–110.

came more and more apparent. On March 27, however, Governor Mills was found in the minority, since he believed that the "long-maintained high level of free reserves had forced excessive liquidity into the economy"; he apparently desired tighter money for both domestic and international reasons. On April 17 Governor Mills was joined by President Hayes of the New York Bank:

> He noted that the country's ability to withstand heavy balance of payments deficits and accompanying gold drains was not unlimited and that he had yet to see any convincing evidence of a real turn in the tide. He expressed particular concern about the volume and breadth of foreign borrowing in the United States, both from banks and through bond offerings. In these circumstances, he felt that the System should edge toward a moderately less easy reserve position, thus encouraging the development of a somewhat higher structure of interest rates, particularly short-term rates.

By May 29, however, Hayes and Mills had returned to the fold and joined in the unanimous adoption of a substantially unchanged directive: possibly unrecorded agreement had been reached that the directive should henceforth be interpreted more restrictively. At any rate at the next meeting on June 19 a fresh directive called for "a somewhat smaller rate of reserve expansion in the banking system than in recent months" and "a moderately firmer tone in money markets." Governor King dissented on the ground that any change should be postponed until the effect of the recent fall in the stock market could be gauged; and Governor Robertson desired an easier policy for domestic reasons. On July 10 Governor Mitchell joined Governor Robertson in this position.

International transactions were steadily expanding and the System account was now authorized to hold British, French, German, Italian, Dutch, Swiss, Belgian, and Canadian currencies. On July 10, 1962, what had been an initial authorization of $500 million was increased to $750 million.

As the summer advanced, the June 19 directive was continued, but on September 11 Governors Mitchell and Robertson were joined by Governor Mills in a minority that desired an easier policy for domestic reasons. Mills "considered the forestalling of further declines in the money supply to be an overriding necessity." Robertson "believed that greater monetary stimulation at this time—when there were unutilized human and material resources and when the gold stock was ample to protect against rumor-spawned speculative raids on the dollar—would contribute to a prosperous and more rapidly growing economy. . . ."

On October 2, 1962, Austrian currency was added to the list of those that might be purchased for the System account and its maximum permitted holding of foreign exchange was raised to $1 billion.

On October 23, the dissenters with respect to domestic policy apparently in reaction to the Cuba crisis, ceased for the time being to press for greater ease. On November 13 the directive of June 19 was again reaffirmed; but on this occasion a bare majority of the Committee were solidly behind the policy. Governors Mills and Mitchell (but not Governor Robertson) would have preferred a greater degree of ease; while Governor Balderston and Presidents Fulton (Cleveland) and Hayes (New York) would have liked to tighten credit, although only the last-named voted in the minority. On December 4 majority sentiment in the Committee is reported as favoring "a policy of slightly less ease" as a response to "a distinct improvement in business psychology," but the formal directive was left unchanged, President Hayes again voting in the negative. On December 18 the tight-money party (if such it may be called) succeeded in modifying the directive at the cost of splitting the Committee. The directive as a whole now read:

> It is the current policy of the Federal Open Market Committee to accommodate further increases in bank credit and the money supply, while aiming at money market conditions that would minimize capital outflows internationally. This policy takes into account the lack of any significant improvement in the U.S. balance of payments and the recent substantial increase in bank credit, but at the same time recognizes the unsatisfactory level of domestic activity, the continuing underutilization of resources, and the absence of inflationary pressures.
>
> To implement this policy, operations for the System Open Market Account during the next 3 weeks shall be conducted with a view to offsetting the anticipated seasonal easing of Treasury bill rates, if necessary through maintaining a firmer tone in money markets, while continuing to provide moderate reserve expansion in the banking system.

Such a directive might indeed be thought—by the uninitiated—to convey all things to all men. But two important changes had been made. The previous directive referred first to "underutilization of resources" and second to avoiding conditions "unduly favorable to capital outflows"; the priorities were now reversed. And where the previous directive had called for "a steady tone," the new one called for "a firmer tone"—albeit "if necessary"—in money markets. Such are the subtleties of language through which the Committee communicates with its agent—or at least chooses to go on record. But the easy-money men had no difficulty in recognizing the new directive for what it was: a manifesto for tighter money. The Committee split as follows:

> For the directive: Chairman Martin, Governors Balderston, King, and Shepardson, and Presidents Hayes (New York), Ellis (Boston), and Fulton (Cleveland).
>
> Against the directive: Governors Mills, Mitchell, and Robertson, and Presidents Bryan (Atlanta), and Deming (Minneapolis).

At the first few meetings of the Open Market Committee during 1963 the policy directive of December 18, 1962, was unanimously renewed without substantial change.[38] No doubt something of a stand-off had been reached between those who wanted tighter money for international and those who wanted easier money for domestic reasons. But, beginning at the meeting of March 26, 1963, President Hayes, on behalf of the New York Bank, launched a campaign for higher short-term rates. On May 7 by majority vote the directive was modified to call for "a slightly greater degree of firmness in the money market than has prevailed in recent weeks." The action split the Committee on lines similar to those of the preceding December, although Governor Mills was not recorded and the representation of Reserve Bank presidents had changed somewhat:

> For the directive: Chairman Martin, Governors Balderston, King, and Shepardson, and Presidents Hayes (New York) and Irons (Dallas).
>
> Against the directive: Governors Mitchell and Robertson, and Presidents Bopp (Philadelphia), Clay (Kansas City), and Scanlon (Chicago).

The policy was confirmed July 16 when the Board of Governors approved discount rate increases from 3% to 3½%. Meanwhile free reserves declined toward the vanishing point and the Treasury bill rate rose from below 3% toward 3½%.

At remaining meetings of the Committee during 1963, President Hayes pressed for tighter and Governor Mills for easier money, but a majority merely preferred to maintain the degree of firmness al-

[38] For the record of policy actions during 1963, see *Annual Report of the Board of Governors for 1963*, pp. 37–125.

ready achieved. The directive approved by the Committee at its final meeting of the year on December 17 read as follows:

> It is the Federal Open Market Committee's current policy to accomodate moderate growth in bank credit, while maintaining conditions in the money market that would contribute to continued improvement in the capital account of the U.S. balance of payments. This policy takes into consideration the fact that domestic economic activity is expanding further, although with a margin of underutilized resources; and the fact that the balance of payments position is still adverse despite a tendency to reduce deficits. It also recognizes the increases in bank credit, money supply, and the reserve base of recent months.
>
> To implement this policy, System open-market operations shall be conducted with a view to maintaining about the same conditions in the money market as have prevailed in recent weeks, while accommodating moderate expansion in aggregate bank reserves.
>
> *For the directive:* Chairman Martin, and Governors Daane, Mitchell, Robertson, and Shepardson, and Presidents Bopp (Philadelphia), Clay (Kansas City), Irons (Dallas), and Scanlon (Chicago).
>
> *Against the directive:* Governor Mills and President Hayes (New York).

Governor King had resigned and had been replaced by J. Dewey Daane, an economist from the Richmond Reserve Bank. The appointment was generally interpreted in the press as an attempt to consolidate the "hard money" party under Chairman Martin, but such a conclusion may well be wide of the mark.

Meanwhile by the end of 1963 the Open Market Committee had authorized the New York Reserve Bank to hold foreign currencies up to $2,050 million under swap arrangements and up to $150 million by outright purchase. In addition to those already mentioned, Swedish and Japanese currencies might now be held.

In the light of prevailing unemployment and the continued failure of Congress to enact a tax cut, one could well sympathize with the minority of the Open Market Committee in desiring a less restrictive monetary policy. Yet its logic might be impugned. So long as U.S. international payments remained out of balance, the majority was probably correct in concluding that cheaper money could only lead to gold exports. Given the "external constraint" imposed by the continued need to sell gold at $35.00 an ounce, the Reserve System unquestionably deserved applause for the success with which it had skirted the thin edge of compromise. Between 1960 and 1964 it probably sacrificed little if any more domestic activity than was absolutely necessary. Granted that Governors Mills, Mitchell, and Robertson, and some of the Bank presidents desired a more expansionist policy: instead of questioning the judgment of the majority, should they not rather have questioned the wisdom of continuing to maintain a fixed exchange value for the dollar?

The Federal Reserve and the Foreign Balance

Despite substantial gold losses in 1958 and 1959, the deficit in the balance of international payments first became a factor in Federal Reserve policy after the run up in the London gold price in October 1960 and the large gold exports during subsequent weeks. Since that time the System has shown a strong desire to maintain interest rates—and particularly short-term interest rates—high enough to ensure that most of the surplus dollars earned by foreigners would remain here and not be used to purchase gold. Since the economy was in recession and the upturn did not come until February 1961, the System was chary at first of actually raising rates. But by the fall of 1961 business clearly was on the upgrade, and the Treasury bill rate was allowed to rise from 2.3% in September to 2.7% early in 1962 and 3.5% in 1963. During 1961 and 1962 free reserves were kept at plus $300–$400 million—a level that in the past had denoted substantial ease. However, excess reserves were concentrated entirely at country banks; and the inclusion of vault cash, which had recently been permitted, was believed to have diminished the excess of actual over desired reserves, and so to have diminished the degree of ease attached to a given level of free reserves. During 1963 free reserves were all but eliminated.

The existence of the dilemma was freely recognized by the System, and it is to be assumed that, had the foreign balance been the only consideration, a much more restrictive policy would have been followed. On the other hand business revival during 1961–1963 was slow and halting, and unemployment continued close to 6% of the labor force; so that domestic considerations indicated an easier policy than that actually pursued. In the Fall of 1962 the Kennedy administration asked for a tax cut "to get the economy moving," i.e., to offset the effects of a necessarily restrictive monetary policy.

I shall argue later that with respect to its domestic effects a tax cut is a rather good substitute for an easing of the money market. Yet in the present context it is far from clear how well fiscal policy might achieve a goal unattainable through monetary policy. For a more rapid revival of business would encourage commodity imports and discourage exports, and thus increase the deficit in the foreign balance. Some improvement might indeed occur in the balance on capital account, but the net result is at best dubious. Hence the dilemma may not be so easily avoided as advocates of a tax cut are inclined to claim. Yet in the awkward situation of the early 1960's a tax cut certainly was a remedy worth trying.

As for monetary policy, it may be pleaded that the Reserve maintained as much ease as the foreign balance would allow; nor did the System claim that its policies would remove the basic deficit in U.S. foreign payments. Granted the need for a substantial surplus on current account to finance foreign aid and long-term investment abroad, the difficulty appeared to lie in an overvaluation of the dollar in terms of foreign currencies. If this diagnosis was correct, the Reserve could contribute to a solution only by a policy of vigorous deflation—a clearly unacceptable alternative. The other possible remedy lay, not with the Federal Reserve, but with the Treasury. It became a question whether the Treasury should not long since have taken steps to convince the International Monetary Fund of the existence of a "fundamental disequilibrium" in the U.S. balance of payments and of the need for a realignment of the exchange value of the dollar.

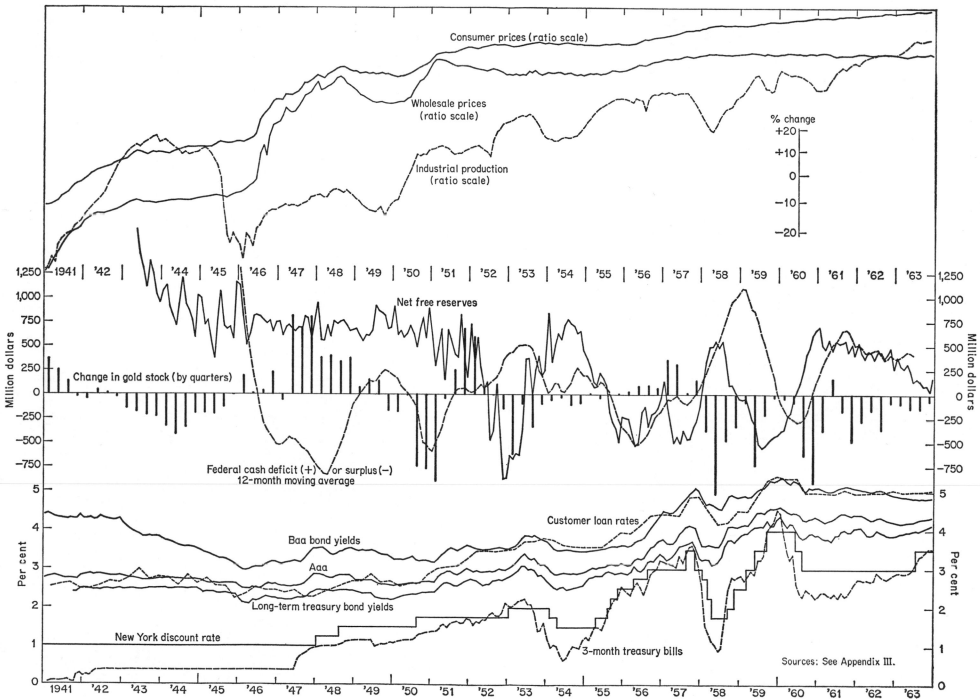

Figure 3. PRODUCTION, PRICES, AND MONEY-MARKET DATA, 1941–1963

Consumer prices (ratio scale)

Wholesale prices (ratio scale)

Industrial production (ratio scale)

% change
+20
+10
0
−10
−20

1,250 1941 | '42 | '43 | '44 | '45 | '46 | '47 | '48 | '49 | '50 | '51 | '52 | '53 | '54 | '55 | '56 | '57 | '58 | '59 | '60 | '61 | '62 | '63 1,250

Million dollars
1,250
1,000
750
500
250
0
−250
−500
−750

Net free reserves

Change in gold stock (by quarters)

Federal cash deficit (+) or surplus (−)
12-month moving average

Million dollars
1,250
1,000
750
500
250
0
−250
−500
−750

Per cent
5
4
3
2
1
0

Customer loan rates

Baa bond yields

Aaa

Long-term treasury bond yields

New York discount rate

3-month treasury bills

Sources: See Appendix III.

Per cent
5
4
3
2
1
0

1941 '42 '43 '44 '45 '46 '47 '48 '49 '50 '51 '52 '53 '54 '55 '56 '57 '58 '59 '60 '61 '62 '63

Chapter 8

The Shift in Policy Aims

> *The secret of success is consistency of purpose.*
>
> —BENJAMIN DISRAELI

As its name implies, the Federal Reserve System was originally established to husband the banking reserves of the nation: that is, to have centrally available at all times a supply of unused lending power, or to act as a "lender of last resort." From the very start of operations in 1914 this passive, or as I have called it, therapeutic, function was well understood by Warburg, Strong, and other System officials. It merely was necessary to adapt the contemporary practice of the Bank of England and other European central banks to American conditions. From time to time the function of lender of last resort might indeed be jeopardized by a mistaken concern on the part of some, e.g., Governor McDougal of the Chicago Bank, for the liquidity of the earning assets of the Reserve Banks themselves. But by and large the emergency supply of liquidity to the economy has been—and continues to be—performed in very much the manner contemplated by the System's founders (except for the substitution of collateral lending for rediscounting). And the proof of success has been the elimination of the old-fashioned financial panic.

To conceive the System's functions thus narrowly, as did the authors of the Federal Reserve Act, seemed very good sense at the time. But this was to imply the false assumption that a passive or neutral policy could be attained merely by noninterference or "following the market." It implied also a failure to understand the instability of credit or to envisage the potentialities of monetary control. During this early period, within wide limits set by the imagined need to husband liquidity, policy criteria were totally lacking and policy seemed a matter of indifference. For the sole legal requirement was that the Reserve Banks should maintain a minimum gold cover, and the sole moral requirement that they should stand ready to discount freely at whatever rates they chose to announce. Hence the groping for policy guidelines, contemporary illustrations of which are Strong's memoranda and the passages in the *Annual Report for 1923* usually attributed to Miller (see above, Chapter 4). Only gradually was monetary policy shifted from a purely therapeutic to a prophylactic role.

Concern both for the System's earnings and for its gold reserve came to influence policy at quite an early date. By and large, the first of these set a limit to contraction, the second to expansion. Earnings were important because of the desire to avoid the need for Congressional appropriations. Gold mattered because of the requirement that the Banks pay it out, yet maintain the minimum reserve prescribed by law.

Major domestic objectives, not contemplated by the authors of the Federal Reserve Act, which came to the fore as the System developed, include: stabilization of the purchasing power of the dollar, full utilization of resources, and the promotion of economic growth.

Earnings

In recent years the System's earnings have been ample to meet its expenses, and large sums have been turned over to the Treasury. Yet anxiety was felt in 1922 from a paucity of discounts and advances, and in 1939–1940 from the low level of prevailing interest rates, lest earnings should prove inadequate to meet expenses. However, the very large size of the System's portfolio since World War II suggests that such lean times are unlikely to recur, and the matter might no longer be worth discussing but for the question of "interest-free financing."

The profits derived from the secular increase in the money stock are divided between the Reserve System and the commercial banks in a ratio that is very sensitive to member-bank reserve requirements. The higher are these requirements, given the volume and distribution of bank deposits, the larger is the fraction of the total earning assets of the banking system held by the Reserve Banks and the smaller the fraction held by commercial banks. Profits from the expansion of the total money stock, when the expansion is accompanied by a growth of earning assets, accrue in a similar ratio. Since the excess earnings of the Reserve Banks are returned to the Treasury, some writers have advocated high commercial-bank reserve requirements as a device to recapture profits on the manufacture of additional means of payment—even to the point of asking 100% reserves (see below, Chapter 10). A majority of the Joint Economic Committee has recently taken a more moderate position, as we saw in the preceding chapter, to the effect that future expansion of bank reserves should be achieved through open-market purchases in preference to reduction of reserve requirements. Whatever view one adopts, the case seems strong for uniform reserve requirements against demand deposits for all commercial banks, member and nonmember.

Ultimately involved is the question not only who should receive profits from the manufacture of means of payment, but also who should bear the costs of monetary management. To this question I return in Chapter 13. Although in the early days earnings unquestionably motivated the Reserve in making policy decisions, today they no longer in any sense represent a policy objective.

Gold

In principle monetary policy could be, and at one time it was thought it should be, regulated entirely by the nation's gold reserve. Such a plan would resemble the practice of the Bank of England during the latter part of the nineteenth century. It would call for credit expansion whenever the metallic reserve increased, contraction whenever the reserve declined. Some critics who call attention to the balance of international payments and the "discipline" that it imposes may still feel that the prescription has virtue. Yet occasions have been infrequent on which the Reserve System has chosen —or has been forced—to pay attention to its gold holding.

The law has indeed required that the System protect its gold reserve (or since 1934, the Treasury's), but this constraint has seldom been compelling. In the early years the reserve was more than ample. When in 1919–1920 gold exports coincided with a large expansion of member-bank borrowing, so endangering the

System's reserve ratio, it happened that other considerations such as price stability in any case called for restraint. The second occasion on which gold losses imposed credit restriction was in 1931: I have argued in Chapter 5 that in this case the tightening of credit could and should have been avoided. The third period during which gold losses influenced policy, i.e., since 1960, is still with us.

During most of the System's history the question was evidently rather, should discretion be exercised to expand credit on the basis of increments in the gold stock? Instead the System sterilized gold, or at best paid no attention to gold movements. Although sometimes a source of embarrassment, as in 1935–1936, gold inflows have never caused policy to be substantially different from what it would have been in their absence.

For those who think that operating the gold standard according to the classical pattern should have been the overriding aim, the System's record is of course a dismal one. By this criterion the case against the System's policies rests upon the assumption that a more liberal credit policy in 1929–1930 (when gold was being received) would have prevented abandonment of gold by other nations, or that a similar policy in 1934–1941, 1946–1948, and 1951 (when gold was also being received) would have caused other nations to return to gold. It seems to me that this view has only to be stated for its absurdity to become apparent. The opinion that it lay within the power of the United States by example to transform the behavior of other nations represents, I believe, a gross overvaluation of its influence and cannot be accepted. The case further rests upon the assumption that the more countries operating the gold standard, the better for all concerned—an assumption in itself open to doubt.

Still more serious is the claim that the System should have initiated a deflationary policy in 1958, or at latest in 1959, in response to gold losses and with a view to the early elimination of the deficit that had appeared in the United States balance of payments. Unquestionably this would have imposed a heavy price on the United States in the shape of business depression and might well have sparked a worldwide credit liquidation.

I do not believe that the Reserve is to be reproached for its comparative neglect of gold as a guide to policy. Rather it should be criticized for unwisely paying on one crucial occasion (1931) far too much attention to the gold situation. By 1961 at the latest it should have been urging the Treasury to seek through the International Monetary Fund a realignment of exchange rates.

The influence of gold on Federal Reserve policy, in sum, has been intermittent and wholly one-sided—toward contraction when gold was being lost. Willingness to sterilize gold imports has meant that they did not induce monetary expansion unless such expansion was desired for other reasons. Hence gold has influenced monetary policy only occasionally and only in one direction—checking the expansion or forcing the contraction of credit.

The Price Level

Since the establishment of the Reserve System, the dollar has lost about two-thirds of its purchasing power. This appears to be a very poor record. However, almost the whole of this loss occurred during or immediately after two world wars and the early months of the war in Korea (before the Accord of 1951), i.e., at times when monetary policy was dominated by the Treasury. If we reject the idea that the Reserve could and should have resisted Treasury influence in wartime, it would indeed seem that the System is rather to be reproached for deflation than for inflation. The violent fall in commodity prices of 1920–1921, and their longer but slower decline during 1929–1933, occurred when the Reserve was a free agent and in no way suffering under Treasury or other duress.

I have argued in Chapter 4 that the deflation of 1920–1921, in part a speculative reaction, went much further than was necessary, mainly owing to lack of appreciation by the System of its powers. The decline in prices which accompanied the Great Depression is a more complicated matter and was discussed at length in Chapter 5. Reasons are given there for believing that much more vigorous open-market purchases should have been made, of bonds as well as short-term securities, during the year 1930. Deflation was further intensified by the System's handling of the gold crisis of 1931. In both these cases the decline in commodity prices was of course closely interlocked with the decline in business activity.

Prior to the passage of the Employment Act of 1946, legislative proposals to instruct the System to push for stability in the purchasing power of money were consistently resisted by the Board and the Banks. More recently the position of the System has been that

it is bound by the Employment Act and that concern for the purchasing power of the dollar is implied by the terms of the Act.
System officials doubtless prefer the present vague mandate to
specific instructions to stabilize the price level.

Reserve officials have always admitted concern for the behavior
of the price level, at least as one among several criteria of policy.
On numerous occasions credit was restricted with a view to preventing a rise in the price level, notably in 1923 and in 1936–1937.
More recently, in 1950–1953, 1955–1957, and 1958–1959, the
edging up of the price level certainly was a factor inducing the
System to tighten credit. Somewhat less clear cut are the cases on
the other side: the cheap money of the 1930's, and especially the
open-market purchases of 1932, were thought of, somewhat desper-
ately it is true, as price-raising measures. Thus while the System
has always hesitated to accept explicit responsibility, there can be
no question but that concern for stability in the purchasing power
of money has been a factor in policy formation.

Business Activity

Prior to the onset of the Great Depression the level of business
activity received far less attention than the price level, perhaps
because it frequently was taken for granted—in the fashion of the
time—that stabilization of the latter would lead automatically to
stabilization of the former. Yet more or less explicit concern with
the state of business clearly influenced Reserve policy at quite an
early date: under Strong's leadership, easing of credit in 1924
and 1927 was intended as a more or less deliberate antidote to
business recession.

Motivations for policy during the Great Depression were more
complex. The cheapening of credit in 1930 can be viewed as the
predictable result of a decline in demand. Not until 1931, or perhaps even 1932, were deliberate steps taken to augment the liquidity
of the economy, and by then matters had gone too far to respond to
any but the most heroic measures—measures too unorthodox for
the System to consider. Nevertheless by 1932 the concern of officials
with the level of business had become acute, powerless as they felt
to influence events.

After his appointment to head the Board in 1934, Eccles held
such strong views on the matter that he actually proposed the in-

clusion of business stabilization in the 1935 banking bill as an instruction to the System. Governor Harrison's views were more conservative and skeptical, but since 1941 when Sproul succeeded him as president of the New York Bank, the stabilization of business, or "maximum sustainable expansion of the economy," has been an—if not indeed the—acknowledged objective of Reserve policy. The new attitude was confirmed and endorsed by the Employment Act of 1946, even though this legislation made no mention of the Reserve System as such. In time Eccles and Sproul were succeeded by Chairman Martin and President Hayes: the commitment to business stabilization continued.

How well has monetary policy achieved this objective? In addition to the Great Depression, which stands in a class by itself and has been discussed at length above, the U.S. economy has experienced eight fairly well-marked recessions in business during the lifetime of the Federal Reserve System. Some aspects of these nine declines in business are compared in Table 8.

As measured by the Reserve Board's own index of industrial production, the dips in business seem to have been getting shorter. Both the time elapsed from peak to trough, and the time taken for recovery to the level of the preceding peak, were on the average slightly less for the four recessions since World War II than for the four recessions between the wars (excluding the Great Depression). The percentage decline in output also averaged somewhat less in the four recent than in the four earlier recessions. The number of instances is, however, not enough to make these differences statistically significant.

More interesting still, the response of the Reserve seems to have been slightly smarter in the later than in the earlier period, although here too data are not numerous enough for results to pass the usual statistical tests of significance. The very prompt application of restraint in February 1928, only three months after the cyclical trough, was of course accidental, and not a deliberate countercyclical policy measure. The most prompt response to a cyclical upswing was in September 1958, only five months after the trough earlier that year. Most persons will agree that the record of the System in dealing with minor recessions has been good. With regard to the Great Depression the case is of course otherwise: the System's responsibility for the depth and duration of the depression of the 1930's

Table 8

NINE DECLINES IN BUSINESS COMPARED[a]

Decline in business	Date of previous peak	Date of trough	Date of recovery to previous peak	Length of		Per cent decline in output	First easing of credit		First tightening of credit	
				Recession (months)	Recovery (months)		Date	Months after peak	Date	Months after trough
Recession of—										
1921	Jan.-Feb. 1920	Mar.-Apr. 1921	Nov. 1922	14	19½	33	April 1921	14½	Feb. 1923	22½
1924	May 1923	July 1924	Nov. 1925	14	16	21	May 1924	12	Feb. 1925	7
1927	Sept.-Oct. 1926	Nov. 1927	Sept. 1928	13½	10	9	Aug. 1927	10½	Feb. 1928	3
Great Depression	June 1929	July 1932	Dec. 1939	37	89	54	-	-	-	-
Recession of—										
1938	April 1937	May 1938	Oct. 1939	13	17	36	-	-	-	-
1949	Oct.-Nov. 1948	July 1949	May 1950	8½	10	17	-	-	Aug. 1950	13
1954	July 1953	May-June 1954	May 1955	10½	11½	10	Feb. 1954	7	April 1955	10½
1958	Dec. 1956[b]	April 1958	March 1959	16[b]	11	14[b]	Nov. 1957	11[b]	Aug. 1958	4
1961	Jan. 1960	Jan. 1961	July 1961	12	6	8	May 1960	4	Oct. 1961	9

[a] All data derived from the Federal Reserve Board index of industrial production.
[b] Data relate to a peak of 147 in Dec. 1956. If the peak is taken to be 145 in Aug. 1957, the recession lasted 8 months (instead of 16), the decline in output was 13% (instead of 14%), and credit was first eased 3 months (instead of 11) after the peak.

will remain controversial, but many will feel that it could have established a far better record than it did.

Economic Growth

The bearing of monetary policy upon the economy's growth rate is at best somewhat indirect. Since growth is the result of capital investment, and since investment spending is larger at full employment than with unused resources, monetary policy can contribute toward growth by promoting full employment. Since low interest rates will stimulate investment, a tight fiscal policy, with a budget in surplus rather than in deficit, will also help. The discouragement of consumer credit will further tend to promote saving and to make lower interest rates possible without inflation.

Concern of the Federal Reserve with the nation's rate of economic growth is a quite recent development. It appeared for the first time in a directive of the Federal Open Market Committee on December 15, 1953, when the objective of "avoiding deflationary tendencies" was changed to "promoting *growth* and stability in the economy by actively maintaining a condition of ease in the money market."[1] Most probably this concern was at first of a negative sort: if real output were to grow, officials wished to ensure that money was available to purchase it. Later, growth figured as something to which the Reserve could contribute indirectly through the stabilization of business activity or of the price level.

By 1959, perhaps because of widespread concern about the lagging rate of growth of the American economy, Chairman Martin was to place "a maximum rate of sustained economic growth" as foremost among objectives for monetary policy.[2] He noted the need in this connection for "real saving and investment," which he claims depends upon "broadly based and justified confidence in a reasonably stable dollar." However, the usefulness of price-level stability as an encouragement to saving and investment is at best uncertain. Reserve officials have never made their view of the connection plain. It has the air of a piece of mythology devised to support anti-inflationary policies that may be desirable on other grounds. The matter will be discussed further in Chapter 12.

[1] *Annual Report of the Board of Governors for 1953*, p. 101. Italics supplied.
[2] See below, pp. 289–90.

Were the Aims Appropriate?

It is not too difficult to see where policy aims came from and how they developed. On the one side were the text of the Federal Reserve Act, public and private pressures to embrace this or that objective, and the day-to-day exigencies of an administrative machine. On the other were the native intelligence, prejudices, and preconceptions of Board members, heads of Reserve Banks, and their advisers. It was perhaps a pity that a public-service institution as important as the Reserve should have been forced to worry about so mundane a matter as the adequacy of its earnings. Yet this anxiety had the incidental result of disclosing the management possibilities of open-market operations.

That the System should pay attention to its gold cover was probably inevitable—whatever we may think of the appropriateness of sacrificing domestic aims to the requirements of convertibility. That it may also be relieved of this obligation, if necessary, was shown in 1933 and may perhaps be demonstrated afresh in the 1960's. For most of its history the System in conducting monetary policy has been free of the "external constraint."

It may be thought that the System should have stuck to its original purpose, and have confined its activities to last-resort lending. But, as will be argued in detail later, this prescription leaves a broad area in which discretion must be exercised and in which no guidance is given on policy matters. A wide variety of policies, that is to say, would enable it to fulfill the therapeutic function—any policies, indeed, which did not dissipate its own cash (or, if it can manufacture cash at will, any policies at all).

How, then, is the discretion to be used? "Sustainable expansion of the economy" seems a worthy aim, provided we can discover what it means. Reserve officials have been far too inclined to interpret this aim simultaneously as a high level of business activity, a stable price level, and a high rate of economic growth. Much talk about fighting inflationary tendencies is justified, not particularly as means toward an honest dollar, but rather on the ground (real or imaginary) that business expansions, when accompanied by inflation, are not "sustainable." That is to say, some degree of stability in the price level is regarded by System officials as a necessary —although no longer, as in the old days, a sufficient—condition for business stability. In truth, this rationalization has enabled the authorities to avoid facing up to the conflict between full employment and price-level stability.

The question whether stability in the purchasing power of the monetary unit is in today's conditions compatible with—so far from being a necessary condition for—full employment of resources has not so far been raised by Reserve officials, at least not publicly. On the other hand the lack of identity between business stabilization (in the countercyclical sense) and full employment presents a mounting problem dramatized by the rising trend in the unemployment percentage throughout the 1950's. On this point the attitude of the System appears to be that unemployment is increasingly structural in nature (a proposition that has been disputed), and therefore not to be laid at the door of monetary policy.

It is very plain that these various objectives are of unequal merit. Moreover disagreement will exist as to their relative worth. It is also plain that some of them may reinforce each other, while others threaten conflict. In Part II we shall turn from what seem to have been the objectives of monetary policy in the past, and shall consider the goals we should press for in the future.

Part Two

Analytical

Chapter 9

What History Teaches

> *So very difficult a matter is it to trace and*
> *find out the truth of anything by history.*
> —PLUTARCH

This book has been written on the assumption that our recent experience with central banking—and equally our earlier experience with the lack of it—are highly relevant to today's perplexities. That is not to say that we should merely take tradition for our guide: far otherwise. An appeal to tradition may indeed merely enable us to repeat the mistakes of the past. I suggested in Chapter 7 that, given suitable conditions, a "bills only" doctrine could lead us to do just that. Yet on the whole the influence of experience—that is, of history—has been overwhelmingly beneficial. Again and again the Federal Reserve System has learned by trial and error, and past mistakes have been ungrudgingly admitted. To learn from the past, we should study history with an open mind and a healthy disrespect for tradition.

What history teaches may be hard to learn. The first and most important lesson, in fact, is that Clio's feet are made of clay. But the muse of history can do much for us if we know how to woo her. She will sometimes suggest which solutions are viable and which are not. And she can often indicate which reforms can be advocated with some hope of adoption, and which cannot.

Our present topic is monetary policy—its scope and potentialities, its weaknesses and limitations. How have public attitudes toward monetary policy varied historically?

To the founders of the Federal Reserve System monetary policy consisted of a single legislative act—the practical establishment of the metallic content of the dollar. For Senator Aldrich and Mr. Warburg, for Congressman Glass and Senator Owen, a central-banking system was above all a means of centralizing and mobilizing banking reserves. They intended it to furnish emergency supplies of liquidity, and generally to act as a "lender of last resort." Discount policy was to be used purely to protect the System's own reserve (i.e., gold) position; and there was no thought that the Reserve Banks would or should have latitude to pursue any independent policy not immediately conditioned by the gold situation.

The great innovator in this regard, ironically, was not Warburg, the European central banker, but Benjamin Strong, a mere commercial banker from New York. As governor of the New York Reserve Bank for a decade and a half, Strong demonstrated the influence of the Bank's investment policy on conditions in the market, and showed that mere adaptation to the market failed to furnish an intelligible policy standard. Nor, Strong felt, could gold movements furnish a unique or, by themselves, a satisfactory guide to policy: hence he looked round for other standards—such as business activity and price-level movements—and so was born monetary management in the modern sense. In the 1920's, Strong's success—for to him may be given almost uniquely the credit—in dealing with incipient recessions in 1924 and 1927, and in stabilizing the level of commodity prices, pushed the prestige of monetary policy to a high level.

But nemesis was just around the corner. Strong had not been in his grave many months when the total incapacity of the System, as then managed by persons who admittedly lacked Strong's ability and insights, to cope with the Great Depression plunged the reputation of central banking, as of other types of financial endeavor, into the abyss. The 1930's were pre-eminently the decade of largely unsuccessful experiments of a fiscal nature and total disillusionment with monetary policy. In 1942 the Treasury took over, and the eclipse of monetary policy was complete.

Yet despite the determined attempts of Secretaries Vinson and Snyder to bury them, the discoveries Strong had made in the 1920's were not lost forever. Eventually the efforts of President Sproul and Chairman Eccles, with the help of Senator Douglas' committee, were successful in ending bond support and resuscitating monetary policy. And since 1951, as in the 1920's, the System has had fair success in stabilizing both business activity and the level of commodity prices. In consequence, the common assessment of the potentialities of monetary policy has undergone a marked revival. But questions have been raised and doubts and difficulties have appeared. These must now be listed for later discussion.

Limitations Suggested by Experience

The most obvious limitation of monetary policy suggested by this nation's experience with central banking is its inability to cope with a serious depression. Since 1951 recessions have been quite minor, and the matter has not been put to the test. But supposing a decline in business comparable to that of 1929–1932 should occur again? Have we any reason to expect a better performance in the future than in the past?

I have given reasons in Chapter 5 for thinking that monetary policy was seriously mismanaged during the Great Depression: the belated and reluctant resort to open-market purchases, the ill-advised and unnecessary credit restriction in 1931, and the unwillingness to buy bonds. The question remains whether different policies would have reduced the decline in business to tolerable proportions. The results of determined efforts to revive the bond market in 1930–1931 might have been spectacular, but we cannot know for sure. If different policies would not have done the trick, might other weapons have been placed in the hands of the monetary authority, or should reliance have been made on fiscal policy? Deficit spending was not notably successful as a recovery measure during the 1930's, but then it was tried at a very late stage. If monetary policy should in the last resort prove incapable of stemming a business decline, we may be fairly certain that fiscal policy—carried out with sufficient vigor—would achieve the objective. But it cannot be said that during the 1930's monetary policy was adequately tested.

The ability of the central bank to check inflation in the contrary situation is, I think, not in doubt. Whenever substantial rises in the price level have occurred, either the Treasury was running a large deficit, or the System's power to raise interest rates was deliberately restricted, or both of these. The power of the System to check inflation in the face of substantial budget deficits by raising interest rates against private borrowers may be questioned, but this is hardly a practical issue except in time of war; and in time of war there are other reasons why inflation may prove inevitable. Necessary reallocation of resources may be hard to achieve without inflation. But in peacetime, with the budget not too far out of balance, there is no reason to doubt the power of the central bank to check inflation. Whether this can always be done without producing unemployment is a further question.

If there are no good reasons for depreciating the power of the Reserve System, experience—analyzed in Chapter 8—suggests that its reactions are delayed. If we may suppose that, at least since 1923, it has wished to iron out cyclical fluctuations, its success has of course chiefly been marred by its failure to cope with the Great Depression. But in each of the seven lesser peacetime downturns since 1923, it has reacted by first easing credit several months after the downturn occurred. Here is a question—whether these time lags can be shortened.

Still other questions remain. As a matter of both economic efficiency and justice, the distribution of the effects of credit restrictions or expansions on different groups may be questioned. It has been alleged that credit policy has greater effects on small business than on large. This matter is tied up with selective credit controls: the control of stock-market credit and consumer credit has been advocated because of the insensitiveness of these areas to general credit conditions.

Are the instruments the Reserve possesses appropriate? Should it be permitted to buy assets or make loans not now permitted to it? Should the System itself be given power to borrow in the market, as has been suggested? Should it be given selective controls over particular types of credit? Have the large volume of public debt and the growth of financial intermediaries since the war made credit control easier or more difficult? These questions must be discussed.

But there is a prior question: to manage or not to manage. It is my conviction that our experience points to the conclusion that paper money will not manage itself. To me, therefore, the worth-while questions are, who should manage it? and, how should it be managed? To these questions Chapters 11 and following are devoted.

But first, in Chapter 10, it is necessary to dispose of a contrary view. There are those who do not accept this "teaching of history" and who believe that paper money can and should be made to manage itself. Since they have no use for central banks or other monetary authorities, I have called those who hold this view the Nihilists.

Chapter 10

The Nihilists

> *. . . thus none would complain of broken promises, but impute their disappointments wholly to fortune, whose shoulders are broader and stronger than those of a ministry.*
>
> —JONATHAN SWIFT, A Voyage to Laputa

That the management of money should be fully automatic is doubtless a dispensation devoutly to be wished. To those who have read thus far it will be obvious that, in common with most writers on this subject, I do not believe that in the nature of things such a dispensation is possible. Yet the contrary has been argued seriously. At different times and on different grounds the claim has been advanced that administrative discretion—i.e., central banking—could, within a suitable legal framework, be eliminated entirely from the management of paper money. This belief deserves examination.

Those who claim that central banking can and should be done away with, I have called the Nihilists. They fall into three groups: (1) the advocates of "free banking," who flourished principally during the first half of the nineteenth century, (2) the advocates in more recent times of a so-called "automatic" gold standard, (3) the small but important group which today believes that discretion can be removed from monetary affairs through the abolition of fractional-reserve banking, i.e., through one or another form of "100% money."

Free Banking[1]

The movement in favor of free banking was essentially an attack upon monopoly. It seems to have originated in England from disgust with the manner in which the Bank of England had used its partial monopoly of note issue. Later it spread to France, Germany, and the United States. Only in New York and Michigan did it give rise to actual legislative experiments.

A central bank had to be either private or public. The idea of a government bank recalled too readily experience with the Continental currency. A private bank, even with government participation, such as the Second Bank of the United States, savored too much of monopoly. The Second Bank had been killed: well and good. But in most states new banks were hard to charter, and their advent was resisted by existing banks. It seemed apparent to many that monopoly in banking had not been eliminated by the demise of the Second Bank. Moreover, as the general suspension of specie payments during the crisis of 1837 showed, the existing situation could bear improvement.

Those who advocated free banking wished to return to a regime in which the state exercised its sovereignty only by defining the metallic content of the currency unit—and by enforcing the bankruptcy laws against bankers as against others. Paper money was to be regulated by insuring its continuous redeemability. Note-issuing banks were to be freely chartered on certain minimum conditions, so eliminating monopoly. Overissue was to be prevented by enforcement of the law that banks failing to redeem their obligations in specie would be liquidated forthwith. However, some writers advocated in addition the deposit of securities with a government agent, so that if banks did fail there could be no question about the redemption of their notes. Inspired by these ideas, the Michigan law of 1837 and the New York law of 1838 provided that banks might be established by simple registration with a minimum of formality. According to Bray Hammond, "the result was that it might be found somewhat harder to become a banker than a bricklayer, but not much"; and he characterizes the free-banking movement as "a retro-

[1] The chief work on the subject is Vera C. Smith, *The Rationale of Central Banking* (London: P. S. King, 1936).

grade effort to restore to the individual the ancient common-law right to be a banker."[2] With respect to its practical results this judgment may stand, but it does less than justice to the intellectual side of the movement.

Politically the movement seems to have owed its origin to general disgust at the corruption with which banks had been chartered by individual enactment. As more general causes, an attack upon privilege was allied with a desire for cheap money. The New York law continued the safety-fund principle (1828) whereby banknotes were issued only upon the pledging of bonds, but there were no restrictions as to the manner in which a deposit business might be conducted. Banking in New York under the free-banking law (1838) was no more edifying than contemporary banking elsewhere in the Republic: yet, regarded as a test of free-banking doctrine, it may well be questioned whether the experiment was a fair one.

In particular, it was politically impossible to enforce the penalty of liquidation as soon as a bank suspended specie payment. The movement's most interesting writer on this side of the Atlantic, Richard Hildreth, recognized this difficulty and invoked the aid of the federal power:

> Institutions have been established under state laws for furnishing [paper] currency, and so far, the federal government is saved from the necessity of intermeddling at all with the matter.
>
> But experience has shown that these state institutions are liable to a certain disorder called *stoppage of specie payments*, which *unbanks* them at once, and changes them into mere machines for manufacturing paper money of no particular value,—a sort of commodity not a whit better than those bills of credit, of which the framers of the constitution had so wholesome an abhorrence. This unhappy disorder is apt occasionally to become epidemical; and what is still worse, the people, or some of them, have got into the habit of meeting together, and insisting that the banks shall stop payment whether they will or no, and then the state legislatures assemble and relieve the delinquent banks from all the penalties they have incurred by thir stoppage. This is a sore evil. Banks that are banks are excellent things, but non-specie-paying banks are the greatest nuisances with which a country can be cursed. This matter is wholly in the power of the federal government, and ought at once to be attended to. The federal government possesses a sovereign medicine against this disorder, which it ought to apply at

[2] *Banks and Politics in America* (Princeton: Princeton University Press, 1957), pp. 572, 573.

once. Let Congress enact a general bankrupt law, as it is specially authorized to do, including banks and other corporations, and placing them upon the same level with other bankrupts, and the thing is done.[3]

Unfortunately the thing never was done, and the grand experiment proposed by the opponents of banking monopoly was not put to the test.

Would free banking have worked? Probably not. The idea is attractive, but in my view its proponents consistently under-rated the forces making for overissue. Certainly ease of redemption was the key to success, and any measure which facilitated redemption would help to prevent overissue. If a bank is the only bank in a given area, and it expands its issues, redemption will be asked mainly by those who have payments to make at a distance—not perhaps a very numerous group. If however there are other banks in the immediate neighborhood, and if they return for redemption the notes of the first bank when they receive them, overissue by the first bank will be checked much more rapidly than in the former case. It might seem therefore that the claim is sound that free banking would eliminate overissue, for with large numbers of banks everywhere competing, overissue by any one bank would be checked rather rapidly. The situation in this regard would have been still further improved, had branch banking been allowed to develop, for the trouble and expense of redemption would have been thereby diminished, since all the branches of a given bank could be required to redeem the notes issued by every other branch.

Yet however much such measures might restrain the tendency of any one bank to overissue, they would afford no obstacle to simultaneous overissue by all the banks in a given area. In a period of business optimism there would be nothing to prevent a *general* upward revision in notions about how much circulation a given specie reserve would support. True, each bank would experience larger redemptions of its own notes; but it would also return to other banks larger amounts of their notes for redemption. The bank expansion would thus be brought to an end only by a drain of specie into circulation or for export. But nineteenth-century experience plainly demonstrated that this was a slow process, often so long delayed as to allow overissue and a resulting crisis.

[3] Richard Hildreth, *Banks, Banking and Paper Currencies* (Boston: Whipple and Damrell, 1840), pp. 176–77. (Italics in original.)

Like other early nineteenth-century writers, the advocates of free banking concentrated their discussion upon note circulation to the neglect of checking deposits. However, substantially the same analysis can be applied to deposit as to note-issue expansion, and the same conclusion applies. Free banking—i.e., general competition among banks—cannot be expected to restrain expansion pursued by all the banks simultaneously. This can be achieved only by a set of rigid rules, as under the National Banking Act; or by the discretion exercised by a central-banking institution.

The "Automatic" Gold Standard

Before the invention of banking, the precious metals had circulated as coin: the element of discretion was confined to the once-and-for-all definition of the weight and fineness of the coin. Thereafter specie was brought to the mint when it was more valuable as coin than as bullion; coin in turn would be melted down when the metal was more valuable as bullion than as coin. The aim of free banking was—by laying heavy penalties on the inconvertibility of paper money—to imitate this system.

Could not the same objective be attained by a central bank with a mandate which deprived it of discretion? Given a system of fractional-reserve banking in which contraction is assured when gold is scarce, and expansion equally assured when gold is plentiful, paper will always circulate on a par with gold. For a single country, small in comparison with the world as a whole, which desires above all to preserve the gold value of its currency unit, this may be an acceptable policy. It was a policy followed, more or less, by the Reichsbank and the Bank of France between the collapse of bimetallism and the First World War. It is certainly a policy implying a minimum of discretion. I do not cite the Bank of England as an example during this period only because Britain was a large enough part of the world economy for the Old Lady to exercise a considerable degree of discretion without seriously endangering the convertibility of sterling.

For a large country like the United States today, even possessed of ample gold reserves, it is a particularly difficult policy to follow. It was a commonplace, even before World War II, to say that the value of gold was fixed by the value of the dollar, rather than the other way round. Today the dollar is not fully convertible: even if it were, the mere maintenance of its convertibility would fall far short of offering a unique prescription for monetary policy. When during the period between the wars the United States was charged with failing to follow the "rules" of the gold-standard "game," the reproach was leveled against the manner in which discretion was exercised by the Reserve System. The charge was, not that the gold convertibility of the dollar was in jeopardy, but that by sterilizing gold, American policy was raising the commodity value of gold in the world at large, something which the Reserve System would be totally unable to do—no matter how much discretion it exercised— were it the central bank of a small country. Thus the United States sterilized gold in 1936–1937, instead of allowing it to expand the credit structure, partly because the gold inflow at that time was thought to represent capital rather than current transactions. But with fractional-reserve banking, an automatic response would imply so far as possible a constant ratio of credit superstructure to metallic base. Convertibility into metal would be assured by such a policy; but convertibility would also be assured by many alternative policies.

Evidently, for a country like the United States, mere convertibility does not eliminate discretion. Maintenance of the international gold standard is seen to be compatible with a wide range of domestic monetary policies. The gold standard cannot so easily be made "automatic." Some additional prescription is needed to remove discretion. It is not immediately clear what that prescription should be.

100% Money: Irving Fisher

History, like hell, is paved with good intentions: free banking as it was to have worked but didn't; the international gold standard as it almost seemed, but just failed to work during the decades before World War I. Both were attempts to eliminate discretion from monetary management—that is to say, to do away with the need for central banking. After World War I neither of these plans any longer promised a solution. The establishment of the Federal Reserve System ruled out automatic regulation through free banking; and the instability of gold inflow and outflow—especially in response to short-term capital movements—made it hard to revive the gold standard along pre-1914 lines. In any case the sentiment for these two remedies was primarily nostalgic. Neither the free-banking laws of the early, nor the gold standard of the late, nineteenth century had given much promise of preventing periodic financial panics. It was hard to argue seriously that either measure would provide a desirable substitute for the discretion embodied in the Federal Reserve Act, which the System was slowly beginning to learn how to use.

As was to be expected, the Great Depression of the 1930's nurtured a budding crop of monetary reformers fertile with ideas. In Congress, as we saw in Chapter 5, the principal pressure was toward giving the Reserve System, if necessary after reorganization, a mandate to raise and then stabilize the level of commodity prices. Meanwhile, especially in academic circles, there developed a movement—with many variations—toward what came to be called "100% money." Not all the proposals grouped under this rubric were designed to diminish the discretion of the monetary authority. But many of them were, and some intended for this purpose still have support today: therefore we must consider them in detail.

The first thoroughgoing plan of this character was put forward by Irving Fisher in 1935. The essence of his proposal was that all commercial banks should be required to keep 100% reserve of cash (currency or balance at Reserve Bank) against their demand deposits. The Federal Reserve Banks, or a special Currency Commission, were to take over enough of the assets of the commercial banks in exchange for cash to achieve this result. To compensate for loss of earning assets, the banks would be expected to charge their customers for service. "Fractional-reserve banking," at least as far as the commercial banks' demand deposits were concerned, would be at an end. Banks would not be permitted to acquire assets through credit creation, but only to the extent of their own capital or by attracting time deposits (to which present reserve provisions would apply). Expansion and contraction of credit would be performed only by the Reserve Banks or the Currency Commission, a prerogative to be exercised under strict limitations. The present arrangement, whereby commercial-bank lending expands or contracts by an amount several times the change in Reserve Bank lending, would have been abolished. The distinction between high-power dollars and low-power dollars, between Reserve money and member-bank money, would have disappeared: all dollars would be low-power dollars.[4]

[4] Irving Fisher, *100% Money* (New York: Adelphi Co., 1935). For variants of Fisher's plan and some critical comments, see Albert G. Hart, "The 'Chicago Plan' of Banking Reform," *Review of Economic Studies*, II (February 1935), 104–16; reprinted in American Economic Association, *Readings in Monetary Theory* (Philadelphia: Blakiston, 1951). pp. 437–56.

For Irving Fisher the 100% proposal was to be coupled with eventual stabilization of the level of commodity prices. Today it seems as important as ever to avoid violent inflation and deflation, and creeping inflation is a new danger against which many have warned. But the rigid stabilization of the level of commodity prices has receded into the background, and today has few apostles. It will not be further discussed. The charms of the 100%-money plan, on the other hand, have proved more durable, and many otherwise reasonable men still are fascinated by them.

In Irving Fisher's mind the purpose of 100% money was to divorce bank lending from the manufacture of means of payment. "Intrinsically," he says at one point, "loans have nothing to do with putting more money or less money into circulation."[5] He wished to bring about this separation because, as he saw matters, variations in the lending activity of the banks gave rise to undesired fluctuations in the volume of means of payment (bank deposits). Perhaps newly-created money should be given away, like manna from heaven: but in our imperfect world it can only get into circulation if, as, and when the issuing agency uses it to acquire an asset or discharge a debt. Of course the asset need not be a customer's note; it could equally well be a bond bought in the market, common stock, title to property, or even a commodity or service.

In effect, the Fisher proposal substitutes government securities acquired by the central monetary authority for the note of a commercial borrower acquired by a commercial bank, as the mechanism whereby new money is to be issued. This change would undoubtedly give the monetary authority somewhat more complete control over the volume of money (currency plus demand deposits) in the hands of the public than it at present possesses. The reason is that the central bank can always find a buyer (or seller) for government securities, at a price; whereas a commercial bank may sometimes have difficulty in finding fresh (or disengaging itself from old) borrowers. That is to say, the market for government securities is less imperfect than the market for the notes of a bank's customers. (Of course a commercial bank, too, may buy government securities, but it may be unwilling to do so when its reserves are increased, either through fear of loss or from respect for conventional asset ratios.) This surely is the reason why the proposal appealed to Irving Fisher: the sharper control it would furnish over the *volume* of money.

[5] Fisher, p. 166.

But the desideratum is greater control, not over money itself, but over the public's spending of money for consumption or investment purposes. In this respect it is not at all clear that Fisher's proposal would change the present situation in any essential way. In a depression, for instance, Fisher thought that the power to prevent a decline, or to assure an increase, in the volume of money would overcome the difficulty that banks could not, or would not, find borrowers, however liquid banks in general might be made. Yet although the central bank can always assure an increase or decrease in the volume of money—a power underscored, but not really altered, by the 100% proposal—it cannot assure that the money will be spent for consumption or investment. That is, it cannot assure turnover of money, or control the velocity of circulation, and it cannot prevent an increase in the volume of money from being offset by a decline in its velocity.

In Fisher's mind, as I have said, the advantage of the proposal was that bank lending would henceforth be divorced from the manufacture of money. But even under our present regime, as when Fisher wrote in 1935, the Reserve Banks can always increase the supply of low-power dollars by buying governments, bank lending or no bank lending. Right now the seller receives a brand-new deposit in a commercial bank, just as he would do under 100% money. Fisher overlooked this point:

> . . . had there been a 100% reserve system in [the years after] 1929 . . . there would have been no need for open-market operations to produce large "excess reserves," i.e., reserves above 10% [the reserve requirement assumed by Fisher as typical]. Reserves to start with would already have been not only above 10%, but 100%, and any open-market operations would have acted on business and the price level directly and promptly instead of, as now, merely piling up unused reserves, which are powerless to act until a good deal of slack is taken up.[6]

But in "piling up unused reserves" in the commercial banks, open-market purchases by the central bank increase commercial-bank customers' deposits under existing conditions exactly as they would under 100% money. And the customers' deposits may be just as idle as the excess reserves. So the reform achieves nothing. On the other hand, after the "slack is taken up," the banks themselves may start lending—which they could not do under 100% money: so that the

[6] *Ibid.*, p. 115.

opportunity to influence business and the price level might even be less under 100% money than it is today.

In truth Fisher grasped the shadow and allowed the substance to elude him:

> If the reader is convinced that this analysis is substantially correct, he cannot but be convinced also that the 10% (i.e., present fractional-reserve) system is largely responsible for the development of depressions. For, under a 100% system, the liquidation of bank loans could not, as we have seen, reduce the quantity of money by a single dollar. With plenty of money, there could be no fall of prices, and without a fall of prices, the subsequent links in the depression chain would be almost non-existent.[7]

Certainly Fisher is correct: under the plan the liquidation of bank loans could not reduce the quantity of money by a single dollar—nor could bank failures. But it does not follow that, with plenty of money, there could be no fall of prices: spending may still decline, and with it the velocity with which the (unchanged) volume of money circulates. It is therefore quite unsafe to conclude, as Fisher did, that 100% money would prevent depressions. This is not to deny that the proposal might have prevented some of the secondary effects of the depression of the 1930's. Since demand deposits could not be wiped out or immobilized through bank failures, one source of aggravation would indeed have been avoided. But this is aside from Fisher's main theme, and he discards mitigation of the effects of bank failures as a merely incidental advantage of his proposal.[8]

The advantages of the plan are therefore illusory. Further, it would cause a considerable upset to banks and their customers. In addition, it would sacrifice an important advantage of our present fractional-reserve system. In manufacturing cash under the plan, the Reserve Banks, or the Currency Commission, must buy securities: and they must buy securities to the full amount of the money to be manufactured. Similarly with selling. Suitable securities might not be available in adequate supply. Under our present fractional-reserve system, on the other hand, when the central bank manufactures money, it can often count on the commercial banks to do the same. The effect is reinforced: the open-market operations of the central bank do not have to be on as large a scale as would be neces-

[7] *Ibid.*, p. 120.
[8] *Ibid.*, p. 177.

sary under the 100% scheme. Fisher claimed the opposite, because he believed, I think mistakenly, that the present system is less stable. But he overlooked the fact that the manufacture of a *given* amount of money requires *larger* open-market operations under the 100% than under our present system.[9]

The principal effect of the plan would evidently be to impose service charges upon the banking public, a corresponding benefit accruing to the Treasury through larger profits of the Reserve Banks (or if the Currency Commission device is used, through retirement of debt turned in to obtain currency. Aggregate profits of the commercial banks are assumed constant). For the long pull, however, since new currency is used (in effect) to retire Treasury obligations, the debt in the hands of the public will gradually be reduced. To put it differently, the profits from manufacturing money would in future accrue to the Treasury instead of to the commercial banks. This seems to me an important long-run benefit, and the only substantial advantage to be derived from the 100% scheme.[10]

Finally, it should be observed that Fisher does not advocate 100% money in order to eliminate, or even to reduce, the element of discretion in the management of money.

> The question now is not at all whether we shall have an automatic (unmanaged) or a discretionary (managed) currency. The question is whether we prefer the present irresponsible management or a responsible management with the definite object of stabilization [of the level of commodity prices].[11]

Indeed, the element of discretion involved in the manufacture of money by Fisher's Currency Commission is at least as great as that lodged with the Federal Reserve System at present. The substantial difference—Fisher is entitled to emphasize it—is that the discretion under his plan is to be exercised in accordance with a definite mandate—price stabilization. His characterization of present management as "irresponsible" seems to be due (1) to the private "minting" of money by commercial banks;[12] and (2) to the fact that the Reserve System had (and has) not embraced his objective of price stability. But in fact (1) the private "minting" of deposits is closely

[9] *Ibid.*, p. 126.
[10] *Ibid.*, pp. 188–92.
[11] *Ibid.*, pp. 195–96.
[12] *Ibid.*, e.g., p. 184.

controlled by the Reserve System; and (2) to accuse the System of irresponsibility merely for having failed to embrace Fisher's own particular policy prescription is to go far afield. The position of later advocates of 100% money is very different from Fisher's. They regard the mere existence of discretion as the very essence of irresponsibility, as we shall now see.

"Rules versus Authorities"

Fisher's plea for the abolition of fractional-reserve banking, written more than a quarter of a century ago, is now mainly of historical interest. The movement in favor of this particular brand of "reform" would not deserve extended treatment but for the fact that the 100% idea has since received powerful support on grounds quite different from those Fisher advanced. I have in mind particularly the writings of Henry C. Simons and Milton Friedman and their followers. Unlike Fisher, this group is inspired, not by any doctrinaire opposition to private manufacture of the means of payment, nor even by a wish to secure the profits of such manufacture for the Treasury, but by a desire to eliminate discretion in monetary matters, to do away with monetary management, or (in Simons' words) to substitute a set of rules for the exercise of discretion by the monetary authority.[13]

To be sure, changes in the discount rate, open-market operations designed to ease or tighten credit, variations in the reserve requirements of commercial banks—all these typical central-banking measures can appear highly arbitrary to the individual businessman. Pressure may be exercised from business or political sources for or against particular policies on the part of the monetary authority. It is not, however, the independence or disinterestedness of the Reserve System that Simons and Friedman call in question. They would still object just as strongly to the exercise of discretion, however objective and impartial, wise and good, those exercising it might be.

---

[13] See Henry C. Simons, "Rules Versus Authorities in Monetary Policy," *Journal of Political Economy,* XLIV (February 1936), 1–30, reprinted in *Economic Policy for a Free Society* (Chicago: University of Chicago Press, 1948). Also Milton Friedman, "A Monetary and Fiscal Framework for Economic Stability," *American Economic Review,* XXXVIII (June 1948), 245–64, and "The Controversy over Monetary Policy," *Review of Economics and Statistics,* XXXIII (August 1951), 186–91, both reprinted in *Essays in Positive Economics* (Chicago: University of Chicago Press, 1953); *A Program for Monetary Stability* (New York: Fordham University Press, 1960); and U.S. Congress, Joint Economic Committee, *Employment, Growth and Price Levels,* Hearings, 86th Cong. 1st Sess., 1959, especially pp. 3029–52.

Certainly monetary policy will influence the fortunes of business-men—indeed of all citizens—in important and unexpected ways. For this reason Simons claims that every business venture is "largely a speculation on the future of monetary policy."[14] But equally, every business venture is a speculation on the outcome of any and all future events that may possibly affect business conditions. Still, if one element of uncertainty could be removed (without increasing other elements), the result would clearly be a net gain.

The Simons-Friedman attack upon discretion in monetary matters rests immediately on the desirability of minimizing the uncertainty surrounding business decisions. But it is in truth still more broadly based on the liberal doctrine of *laissez faire* which argues against the concentration of power in any public body—however wise or well intentioned. This modern attack upon central banking therefore rests upon very secure intellectual foundations running clear back to the economic liberalism of the eighteenth century. It is strictly in the tradition which sponsored, first free banking, and then the auto-matic operation of an international gold standard. The objective of this school—the simple abolition of central banking—is obviously a highly desirable one. In principle. The question to be resolved is, whether we can get along without central banking. Could the man-agement of money be made fully automatic? Or would such a plan bring intolerable difficulties in its wake? Is the elimination of discre-tion in monetary affairs a workable proposal in the light of the insti-tutional framework of a modern economy? I do not ask, is it politi-cally feasible, for its workability is the prior question.

As Simons recognizes, the ultimate desideratum for economic liberals is a completely neutral money supply. This is a highly ab-stract concept. It calls for a volume of money, or a set of interest rates, such that the entire economy would behave exactly as if money did not exist. Disturbances from the side of money would be absent.[15] A good way to judge any monetary policy is by the degree to which it conforms to this criterion. If the case for central banking is to be established, it must be through the probability that we will come

---

[14] *Economic Policy for a Free Society*, p. 161.

[15] The idea originated with Wicksell (*Geldzins und Güterpreise* [Jena: Fischer, 1896]). See also Friedrich A. Hayek, *Prices and Production* (London: Routledge, 1931), Lecture IV: J. G. Koopmans "Zum Problem des 'neutralen' Geldes," *Beiträge zur Geldtheorie* (ed. Hayek) (Vienna: Springer, 1933); Harold Barger, "Neutral Money and the Trade Cycle," *Economica*, II, N.S. (November 1935), pp. 429–47.

closer to a neutral money supply with a central bank than without one. This is—as Simons and Friedman justly imply—not obvious from intuition, and careful demonstration is necessary if the case is to be made out.

Let us then examine the alternatives to central banking put forward by its critics. Simons begins with this proposal:

> (a) putting demand-deposit banking on a 100% reserve basis and, more tentatively, (b) eventual fixing of the total quantity of circulating media (currency plus demand deposits).[16]

But Simons felt that this prescription would not achieve stability because of variations in velocity, and the substitution of "near-moneys" (such as time deposits) for money in some of its uses. Put otherwise, the fixing of the volume of money would not prevent expansion (or contraction) of total spending through more (or less) intensive use of money or through greater (or diminished) use of money substitutes. For Simons the 100% plan is therefore merely the first step in a more extensive program of reform. Money substitutes would be restricted, or even abolished, by making call and short-term lending illegal.

To deal with shifts in velocity, discretion—that is to say, management—will still be needed. But discretion is not to be given to a central bank, apparently because central banks customarily deal in the prohibited short-term obligations, and also because they arbitrarily influence the direction of investment by favoring certain types of assets over others. Instead, Simons proposes to stabilize via fiscal policy, the necessary discretion over borrowing and lending, taxing and spending, being confided to the Treasury. Fiscal policy is a powerful weapon, but it has all the disadvantages of political complication and delay. Simons would have the Treasury issue only legal-tender currency on the one hand and on the other long-term obligations. But a central bank could also operate under these restrictions if desired. (Moreover, if discretion is entrusted to the central bank rather than the Treasury, the former can offset shifts between money and near-moneys, thus making it unnecessary to take the drastic step of prohibiting short-term borrowing and lending.) After exploring these various alternatives, Simons concludes that to remove discretion from the system is an unattainable ideal. In the end he settles

[16] *Economic Policy for a Free Society*, p. 163.

for the grant to the monetary authority (whether Treasury or central bank) of a definite mandate, preferably to stabilize some price level. So that he ends up in much the same position as Fisher.

The Simons proposals have been modified and extended by Milton Friedman. Although sympathetic to the stabilization of some commodity-price level, Friedman prefers a rule whereby the money stock would be increased every year by the same predetermined percentage. In earlier proposals he followed Simons in desiring to place upon fiscal policy the burden of securing this result: expenditure programs and tax rates were to be adjusted to produce an annual *average* deficit of the required magnitude, the *actual* deficit varying with residual fluctuations in the economy.[17] More recently he has suggested that a steady increase in the money stock might perhaps best be achieved through open-market operations by the Reserve System.[18]

Friedman would remove discretion from monetary policy by giving the Reserve System a single, new, precise, and unambiguous mandate: to increase the money stock (demand deposits plus currency outside banks) by, say, 4% yearly. To make it easier to implement this "rule"—his central objective—he proposes several measures of banking reform. (1) To reinforce control of the money stock, the Federal Reserve would no longer lend to member banks, would publish no discount rates, and would give up the power to vary member-bank reserve requirements. (2) Commercial banks would be required to hold 100% reserves against demand deposits, would receive interest on these reserves, and would be permitted to pay interest on demand as well as on time deposits.

To be sure, open-market operations have rightly become by far the most important instrument of monetary policy in the United States. The main objections to discount policy and to the variation of reserve requirements are the large steps in which they must be carried out and their sometimes unfortunate announcement effects. Whether the federal-funds market is as yet well enough organized to prevent unintended local tightness, it is difficult to say, but if so the need for member-bank borrowing has largely disappeared. As for the variation of reserve requirements, its effect upon member-bank earnings is undesirable, and has led to pointless political difficulties

---

[17] "A Monetary and Fiscal Framework for Monetary Stability."
[18] *A Program for Monetary Stability*, pp. 84–99.

for the System.[19] The abolition of rediscounting and of variation in member-bank reserve requirements can of course be advocated quite independently of Friedman's "rule" and may have merit even if no virtue is seen in the latter. If undertaken, these reforms probably should be coupled with others, e.g., the grant of power to the System to purchase a broad range of corporate obligations, and also to sell its own obligations in the market.

As to his second group of proposals, Friedman advocates 100% reserves for commercial banks, neither to divorce lending from the manufacture of money and gradually reduce the burden of the public debt (Fisher), nor to eliminate the supply of money substitutes (Simons). For Friedman the purpose of this drastic change would be to give the Reserve System complete and unambiguous control over the money stock, and especially to bring to an end the perverse effect on the money market of changes in the public's desire to hold currency as against bank deposits. A major practical objection to earlier proposals to abolish fractional-reserve banking was the obvious need for commercial banks to find new sources of earnings, through higher service charges or otherwise. Friedman sidesteps this difficulty by having the Reserve Banks pay interest on member-bank reserve balances—which with a larger portfolio they could well afford to do. In addition commercial banks would be permitted to pay interest on demand deposits, the purpose being to prevent present wasteful efforts on the public's part to economize money balances. The end result would be—as at present—to divide most of the profits from the manufacture of money between bank stockholders and bank depositors, instead of using them to reduce the public debt.

While Friedman's proposals for banking reform are unquestionably worth discussion on their own merits, and we shall return to the more interesting of them in Chapter 13, his general position stands or falls by his central idea that the money stock should be made to grow at some predetermined rate intended to match the growth of the economy. In the past considerable fluctuations in economic activity have occurred without corresponding variations in the money stock, so that the proposition that a steady increase in the money stock will make a worth-while contribution to stability is not obvious. Principally we should ask: how would the Friedman "rule" affect cyclical fluctuations? and how would it cope with the cost-push?

[19] See above, pp. 208–12.

Automatic Stabilizers

For moderating short-run fluctuations in economic activity Friedman would rely entirely upon automatic stabilizers:

> Deficits or surpluses themselves become automatic consequences of changes in the level of business activity. When national money income is high, tax receipts will be large and transfer payments small; so a surplus will tend to be created, and, the higher the level of income, the larger the surplus. This extraction of funds from the current income stream makes aggregate demand lower than it otherwise would be and reduces the volume of money, thereby tending to offset the factors making for a further increase in income. When national money income is low, tax receipts will be small and transfer payments large, so a deficit will tend to be created, and, the lower the level of income, the larger the deficit. This additiion of funds to the current income stream makes aggregate demand higher than it otherwise would be and increases the quantity of money, thereby tending to offset the factors making for a further decline in income.[20]

But would these deficits and surpluses appear promptly enough and be large enough to keep business at a satisfactory level? Friedman's belief that they would depends partly on his claim that discretionary monetary policy has in the past been destabilizing, and that once this source of instability has been removed automatic fiscal stabilizers can do the job.

First, Friedman attempts to show that automatic stabilizers are less subject to time lags in operation than are—or can be—our present discretionary controls. These are not of course true alternatives, for we already have automatic stabilizers and no one proposes to abolish them. The question is rather whether our present—or indeed any conceivable—discretionary controls can contribute additional stability to that furnished by automatic stabilizers. To this question the matter of time lags clearly is relevant.

Friedman distinguishes three varieties of time lag:

> (1) the lag between the need for action and the recognition of this need; (2) the lag between recognition of the need for action and the taking of action; and (3) the lag between the action and its effects.[21]

Friedman points out that the first kind of lag is absent for an induced budgetary deficit, but must remain appreciable (in the absence of

---

[20] *Essays in Positive Economics,* pp. 140–41. Copyright 1953 by the University of Chicago.
[21] *Ibid.,* p. 145.

satisfactory forecasting) for any kind of discretionary control. With suitable administrative arrangements (pay-as-you-earn taxes, prompt payment of unemployment compensation), automatic fiscal stabilizers would also score well with respect to the second kind of lag— the lag between recognition and action. Here discretionary action in the monetary field also scores well, at least when monetary policy is centralized, as it has been in the Federal Reserve System since 1935. (On the other hand *discretionary* action in the *fiscal* field scores badly with respect to the second lag, for changes in tax and expenditure *policies* can come about only slowly.)

The most important lags are probably those of the third kind— between taking action and its results—and them we know least about. Automatic fiscal stabilizers expand personal income distributed by governmental units and reduce income withheld by such units. The immediate effect upon spending for GNP is practically confined to consumer spending, can hardly be as large as (least of all larger than) the initial change in income, and will be subject to some such time lag as one income period (roughly). Since there is no direct effect upon interest rates or the availability of credit, any influence on investment spending will have to wait upon changes in the derived demand from consumer spending. Hence for automatic stabilizers the third type of lag is clearly considerable, as Friedman admits.

In "A Monetary and Fiscal Framework" Friedman claims that the third type of lag will be equally long for (discretionary) monetary policy.[22] Here consumer incomes are not directly affected, but instead a reduction of interest rates or increase in the availability of credit will follow directly from the expansion of the money supply; for the new money, instead of being placed initially in the hands of income receivers or clients of the government, is lent out on the capital market. Here Friedman claims that the lag surely must be long, for "balance-sheet adjustments are sluggish."[23] But are they?

[22] Friedman's own attempts at empirical investigation, as yet only available in summary, have shown that peaks and troughs in the rate of change of the stock of money precede peaks and troughs in general business by from 12 to 16 months, but the relevance of this discovery is obscure, for the former seem a poor way of dating changes in monetary policy, and the latter seem an equally poor way of dating their effects. See Joint Economic Committee, *The Relationship of Prices to Economic Stability and Growth*, Compendium of Papers submitted by Panelists, 85th Cong. 2nd Sess., 1958, pp. 241–56; and exchanges between Friedman and J. M. Culbertson on "The Lag in Effect of Monetary Policy," *Journal of Political Economy*, LXVIII (December 1960), 617–21 and LXIX (October 1961), 447–77.

[23] *Journal of Political Economy*, LXIX, pp. 462–63; see also Culbertson's comments, *ibid.*, pp. 475–76.

Some may be, others not. If a firm, previously denied credit, suddenly finds it can borrow, will it not react immediately?[24]

We may note that the ability quickly to influence the rates of interest upon which entrepreneurs base their calculations—and the availability of funds in the markets in which they borrow—is somewhat restricted if the central bank deals only in short-term obligations, for arbitrage often works but slowly. Time lags of the third type will be shortest if the monetary authority buys and sells assets of a kind most closely resembling those sold or bought by entrepreneurs. The time lag will be minimized if the central bank buys, not merely long-term Treasury obligations, but corporate bonds or even common stocks. The third type of lag will surely be shorter, and perhaps very much shorter, for monetary than for fiscal policy. In his 1948 paper Friedman maintains the opposite.[25] Yet in another paper, published three years later, in 1951, he defends the effectiveness of open-market operations—albeit in the direction of restraint—and, although he does not mention time lags, the implication clearly is that they are unimportant.[26]

While admitting that the analysis is highly conjectural, Friedman concludes that the time lag is "definitely longer" for discretionary actions in the monetary field than for the automatic fiscal reactions upon which he proposes to rely, since each of the three parts into which the total lag is divided is longer.[27] I do not believe that this conclusion will stand up. The discussion suggests that only the first type of lag is longer for discretionary monetary action: between the need for action and its recognition. The second—between recognition and action—may well be shorter; and the third—between action and result—seems most probably much shorter. Certainly there is need for empirical investigation.

[24] The third type of lag has been estimated for monetary policy by Thomas Mayer in "The Inflexibility of Monetary Policy," *Review of Economics and Statistics*, XL (November 1958), 358–74. His conclusion is that "a restrictive policy reaches only half its effectiveness five months after the change in credit availability and reaches three quarters effectiveness only after nine months. An expansionary policy takes even longer—seven months to reach the 50 per cent level and ten months to reach the 75 per cent level." The calculation was made by asking businessmen how long it takes them to spend for capital purposes after deciding to do so, and takes no account of speculative anticipation or of multiplier and acceleration effects. For other reasons why Mayer may have overestimated the length of the lag, see William H. White, "The Flexibility of Anticyclical Monetary Policy," *Review of Economics and Statistics*, XLIII (May 1961), 142–47.

[25] *Essays in Positive Economics*, p. 147.

[26] *Ibid.*, pp. 263–73.

[27] *Ibid.*, p. 148.

So much for the situation—scarcely conclusive—in regard to time lags. Otherwise the Friedman proposal would seem to suffer from a serious weakness in the limited potentialities of automatic stabilizers. Under usual arrangements marginal rates of tax-receipt-plus-transfer-payment are less than unity. That is to say, if income declines $100, the consequent decline in tax receipts plus the increase in transfer payments (unemployment compensation) will together normally amount to less than $100.[28] Therefore automatic fiscal stabilizers can at best slow the decline in income, but cannot of themselves reverse it. The discretionary use of monetary policy is not subject to this limitation. There is in principle no limit to the volume of assets a central bank can acquire: nor, given appropriate borrowing powers, to the volume of assets which it can force the market to absorb. Hence, provided the elasticity of the supply of assets is less than infinite, it can always raise their price—i.e., reduce the cost of borrowing. And provided the elasticity of investment spending with respect to the cost of financing it is less than zero, the central bank can always influence investment—provided it pursues a sufficiently vigorous policy. The elasticity conditions can scarcely be considered restrictive. In potential effectiveness, then, monetary action, which is of course (alas!) essentially discretionary in nature, must seem greatly superior to automatic fiscal stabilizers. Its weaknesses lie in time lags (albeit shorter than suggested by Friedman) and in the instability of the supply schedule for financial assets and the demand schedule for real capital which, although they have the right elasticities, embody and are subject to the waywardness of entrepreneurial expectations. But automatic fiscal stabilizers and discretionary monetary policy are not in any real sense, or indeed necessarily, alternatives; both are needed. By moderating fluctuations in income, automatic reactions on Treasury receipts and disbursements will make the task of monetary control easier but cannot plausibly be thought of as a substitute for the latter. To slow down a contraction in income, or even to bring it to an end, is not the same thing as to reverse such a contraction and initiate an expansion.

[28] The actual figure of course depends upon institutional arrangements. For the United States in recent years it has been estimated that automatic fiscal stabilizers offset about 60% of a decline in income during recession and about 40% of a rise in income during expansion: see Nevins D. Baxter, "Built-in Fiscal Stabilizers in the United States," *Zeitschrift für Nationalökonomie*, XXII (1962), pp. 145–52. Similar conclusions are reached by M. O. Clement, "The Quantitative Impact of Automatic Stabilizers," *Review of Economics and Statistics*, XLII (February 1960), 56–61.

The Friedman "Rule"

Whatever the value of automatic stabilizers, the kernel of Friedman's proposal is to give monetary policy the task of increasing the stock of money in a defined ratio from one month to the next. The practical consequences of implementing such a "rule" are hard to assess. I assume the reader will be willing to reject the hypothesis that cyclical fluctuations are the simple result of unwise discretionary action and will therefore disappear completely once the rule is substituted: we may suppose that tendencies to fluctuation still would persist under the rule. How would the changed temporal pattern in the growth of the money stock react with these tendencies?

Let us interpret the rule as a steady annual 3% growth in demand deposits plus currency. This somewhat exceeds actual growth in recent years, which has averaged about 2% since 1947. To be sure, for many months at a time the money stock grew more rapidly than 3% annually, but at other times it actually declined. An examination of the Federal Reserve's seasonally adjusted series[29] yields the following conclusions. (1) The growth in the money stock has been most rapid around cyclical troughs and during the early months of business expansion: a 3% rule would have called for less ease and have slowed monetary growth at such times. (2) In the later stages of business expansion and the months following a downturn, the money stock has typically grown at less than 3% or has actually declined: the rule would have required easier money and a more rapid growth of the stock during these phases of the cycle.

The implication of these two observations is far from straightforward. Observation (1) certainly suggests that under the rule business expansions would get under way more slowly and take longer to acquire momentum than they now do, but observation (2) implies that once under way they would proceed further and reach greater heights of activity. It might be thought that the converse would hold for recessions, which would be slowed down at first by cheaper money under (2), but eventually prolonged by dearer money under (1). In that case we could predict that the rule would increase both the amplitude and duration of business cycles, i.e., be clearly destabilizing.

But matters are not that simple, for the effect of the rule on reces-

[29] *Federal Reserve Bulletin*, 48 (August 1962), 946.

sions need not parallel that on expansions. For the effect of (2)—
essentially a more prompt response to a business downturn—might
well be to lessen the magnitude and duration of a decline in business,
swamping any adverse effect of (1) later in the recession. On the
other hand the absence of any provision for last-resort lending,
especially since the rule would cheapen money (relative to present
conditions) as the expansion proceeded, might provoke the kind of
financial panic that has not been experienced since the Reserve was
founded.

The longer-range effects of the rule are also hard to assess. The
chosen rate of increase in the money stock assumes a knowledge of
the future rate of growth of the demand for money, and especially of
the influence upon this demand of the supply of money substitutes,
knowledge we do not possess.[30] A too rapid increase in the money
stock would have inflationary effects, while too slow an increase
might well act as a drag upon the economy.

Friedman concedes that price rigidities could interfere with the
plan's operation. For example, an accidental or autonomous increase
in wage rates in some sector, uncompensated by a decline in any
other sector, would lead to permanent underemployment. Employment could be restored, under the given conditions, as Friedman
rightly says, by a dose of inflation. But under the proposal, if it is
taken seriously, discretion being absent, the community has relin-
quished the opportunity to choose between unemployment and inflation: it must accept the unemployment.

Where does this leave the good old liberal doctrine of the desirability of a neutral money supply? If you believe that the misuse
of resources that results from an inappropriate level of total spending dwarfs other mistakes in the allocation of resources, the answer
is plain. A weakening of control over the level of activity is too high
a price to pay for automatic regulation. The monetary authority has
the power. We must take the risk that it may not always be used as
promptly or as wisely as we could wish.

[30] See comment by John G. Gurley and E. S. Shaw, "Financial Aspects of Economic
Development," *American Economic Review*, XLV (September 1955), especially pp.
534–35.

Chapter 11

Who Should Manage Money?[1]

> *For forms of government let fools contest;*
> *Whate'er is best administered is best.*
> —ALEXANDER POPE, Essay on Man

In the preceding chapter I have attempted to refute the notion that a self-adjusting monetary system—or combination of monetary and fiscal arrangements—could be set up in such fashion that all conscious administrative or discretionary management might be dispensed with. In the remaining chapters I shall proceed on the assumption that management is necessary—if you will, a necessary evil. There remain the vital questions: Where should management be located? What should be its objectives? What forms should it take? Answers to these questions will be attempted in this and the two succeeding chapters.

Down to 1914, as we saw in Chapter 2, little management was exercised except at times of crisis when the Treasury and the clearing-house associations would furnish the market with such small amounts of emergency cash as they chanced to possess or were able to manufacture. Since 1914 management has mainly reposed in the Federal Reserve System. Yet the Treasury has continued to wield certain minor monetary powers; and it also plays a role, in conjunction with the Bureau of the Budget and the usual Congressional committees, in shaping fiscal policy.

Questions to be considered in this chapter are: (1) the significance

---

[1] For a useful discussion from the standpoint of politics and public administration of the questions raised in this chapter, see Michael D. Reagan, "The Political Structure of the Federal Reserve System," *American Political Science Review,* LV (March 1961), 64–86.

of such residual monetary powers as at present rest with the Treasury; (2) in what sense (if any) the Federal Reserve ought to be independent of the administration of the day; (3) the location of monetary control within the System itself; and (4) the coordination and ultimate direction of the monetary and fiscal policies of the economy.

Residual Powers of the Treasury

It often has been observed that any agency, public or private, if possessed of sufficient resources, could, by alternately releasing and immobilizing funds, exercise what are in effect central-banking functions. In the United States, as in other countries, the only agency (other than the central bank) able to operate on a sufficient scale to be worth considering in this connection is the Treasury. We may speak of these powers as residual, since the Treasury can exercise them independently and without the acquiescence of the Reserve System. They belong to monetary rather than fiscal policy, since their use does not depend upon whether the federal budget is in deficit or surplus. They consist of the release and absorption of cash otherwise than through current revenue and expenditure, and of changes in the form of the publicly-held debt.

From time to time the United States Treasury has been justly reproached for a bias in favor of cheap money and a display of inflationary proclivities. Yet it happens that—paradoxically—its own freedom of action is far greater in *contracting* than in expanding the money supply. By moving balances from the commercial banks to the Reserve Banks and by immobilizing funds borrowed in the market, the Treasury can cut bank reserves sharply.

By contrast, the Treasury's independent power to *expand* credit is quite limited. Expansion of the money supply by the Treasury no longer empowered itself to manufacture currency, is limited by the size of its existing balances—unless or until the Reserve is willing to acquiesce in the expansion by furnishing additional means of payment. That is to say, the Treasury can disburse cash, for instance by repaying debt, but only within the limits of what cash is available to it. This painful fact impressed itself—as we saw in Chapter 2—upon a long succession of Secretaries of the Treasury, from Guthrie in the 1850's to Shaw half a century later.

Minor modifications have occurred. Since 1935 the independent power of the Treasury to expand credit has sometimes been bolstered by the fact that the old-age provisions of the Social Security Act require large trust funds to be invested in Treasury obligations. The assurance that an administratively balanced budget will normally yield a cash surplus has tended to keep the Treasury rather well supplied with cash resources so long as the administrative budget was not seriously in deficit. By hoarding cash the Treasury can acquire a mass of maneuver which has increased its freedom of action in managing the debt, and has occasionally enhanced its short-range bargaining power in dealing with the Reserve. But the fact remains that the Treasury can only put money into the market which it has previously abstracted from the market (by taxes or borrowing), or which the Reserve has been willing to create in its favor. Thus the *independent* powers of expansion possessed by the Treasury are—except in the very short run—quite limited. They contrast with the vast powers of expansion, subject to quite distant legal limitations, of the Reserve. The pressure upon the Reserve which it exerted during the bond-pegging period was in fact a tribute to the impotence of the Treasury in monetary matters. Thus the reputation of the Treasury as an engine of inflation during and after two world wars rests upon its success in inducing the Reserve System to acquiesce in its policies and to create the additional cash it sought.

Unlike its power to expand credit, the Reserve System's power to take money out of the market is actually much less than that of the Treasury. Open-market sales of securities are limited by the size of the System's portfolio and by the practical need of the Reserve Banks to earn their expenses—a consideration not now critical, but important in the past and possibly in the future. The System's leeway in contracting credit, or in restraining expansion, would of course be larger if it had the power to borrow, and if its expenses could be met in some way other than through earnings on its portfolio. But as things stand, the Reserve's weakness in this regard is matched by the Treasury's strength. On a number of occasions the Treasury was called on to assist the Reserve for this very reason. In 1936–1937, at the request of the Reserve, the Treasury by borrowing in the market sterilized over $1 billion of incoming gold which the Reserve unaided could only with difficulty have prevented from expanding domestic credit. Less significantly, in 1946–1948 the Treasury used surplus cash to retire bank-held debt, and so reduced the need for restrictive action on the part of the Reserve: however, in this instance the benefit (such as it was) may be said to have accrued to the Treasury, since the Reserve was perfectly able to keep the money supply under control by normal methods, but in doing so would have raised the cost of Treasury borrowing.

In sum: leaving on one side the effects of budget deficits and surpluses (i.e., fiscal policy), we may say that—with respect to monetary management—the power of the Treasury is greatest where that of the Reserve is least (i.e., in restraining credit); and the power of the Treasury is least where that of the Reserve is greatest (i.e., in inducing expansion).

The monetary powers of the Treasury are not confined to the release and absorption of cash, for it can also alter the form of the publicly-held debt. Thus lengthening, i.e., increasing the average maturity of the debt (funding) decreases the supply of liquid assets (money substitutes) and so may be considered a restrictive measure. Not only does lengthening the debt cut liquidity, it tends to raise long-term rates of interest relative to short; and, to the extent that investment spending is sensitive to long rather than short rates, it will cut investment spending. In the same way, shortening the debt ("unfunding") will swell the supply of liquid assets available to the public and lower long-term rates of interest relative to short, and therefore tend toward expansion.

It is obvious that—quite apart from the interaction of fiscal and monetary measures—the efficient conduct even of monetary management is impossible without close cooperation between the Federal Reserve and the Treasury. The large opportunities for short-run disturbances to the money market from variation in Treasury balances and from debt management, not to speak of the limitation in some circumstances of the Reserve's ability to restrain expansion, make coordination of policies imperative. Yet it is hardly surprising if the Reserve, with primary responsibility for monetary management, has sometimes felt that the price exacted by the Treasury for cooperation seemed excessive. The altogether exaggerated concern of Secretaries Morgenthau, Vinson, and Snyder with the dollar cost of debt service to the exclusion of all other policy criteria necessarily pushed the Reserve in the direction of "going it alone."

Yet "going it alone" is not in the long run a feasible attitude for a central bank. To be sure, in its negative or defensive aspect, central banking consists in offsetting disturbances to the money market from whatever direction they may arise. If a treasury has concerns of its own that conflict with the views of the central bank about monetary policy, a truly independent and dedicated central bank might well feel that it should offset disturbances induced by treasury behavior just as it would any other disturbances. In the United States such a division of labor could be made explicit, were Congress to charge the Treasury with minimizing the cost of the debt, while giving the Reserve responsibility for stabilizing the economy. However, the financial operations of the federal government today are on such a scale that the Reserve System probably does not have the power—even in a technical sense—to defy the Treasury. To possess such power it might well need to retain more of its earnings, to be able to abstract funds from the market by borrowing, to have power to vary commercial-bank reserve requirements over a wider range than at present, and possibly even to have its expenses underwritten by Congress in case its earnings proved insufficient.

The wisdom of any such approach remains highly suspect, for the public and private disadvantages of open opposition between the two agencies are manifest. Yet, fantasy though it be, to consider the effects of stripping the Treasury of its monetary functions has its uses. For it enables us to see the hollowness of the argument that by the nature of its operations the Treasury must inevitably exercise central-banking functions. There is no *technical* reason why the Reserve, with adequate powers, could not be given a monopoly of monetary management and be instructed to offset any and all disturbances due to Treasury operations. It was Benjamin Strong who, no doubt in a moment of temporary desperation, opined that the Treasury should be treated "like any other customer."[2]

The objections to total independence for the Reserve—to the point if necessary of defiance of the Treasury—relate not to monetary technique but to political power and responsibility. The question was brought to the fore by the extreme irresponsibility of the Treasury under Secretaries Vinson and Snyder during the first six years after the conclusion of World War II. At that period the Reserve could certainly have had its way without additional powers, and the obstacles to its independence were not technical, but lay in the unwillingness of Reserve officials to defy the Treasury.

To give the entire responsibility for monetary management to the Reserve System, to absolve the Treasury from all concern for mone-

[2] Hamlin diary, November 7, 1919.

tary affairs, and to leave it to the Reserve to offset disturbances caused by the Treasury, as those from any other source, is technically feasible but unlikely to result in the most efficient conduct of the public business. The choice can be illustrated by the controversy as to *when* the Treasury should attempt to lengthen the debt. If it has no responsibility for monetary management, it will obviously choose to refund in periods of monetary ease, i.e., recession. But this may interfere with the Reserve's efforts to cheapen credit, so that the destabilizing action of the Treasury will have to be countered by stronger action on the part of the Reserve than would have otherwise been required. On the other hand, if the Treasury shoulders responsibility in the monetary field and aids and abets the Reserve, it will refund in boom periods when interest rates are high or rising. In this instance the choice may not be vital, but in other situations Treasury cooperation may prove indispensable. If at some future time, possibly through a further devaluation of the dollar, the 1937 situation should be repeated in aggravated form and a flood of gold denude the Reserve Banks of earning assets, Treasury cooperation would become a clear necessity.

The "Independence" of the Reserve

In 1913 Secretary of the Treasury McAdoo proposed that a bureau within the Treasury be set up with central-banking functions. Instead the Federal Reserve Act established a more or less independent central-banking organization whose main connection with the Treasury was that two out of seven (later eight) members of the Federal Reserve Board consisted of the Secretary of the Treasury and the Comptroller of the Currency. In 1935 even this connection was sundered through the removal of these two officials from the Board. The Congressional debates show that in 1913 independence was desired because the new agency was to issue currency, and the Treasury had been distrusted as a source of currency ever since the Revolutionary War. The argument for independence in more recent times is based rather on the belief that the Treasury's interest in cheap money to finance the public debt caused inflation after two World Wars.[3]

---

[3] See, e.g., *Monetary, Credit and Fiscal Policies*, Report of the (Douglas) Subcommittee of the Joint Committee on the Economic Report, 81st Cong. 2nd Sess., Senate Document 129, 1950, pp. 17–32.

The two agencies have rather similar constitutional status but quite different political standing. Each was created by act of Congress. The members of the Reserve Board, like the Secretary of the Treasury and his bureau chiefs, are appointed by the President subject to confirmation by the Senate. Yet the Secretary is a cabinet officer, responsible for Administration policies in his field, who is replaced upon a change of Administration. On the other hand the Governors of the Reserve System are appointed for 14-year terms and are not in any ordinary circumstances removable. Both agencies represent the public interest. How is a conflict between them to be interpreted?

Apart from party-political advantage, which does not seriously enter the question, differences obviously reflect differing judgments as to what constitutes the public interest. An Eccles will feel that a Snyder over-rates the importance of keeping down the cost of the debt and under-rates the danger of inflation: a Snyder will feel that an Eccles under-rates the importance of keeping down the cost of the debt and over-rates the danger of inflation. Who shall decide?[4]

The ultimate appeal evidently is to the President or to Congress. Yet neither appeal is easy to make. It is obvious that in February 1951, when appeal was made to President Truman, he was not brought to an understanding of the issues. Yet the ultimate responsibility for economic policy must rest with the Administration of the day. The appeal to Congress is even more difficult to undertake. Repeatedly between 1945 and 1951, the Board of Governors called attention to the inflationary implications of bond support, and asked Congress for direction as to whether or not it should continue to go along with the Treasury's wishes. But, as with the appeal to the President in 1951, the issues were technical in nature: in the absence of outright and obvious emergency, a consensus is hard to develop in a large legislative body. In the end, growing Congressional support for the Reserve System, sparked by the educational efforts of Senator Douglas' subcommittee, probably had much to do with the System's belated victory over the Treasury in March 1951. How much better had the question been resolved in 1945!

The case for making the Reserve independent of the Treasury

---

[4] Snyder's answer is that the President should mediate; see Joint Committee on the Economic Report, *Monetary Policy and the Management of the Public Debt*, Replies to Questions, Part I, 82nd Cong. 2nd Sess., 1952, pp. 28–32.

rests upon the long record of the latter in subordinating other considerations to the dollar cost of the debt. It may also be said that the Secretary of the Treasury is a busy man to whose attention monetary policy comes only intermittently. It may further be claimed on behalf of the System that in the past it has had more and better research facilities; its personnel have been in closer touch with the money market; and, finally, its policy makers have generally (although not always) shown a better grasp of the fundamentals of monetary management—here we need only contrast a Strong, an Eccles, or a Sproul with a Vinson, a Snyder, or a Murphy.

Broadly speaking, this argues for the Treasury to accommodate itself to the Reserve, rather than the other way around. This was the position taken by Senator Douglas' subcommittee, which in 1950 asked Congress for a joint resolution to the effect that

> the primary power and responsibility for regulating the supply, availability, and cost of credit in general shall be vested in the duly constituted authorities of the Federal Reserve System, and that Treasury actions relative to money, credit, and transactions in the federal debt shall be made consistent with the policies of the Federal Reserve.[5]

No such resolution was ever passed and it may be anticipated that any Secretary of the Treasury would feel bound to resist such an expression of opinion by Congress.

So much for independence of the Federal Reserve from the Treasury; what of independence from the White House? The opinion that the Reserve should not take orders from the President of the day originated in the fear that he might adapt monetary policy to short-sighted political ends (e.g., attempt to use cheap money to win an election[6]).

Moreover, necessary anti-inflationary measures may be unpopular, and may prove more readily acceptable if dispensed by a quasi-judicial body removed from public pressures. Finally, Congressional review after the fact provides adequate assurance that the System will act in the public interest. To these earlier arguments for independence from the White House was added the fear that in attempting to exercise his authority over the Reserve the President

---

[5] *Monetary, Credit and Fiscal Policies*, p. 18.

[6] Governor Harding claims that he resisted political pressure for lower rates prior to the 1920 election (*The Formative Period of the Federal Reserve System* [Boston: Houghton Mifflin, 1925], p. 187).

would depend heavily for advice upon his Secretary of the Treasury, so compromising independence of the Reserve from the Treasury: however since 1947 Presidents have had an alternative source of advice in the Council of Economic Advisers.

The truth seems to be that, so long as monetary policy is a substantial part of national economic policy, the Administration *must* have a say in the matter. Major questions of social priority are involved: for instance, the choice between full employment and price-level stability. For the Reserve to pursue a policy at cross purposes with that laid down by the Administration of the day would clearly be intolerable and would subvert the democratic process as we understand it. Long-run accountability to Congress is no safeguard here.

It has been claimed, paradoxically enough, that this issue was settled by the passage of the Employment Act of 1946 which does not so much as mention monetary policy or the Federal Reserve System. This Act gave the Council of Economic Advisers the statutory duty to recommend "national economic policies . . . to avoid economic fluctuations or to diminish the effects thereof, and to maintain employment, production, and purchasing power." Further, the Act requires the President in his Economic Report to set forth "a program . . . to promote maximum employment, production, and purchasing power." Obviously such a program may—indeed must—include monetary measures; and it would be absurd for the President to propose monetary measures which he had no means of implementing. It is to be noted that, largely for this reason, virtually all other countries have submitted monetary policy to the formal direction of the government of the day.

What form should the control of the executive over monetary policy take? A first step is more opportunity for an incoming President to influence the personnel of the Board of Governors. Although a governor's term expires every two years, it does so in January of even-numbered years. If the change were made to odd-numbered years, an incoming President would always have a chance to appoint one of the seven governors. Furthermore, the 1935 Act specified a four-year term for Board chairman, but failed to provide that such term should coincide with the Presidential term of office. Either the terms should be made to coincide, or the governor who serves as

Board chairman should do so at the pleasure of the President.

If monetary policy stood alone as an "independent" function, these reforms might be sufficient. I argue below that, because of the need to coordinate monetary with fiscal policy, a more formal subordination of the System and its policies to Presidential direction may now have become necessary. First, however, we must note where policy making lies within the System itself.

The Locus of Decision Making

If decisions about monetary policy are the function of the Federal Reserve System, whether or not subject to the over-all direction of the Administration of the day, at what point within the System should decisions be made?

At present formal responsibility is divided as follows. By tradition rather than by strict legal requirement, discount-rate changes are initiated by directors of Reserve Banks, although the Board in Washington has final responsibility. Member-bank reserve requirements are the exclusive responsibility of the Board. Open-market operations are in the hands of a twelve-man committee—the seven-member Board and five Reserve Bank presidents. These arrangements represent a decided improvement over the situation that existed prior to the 1935 Act. Then the Board had the final say in regard to discount policy, although the initiative for changes had to come from the Banks; but open-market operations were conducted by a committee of Bank officials with almost no control by the Board.

It is hardly surprising that decisiveness has not been the most marked attribute of Federal Reserve policy making. Whether the System is able to make up its mind turns in practice upon whether or not the chairman of the Board is a dominating personality, and whether or not he gets along with the president of the New York Bank. The New York Bank has been run mostly by vigorous executives who knew their own minds—Strong, Harrison, and Sproul. On the other hand between the time that W. P. G. Harding left Washington in 1922 and the arrival of Marriner Eccles in 1934, the Board suffered from a succession of weak executives, and the System as a whole from indecisiveness. In 1927 the handling of the Chicago rate case was clumsy; in 1929 policy remained unresolved for months; the open-market operations of late 1929 and early 1930 were carried out by Governor Harrison without consulting the Board. After Eccles arrived to give the Board direction, he usually had his way—sometimes over Harrison's opposition, but usually with Sproul's agreement. After 1940, indeed, the struggle with the Treasury tended to unify the System, but indecision again became evident when McCabe succeeded Eccles as Board Chairman in 1948—indecision which was only resolved three years later by the Accord of 1951 and the advent of Chairman Martin. Unquestionably Mr. Martin is a strong executive and he has not allowed differences of opinion—for example, between Washington and New York on the subject of "bills only"—to prevent firm and prompt policy making.

This history suggests that the effectiveness of the System's policy making processes still depends too heavily upon the accident of personality. First, the decision-making power is too widely spread. Second, it is distributed differently for different policy instruments.

The Reserve Banks' role in discount policy represents a desire for sensitivity to regional circumstances that is wholly out of place today. National economic policy must be nationwide, and the gradual disappearance of regional differentials in interest rates is a symptom of the Reserve's own involvement in national policy. The Banks' role in open-market policy (through the Open Market Committee) recognizes at least in part the need for operating experience and contact with the market not readily available in Washington. On the other hand the exclusive concentration in the Board of Governors of the power to vary reserve requirements recognizes the direct connection between reserve ratios and commercial-bank earnings: Congress refrained from giving member banks the power, even very indirectly, to influence their own earnings.

To concentrate decision-making power, discount policy, open-market policy, and the variation of reserve requirements should all be located in one place, preferably the Board of Governors, if necessary with a somewhat modified membership. This would imply abolition of the present Open Market Committee. The present Committee is unwieldy: in addition to the twelve voting members (the Board and five Reserve Bank presidents), the seven nonvoting presidents attend, and perhaps a dozen staff (including of course the manager of the open-market account), making thirty or more persons altogether. Difficulty and delay in reaching a consensus is at times apparent from the published record. Even the Board is perhaps large for its purpose and might be reduced from seven governors with 14-year terms to five with 10-year terms.[7] As mentioned in the preceding section, terms should end in odd- rather than even-numbered years. It is obvious that many of the duties at present performed by governors in person could equally well be carried out by hearing examiners or other staff members, or should be transferred to other agencies (see Chapter 14).

As an objection to concentration of policy making in the Board I do not regard the regional issue as relevant. It is high time that we recognized that what we need—and what we already essentially have—is a central bank located in Washington with 12 major and 24 minor branch offices spread across the nation.

The objection that the Board is too far removed from the money market to be able to control open-market operations effectively appears more substantial. Yet the present division of function between the Open Market Committee (which makes policy) and the management of the account (which carries it out) seems to work well enough. It is hard to see why the Board should not make policy just as the Committee does today.

A further argument for concentrating all policy making in the Board is based, although not too solidly, on the notion, acceptable enough in itself, that commercial bankers should not regulate themselves. Three directors of each Reserve Bank are commercial bankers; three more are elected by bankers; the remaining three are appointed to represent the public. Boards of directors nominate Reserve Bank presidents (subject to approval by the Board of Governors); Reserve Bank presidents sit upon the Open Market Committee. The possibility that member banks might influence open-market policy is not as significant as it sounds, for Reserve Bank presidents tend to be career officials, not subject to detailed control by their directors; and in any case they form a minority of the Committee. Nontheless this question has generated so much heat, in Congressional committees and elsewhere, that it would seem worth

[7] G. L. Bach, whose preference is for a single administrator, favors a three-man Board with six-year terms (*Federal Reserve Policy-Making* [New York: Knopf, 1950], pp. 222–27) on the ground that the Reserve must negotiate with the Treasury and other agencies, and a negotiating body should be as small as possible.

while to remove even the appearance of banker representation in Reserve policy making.

The Over-all Management of Macroeconomic Policy

So long as the management of the economy in a macroeconomic sense consisted solely of monetary policy, the question of the "independence" of the Reserve System, and the locus of decision making within it, could be left in the terms discussed above. The partial and as yet incomplete transformation of fiscal influences from mere unwanted disturbances to deliberate measures of macroeconomic policy has changed all this. Although still in its infancy, discretionary fiscal policy will probably come to play an ever larger role in the regulation of economic activity. The coordination and over-all direction of these two types of economic policy is already an urgent matter.

In some cases fiscal policy may usefully supplement or reinforce monetary measures. Although during the 1930's monetary measures were not pushed to the limit, their effectiveness in a severe depression is questionable. The deficit spending of that period also was relatively ineffective, mainly because of its delayed application and modest scale in comparison with the severity of the depression. Whether or not fiscal measures are more powerful than monetary, all will agree that both influences working in the same direction can achieve more than either taken separately. Public reaction to recent business recessions suggests that fiscal measures, deliberately undertaken, are likely to become a regular feature of stabilization policy: recessions will be met with a tax cut, or larger federal spending, or both. Thus will fiscal be brought to the aid of monetary policy.

We need not expect fiscal always to reinforce monetary management, for occasions may arise when the influence of the one may appropriately be used to offset the effects of the other. In 1946-1948, budget surpluses were used to cancel, in part, the inflationary consequences of cheap money. In 1961–1963, a Treasury deficit partly compensated for the deflationary effects of relatively high interest rates induced by gold losses. If a determined effort is ever made to raise the growth rate of the American economy, it will call (amongst other measures) for monetary ease coupled with Treasury surpluses. Combinations of fiscal and monetary measures, appropriate for the purpose in hand, may enable us to reach objectives we could not reach with either taken separately. But we shall fail to reach our objectives and to realize the full potential of the weapons of economic policy available to us, unless fiscal and monetary policies are coordinated and—at least in broad outline—given unified direction.

The locus of monetary decision making we discussed above. On the fiscal front, management is formally in the hands of the President, in the sense that he regularly transmits budgetary proposals to Congress—proposals of a kind he has hitherto not been expected to make in the field of monetary policy. Also involved are the Bureau of the Budget, which formulates proposals for spending, the Treasury, which formulates tax proposals—and of course Congress, which has the last word with respect to both. It might be thought that the Treasury would be the logical source of fiscal policy making, but its lack of contact with expenditure policy is at present a serious weakness.[8] It is evident that the locus of decision making here is far more dispersed than in the case of monetary management.

Who can furnish the necessary direction? The Reserve Board Chairman, the Secretary of the Treasury, some new "czar" appointed for the purpose, or a cabinet-level committee? Such alternatives have only to be stated to be discarded. The Reserve Board Chairman has no authority in the fiscal field and could not reasonably be given any; the Secretary of the Treasury has monetary and fiscal functions, but both are attenuated, and his prime interest and main responsibility might almost be said to lie in debt management; no new "czar" could be expected to influence the Reserve System on the one hand or Congress on the other; a cabinet-level committee may have value in reconciling divergent viewpoints, but its ultimate role could be no more than advisory. I conclude that the President alone can effectively shoulder the responsibility and provide the leadership that is required.

Although frequently recommended, it seems doubtful that a cabinet committee can be much help to the President. The Douglas subcommittee proposed a National Monetary and Credit Council

[8] This lack of contact has frequently been illustrated. In January 1957 when Secretary Humphrey predicted "a depression that will curl your hair" if taxes were not reduced, he also said "there are a lot of places where the budget can be cut"—thereby disclaiming responsibility for the budget for 1957–1958 that had been drawn up by the Bureau of the Budget and had just been laid before Congress by President Eisenhower. Shortly thereafter, W. Randolph Burgess, Humphrey's deputy, told the Senate Finance Committee that cuts of $2 to $3 billion should be made. See A. E. Holmans, *United States Fiscal Policy 1945–1959* (London: Oxford University Press, 1961), p. 262.

of a purely advisory character under the Chairman of the Council of Economic Advisers.[9] In 1953 President Eisenhower established an Advisory Board for Economic Growth and Stability, in which the Chairman of the CEA presided over a group of undersecretaries (or the equivalent) from the Federal Reserve, the Departments of State, Treasury, Agriculture, Commerce, Labor, and Health, Education and Welfare, the Housing and Home Finance Administration, and the Bureau of the Budget. Dormant in the Kennedy Administration, the reactivation of the Advisory Board has been proposed by the Commission on Money and Credit.

Such a cabinet- or subcabinet-level committee may be useful in explaining policy and resolving differences of view. But only the President can choose the monetary-fiscal policy mix appropriate to the given situation with some hope of seeing it implemented. He should be able to obtain all the *advice* he needs from the Council of Economic Advisers and its staff. When he has decided what policy is appropriate, his main task remains: to persuade the Federal Reserve to adopt monetary measures and Congress to adopt fiscal measures to carry it out. It seems unlikely that a committee, however high-level, could give him much help in this regard.

If we view the matter in this fashion, the issue of the "independence" of the Reserve System takes on a somewhat novel aspect. The traditional case for independence of the central bank from the Treasury rests upon the desire of the latter to minimize the burden of servicing the public debt, even at the cost of cheap money that could promote inflation. The case for a monetary authority independent of the chief executive or the government of the day is somewhat different. It rests upon the notion that monetary policy is a technical matter not readily understood by laymen, and that so far as a president or prime minister does understand it he may be tempted in a shortsighted fashion to cheapen money in an attempt to win an election. Negatively, the case for the central bank's independence has in the past rested upon the absence or unimportance of other types of macroeconomic policy, such as fiscal measures, with which monetary policy needed to be coordinated.

Other countries have chosen other ways to coordinate fiscal and

---

[9] Subcommittee on Monetary, Credit, and Fiscal Policies of the Joint Committee on the Economic Report, *Monetary, Credit and Fiscal Policies*, Senate Document 129, 81st Cong. 2nd Sess., 1950, p. 48. For a similar proposal, see Bach, Ch. XII.

monetary policy. In Britain for example since World War II the Chancellor of the Exchequer has initiated both fiscal and monetary measures—the former by legislation proposed to Parliament, the latter by direction (to date informal, but if necessary formal) to the Bank of England. In the United States it is scarcely possible to imagine the Secretary of the Treasury fulfilling such a role. As we have seen, not even within the Administration itself is he uniquely responsible for the formulation of fiscal policy. Moreover, any proposal to subject the Federal Reserve to Treasury direction would—in the light of history—inevitably be resisted. Not since the untroubled days of Secretary Mellon has the U.S. Treasury enjoyed the prestige and goodwill that could qualify it as the source of overall economic policy.

Therefore the burden falls squarely on the President. But effective leadership by the President in the formulation and implementation of policy will require major changes in our ways of doing things. In the first place it will involve subordination of the Federal Reserve System to the White House with respect to the larger aspects of monetary policy. Second, with respect to fiscal policy, it will demand some delegation, or even renunciation, of power by Congress.

The first of these reforms is probably the easier to achieve. The intention of the Banking Act of 1935 was to give each incoming administration the opportunity to appoint a Reserve Board Chairman. The intention was vitiated by the phraseology of the 1935 Act and the accident of retirement, but there seems no reason why the existing four-year term of Chairman should not be made regularly coextensive with the Presidential term of office. At any rate the coordination of monetary with fiscal policy in a modern economy seems to demand that the Federal Reserve follow Presidential directives that state broadly how easy or tight money should be. The choice of instruments and the detailed management of the money market can of course be left to the Reserve.

The second reform, for the coordination of fiscal policy, looks to be much more difficult to achieve. Too often the President proposes, Congress disposes. The need for (say) a tax cut is evidenced by the economic situation; but the economic situation may be read differently by different people. Further, as we have seen recently, proposals for a tax cut generate controversy on account of the principles involved: "fiscal orthodoxy" and other irrelevancies may be in-

voked. In acting upon controversial legislation Congress is notorious-
ly dilatory, although it can act fast where a clear emergency has
stilled controversy. Hence such a tax cut may not become law until
many months after it was first proposed, by which time it may be no
longer desirable. There are good reasons for pressing for (1)
formula flexibility, or (2) Presidential discretion. Both, but especially the second, were urged by the Commission on Money and
Credit.[10]

Formula flexibility would vary the tax schedule on the basis of
some prescribed economic indicator, for instance the unemployment
percentage. Such an arrangement would secure rapid action, but not
necessarily of just the amount required. Much superior would be a
grant of Presidential discretion, for instance to vary the first-bracket
rate of the individual income tax by a defined number of percentage
points. Either plan would enable Congress to debate the controversial
principles involved at leisure; then, if the standby power were enacted, it could be used without delay whenever needed.

Unquestionably these reforms would greatly increase the power
of the President over the management of the economy. The record of
chief executives in understanding these matters is not good. Even if
it were, the President would obviously need advice, and the obvious
place for him to turn is to his Council of Economic Advisers and its
chairman. The latter would of course discuss upcoming policy proposals with the Chairman of the Federal Reserve Board of Governors, the Secretary of the Treasury, and the Chairmen of the House
Ways and Means Committee and the Senate Finance Committee. It is
to be supposed, too, that the Chairman of the CEA would write necessary directives for Presidential approval.

These appear to be, and are, substantial changes in our ways of
doing things. But the true management of money implies the management of the economy in a macroeconomic sense: it has passed out
of the hands of the central bank, but it has not yet been lodged elsewhere in a fully conscious and consistent fashion. The management
of the economy is a function of government, and in a democratic
society must rest with the chief executive.

[10] *Report of the Commission on Money and Credit* (Englewood Cliffs, N.J.: Prentice-
Hall, 1961), Ch. 5.

Chapter 12

Objectives for Management

> It is certain that the world will not much longer tolerate the unemployment which, apart from brief intervals of excitement, is associated—and, in my opinion, inevitably associated—with present-day capitalistic individualism. But it may be possible by a right analysis of the problem to cure the disease whilst preserving efficiency and freedom.
>
> —Keynes, The General Theory

What should be the objectives of macroeconomic policy for a modern industrial nation such as the United States? Today fiscal as well as monetary policy comes in question, although historically the debate has centered on the narrower issue, What mandate ought to be given to the monetary authority? If fiscal measures also are available, the task of control may be eased and the range of possible objectives broadened somewhat, but the need for a priority ranking of goals remains.

The Absence of a Mandate

Congress has given the Federal Reserve System few guideposts. The preamble to the Federal Reserve Act, as originally passed, gives as its purpose "to furnish an elastic currency, to afford means of rediscounting commercial paper, to establish a more effective supervision of banking in the United States . . ." and Section 14 provides that rates of discount "shall be fixed with a view of accommodating commerce and business . . . ." These monuments of vagueness in the original text have not been changed or elaborated since, despite wholesale rewriting of other portions of the Act. The principal attempts to persuade Congress to furnish the System with a more specific mandate proposed a stabilization, in one form or another, of the commodity-price level. These attempts, made prior to World War II, were chiefly blocked by the resistance of Reserve officials to having their hands tied; they were reviewed in Chapters 4 and 5.

Although Congress has refused to give the Reserve System any more explicit mandate than that quoted, the declaration contained in the Employment Act of 1946 can be regarded as a partial substitute for more specific instructions. This Act, which (as we saw in Chapter 5) was in some measure anticipated by the Patman bill of 1938, declared that "it is the continuing policy and responsibility of the Federal Government . . . to promote maximum employment, production and purchasing power." The Federal Reserve is not mentioned explicitly, and the Act gives no guidance as to the degree to which, or the manner in which, it is expected to share in this "responsibility." Although a hybrid, and in some respects constitutionally independent, the System obviously is to be included in the term "Federal Government." Hence the Employment Act can be interpreted as furnishing the Reserve with an implied mandate in regard to employment stabilization—in company, of course, with all other federal agencies, and especially (we may assume) the Treasury Department. We can also think of it as furnishing the Reserve with retrospective justification for its past concern with the state of business.

On the other hand the Act says nothing about inflation. It offers absolutely no guidance as to how much attention the System should devote to the avoidance of inflation. Nor does it suggest what kind of compromise (if any) it should make between maintaining employment and avoiding inflation, should a conflict between these objectives arise.

We can indeed go somewhat further than this. For on the one hand the Act of 1946 implies that maximum employment is always to be the over-riding consideration for government agencies in setting their policies. On the other hand Congress has rejected a long series of proposals to make some form of price-level stabilization an objective of Reserve policy. The conclusion seems inescapable that the will of Congress gives a higher priority to stable employment than to stable prices.

It is true that the 1946 Employment Act demands that an effort be made to attain maximum "purchasing power" as well as employment. It has been said that this could refer to price-level stability. But if the phrase means purchasing power *of the dollar*, the adjective "maximum" implies the lowest possible price level, not stability of any price level. So this interpretation is ruled out. More likely, "purchasing power," like "production," is to be taken as a synonym for or variant of "employment," and the language means that consumer purchasing power, in money or (more probably) real terms, is to be maximized. So far as I can see, price-level stability can be brought within the objectives of the Employment Act only by arguing that it is a necessary condition for employment stabilization, and this seems to me an oversophisticated interpretation. Indeed the two aims seem more likely to be competitive than complementary.

Arthur F. Burns, writing in 1957 after having served for several years as Chairman of the Council of Economic Advisers, believes that the time finally has come for Congress to legislate in favor of price stability.

> What we need more than anything else at this juncture of our great experiment in the management of prosperity is a national declaration of purpose with regard to the level of prices that could have a moral force such as the Employment Act already exercises with regard to our levels of production and employment. This can be simply accomplished by including reasonable stability of the consumer price level among the objectives of the Employment Act which "it is the continuing policy and responsibility of the federal government to use all practicable means" to promote . . . . One of the main factors in the inflation that we have had since the end of World War II is that many consumers, businessmen, and trade union leaders expected prices to rise and therefore acted in ways that helped to bring about this result. A declaration by the Congress that it is the continuing policy of the federal government to promote reasonable stability of the consumer price level, as well as "maximum employment, production, and purchasing power," could go a considerable distance in dissipating the widespread belief that we are living in an age of inflation and that our government, despite official assertions and even actions to the contrary, is likely to pursue an inflationary course over the long run.[1]

[1] Arthur F. Burns, *Prosperity without Inflation* (New York: Fordham University Press, 1957), p. 71.

Should the Employment Act be amended to declare stability of the price level to be an aim of federal economic policy, on a par with "maximum employment"? In 1959 Senator Prescott Bush of Connecticut introduced a bill (S. 64) for this purpose, which attracted the support of the Eisenhower administration but was not enacted.[2]

Views may differ, both as to how widespread the belief is that we are living in an age of inflation, and as to how effectively a declaration of the sort indicated would dissipate such a belief. To be sure attention has increasingly been devoted by economists and financial analysts to the possibility of a secular decline in the purchasing power of the dollar, and some practical steps have been taken with this possibility in mind. For example, certain insurance companies have for some time past sold annuities with partial protection against inflation through investment in common stocks; while in 1963 pensions to be paid to federal employees were geared for the first time to the consumer price index. Yet I do not think that many consumers, businessmen, or labor leaders think much about the matter, or really believe that the purchasing power of the dollar will continue to shrink. Or if they do believe it, they are not sufficiently convinced to shift in any wholesale fashion out of obligations fixed in money terms. In 1959 the difficulty of selling long-term government bonds was often cited as evidence of a crumbling money illusion and an incipient flight from the dollar. But the low prices of governments and the need to raise the interest ceiling can be adequately explained by the unwillingness of the Reserve to create large amounts of additional cash in the face of burgeoning private capital expenditures. A flight from the dollar will not be in question so long as savings banks and life insurance companies continue to flourish by selling fixed money contracts. The money illusion dies hard, as we well know from studying the early phases of hyperinflation.

Furthermore, it seems to me extremely unlikely that, if the public at large came to believe in the probability of continuing inflation, a mere declaration of Congressional intent could play a significant role in altering this belief. Therefore the reasons given by Burns for desiring a change in the law do not seem to me compelling.

On the other hand, from the standpoint of the Reserve System's mandate, and its relations with the Treasury and other government

[2] See Senate Committee on Banking and Currency, *Employment Act Amendments*, Hearings, 86th Cong. 2nd Sess., 1960, especially pp. 1–5, 129–32, 198.

agencies, the situation is quite otherwise. A Congressional declaration about price-level policy might solidify opinion within the System and furnish the Reserve with a fresh argument in dealing with the Treasury. It might also help the Reserve in meeting public criticism. Credit restriction is never popular: if it can be defended as necessary for price stability, and price stability has Congressional endorsement, the public relations of the System might well benefit thereby.

How much emphasis do we want to place on a stable price level, and how much emphasis on other objectives?

Current Reserve Thinking about Objectives

Federal Reserve officials have committed themselves to multiple objectives. Their philosophy has developed only slowly and they have not always been articulate about it. Particularly since the Accord, the need for explicit formulation of policy objectives has become urgent. To the Joint Economic Committee, for instance, in 1959 Chairman Martin acknowledged the following four objectives:

(1) *Bringing about a maximum rate of sustained economic growth.* Manifested in part by a rising level of living through increasing consumption per capita, this requires rising output per worker: that is, higher productivity through advancing technology. One essential for sustained growth is a volume of real saving and investment sufficient to support continuous renewal, adjustment, and expansion of capital resources. The maintenance of adequate saving and investment depends, in turn, upon broadly based and justified confidence in a reasonably stable dollar.

(2) *Keeping down unemployment.* There are many types of unemployment and many causes of unemployment, and all the factors that go into unemployment must be carefully considered and sympathetically studied in relation to public policy decisions in numerous fields. While we have unemployment compensation benefits for residual or temporary unemployment, the major problem is how to keep people at work and in jobs that will be permanent and profitable.

(3) *Maintaining the value of the dollar.* Reasonable stability of the general price level is important from the point of view of equity and social justice for all who receive or hold money or claims in money terms. It is essential to adequate saving and investment and hence to sustained economic growth, as noted above, and also contributes to the maintenance of relationships between the various individual prices that help to allocate resources in a way to foster over-all economic growth.

(4) *Developing and maintaining balance in international payments.*
The financial position of the United States *vis-à-vis* the rest of the world
is in general very strong, but it will continue necessary in the long run
for this country's foreign trade and payments to be in sustainable balance. This is related, in turn, to keeping an appropriate relationship
between the value of the dollar, in terms of goods and services, and
foreign price levels.[3]

No doubt the System may have, or could be given, numerous other
objectives, such as to discourage speculation in stocks or commodities, to encourage competition among commercial banks, or
even to promote public understanding of our financial system. But
these are minor objectives. As major goals of macroeconomic policy,
the four listed in Chairman Martin's statement may be considered
adequately inclusive. Let us examine them.

The Growth Rate

There will be little disagreement that the speed with which output
per manhour rises depends upon (1) technological advance, and (2)
the level of investment spending. The two things are of course closely
connected, for on the one hand technological change can seldom be
put into effect without fresh investment, while on the other technological advance mostly occurs as a consequence of investment in
research. The contribution that fiscal and monetary policy can make
toward a higher growth rate is concerned with the level of investment
spending.

Certainly for faster growth public investment in research, and perhaps also in productive facilities, may be necessary. The main task
of fiscal and monetary policy, however, must be to raise the level of
private investment. If private investment is not completely interest
inelastic—and in the long run and with respect to long-term interest
rates it is impossible to believe it can be—then monetary expansion
will be effective. On the assumption that it is desired to prevent inflation, the scope for such monetary action can be enlarged through

[3] Joint Economic Committee, *Employment, Growth and Price Levels*, Hearings, 86th
Cong. 1st Sess., 1959, Part 10, pp. 3383–84. This sounds like a committee job. A cap-
tious critic might well ask, in relation to public policy decisions, in what fields factors
that go into unemployment must be studied, to what relationships between individual
prices maintenance of the general price level contributes, and in what sense it is true
to say that the financial position of the United States *vis-à-vis* the rest of the world is
strong at the present time. More substantial exception may be taken, as noted in the text,
to the statement that stability of the general price level is a prerequisite to an adequate
level of saving and investment.

restrictive fiscal action: a budget surplus used for debt repayment will expand the community's saving and supply funds to
the capital market. (If the money in question is hoarded by the
Treasury or by the former owners of public debt, the scope for noninflationary bank expansion is correspondingly increased.) The prescription for growth is therefore an easy monetary coupled with a
tight fiscal policy.

How does this prescription jibe with the requirements of full employment and a stable price level?

With a given percentage of GNP taking the form of investment,
the level of investment will be higher, the larger is GNP, i.e., the
closer the economy is to full employment. But the percentage of
GNP going into investment is correlated with the level of GNP: the
reason is that the public saves a higher percentage of a full-employment income than of a smaller income. All the more, therefore, will
investment be larger, the closer the economy is to full employment.
Consequently, full—or at least a high level of—employment appears
to be not merely compatible with, but a factor favoring a high rate of
growth.

The relation between a high rate of growth and a stable price level
is much more ambiguous. So far as growth is concerned, the first
half of the above prescription is the operative clause: an easy monetary policy to encourage investment. The second half—a tight fiscal
policy—is inserted in order to combine a stable price level with a
high rate of growth. But that a stable price level will contribute to a
high rate of growth is far from obvious. Candor forces us to admit
the possibility that a gently rising commodity-price level might
promote investment by swelling business profits, furnishing "forced
saving," and lightening the debt burden of the entrepreneur. Empirical evidence on this point is conflicting: countries have attained
rapid growth—and equally have stagnated—with rising, with stable,
and with falling price levels.[4] At the very least I must deny having
seen any evidence to support Chairman Martin's assertion that "reasonable stability of the general price level . . . is essential to adequate saving and investment and hence to sustained economic
growth."

---

[4] See, e.g., Otto Eckstein, "Inflation, the Wage-Price Spiral and Economic Growth,"
Joint Economic Committee, *The Relation of Prices to Economic Growth and Stability*,
Compendium of Papers submitted by Panelists, 85th Cong. 2nd Sess., 1958, pp. 361–74.

While the broad prescription for economic growth in an economy such as our own is an easy monetary policy coupled with a tight fiscal policy, many other policy measures can contribute to the desired end. For instance, in the field of monetary management, curbs upon consumer credit can help channel resources into investment. In the fiscal field taxes on consumption and tax credits on investment spending can achieve the same result. But the most important requirement is perhaps expenditure for research, basic and applied, especially by the Treasury. Hence the contribution which monetary and fiscal policy can make toward growth, although considerable, may not be decisive.

The Unemployment Problem

The contribution that monetary and fiscal policy can make in this area depends very much upon the nature of the unemployment from which the economy suffers. It is convenient to discuss four kinds of unemployment:

(1) *Frictional unemployment.* New entrants to the labor market who have not yet found a job, persons laid off briefly (e.g., during model changes), and especially those who have quit their jobs to look for others, fall into this category.

(2) *Seasonal unemployment.* Workers in construction and in agriculture find fewer jobs available in Winter than in Summer. Retailing is busiest before Christmas, and many other trades vary in activity from one season of the year to another. Seasonal joblessness, although by its nature temporary, is regularly repeated.

(3) *Structural unemployment.* Where technological changes have rendered a product obsolete, or superseded the skill formerly needed to make it, or where industry has moved away to some other locality, we speak of "structural unemployment"—because the structure of the economy has changed. The resulting unemployment may be far from temporary, for the best that the displaced worker can hope for may be a job in another occupation in another section of the country. If he is no longer young, and does not care to move his home, he may possibly never find another steady job, or may at best be forced to accept a position demanding less skill and paying less money than his former occupation.

(4) *General unemployment.* In addition to the above causes, people may lack jobs because of an insufficiency of aggregate spend-

ing. One reason for such an insufficiency is the fact that the level of demand fluctuates cyclically. However, general unemployment cannot be blamed entirely on the business cycle, since it is not always wiped out at cyclical peaks in business. It should be noted that, if aggregate spending (GNP) is not high enough to employ everybody who wants a job at existing wage and salary levels, there is in general no way of determining which component—consumption, investment, or government purchases—is deficient. All we can say is that general unemployment exists if an increase in demand will increase employment—whether or not it also raises commodity prices.

It will be obvious that not all unemployed persons can be classified unambiguously into one or another of the above four categories. Yet such a classification affords an indispensable means of arriving at policy prescriptions for dealing with the unemployment problem. For measures to increase the level of demand can—by themselves— be effective only in dealing with the fourth category. The first three categories require other measures.

Although crucial from a policy standpoint, the four categories do not lend themselves readily to empirical assessment. Nevertheless a careful study by the United States Bureau of Labor Statistics, based mainly upon the length of time that unemployed persons had been out of work, offers the following estimates for 1955–1957 for the first three categories (figures represent per cent of the labor force):[5]

Frictional unemployment, about 1.3%

Seasonal unemployment, about 9%

Structural unemployment, at least 4%

This gives a total of 2.6% of the labor force. However, the Bureau feels its estimate for structural unemployment is probably an understatement. Therefore we might be wiser to take a figure of, say, 3% as the level of frictional, seasonal, and structural unemployment in 1955–1957. For these three years total unemployment averaged 4.3% of the labor force, which leaves 1.3% as the volume of general unemployment.

These figures suggest that, if full employment is to be the target for monetary and fiscal policy, it should be defined as, say, 97% (not 100%) of the labor force.

[5] Joint Economic Committee, *Employment, Growth and Price Levels*, Study Paper No. 6, "The Extent and Nature of Frictional Unemployment," 86th Cong. 1st Sess., 1959.

To the extent that frictional unemployment results from persons quitting their jobs voluntarily, our concern is correspondingly reduced. Inasmuch as frictional and seasonal unemployment are of short duration, they cannot be regarded as a serious social evil, as must structural and general unemployment. To cut frictional unemployment we need to shorten the time it takes a man to change jobs; to cut seasonal unemployment we need to furnish other employment during the slack season. For such improved mobility of labor, better labor-market information is probably the main need.

Structural differs from frictional unemployment only in degree, but the difference in degree amounts to a difference in kind. When a man must acquire new skills, or move to another section of the country, in order to find a job, the problem, although still a matter of mobility, is of a different order. In the past men have acquired new skills or have "gone west" on their own initiative, and no doubt will still do so in the future. A supply of unfilled jobs in the new occupation and location is a necessary condition—that is, the maintenance of aggregate demand. To be sure, monetary or fiscal policy alone will not do much to accelerate the process. Better labor-market information may help. But to make a real dent in structural unemployment stronger measures are needed. Public facilities for retraining and aid to migration probably afford the best means of attack. To some extent, too, government may be able to influence industrial location, but in most cases it probably is more efficient to move workers to jobs than jobs to workers. The Area Redevelopment and Manpower Training Acts offer an opportunity to experiment.

The net of this discussion is that the maintenance of an adequate level of demand is a necessary condition for reducing frictional, seasonal, and structural unemployment, but no more than a necessary condition. Unless combined with other measures of an entirely different order, monetary and fiscal policy will achieve little in this area.

With general or cyclical unemployment the matter stands otherwise: a more adequate level of demand is the prime condition for reducing or eliminating it. To inquire how much monetary and fiscal policy can achieve is to ask what fraction of the unemployment existing at any time is general in character.

As we have seen, in 1955–1957 when total unemployment averaged 4.3% of the labor force, general unemployment may be placed at about 1.3%. Recently the total has averaged 6% or more. How much of a 6% rate in the early 1960's should be considered general, and how much structural, seasonal, or frictional?

The unemployment rate appears to show an upward trend since 1952 or 1953: in peak years, for example, it averaged 2.9% in 1953, 4.3% in 1957, and 5.6% in 1960. Does this upward trend reflect an increase in structural unemployment? The idea is supported by first impressions: the prominence of "automation" as the villain in many public discussions of the unemployment problem, the increase in the number of persons out of work for more than 26 weeks, and the high rates of unemployment in some areas from which industry has evidently ebbed away. That structural unemployment has become more severe appears to be the view of the Federal Reserve System as expressed by Chairman Martin.[6] Such a view takes the Reserve off the hook and implies growing impotence of monetary and fiscal policy in dealing with the unemployment problem.

That the upward trend in unemployment has been due to an upward trend in the structural component has been denied by James Tobin on behalf of the Council of Economic Advisers[7] and in a report prepared for the Joint Economic Committee by James W. Knowles, a member of its staff.[8] Tobin's position rests upon comparisons between 1953, 1957, and 1960, of unemployment broken by as many characteristics as data allow: age, sex, occupation, industry, locality, marital status, and education. He argues that increased structural unemployment should show up in increased concentration of unemployed in some age brackets, occupations, etc. Instead he finds unemployment to be more or less uniformly higher in 1960 than in 1957 in all age brackets, occupations, etc. The higher unemployment rates of recent years are shown not to be the result of relatively heavier unemployment in upper-age brackets, declining industries, or labor-surplus areas. This conclusion seems rather well supported by the Council's data, although it might possibly be upset by inspection of more detailed occupational, industrial, or topographic

---

[6] "The problem of structural unemployment is manifest in the higher total of those left unemployed after each wave of the three most recent business cycles. . . ." Joint Economic Committee, *January 1961 Economic Report*, Hearings, 87th Cong. 1st Sess., 1961, pp. 470–71; see also pp. 480–82, 485–87. See same, *January 1962 Economic Report*, Hearings, 87th Cong. 2nd Sess., 1962, pp. 171–72, 193–95.

[7] Joint Economic Committee, *January 1961 Economic Report*, Hearings, 87th Cong. 1st Sess., 1961, pp. 295, 378–92.

[8] Joint Economic Committee, Subcommittee on Economic Statistics, *Higher Unemployment Rates, 1957–60: Structural Transformation or Inadequate Demand*, 87th Cong. 1st Sess., 1961.

breakdowns. Tobin's results are confirmed by the broadly similar but more detailed study by Knowles using data for the period 1948–1960.

It should be emphasized that this difference of opinion between the Council of Economic Advisers and the Reserve System relates to the question whether structural unemployment has been *increasing* during the past decade. The Council does not deny the *existence* of structural unemployment, or the desirability of dealing with it by measures to raise the mobility of labor—rather than by fiscal and monetary policy. The weight of evidence is that structural unemployment has *not* been increasing, and that it still measures perhaps as little as ½%—and certainly less than 1%—of the labor force, just as it did in 1955–1957. If we assume that frictional and seasonal unemployment combined have remained at something over 2%, we may safely continue to regard frictional, seasonal, and structural unemployment as together constituting roughly 3% of the labor force. Whenever the unemployment rate is above 3%, we may conclude that the excess represents general unemployment—i.e., joblessness which in principle should yield to monetary and fiscal policy.

Since unemployment rates have averaged 5% and 6% in recent years, it would seem that the scope for monetary and fiscal policy in a direct attack upon the unemployment problem is considerable. We should remember, too, that an adequate level of demand is needed as a condition of success if other measures are to be used to attack structural unemployment. Whether a higher level of aggregate demand would have entailed greater instability of the price level is a question discussed below.

The Inflation Problem

An increase in aggregate spending will reduce the amount of general unemployment, but it may also raise commodity prices and wage rates. Indeed if the level of demand is increased beyond the point at which general unemployment disappears, a rise in price and wage levels is certain to occur. By inflation I mean here any rise in the commodity-price level.[9] (1) Creeping inflation implies a rise in the price level not fast enough to scare people out of holding claims

[9] For most purposes the wholesale or the consumer-price index is an acceptable measure of the price level: both become available fairly promptly. However, since the price level of output is in question, and output means the constituents of GNP, the GNP deflator (available less promptly) obviously is a preferable measure.

fixed in money terms—a rise of (say) up to 5% yearly. (2) A more rapid rise in the price level, to be called trotting or galloping inflation, leads to widespread anticipations that the return obtainable on money claims will be inadequate to compensate the holder for depreciation in the monetary unit. Just what rate of price increase will lead to such anticipations depends upon a wide range of circumstances, of which the observed depreciation in the recent past is merely the chief. (3) With hyperinflation, or disappearance of value in the monetary unit, we shall scarcely be concerned.

Without question monetary and fiscal policy can promote or discourage inflationary tendencies in the economy. Moreover an inflationary fiscal policy can in great measure be neutralized by a deflationary monetary policy, and vice versa. When the two types of policy are fully coordinated and working in the same direction, they have virtually complete control over aggregate spending or the dollar volume of GNP.

On the other hand the relation between GNP measured in dollars and output and employment is complex and not too well understood. (1) With given factor prices and factor productivity, the supply curve of output may well decline at low levels of output, but must be horizontal or slowly rising as output approaches "full employment," sharply rising as output is pressed beyond that point. Hence an increase in the level of demand from any but a very low level of output is certain to cause some inflation, however mild. Beyond full employment the inflation will become more severe. If unemployment is cyclical and commodity prices fell during the recession, their return to their former level could conveniently be called "reflation." Under these circumstances the price level is positively correlated with output and employment, but there is no upward trend in the full-employment price level. Fiscal and monetary policies can be directed toward full employment and no "inflation problem" exists. If aggregate spending is pushed up beyond the full-employment level, "demand-pull" inflation occurs.

(2) If productivity is steady and factor prices rise, or if factor prices rise more rapidly than productivity, the supply curve of output is shifted upward. If the dollar volume of GNP is maintained unchanged—the shift in the supply curve notwithstanding—then, of course, output and employment must fall and commodity prices rise. Inflation (as we have defined it) will occur to some extent, what-

ever the policy of the authorities, unless they successfully pursue a restriction designed to lower factor prices to their former level. In order to maintain the previous level of employment and output, the authorities will actually be forced to increase the dollar volume of GNP and raise commodity prices still further. Here the pursuit of full employment involves a problem of inflation—"cost-push" inflation. An analytically similar situation occurs when commodity prices are fixed, administered, or the subject of widespread price leadership.

The distinction between demand-pull and cost-push inflation has been challenged on the ground that, since the inflation cannot proceed any distance unless the authorities allow an increase in the dollar volume of GNP, cost-push is really a form of demand-pull. Yet to say that the central bank acquiesces in a rise in commodity prices that results from a rise in factor prices, is not to say that the initiative came from monetary policy. To distinguish in practice between the two kinds of inflation may be difficult, but the distinction in principle seems clear and the problems raised by each are quite different.

The External Value of the Dollar

The fourth objective of Reserve policy mentioned by Chairman Martin, developing and maintaining balance in international payments, is an implied requirement of the Federal Reserve Act in that it sets minimum gold-certificate reserves for Reserve Bank liabilities. Nevertheless this objective stands on a somewhat different footing from the others. Growth, employment, and a stable price level are all major goals of domestic policy; by our success or failure in attaining them the performance of our mixed public-private economy must ultimately be judged. Stable exchange rates with other currencies and a stable gold value for the dollar are nice to have, but nobody can claim that their attainment constitutes a test of our system. Hence the fourth objective is entitled to a far lower priority than the other three.

To be sure, this position represents a reversal of classical notions about money. Time was when monetary policy consisted merely in the free coinage of gold: those were the days when paper money was not yet important and money would manage itself. Later the gold standard became a guard against paper-money inflation and a model for the automatic regulation of money. But nations found that they had to sacrifice domestic objectives that they valued, if they were to succeed in maintaining international convertibility at a fixed rate in terms of gold or currencies other than their own.

Advantages to world trade and investment accrue from fixed exchange rates; yet these advantages can be purchased at too high a price. In some respects the situation of the United States is special: it has been claimed that we have an obligation to maintain the external value of the dollar, both because of our membership in the International Monetary Fund and because many other nations keep part of their monetary reserves in dollars. But these are not irrevocable commitments. We can, if we wish, withdraw from the IMF and we can relinquish our role as a key-currency nation.

In the long run a country cannot maintain a fixed external value for its currency unless its commodity and factor prices are in some degree flexible. So long as the world situation remains even mildly inflationary, downward flexibility may not be necessary, but some control over the upward movement of prices and wages is indispensable. In recent years inflation has lowered the commodity value of gold throughout the world, but inflation has proceeded more rapidly in some countries than in others. Fixed exchange rates require that nations keep in step.

Differing rates of productivity introduce further obstacles to equilibrium under fixed exchange rates. Even were factor prices, and especially wage rates, to remain stable or to move in a similar fashion in different countries, those with rapidly rising productivity would develop chronic surpluses in their balances of payments; those with lagging productivity, deficits. But factor prices do not move together; in some countries they tend to be stable, in others to be subject to cost-push inflation.

The small size of the world's gold reserves compared with the volume of its international trade argues for a general increase in the price of gold in terms of all currency units. Yet we should recognize that a mere increase in the dollar price of gold is not likely to relieve the United States balance of payments permanently. Provided that the cut in the gold content of the dollar is bigger than the average cut for the world's currencies at large, temporary relief may indeed be furnished. But cost-push inflation is likely to re-assert itself in the United States. So long as its external value is fixed, the dollar is likely in time to become overvalued again. Therefore a floating exchange rate seems by far the wisest regime for the United States.

Whether the external value of the dollar should be left wholly to the free play of the market, or whether the Exchange Fund should attempt to diminish fluctuations by engaging in the difficult art of counterspeculation, is a secondary question about which I have no strong views. The important thing is not to commit ourselves to a fresh fixed parity, with gold or other leading currencies, either immediately or at some time in the future. For the fact that such a parity must inevitably in time become obsolete is only one objection to it. The other objection is that, if we adopt a fresh fixed parity, all other nations may devalue by the same amount. Should this happen, the world's metallic currency reserves would indeed be increased, but the opportunity to remove the present relative overvaluation of the dollar would have been lost.

A growth rate of a given size, full employment of resources, or a stable price level cannot be achieved automatically; they have to be worked for and engineered; they are legitimate objects of policy. Not so "developing and maintaining balance in international payments," Chairman Martin's fourth objective. In no sense is it an aim with which monetary and fiscal policy should concern itself. For balance in international payments is something that can and should come about of its own accord through the market—provided only that we do not insist upon artificial stability in the external value of our currency.

Compatibility of Objectives

Four objectives can be combined into six pairs, so that six different types of incompatibility might be worth discussing. However I do not propose to dignify maintenance of the external value of the dollar as an objective for which we should be prepared to sacrifice any one of the other three major aims. Incompatibilities to be seriously considered are thereby reduced to three. Furthermore, no difficulty is at present visible in combining a high rate of economic growth with full employment. The problem of compatibility therefore reduces itself to a single major issue: how far can full employment (and economic growth) be combined with price-level stability?

In this context "full employment" means an absence of general unemployment—or, say, 97% of the labor force in jobs. The level of demand required to accomplish this goal is of course a function, not only of the physical amount of factors available to the economy (e.g., the labor force), but also of their prices. If factor prices are stable, sluggish, custom-bound, or conventional—in a word not easily altered—the level of spending required for full employment will lead to a stable price level if technology is stationary, or to a slowly declining price level if technology is advancing. With stable factor prices, or with factor prices which rise no more rapidly than technology advances, we need not worry about a conflict between full employment on the one hand and price stabilization on the other.

But will factor prices remain stable in a full-employment environment? If some degree of monopoly exists in commodity markets, full employment may produce an upward pressure on profit margins, as business raises product prices over which it has control. More important, probably, is the nature of the wage bargain. If full employment allows unions to force up wages more rapidly than productivity is increasing, employers may transmit their higher costs through higher prices to their customers. In either case the level of demand that produced full employment will be insufficient to maintain it. If fiscal and monetary policy perpetuates this level of spending, employers will offer less employment. As the level of output declines, the upward pressure on profits and wages will decline too, until both reach equilibrium. This is of course an underemployment equilibrium, with the same current-dollar GNP as before, but higher commodity prices and lower employment and output.

Advancing technology may help to ease the situation temporarily, bringing prices down and expanding output and employment once again. But as full employment is once more approached, the cost-push may be expected to reassert itself, so that unemployment will reappear.

To be sure, when an autonomous rise in labor cost yields an underemployment equilibrium, it is not likely that the level of aggregate spending will remain indefinitely at its pristine level. Sooner or later the monetary authority will allow the level of spending to rise—and so, in effect, acquiesce in the higher level of factor prices. Of course such acquiescence will also raise commodity prices, since the economy operates upon a rising supply curve of output. If the level of spending is raised by an amount sufficient to eliminate unemployment, commodity prices must rise to the extent that the rise in factor prices exceeds the increase in productivity due to technological change. Such is the dilemma.

It may be objected that higher wages can and should be paid "out of profits." The scope for this escape is very limited. It will be found, if allowance is made for the decline in the number of self-employed, that the wage bill has been an extraordinarily stable fraction of national income over the years. The scope for permanently changing the distribution of national income appears to be small. It may also be objected that wage increases stimulate productivity. If so, the scope for increasing total spending without raising prices is thereby enlarged. But the evidence is slim.

The temporary advantage gained by any group—of workers or business firms—is real enough, but their gain is rapidly eroded as other groups improve *their* position and the purchasing power of the dollar falls. You have to run in order to stay in the same place. And some groups will fall behind. Perhaps in the end, as these matters come to be more thoroughly understood by the public at large, some agreed national wage policy may emerge. The "guideposts" for noninflationary wage settlements offered by the Council of Economic Advisers in 1962 represented a first step in that direction.

Meanwhile, which horn of the dilemma should public policy embrace: unemployment or inflation? If the choice has to be made, I do not think it can be made on grounds of principle. On the one hand it can be claimed that for Uncle Sam to debase the dollar is the height of immorality, especially since he is net debtor for a large amount. On the other hand it can equally well be urged that nothing is more immoral than the deliberate adoption of a policy that must create unemployment, cause businesses to fail, and lead to the loss of billions of dollars' worth of output. Hence, as with so many other choices in this unhappy world, the rate of substitution is critical. Obviously the wrecking of the currency through inflation would be too high a price to pay for the avoidance of a small amount of unemployment. Nor would a 10–15% unemployment rate be a price worth paying simply to avoid a trivial rise in the price level. Unfortunately it is extremely difficult to gauge the rate of substitution available to us, now or in the future. The terms of the trade-off are highly uncertain.

In an attempt to estimate the postwar rate of substitution in the United States, Joseph Aschheim concluded that "the minimal volume of unemployment necessary for price level stability is much closer to 5 per cent of the civilian labor force than 10 per cent."[10] More recently Samuelson and Solow have placed the same minimum unemployment rate at "something like 5 to 6 per cent. . . . That much unemployment would appear to be the cost of price stability in the years immediately ahead." Conversely, they estimate that to keep unemployment down to 3%, "the price index might have to rise by as much as 4 to 5 per cent per year. That much price rise would seem to be the necessary cost of high employment and production in the years immediately ahead."[11]

The history of Reserve policy lends some support to the view that on the whole the System regards inflation as the greater evil. Certainly in peacetime it always has shown a desire to counter inflationary tendencies. In 1923 credit was restricted with this danger in mind; a similar concern dominated policy in 1937. It is abundantly clear that after World War II inflation was the System's prime worry, although its determination to buck the Treasury on this issue did not reach the sticking point until almost six years after the war was over. More recently the restraints imposed on credit in 1953 and in 1956–1957 also show the sensitiveness of the System to the inflation danger. To be sure, the Reserve fought the downswings in employment as best it knew how, but its prime preoccupation in recent years has been the inflationary potentialities of such trends as monetization of the federal debt, rising consumer installment debt, and low-cost mortgages.

Yet a preference, if it exists, for fighting inflation rather than maintaining employment cannot be justified by an appeal to Congressional sentiment. I have argued that what little direction Congress has given argues for the opposite—fighting unemployment rather than battling inflation—as the first priority. To be sure, Congressional direction has been so inexplicit that no indictment of the Reserve for embracing the wrong horn of the dilemma could well

[10] Joint Economic Committee, *The Relationship of Prices to Economic Stability and Growth*, Compendium of papers submitted by panelists, 85th Cong. 2nd Sess., 1958, p. 25. See also A. W. Phillips, "The Relation between Unemployment and the Rate of Change of Money Wage Rates in the United Kingdom, 1861–1957," *Economica*, N. S. XXV (November 1958), 283–300.

[11] Paul A. Samuelson and Robert A. Solow, "Analytical Aspects of Anti-Inflation Policy," *American Economic Review* (May 1960), p. 192.

be returned. Moreover, even if I read the record correctly, I would not want to argue that the Reserve has in fact shown any consistent preference for one horn or the other.

Yet if a choice should have to be made, there are grounds, I believe, for gearing policy to employment rather than the price level. These grounds are independent of any mandate which Congress may or may not be conceived to have given on this point. The issue is scarcely matter for a Gallup poll. Yet it is my belief that the public at large, if fully informed and properly consulted, would prefer a moderate dose of inflation to moderate unemployment—if useful meanings can be given to the word "moderate" in what must remain an essentially vague comparison. I base this view on common observation of the public's reaction in the two cases. News of unemployment is occasion for widespread indignation and for wry comparisons with the Soviet economy. On the other hand, in our affluent society the high cost of living has, so it seems to me, long ceased to be a live political issue. It is recognized, too, that from the standpoint of equity, unemployment hits given localities and individuals, whereas the cost of rising prices is much more widely shared. Despite numerous distortions, a booming economy operates far more efficiently than one in which resources are running to waste.

These considerations, which favor priority for the maintenance of employment, would be outweighed were either of two propositions established. First, should it be true that priority for high employment at the expense of price-level instability would cumulate disturbances and yield violent and uncontrollable cyclical fluctuations, then the employment policy would evidently prove self-defeating. I see no real evidence that this proposition is true. Since World War II, despite quite violent upswings in business, the recessions that followed have been mild and have yielded rapidly to treatment (see above, Table 8). Second, should it be true that moderate inflation could easily lead unbeknownst to galloping inflation and the destruction of the monetary unit, then the cost of following a full-employment policy would clearly be excessive. I see no evidence that this proposition is true either. The halving of the value of the dollar in less than a decade has failed appreciably to reduce the popularity of fixed money obligations as a repository for savings. The money illusion dies hard, very hard.

I conclude that on present evidence as to the terms of the trade-off and the value scales of the public, policy should in general prefer a high level of employment to a stable price level. I conclude further that Congressional emphasis on employment policy and coolness toward price-level stabilization is well grounded in the preferences of the American public at large.

Chapter 13

Instruments of Management

> *To alter the terms on which the community*
> *will accumulate real capital—that is what*
> *monetary policy is all about.*
> —JAMES TOBIN and WILLIAM C. BRAINARD

The three principal instruments of monetary policy—discount-rate changes, open-market purchases and sales, and the variation of member-bank reserve requirements—furnish a battery of quantitative or nonselective controls over the volume of money, interest rates, and the availability of credit, and through these, upon the level of the community's spending for output. Such instruments are called *general* credit controls because, while it cannot be said that they have an absolutely uniform effect on all borrowers, they do not *intentionally* discriminate between uses of credit. The virtue of nondiscrimination is that just so much credit as can safely be made available finds its use according to its price. The presumption is that the practical, impersonal test of the market will distribute what credit is available more fairly and efficiently than any measure that regulates the price or availability of credit in a single use, or to any single class of borrowers.

How far is this presumption justified? To what extent do imperfections in the credit and capital markets cause general credit controls to act in a discriminatory fashion? On the one hand it has been charged that credit restriction bears with particular severity upon residential construction, state and local governments, and small business. In the case of home mortgages and state and local borrowing, difficulties arise because of legal limitations upon interest rates imposed in the first case by the Veterans Administration or the Federal Housing Administration and in the second by local law. Here the market imperfection has been deliberately created. Difficulties of small business in the credit field, to the extent that they exist, seem to reflect one aspect among many in which smallness is a disadvantage; if small business is desirable for its own sake, it should be subsidized or given preferential tax treatment.[1]

In the case of consumer credit, on the other hand, the opposite has been charged: instead of bearing with exceptional severity, a credit restriction has little effect, so that its weight must be borne by other sectors. This question will be discussed below in connection with selective controls. The System has, or has had, power to regulate stock-market credit, consumer credit, and residential-mortgage credit. I shall first consider the adequacy and appropriateness of general credit controls; thereafter I shall discuss the regulation of particular types of credit, and of financial institutions other than commercial banks.

Open-market policy has its primary impact upon the magnitude of member-bank reserve balances; discount policy governs the cost of replenishing them; and changes in reserve requirements of member banks influence the level of earning assets which a given volume of reserve balances will support. Since commercial banks normally seek to acquire all the earning assets that the law allows, these three instruments together give the Reserve System a large measure of control over the aggregate volume of earning assets possessed by the commercial banks. But when a bank acquires an asset, it creates a demand deposit in favor of the seller, and when it parts with an asset it destroys a deposit owned by the buyer. Hence the System can in practice regulate the volume of deposits in the commercial banks, except perhaps in times of severe depression when excess reserves are large.

But the volume of bank deposits is at best a proximate and qualified objective. What we need to ask ourselves is, to what extent this mechanism gives the System control: first, over the quantity of money (defined in any useful manner), the rate of interest, and the availability of credit; second, over the aggregate level of the

[1] For references and a useful review of the evidence on discrimination, see James R. Schlesinger, "Monetary Policy and its Critics," *Journal of Political Economy*, LXVIII (December 1960), 608–12.

community's spending (effective demand); and third, over the state of business and the level of employment?

Open-Market Operations

As noted in Chapter 4, the power to influence the general credit situation—to make money easier or tighter—by acquiring or parting with assets in the open market was only slowly understood. Between 1923 and 1935 the control of open-market sales and purchases was the subject of considerable bickering between the Board, which had the power to make "regulations," and the Banks, in whose hands lay the actual business of acquiring assets from or supplying assets to the market. The compromise embodied in the 1935 Act placed open-market policy decisions in the Federal Open Market Committee of twelve, composed of the Board of Governors and five of the Reserve Bank presidents (one of whom is always the president of the New York Bank). The Committee meets every two to three weeks to formulate a directive to the manager of the open-market account in New York. The implementation of the directive is the subject of a daily telephone conference at 11 a.m. between the manager of the account and the president of the New York Bank, and one or more members of the Board of Governors or other members of the Open Market Committee or their alternates.[2]

When first developed as a policy instrument in the 1920's, open-market operations were viewed as a means of "making the discount rate effective," i.e., of starving member banks of reserves and forcing them to borrow from their Reserve Bank. But this is a totally inadequate description of open-market policy as understood today. So far as concerns the effect on the banks, the earlier doctrine had to be adapted to the coming of excess reserves—originally a consequence of the Depression. An individual bank feels pressure to contract when indebted to the Reserve System, and pressure to expand when it possesses excess reserves. From this general observation it follows that the commercial banks as a whole will be more or less inclined to lend, according as their collective "free reserves" (excess reserves minus indebtedness) are large or small, positive or negative. Open-market operations furnish an extremely flexible method of influencing the volume of free reserves. This is the modern analog of the earlier notion of "making the discount rate effective."

[2] Joint Economic Committee, *Review of Annual Report of the Federal Reserve System for 1960*, Hearings, 87th Cong. 1st Sess., 1961, pp. 7–8.

Free reserves have long been used by analysts as an index of ease or tightness in the money market[3] and have also figured in discussions of the Open Market Committee as one among several proximate objectives of control. They are shown month by month for the postwar period in Fig. 3. However, their value as an index of money-market conditions is subject to several qualifications. First, the development over the past decade of the federal funds market, enabling reserves to be lent from one bank to another, appears gradually to have improved the efficiency with which reserves are used, so that a given level of free reserves (other things equal) probably denotes an easier money market than formerly. Second, on the other hand, the inclusion since 1959 of vault cash within required reserves seems certain to have had the opposite effect: their vault cash being now immobilized unless the banks hold excess reserves, their desire to hold such must have been increased, so that on this account given free reserves imply a tighter money market than formerly.[4] Third, in addition to these secular changes, there is evidence that the desired level of free reserves varies negatively with interest rates and is also subject to seasonal variation.[5] Yet for lack of any other single measure that might be superior, "net free reserves" probably will continue to be used as an index of monetary ease or tightness.

To be sure, open-market operations are not important merely for their effect on bank reserves. Gradually it came to be realized that such operations also cause changes in the prices of the particular assets bought and sold. This feature distinguishes open-market operations from other instruments of central-banking policy, for it enables the monetary authority to influence directly persons and institutions other than commercial banks. Open-market operations are therefore extremely versatile, for the central bank can deal—within limits fixed by law—in obligations of widely varying maturity and type of debtor. Thus monetary policy can select which groups it wishes to make more or less liquid, and decide for which borrowers it wishes to raise or lower the cost of capital. To the degree that open-market operations can discriminate in this fashion,

[3] See, e.g., Harold Barger, *Money, Banking and Public Policy* (Chicago: Rand McNally, 1962), Ch. 10, "Money-Market Measurements."

[4] See Milton Friedman, "Vault Cash and Free Reserves," *Journal of Political Economy*, LXIX (April 1961), 181–82.

[5] A. James Meigs, *Free Reserves and the Money Supply* (Chicago: University of Chicago Press, 1962), Ch. V.

they perhaps fail to conform fully to the definition of *general* controls of credit. To be sure, they have a general aspect—influence on bank reserves—and also a special aspect—effect on the price of the particular asset bought or sold. The interest of the central bank in the matter is (or should be) not in discriminating between one use of credit and another, but in making sure that its policies do in fact have the desired result of reducing or increasing aggregate demand.

Certainly the scope of open-market policy has in practice been restricted by limitations of various kinds. The Federal Reserve System, for example, is allowed by law to buy commercial and municipal obligations only when these are of short maturity; in the long-term market it must confine itself to U.S. Treasury securities. Even in the case of federal obligations it has mostly preferred those of short maturity (commonly less than a year). The occasions when the System has bought appreciable amounts of bonds have been few enough to be listed readily: most of them have been mentioned in earlier chapters.

In 1922 the Reserve Banks of Minneapolis and San Francisco bought small quantities of 4¼% Liberty bonds due 1928, no doubt with a view to earnings. But such purchases by individual Reserve Banks were exceptional. As open-market operations gradually became centralized in the System account under the jurisdiction of the Open Market Committee, the practice was to buy nothing longer than 3- or 4-year notes, and but small quantities of these. In November 1929, in the course of helping the New York banks to assume out-of-town obligations in the wake of the crash, the System bought $34 million (or 10% of its portfolio) of Liberty bonds callable November 1933 and due 1938 (really a 4-year obligation, since it was the habit of the Treasury to call at the earliest possible date); but it sold them again—at a profit—shortly thereafter. The first permanent acquisition of bonds by the System account occurred during the slump in the bond market produced by the credit restriction of October-December 1931. To aid member banks the System acquired sizable amounts (about $200 million altogether) of First 3½% Libertys 1932–1947 and Fourth 4¼% Libertys 1933–1938. No doubt officials salved their consciences by reflecting that these obligations ran under two years to first call date, although in view of the depressed state of the market they were unlikely to be (and were not in fact) redeemed so soon. These distress acquisitions, which at the end of 1931 had put nearly one half of the System account into Libertys, were mostly retained until redeemed or converted; but the large open-market purchases of bills and notes during 1932 and 1933 put these bond-holdings (such as they were) completely in the shade.

In the Spring of 1932, as described in Chapter 5, proposals for bond purchases to revive the bond market were resisted by Governors Meyer and Harrison on the ground that such assets would make the System illiquid. The large open-market purchases of 1932 were mostly of bills; but small additions were made to the 1933–1938 Libertys (then not much over a year to first call!). Under pressure from Secretary Morgenthau and with a side glance at earnings, these Libertys, when called April 16, 1934, were converted into 3¼'s 1944–1946, thus giving the System for the first time in its history an obligation maturing in 10 years or longer. However, at midyear 1934 the System held only $79 million of such long-term bonds out of a portfolio of $2,432 million.[6]

In July 1936, at the time of the first increase in member-bank reserve requirements, about $100 million of bonds were bought, and a corresponding amount of shorter maturities sold, to stabilize the market, but the due dates of these bonds are not known. Another $100 million were bought in December, and some $210 million in March and April 1937 at the time of the second increase in reserve requirements: these had maturities in excess of five years.[7] Since all these purchases were to offset bond sales by commercial banks, it is to be assumed that they were mainly if not wholly of maturities less than 10 years. By mid-1937, 27% of the System's holding consisted of bonds with a maturity of 5 years or more. Further bond purchases at intervals—and corresponding sales of shorts—brought the ratio to 34% by August 1939.

Support of the bond market at the outbreak of war in Europe in September 1939 carried bond-holdings to over $1 billion and their share of the entire portfolio to just over 50%. Despite some sales (at a profit) as the bond market recovered in 1940, this situa-

---

[6] George L. Harrison papers, "Governors' Conference," May 2, 1922; "Open Market Committee," especially Vol. I, January 24, 1930, and Vol. III, May 23, 1934.

[7] July 1936 is the earliest date for which a published maturity distribution of the System's portfolio is available; but not until October 1950 are "5 to 10 years" and "over 10 years" shown separately (*Federal Reserve Bulletin*; also the System's *Banking and Monetary Statistics*). See also pp. 126–29 above.

tion did not change materially until mid-1942, when the vastly in-creased output of Treasury bills had to be bought by the Reserve to support the "pattern." Bond-holdings declined both absolutely and relatively until by 1947 they amounted to under 3% of the portfolio. But within a year thereafter bond support had pushed bond-holdings from $½ billion up to a peak of more than $9 billion, or just 40% of the account (see Fig. 2). Moreover, these bonds were almost entirely the 2½'s of 1967–1972—i.e., in excess of 10 years to first call. After the Accord bond-holdings were reduced to the present figure of about $2 billion, most of which are under 10 years to maturity.

Thus bonds have been purchased at one time or another with a variety of motives: to expand System earnings, to salvage member banks, to maintain an orderly market in bonds, and—in the grand experiment of 1947–1951—to stabilize the long-term rate of inter-est at the desire of the Treasury. But it can scarcely be said that the Reserve has ever yet entered the long-term market as an integral part of a monetary policy objective, i.e., to influence the level of aggregate demand. Indeed, except for a brief excursion in 1961 described in Chapter 7, the tendency since 1953 under the Reserve's present management has been entirely in the other direction. Under the influence of the "bills only" doctrine the System has chosen to deal almost exclusively in maturities extending no further than 15 months.

To be sure, to operate only in a given maturity or only in the obligations of a single class of debtor may be regarded as discrimi-nation. Whatever is bought and sold, the effect upon bank reserves is the same. Yet the effect on the volume of spending is not uniquely correlated with the change in bank reserves. One would expect the purchase of corporate bonds, for instance, to influence investment spending much more immediately than the purchase of Treasury bills, yet the effect on bank reserves is identical. It makes sense to operate in that part of the market where the desired effect is most direct. On the one hand such a policy will minimize time lags; on the other, it will avoid creating unnecessary surpluses or shortages of liquidity that may give trouble later. If the market were perfect, these considerations would of course have no application.

It is my contention that the limited scope of open-market policy in the past has led to far too modest an assessment of the potential effectiveness of monetary policy. During the Great Depression open-market purchases were, for that time, on a large scale, but they failed to stem the tide of deflation. Largely as a result of this experience, interest shifted toward fiscal measures as a means of stabilizing business. But the purchases in question were almost entirely of short-term securities, and tell us nothing about what would have happened had the System bought comparable amounts of long-term obligations.

This argument leads to the conclusion that the range of assets in which a central bank is permitted by law, or itself decides, to deal should depend upon how much power we wish it to have. To answer that question we need to know what we want it to achieve. Despite frequent proposals for a more specific mandate, Congress has refrained from spelling out objectives for Reserve policy. Yet, as we saw in the preceding chapter, since the Great Depression a rather clear consensus has emerged, both within and without the Reserve System, that it should concern itself with the stabilization of business and employment. But stabilization is a difficult task and calls for the most potent weapons at hand. I conclude that open-market operations should be subject to as few restrictions, self-imposed or otherwise, as possible.

Discount Rates

Discount policy was the principal if not the only instrument contemplated by the founders of the System. The Reserve Banks were to be simply lenders of last resort and, as such, purely passive agents. In 1914 nobody seems to have realized that the deliberate purchase or sale of assets could influence the money market; and of course the control of member-bank reserve requirements lay in the dim and distant future. But in drafting the Federal Reserve Act, Congress devoted much attention to the power to fix discount rates. There emerged the ambiguous compromise whereby the initiative for rate changes rested with the Banks but final decisions with the Board. Even before the revision of the law in 1935, the Attorney-General had decided that ultimate power in this matter rested with the Board, and the 1935 Act gave the power to the Board unambiguously.

The discount rate is the price of access to emergency cash. Originally the cash was to be supplied to the banks through the rediscount of commercial paper held by them. It was soon found more convenient for member banks to discount their own notes secured by collateral. In the early years Reserve Banks quoted a wide variety of rates for rediscount according to type and maturity of the paper, and immediately after World War I under the Phelan Act some of them charged progressively higher rates according to the amount borrowed by the individual member bank.[8] But these experiments were soon discarded and by 1921 a single discount rate at each bank applicable to all transactions became the rule. Since that time exceptions have been made only for certain types of emergency lending during the Great Depression (a higher rate) and loans secured by short-term government paper during World War II (a lower rate).

By the middle 1930's the volume of excess reserves was so large that the importance of discount policy appeared much reduced. During World War II and after, policy was subordinated to the wishes of the Treasury. Since the Accord of 1951, however, member-bank borrowing has been substantial at times of credit restraint. Accordingly the practical importance of the discount rate has revived, and by 1956–1957 was greater than at any time since late 1931.

Changes in discount rates are often said to have psychological importance out of proportion to the transactions to which they apply, signaling to the market the central bank's encouragement or warning, as the case may be. Yet they tend to "follow the market," confirming a trend in interest rates already initiated by open-market operations or changes in member-bank reserve requirements, or by a turn in business activity. For it would make no sense to keep discount rates low (or high) when other measures were being taken to tighten (or relax) credit. However this may be, it is certain that the independent power of discount policy, psychological or otherwise, has declined with the years.

As a signal, a change in the discount rate has uncertain meaning and may be misunderstood. A variation of, say, half a per cent may herald a sharp change in credit conditions in some circumstances, only a mild change in other circumstances. Moreover there is the possibility that a rise may be taken as a bullish appraisal of the business outlook by the Federal Reserve, or a fall as a bearish

[8] H. Parker Willis, *The Federal Reserve System* (New York: Ronald Press, 1923), pp. 894–96, 1341–44.

appraisal, thus yielding perverse responses on the part of the business community. These considerations have led to proposals that the discount rate vary automatically with the Treasury bill rate, as it was made to do in Canada from 1956 to 1962.[9] Such a proposal has merit; still better, the System could follow this practice normally, reserving the right to vary it in emergency situations in case a psychological shock seemed desirable.

Of course the borrowing of reserves can prevent the System from unambiguously controlling the money stock, and this has led Friedman to advocate the total abolition of borrowing by member banks.[10] The sensitive control of bank reserves made possible by open-market operations, coupled with the availability of the federal-funds market, make such a proposal feasible. Yet if the control of aggregate spending for output is the desideratum, the terms on which money is supplied and the cost of holding it are the important things to regulate, rather than the size of the money stock. Such regulation is not diminished by the existence of the discount window, and the ability to borrow—at a penalty rate—may have value in case the System fails to forecast accurately the demand for money in the short run.

Reserve Requirements

Since 1933 the Reserve Board has had power to vary the reserve requirements of member banks. As we have seen, this power has been rather frequently exercised—sometimes, as in the Spring of 1937, with unfortunate results. The variation of reserve requirements resembles open-market operations in that it produces immediate and well-defined changes in the aggregate free reserves of the commercial banks. Compared with open-market policy, however, changes in reserve requirements lack flexibility. Such changes must be made in a whole number or convenient fraction of percentage points, and the effect is therefore large and sudden. Moreover such changes affect all member banks in a given class, and so create widespread need for adjustment of reserves between banks. In some situations a sharp jolt of this kind may have merit, but most of the

[9] Warren L. Smith, "The Discount Rate as a Credit-Control Weapon," *Journal of Political Economy*, LXVI (April 1958), 171–77. See also Joint Economic Committee, *Employment, Growth and Price Levels*, Staff Report, 86th Cong. 1st Sess., 1959, p. 405.
[10] Milton Friedman, *A Program for Monetary Stability* (New York: Fordham University Press, 1960), pp. 35–45.

time these characteristics would seem to be a disadvantage. For this reason some have claimed that the power to change reserve requirements should be kept in hand, and used only when it is desired to move—more or less permanently—from one level of reserve requirements to a different level. For the record of changes in requirements, see Appendix III, Table B.

The variation of reserve requirements is also inferior to open-market policy on another and different ground. Open-market purchases and sales enable the central bank to influence interest rates directly through alterations in its asset holdings, as well as indirectly through member-bank reserves. When member-bank reserve requirements are changed, however, Reserve Bank asset holdings are not altered in any way. Consequential changes will indeed occur in member-bank asset holdings—as always when free reserves alter—but the central bank has no control over the type of assets of which the commercial banks decide to diminish or increase their holdings. The effect on interest rates is indirect and may be delayed.

The usefulness of changes in reserve requirements as an instrument of monetary policy is further limited by the fact that the optimum long-run level of requirements is governed by factors having nothing to do with monetary policy. Since cash in vault and deposits at Reserve Banks earn nothing, reserve requirements represent a tax upon member banks, and indirectly upon their customers. This tax can be thought of as a contribution to the cost of running the monetary system, or a franchise for the right to manufacture means of payment. The higher the level of requirements, the larger the contribution. Perhaps the commonest criterion for the level of requirements would pitch them high enough to secure adequate earnings to, and independence of Congressional appropriations for, the Reserve Banks. Since the System's portfolio grew to its present level as a result of World War II, this criterion has been amply satisfied and large sums have in fact been turned over to the Treasury.

A practical ceiling on reserve requirements is set by the continued existence of nonmember banks, whose competition member banks have to meet. However, as System officials have recognized, the probability is that the expansion of the economy will call for a gradually expanding stock of money in the future. This means that there will be scope for reducing reserve requirements, or increasing the System's portfolio, or a combination of both. The need for higher reserve requirements appears remote, unless (1) there should be a large accretion to the monetary gold stock, or (2) it should be desired deliberately to restrict or abolish fractional-reserve banking for one or other of the reasons discussed in Chapter 10.

If expansion of the money stock is effected by reducing reserve requirements, the whole of the resulting profits accrues to the commercial banks or their customers; if it is effected by adding to the Reserve System's portfolio, part of the profits go (eventually) to the Treasury. For in the latter case the System will come to hold ever larger quantities of federal debt, and turn over ever larger earnings to the Treasury. As explained in Chapter 7, this matter has become something of an issue between certain members of Congress, particularly Senator Douglas and Representatives Patman and Reuss, on the one hand and Chairman Martin on the other. Without making any explicit declaration of policy, the Board of Governors has worked toward lower requirements in recent years in a manner suggesting that it believes the secular increase in the money stock appropriate to the growth of the economy should be furnished by this method rather than by open-market purchases, at least until reserve requirements are much lower than they are at present. In 1959 the System proposed, not only that vault cash should be counted as reserve, but that the permissible range of requirements in the then central reserve cities (New York and Chicago) be lowered to correspond with the range for reserve cities. This proposal led Congress, under pressure from New York and Chicago banks, to abolish the reserve city classification altogether, which was not the Reserve's intention. Actual requirements for city member banks were lowered from well over 20% of demand deposits in 1948 to 16½% in 1960, and for country banks from 16% to 12%. Between 1952 and 1959 member-bank reserves grew by $8½ billion, of which roughly half was furnished through open-market purchases and half through reductions in member-bank reserve requirements effected during the 1954 and 1958 recessions.[11] No estimates are available for the increase in the annual gross earnings of member banks as a result of these reductions, but it must have been substantial.

The question concerns the division of gross earnings obtained by supplying the community with money between the Federal Reserve

[11] Joint Economic Committee, *Employment, Growth and Price Levels*, Hearings, 86th Cong. 1st Sess., 1959, p. 1494.

System (and therefore ultimately the taxpayer) on the one hand and the commercial banks and their customers on the other. The open-market method will secure a fraction (with 100% reserves the whole) of these profits to the Treasury. The reduced reserve requirements method gives the whole of the profits to the banks. Of course competition may eventually cause the banks to transfer the benefit to their customers, so that the ultimate choice could be whether profits from adding to the money stock should go to taxpayers or to customers of banks. Since these two classes are pretty well coterminous, it might be thought a matter of indifference. However, (1) barriers to entry and restricted competition in banking suggest that a considerable share will accrue to bank stockholders rather than depositors; (2) relief to taxpayers should conform better to canons of equity than would higher interest payments or lower service charges to bank customers. These considerations favor the open-market method. On the other hand, especially but not exclusively if banks were allowed to pay interest on demand deposits, (3) a reduction in the cost of holding money would prevent wasteful efforts to economize money balances (see above, Chapter 10). The net of the argument would appear to favor open-market purchases over the reduction of reserve requirements.

Chairman Martin has been curiously hesitant in developing a substantive defense of his preference for the reduction of reserve requirements, and his claim that they ought to be lower than they now are. His oral testimony on the subject (pp. 208–12 above) is not to the point, and his evasiveness obviously infuriated his critics. In substance, all he said was that a sense-of-Congress resolution favoring the open-market method would imply criticism of the Reserve and thereby frighten foreign observers into a belief that inflationary policies were about to be adopted.

From scattered testimony and System memoranda, it would appear that Martin's desire for lower reserve requirements rests on three grounds: (1) present (or recent) requirements are high by historical standards.[12] An average required reserve against demand deposits of 15% in 1959 or 14% in 1962 is high compared with the average of close to 10% from 1917 to 1936, but low compared with the 25% for city banks and 15% for country banks that obtained from 1863 to 1914. But the relevance of historical levels is obscure.

[12] *Ibid.,* p. 1498.

It is also argued (2) that member-bank capital ratios have declined sharply since 1940, and that (higher?) profits are needed as a condition for, if not as a source of, additional capital.[13] Bank profits as a percentage of net worth have in fact been well maintained, but banks do not seem to feel that they need more capital. It is far from clear that even larger profits in the future will necessarily lead to higher capital ratios. If such higher ratios really are desirable, which seems doubtful, legislative regulation would seem to be the appropriate method of securing them. If retained earnings are insufficient, most banks would have no difficulty in raising outside capital.

Strangest is the argument (3) that requirements have necessarily to be reduced over time, because it is expedient to reduce them in recessions but inexpedient to raise them in boom periods. If this doctrine has not been given explicit form, it is nonetheless implicit in positions taken by Chairman Martin.[14] To him the lowering of reserve requirements is the preferred method of easing credit in a recession because its effect is felt rapidly in all corners of the country, whereas open-market purchases directly influence only the money-market banks; also, bankers apparently regard a change in requirements as a more permanent measure, so that they may be more inclined to make long-term commitments when reserves are released in this way, than in the case of open-market purchases. The Chairman feels that, by contrast, when business expands, no actual absorption of reserves may be necessary, but merely a slackening of their rate of growth; and that, if such absorption should be necessary, raising of reserve requirements is too "blunt" a weapon and much inferior to open-market sales. The practical consequence is that, although demand deposits are subject to a long-term upward trend conforming to the growth of the economy, bank reserves should continue to fluctuate around their present level—at least until reserve requirements are much lower than they now are!

In sum, so small a change in requirements as ½% raises or lowers reserves by nearly half a billion dollars, and the effect—depending

---

[13] See brief on "Proposed Legislation for Revision of Reserve Requirements, January 29, 1959," by the staff of the Board of Governors, reprinted in Senate Committee on Banking and Currency, *Member Bank Reserve Requirements*, Hearings on S. 860 and S. 1120, 86th Cong. 1st Sess., 1959, pp. 114–15; also in House Committee Hearings on H.R. 5237, pp. 26–28. See also Chairman Martin's written reply to Representative Coffin, *Employment, Growth and Price Levels*, Hearings, p. 1499.

[14] See *Employment, Growth and Price Levels*, Hearings, pp. 1457, 1462–65, 1497–98.

upon the existing distribution of reserves—is often hard to predict.
This has suggested to many commentators that such changes should
be used rarely, perhaps only in emergency. The additional fact that
such changes have a rather direct immediate effect upon member-
bank earnings gives this weapon peculiar political overtones. Possibly the wisest plan would be to follow Milton Friedman's advice
and stabilize requirements once and for all. The existing differential
in favor of country banks is an anachronism and should be eliminated.

The Rate of Interest and the Availability of Credit

To what extent is control over the quantity of money and the level
of interest rates assured through the instruments described in the
preceding sections?

Let us define money as demand deposits plus currency outside
banks. In that case control over bank reserves and reserve requirements would appear to assure control over the quantity of money
except in rare situations. (1) Commercial banks may fail to acquire
all the earning assets that the law permits. This can happen if the
banks cannot find a supply of the particular assets to which they are
accustomed, or if they have an exaggerated concern for their own
liquidity. Such a situation may occur in acute depression. (2) The
ratio of demand to time deposits may change. However, this merely
alters the lengths to which the Reserve has to go to produce a given
change in demand deposits. (3) The ratio of demand deposits to
currency outside banks may change. Again, this merely alters the
lengths to which the Reserve must go, although a general distrust of
bank deposits (unlikely with deposit insurance) could make things
awkward. Collectively these qualifications are unimportant, and we
may say that the System's control over the volume of money, as defined, is substantially complete.

With control over the volume of money goes control over interest
rates. Yields must be sufficient to induce the public to hold all assets
not held by the banking system. Broadly speaking, it is true, the size
of the stock of money defines the volume of such assets, and in a
perfect market would determine all interest rates. In practice the
connection between the stock of money and the level of interest rates,
and between one interest rate and another, is somewhat loose, especially in the short run. As the money supply changes, the yields most

immediately affected are those on the particular assets that the central bank or the commercial banks are currently buying or selling. Rates on some types of marketable issue, however, may be quite sluggish, and the cost of bank borrowing may not move at all. It is therefore necessary to discuss the availability of credit as well as its cost.

To relatively few borrowers is the supply of capital solely a function of the rate of interest which they are prepared to pay. Even the United States Treasury is not always in this happy position with respect to all maturities, unless indeed the Federal Reserve underwrites the issue. More commonly, lenders apply varying degrees of rationing to borrowers: a larger supply of funds may not be available even at higher interest rates.

In the short-term market commercial banks often prefer to vary the credit standards they impose on borrowers, or loan terms other than interest cost, instead of changing their customer-loan rates. Those who for the moment cannot get credit at prevailing rates, but who would be supplied if the banks had more reserves, are known as the "fringe of unsatisfied borrowers."

In the long-term market analogous conditions may be observed. A small rise in interest rates may dry up funds for investment spending, not by cutting the volume of funds borrowers demand at prevailing rates, but by making lenders unwilling to lend. Underwriters, fearing still higher interest rates, may discourage corporate borrowers from offering securities to the public. Insurance companies may be reluctant to realize losses, already incurred on paper, by selling governments: a common rule of thumb is said to prevent the taking of a loss unless the increase in yield obtainable by reinvesting the funds will allow the loss to be written off within twelve months. Mortgage money and private placings may be rationed among clients who lack alternative sources of capital supply. As the speed declines with which the market digests bond issues, a line of would-be borrowers forms outside the offices of underwriters. Yet almost no visible change may have occurred in interest rates.[15]

More commonly an upward movement of interest rates is accom-

[15] A partial list of references on credit availability includes: John Maynard Keynes, *A Treatise on Money* (London: Macmillan, 1930), II, 364–67; Robert V. Roosa, "Interest Rates and the Central Bank," in *Money, Trade and Economic Growth* (New York: Macmillan, 1951); Joint Committee on the Economic Report, *Monetary Policy and the Management of the Public Dept*, Subcommittee Hearings, 82nd Cong., 2nd Sess., 1952, pp. 691–98, and Replies to Questions, 1952, I, pp. 370–73.

panied by reduced availability of credit, a decline in interest rates by greater credit availability. While changes in availability may occur with unchanged interest rates, their normal role is to reinforce the effects of interest-rate changes. Unfortunately no direct quantitative measure of variations in credit availability is available. Moreover interest-rate changes do not have the unique significance they would possess in a perfect market. Although an appropriate level for the cost and availability of credit—long or short—is a proximate goal of monetary policy, it is a goal whose achievement cannot be measured or tested directly. Hence comes the need to use other indicators, e.g., free reserves, total bank reserves, demand deposits, or the money stock, as a measure and description of monetary policy in any given situation.

General Credit Controls and Macroeconomic Policy

The size of the money stock, the level of interest rates, and the degree of credit availability are but proximate, qualified objectives for policy. The ultimate goals are control of the aggregate volume of spending in the economy and the maintenance of business activity at an acceptable level.

Let us take the "volume of spending" to mean effective demand for final output (GNP). To influence aggregate demand the Reserve must influence either (1) consumer spending, (2) investment spending by private business, or (3) government spending.

(1) The possibility of influencing *consumer* spending directly via general credit controls is slight. Personal saving is thought to be interest inelastic; consumer credit appears to be insensitive to ordinary credit controls. The selective control of consumer credit is discussed below.

(2) *Private investment spending* is a more hopeful category, for it is sensitive to some degree at least both to interest rates and to the availability of credit. Whenever the Reserve increases the quantity of money, there will be *some* tendency for investment spending to expand. But since the market is imperfect, a given increase in the money stock will have maximum effect if the assets acquired by the Reserve (and of course by the commercial banks, too!) are in that part of the market where the interest elasticity of investment spending is greatest. In general, this means securities of a kind used to finance long-term and perhaps equity capital. The Reserve Banks are

not at present authorized to purchase long-term corporate obligations. Moreover, from 1953 to 1961, in accordance with Chairman Martin's "bills only" doctrine, the System denied itself the purchase (and therefore also the sale) of the next-best item—long-term Treasury obligations. Even though the formal "bills only" instruction was rescinded by the Open Market Committee in December 1961, it is plain that opinion in the System still is strongly adverse to operations in the long-term market. It happens that since the end of World War II, business has been quite sensitive to Reserve policy, so that tho restrictions just discussed—whether statutory or self-imposed—have not had important effects. But the time could come in the future, as it did in the 1930's, when the purchase of short-term governments, on no matter what scale, would be insufficient to stimulate business.

The sensitivity of investment spending even with respect to the long-term rate of interest has indeed been questioned. Empirical studies have cast doubt upon the importance of the interest rate in entrepreneurial calculations.[16] These studies may in fact be criticized on several grounds. They rely upon a canvass of businessmen's expressed opinions as to how their decisions are motivated; hence the data are subjective in nature. Nor were the samples large upon which the conclusions were based. Some of the results are contradictory.

To contemplate what might be done with really cheap long-term capital, e.g., 1% for prime corporate borrowing, is to induce skepticism about the claim that investment spending is insensitive to interest rates. Not only private, but semi-public, and state and local enterprise would, it seems to me, go overboard on power, highways, urban housing, water supply, sewage, and a dozen other types of project. It will be objected that financing costs and other institutional factors would in practice prevent such a decline in long-term rates. Maybe so; in which case, if the *equilibrium* rate were that low, some Treasury guarantee or subsidy could be indicated. But the possible existence of a floor below the *supply* price of long-term capital is no evidence of downward inelasticity in the *demand* for capital!

The consensus at the present time would probably be that (*pace* Hawtrey) inventory investment is insensitive to rates of interest, that

[16] Thomas Wilson and P. W. S. Andrews, *Oxford Studies in the Price Mechanism* (Oxford: Clarendon Press, 1951) ; Friedrich A. Lutz, "The Interest Rate and Investment in a Dynamic Economy," *American Economic Review*, XXXV (December 1945), 811–30; G. L. S. Shackle, "Interest Rates and the Pace of Investment," *Economic Journal*, LVI (March, 1946), 1–17. For a useful summary see John R. Meyer and E. Kuh, *The Investment Decision* (Cambridge: Harvard University Press, 1957), Ch. II and Appendix.

investment in plant and equipment is not very sensitive, and that public-utility investment, residential construction, and public construction at the state and local level are quite sensitive. Yet to an important degree the ability of monetary policy to influence investment spending does not depend upon its sensitivity to interest-rate changes. In an imperfect market variations in the willingness of lenders to lend may produce the same effect upon the amounts lent (borrowed) as changes in interest rates. Thus changes in the availability of credit tend to reinforce the effects of changes in interest rates. Commercial banks become less (more) willing to lend at short term; through the working of financial intermediaries corporate obligations become less (more) readily salable and mortgages less (more) easily obtainable.

The interest elasticity of investment would be a true measure of the effectiveness of monetary policy only in a perfect market. Should it turn out that investment is quite insensitive to interest rates and monetary policy depends entirely upon changes in the availability of credit, we would have to admit that in a perfect market monetary policy might not work smoothly—or indeed at all. But as things are, monetary policy does not depend uniquely upon interest-rate changes for its ability to influence investment.

It follows that the possibility that important types of investment spending may be interest inelastic in no way reflects upon the effectiveness of monetary management. For the capital market is imperfect: borrowers have preferences for lenders and lenders for borrowers, even where no stronger monopoly elements are present. Credit standards may be applied harshly or lightly; terms of the loan contract other than the interest rate may be varied. Credit expansion and contraction, and changes in investment spending, could in principle proceed with no change whatever in interest rates: yet normally interest rates will change, and their movement reflects changes in the availability of credit—the degree to which credit is currently being rationed. These considerations explain how the obvious effectiveness of monetary policy on many occasions in the past can be reconciled with a quite limited sensitivity of investment to the rate of interest. We may note that, were capital markets more perfectly competitive, if investment is indeed interest inelastic, fluctuations in interest rates would have to be extremely violent for monetary policy to be effective. It is quite possible that in the world as we know it we owe the effectiveness of relatively moderate changes in interest rates to the associated changes that occur in the availability of credit. So much for investment spending.

(3) *Government spending.* Federal spending may be assumed to be insensitive to monetary policy; as an aspect of fiscal policy it will be discussed below. The spending of state and local governments on the other hand, not properly a part of fiscal policy in this context, seems to be quite interest elastic, at least in the short run.[17] Unfortunately the law at present limits the System to the purchase of *short-term* state and local obligations, so that it cannot influence directly the terms on which municipal bonds are salable. However the popularity of the latter with commercial banks no doubt goes far to remedy this defect.

Even if the Reserve can regulate the level of spending in the economy, it does not of course follow that it can control the state of business and employment. Normally indeed the connection is close: increased spending means greater business activity and more employment, decreased spending means slackened activity and less employment. But qualifications are necessary. If spending expands at only a moderate pace, and the wage level is pushed up very rapidly— through collective agreements, arbitration, or escalator clauses—the increased spending may not lead to increased output and employment. More likely, employment will be maintained, but prices will rise. The most serious dilemma we may expect seems to be that between stabilizing the level of employment and stabilizing the price level (Chapter 12).

Institutional Changes and the Effectiveness of Monetary Policy

In economic matters the relevance of past experience to present problems rests upon the existence of some minimum degree of continuity in the institutional framework of society. I believe such continuity exists, or I would not have written this book. Recently, however, some writers have claimed that institutional changes have occurred on so considerable a scale since World War II as greatly to qualify the value of earlier experience.[18] Two such changes are

[17] Municipal bond issues have been postponed on a number of occasions owing to high interest rates: see, e.g., Joint Economic Committee, *Monetary Policy 1955–56*, Hearings, 84th Cong. 2nd Sess., 1957, p. 27.

[18] See, e.g., Ervin Miller, "Monetary Policy in a Changing World," *Quarterly Journal of Economics*, LXX (February 1956), 23–43; Warren L. Smith, "On the Effectiveness of Monetary Policy," *American Economic Review*, XLVI (September 1956), 588–606; Hyman P. Minsky, "Central Banking and Money Market Changes," *Quarterly Journal of Economics*, LXXI (May 1957), 171–87.

principally cited: the growth in the federal debt and the increased importance of financial intermediaries. Perhaps because much of the time since 1945 the practical problem has seemed to be to curb inflationary tendencies, these two changes commonly are cited as obstacles to the effective restriction (but not to the expansion) of demand through monetary policy.

The size of the federal debt. The federal debt today bears much higher ratios to private debt and to the national wealth than it did before World War II, and a much higher proportion is owned by the banking system—although all three ratios have declined steadily since 1945. Now a credit restriction, intended to raise interest rates, must (1) produce a fall in the prices of marketable debt which could render banks and other financial institutions technically insolvent, and (2) make Treasury refinancing more expensive. Yet the problem for commercial banks, at least, is not a serious one so long as examiners allow them to report governments at cost. The greater burden to the Treasury of servicing the debt must, in my view, be regarded as one of the costs inherent in monetary management— that is, in the efficient operation of our kind of economy. To some extent, at least, the matter was put to the test in 1959–1960 when interest rates rose to about twice the level of a decade previously. No group of financial institutions got into difficulties and the Treasury gracefully resigned itself to the situation. I do not think it can be conceded that either of these consequences of higher interest rates in any way compromises the effectiveness of central-bank action.

A further consequence of the large public debt, and especially of the plentiful supply of short-term Treasury obligations, is the enhanced supply of liquid assets available as an alternative to money balances. It is true that, with a rise in the yields of such assets, holders of idle demand deposits (either financial intermediaries or nonfinancial corporations) will switch into such assets, purchasing them from commercial banks or business firms, releasing demand deposits for lending by the former and spending by the latter, especially for investment purposes. Such switching no doubt occurred, and may help to explain the rise in the velocity of demand deposits between 1945 and 1950 when short-term interest rates were rising. But this possibility does not suggest that a monetary policy directed toward the raising of interest rates (or reduction in the availability of credit) would be any less effective on that account in restraining investment spending: nothing has occurred to lessen the interest elasticity of the demand for capital. To be sure, the larger volume of liquid assets, and the greater possibility of switching, may require a somewhat lower level of demand deposits to achieve a given level of interest rates (or reduction in the availability of credit) than would otherwise be the case. There is no reason to suppose that the level of interest rates needed to check inflation (chiefly determined, after all, by the demand for capital) is higher than it would have been had the supply of money substitutes been (relatively) no larger than in 1940.

A practical central banker has claimed that, far from having lessened the effectiveness of monetary policy, the large size of the federal debt has actually increased it. Writing in 1950, Allan Sproul, then President of the Federal Reserve Bank of New York, had this to say:

> . . . the central banking system is now in direct contact with the capital market. It no longer has to rely entirely on the indirect effects of an expansion or contraction of the reserve funds of commercial banks to influence the volume, or at least the timing, of capital expenditures. Through its open-market operations the Federal Reserve System can bring the weight of its policies to bear directly on the prices and yields of government securities of all maturities. Because of the tremendous volume of government debt in relation to all debt public and private, because of the large holdings of government securities in the banking system and in the portfolios of institutional investors, and because government securities are the basic "risk free" obligation in our economy, the whole of the capital market tends to take its cue from what is happening in the government security market.[19]

But the "bills only" doctrine, discussed in Chapter 5, of course severely limits this advantage.

The growth of financial intermediaries. Closely related to the higher level of the public debt is the enhanced importance since World War II of financial intermediaries—insurance companies, pension funds, savings banks, savings and loan associations, sales-finance companies, and the like. It has been claimed, notably by Gurley and Shaw, that financial intermediaries function in such a

---

[19] *Money, Trade and Economic Growth* (New York: Macmillan, 1951), pp. 322–23.

way as to diminish the effectiveness of monetary policy, especially if a restriction of credit is in question.[20] Certainly they facilitate the conversion of idle into active demand deposits at commercial banks in response to a rise in interest rates. Insurance companies and pension funds may lend their own idle deposits; insurance companies may sell assets (especially governments) to the public in exchange for idle deposits which they proceed to lend out; savings banks and savings and loan associations may receive cash—in response to higher deposit rates—and relend it.[21] Hence borrowers, turned away by commercial banks, resort to nonbank intermediaries to obtain needed funds and in consequence—so it is alleged—the attempt of the authorities to restrict credit has been defeated. Therefore controls should be extended to intermediaries with respect to their cash ratios, portfolio policies, or what have you.

But in fact the attempt to restrict credit has *not* been defeated, as is shown by the rise in interest rates (without which the idle balances would not have been activated). A price has been paid for "circumventing" control; interest rates have risen and credit is less available; the usual (and, we must assume, desired) effects upon aggregate demand may be anticipated. The rise in velocity may be a safety valve, but it is no escape route.[22]

Unquestionably improved financial organization facilitates the conversion of idle into active balances when interest rates rise. It also reduces the rise in interest rates consequent upon a given reduction in the money stock. But it does not eliminate the rise in interest rates, nor does it limit the freedom of the central bank to raise them.

Gurley and Shaw complain that the Reserve System controls (directly) only a portion of the supply of short-term credit. As indi-

---

[20] See John G. Gurley and E. S. Shaw, "Financial Aspects of Economic Development," *American Economic Review*, XLV (September 1955), 515–38; Joint Economic Committee, *Employment, Growth and Price Levels*, Study Paper No. 14, "Liquidity and Financial Institutions in the Postwar Period," by J. G. Gurley, 86th Cong. 1st Sess., 1960. For criticism of the Gurley-Shaw thesis, see Joseph Aschheim, "Commercial Banks and Financial Intermediaries: Fallacies and Policy Implications," *Journal of Political Economy*, LXVII (February 1959), 59–71; also J. M. Culbertson, "Intermediaries and Monetary Theory: A Criticism of the Gurley-Shaw Theory," and reply, *American Economic Review*, XLVIII (March 1958), 119–38.

[21] Of course, commercial banks themselves may receive time deposits and lend them out, in which case they too activate previously idle demand deposits.

[22] An analogy may help: suppose the Reserve sells securities; if member-bank indebtedness should rise, but member-bank reserves remain unchanged, would Gurley and Shaw claim that the open-market sales have been without effect?

cated, there is no basis for supposing that such marginal control is insufficient for purposes of monetary policy. They further complain that the Reserve has no control over the issue of long-term securities; this point is not well taken, for control over short-term interest rates can influence long-term rates through arbitrage, while the System is always able itself to operate directly in the long-term market. Finally Gurley and Shaw are disturbed by the ability of business to finance itself from internal sources, whether or not outside funds are available. Here again the critical requirement for monetary policy is that the authorities shall be able to influence *total* funds available to business at the *margin*. If some particular form of finance (or group of borrowers) is in fact immune or exempt from market forces, we may regret the discrimination, for tightness or ease will fall all the more sharply on others; but it will not do to say on this account that monetary policy is ineffective. As for self-financing, internal funds are by no means completely immune to market influence, for if rates are high enough such resources may be lent out instead of being used within the firm.

The most that can be claimed with accuracy is that the existence of financial intermediaries may force the Reserve System to effect a somewhat larger reduction in the money stock in order to achieve a given reduction in aggregate spending.[23] The imposition of reserve requirements on mutual savings banks and savings and loan associations and the regulation of the investment policies of insurance companies, proposed by the critics, might ease the task of the monetary authority but could scarcely enable it to do anything it cannot now do. One critic has even proposed that all long-term governments held by commercial banks should be rendered nonmarketable.[24] To put it mildly, none of these controls appears worth its cost in political friction and administrative complication.

The substantial point made by Gurley and Shaw is not really concerned with the actual or potential effectiveness of monetary policy,

[23] Gurley, at least, seems to agree: "The inflationary effect of growth in nonmonetary intermediaries can be offset by the monetary authorities. All they need do is to restrain, more than they would otherwise have to do, the growth of money and time deposits. This . . . will compensate for the rapid growth of financial intermediaries that lie outside of the controlled area" (Joint Economic Committee, *Employment, Growth and Price Levels*, Hearings, 86th Cong. 1st Sess., 1959, p. 855). Cf. James Tobin and W. C. Brainard, "Financial Intermediaries and the Effectiveness of Monetary Controls," *American Economic Review*, LIII (May 1963), 383–400.

[24] See David A. Alhadeff, "Credit Controls and Financial Intermediaries," *American Economic Review*, L (September 1960), 658.

but with the equity of imposing reserve requirements upon commercial banks but not upon nonmonetary intermediaries that compete with them. To be sure the inequity of imposing reserve requirements against commercial-bank time deposits but not against deposits in savings banks is manifest: a good case exists for abolishing the former. But it is hard to see any unfairness in the requirement that commercial banks maintain reserves against demand deposits, for they alone offer a supply of such. Gurley and Shaw regard the fact that commercial banks have grown less rapidly than other financial institutions as an indication that the former have been discriminated against. Yet would one not expect new types of financial institution to spring up in a developing economy to meet new needs? If so, must not the new types, while young, grow more rapidly than the old?

Compensating for changes in velocity. It may well be that since World War II improved financial organization and the enhanced supply of money substitutes have increased the variability of the velocity of circulation of money proper (demand deposits plus currency outside banks). If so, these changes have further diminished the reliability (never great) of the quantity of money as a guide to central-banking policy. The notion that by stabilizing the volume of money, or allowing it to increase at a steady rate (as Friedman has proposed), may lead to the stabilization of business activity or of commodity prices, and that changes in velocity need be of no concern, is a notion that surely should not have survived the Great Depression. The large increases in the money stock during 1932, for instance, which went unaccompanied by any expansion of business or rise in commodity prices, should have served as a warning. Per contra, in the postwar period we have seen a much more rapid growth in spending than in the money supply.

A good example of the danger of concentrating attention upon the money stock to the exclusion of other variables occurred in 1946–1948. Was Federal Reserve policy inflationary during this period? President Sproul of the New York Reserve Bank took what must seem quite unjustified satisfaction in the fact that adjusted demand deposits plus money in circulation was no larger in March 1948 than in December 1946.[25] But the BLS index of wholesale prices rose almost 15% between the two dates, and—since output

[25] Joint Committee on the Economic Report, *Credit Policies*, Hearings, 80th Cong. 2nd Sess., 1948, p. 89.

rose—velocity increased even more. This should have been expected. In the 1920's GNP ranged between 3½ and 4 times currency plus demand deposits; the ratio fell during the 1930's and credit expansion during World War II reduced it further to an all-time low of 1.99 in 1946. By 1948 it had risen again to 2.39, by 1957 to 3.30. Between 1946 and 1948 a noninflationary monetary policy surely would have called for a sharp reduction in the quantity of money to offset the increase in velocity.[26]

The true purpose of monetary policy is to regulate the price and availability of capital, and the appropriateness of the volume of money must be judged by this test. I conclude that neither the growth of the public debt, nor the rise of financial intermediaries, have lessened the effectiveness of Reserve policies in controlling credit availability and rates of interest. The first has increased the supply of money substitutes; the second has facilitated the adjustment of asset holdings. Both developments may have tended to increase the velocity of circulation (though this elusive ratio still is below the level of the 1920's). They may also have contributed to instability in velocity. But the System can always, or almost always, counter undesired changes in velocity by arranging for opposite changes in the supply of money.

Selective Credit Controls

Evidently general credit controls in most circumstances offer a powerful method of regulating aggregate demand. Consequently the case for selective controls rests upon the possibilities (1) that on the rare occasions when general controls are ineffective, selective regulation may be useful in helping to control aggregate spending, and (2) that good reasons exist for wishing to discriminate between different classes of spending.

I begin by briefly reviewing the three principal selective measures that have been tried.

[26] Quite inappropriately, it seems to me, Alvin Hansen rushed to the defense of the Reserve System against its own 1954 account of its pre-Accord stewardship. He points out correctly that on balance the public debt actually was monetized to a negligible extent during 1946–1950, however much it might have been monetized under the policy of pegging bonds had things developed less fortunately. But he is then mistakenly led to imply that the System had brought inflation to an end between December 1946 and June 1948, since between the two dates it achieved a small reduction in currency plus demand deposits. He takes no note of the fact that the BLS price index rose 18% and that an increase in velocity took place which called for a much larger reduction in the stock of money than actually occurred. See Alvin H. Hansen, "Monetary Policy," *Review of Economics and Statistics*, XXXVII (May 1955), 116–17.

Stock-market credit. The Securities and Exchange Act of 1934 gives power to restrict the amount of funds brokers may obtain for their customers in buying stocks on margin. Under the Act minimum margin requirements are set by the Federal Reserve Board (Regulations T and U). If the requirement is set at 100%, all transactions are upon a cash basis. The percentage permitted has been varied by the Board rather frequently, although the logic governing the use of this particular instrument of credit policy is far from clear.

During the stock-market boom of 1927–1929 much of the money lent to the stock market was eventually used for subscriptions to new equity issues, as explained in Chapter 4. Under such circumstances a rise in margin requirements may make it harder to issue common stocks and thereby exercise a restraint upon investment spending. In other circumstances, particularly when call-money rates are low, much of the money reaching the stock market, after use by the bulls in making purchases, will end up in the idle balances of bears: in that case the influence of margin requirements on investment spending would be slight or negligible.

Residential-mortgage credit. Under the Defense Production Act of 1950 the Board was given power to fix maximum loan-values and maturities for mortgages on new residential construction (Regulation X). Loans made, insured, or guaranteed by federal agencies were exempted. Regulation X was issued in September 1950, shortly after the outbreak of the Korean War, and was suspended in 1952. Power to control mortgage lending expired June 30, 1953, and has not been renewed.

Consumer credit. In August 1941, under an Executive Order of the President, the Board issued Regulation W setting maximum maturities and minimum down-payments for credit sales of durable consumer-goods. This power was renewed and finally expired November 1, 1947. Under the Defense Production Act of 1950, after the outbreak of the Korean War, the Board was again given power to regulate consumer credit, and Regulation W was promptly revived (September 1950). The Regulation was suspended in May 1952, and on June 30, 1952, the Board's powers in the matter expired. However proposals have not been wanting for legislation to re-establish standby power to regulate consumer credit.[27]

[27] The System sponsored an elaborate inquiry into the subject but has not itself taken a position on the desirability of standby powers. See Board of Governors of the Federal Reserve System, *Consumer Instalment Credit* (four parts in six volumes), 1957.

Selective or qualitative controls of the kind listed above have provoked much controversy. The questions at issue ramify widely. It will be convenient first to list the objections and then the arguments in favor of selective controls.

The case against selective controls. (1) When spending needs to be expanded or contracted, there is seldom a presumption that any one particular form of spending is out of line. It is not usually possible to argue that the required expansion or contraction should be concentrated in one particular area. In most cases demand in general just is too high for the economy to support without inflation, or too low to elicit the full capabilities of the economy. In principle it should be left to the market to decide *which* kinds of spending need correction: the nonselective control of credit should enable the market to make this decision. In principle selective credit controls are inferior to nonselective or general controls, in that the former abridge the freedom of the market.

I have qualified the above argument by saying "in principle," because various possible exceptions may be noted. If unused resources are concentrated in certain industries or localities, spending of a kind most likely to re-employ these resources may be desired. But selective credit control is not well adapted to this type of discrimination; moreover demand for the resources concerned may be in secular decline, in which case an effort to re-employ them does not make sense.

A more important exception to the principle enunciated above relates to market imperfection. In allocating resources, only perfectly competitive markets are clearly superior to administrative decisions, and the more imperfect a given market is, the weaker the presumption that it can do a better job than an administrative agency. In two of the three cases listed above the imperfections are in fact rather serious: stock-market and consumer credit are both insensitive to the general credit situation. Hence the general objection to selective controls is weaker in these two cases than in the case of residential-mortgage credit. For example a general credit restriction may be expected to have a greater impact upon residential-mortgage credit than upon consumer credit—upon spending for residential construction than upon spending for consumer durables. From this standpoint special restrictions applied to consumer credit can be viewed as a means of counteracting discrimination inherent in the operation of general credit controls. The Reserve System might perhaps have been justified in using such controls, had it possessed them, to check the very rapid rise in consumer credit in 1955–1956.

The regulation of consumer credit has received support from those who wish to discourage the purchase of durable consumer-goods by people who cannot afford them. Similarly the regulation of stock-market credit has been defended by those who regard speculation as immoral, demoralizing, a danger to the uninitiated, or a waste of resources. But these arguments are concerned with a long-run policy of restriction as such and do not call for or justify discretionary variation in the degree of restriction. They have no application to monetary policy.

(2) From time to time the management of money inevitably involves stepping on somebody's toes. Any move by the central bank that makes credit less plentiful surely will upset somebody's plans to finance himself. But insofar as the credit restriction is nonselective, i.e., applies to everyone, nobody can be said to have a legitimate grievance. Some demands for credit must (in the judgment of the monetary authority) go unsatisfied owing to the general economic situation, and price (or its correlative, availability) will decide which. But if the supply of credit to some particular group of borrowers is explicitly restricted, those affected may well ask pointedly why they have been singled out. It is impossible not to sympathize with automobile dealers who complain when instalment credit is restricted, and with builders who object to the (to them highly arbitrary) control of residential-mortgage terms. Injustice may be presumed in individual cases; worse still, the very principle of credit control itself could in the end be rejected. Of course in wartime the case for selective controls is better based, since their purpose is to prevent the use of scarce resources for specific nonessential purposes: selective control of credit becomes just one method of channeling resources into the war effort.

(3) Selective credit controls impose substantial burdens upon the agency administering them. The large numbers of lenders and borrowers, and the great variety of methods used to extend credit, imply elaborate regulations and considerable enforcement effort. Of the three selective instruments discussed, this objection is strong-

est in the case of consumer credit and weakest in the case of stock-market credit.

The case for selective controls. (1) The major case for selective controls will be found to rest upon imperfections in the market for credit. Monetary policy has been reproached with unevenness of application. Thus it has been claimed that some groups, e.g., small business and other enterprises that need to borrow heavily, are especially sensitive to a credit restriction, while others escape its effects. In principle, selective controls could be used to make a credit restriction more uniform in its effects.[28] On the other hand, the practical difficulty of designing controls that would achieve much in this direction is very great.

(2) Those who doubt the over-all efficacy of general credit control in influencing the state of business or the commodity-price level should welcome selective controls as a reinforcement for more orthodox central-banking policy. If the ability of open-market policy and changes in reserve requirements to restrain an undesired expansion of spending is questioned, then regulation of consumer credit and residential-mortgage credit represents so much added leverage in this regard. Given time for it to work, doubts about the ability of general credit control to restrain spending, to be sure, can scarcely be entertained. Yet the effects of a general credit restriction may take time to show up: in the boom of 1955–1957, for example, selective controls might have brought quicker results.

On the other hand, if we are concerned about the effectiveness of general credit controls in inducing expansion, we cannot expect much help. For the expansionary possibilities of selective credit controls are clearly very limited.

(3) General credit controls raise and lower the cost of borrowing by government. It has been claimed that the amount that a government needs to borrow does not or should not depend upon the rate of interest. Whether this is so or not, it is clear that when public debt has to be refinanced, the government's demand for credit is extremely inelastic. If high rates of interest will *not* curb the government's use of resources, why force it to borrow at high rates? The quick answer is, because others who *will* economize their use

[28] See Warren L. Smith, "Consumer Instalment Credit," *American Economic Review*, XLVII (December 1957), 980–81.

of resources must be forced to do so. However the use of selective credit controls could lessen the rise of interest rates needed to prevent inflation, and so cut the cost of the public debt.[29] But the application of this argument is limited to federal borrowing, for state and local borrowing is rather sensitive to its cost:[30] it would be difficult to argue that this sensitivity should not be respected, i.e., that it does not reflect a proper balancing of social choices. Also, the use of selective controls for the purpose indicated might well lead to complaints that spending for consumer-durables and residential construction was being hit for the benefit of business and local-government borrowers, who would pay higher interest charges but for these controls.

The fact that the tightening of consumer and residential-mortgage credit does not, directly at least, depress capital values—unlike a tightening of credit in general—has been cited as an advantage of the former.[31] But this conclusion is unsound. The decline in the prices of fixed-money obligations that accompanies general credit restraint is part and parcel of its effectiveness. It is greatly to be doubted whether selective credit restriction can achieve the desired effect without also producing indirectly a comparable fall in capital values.

(4) A special case can be made out for discretionary control over the terms of consumer credit. As already remarked, the volume and rate of growth of consumer instalment-credit appears to be quite remarkably insensitive to changing rates of interest. All that the buyer of an automobile asks is, "How much a month?" He is not aware, and does not inquire, what rate of interest is charged. Nor does he compare the total payments called for by his instalment contract with what he could obtain the automobile for on a cash basis. He compounds ignorance with irrationality. If this judgment is correct, the insensitiveness of the consumer to general credit control may be ascribed to a market imperfection. Looking at the matter in this way, we can see that, if the terms for consumer credit (maturity and down-payment) are varied in congruence with the cost

[29] Ervin Miller, "Monetary Policy in a Changing World," *Quarterly Journal of Economics,* LXX (February 1956), 23–43.

[30] See, e.g., testimony by Arthur Levitt, Comptroller of the State of New York, in Joint Economic Committee, *Monetary Policy 1955–56,* Hearings, 84th Cong. 2nd Sess., 1957, p. 27.

[31] Miller, *op. cit.,* p. 38.

and availability of credit in general, the result may quite possibly be to eliminate the effects of the market imperfection. That is to say, the distribution of credit, and of spending, between consumers and others may approach that which would obtain in the absence of consumer-credit control, supposing that consumers were better informed and more rational than they in fact are.

Evidently the case for and against selective credit controls is exceedingly complex. Of the three forms discussed, the best case can perhaps be made in favor of control over consumer credit.

The Fiscal Instruments

Budgeting for a surplus or a deficit affords, it is now generally agreed, a powerful means of diminishing or increasing aggregate demand within the economy. Although the kinds of spending influenced by monetary and by fiscal policy may differ, we can assume that, for any given shift in monetary policy, there exists as an alternative a possible shift in fiscal policy which would produce roughly the same effect upon the level of economic activity. For in a technical sense the two types of policy are in large measure substitutes. Such qualification as this statement needs relates chiefly—as we saw in Chapter 10—to the matter of time lags, which may differ somewhat in the two cases.

The substantial and dramatic contrast between monetary policy on the one hand and fiscal policy on the other lies not in the manner in which they operate and produce results, but rather in the manner in which decisions come to be made in the two cases. Federal taxing and spending policies are the outcome of prolonged negotiation and debate in Congress. Not until Congress enacts a measure of Presidential discretion with regard to tax rates (as has been done recently in Britain) will it be possible to treat fiscal policy as the practical substitute for monetary policy which it ought to be. Among fiscal instruments I give pride of place to variation in tax rates because of its obvious superiority, for administrative and other reasons, over variation in government outlays. But neither type of variation can yet be regarded as an instrument regularly available for the day-to-day control of the economy.

Why not? Only partly because of the long delay and considerable compromises needed to reach fiscal decisions. Partly also because the deliberate use of federal surpluses and deficits as a means of regulating effective demand has not as yet been fully accepted by the public, by members of Congress, or even perhaps by cabinet officers.[32] Some progress of a negative sort, to be sure, has occurred since the 1930's. In one sense, indeed, the desirability of compensatory fiscal policy may now be regarded as part of the "American consensus,"[33] just as it has come to be accepted in most other countries. Not since 1933, except possibly in 1949, have serious attempts been made to increase taxes or to cut expenditures in order unwisely to eliminate a recession-induced budget deficit.[34] Both in 1954 and in 1958 belated increases were made in federal expenditures, mainly in transfer payments and highway construction, in response to the decline in business. Although tax cuts were proposed, in neither case were they enacted. The engineering of budget surpluses to fight inflation is also widely endorsed: ideologically easier to swallow, such a policy may yet be harder to implement than its opposite, required in the reverse case. In practice the achievement of surpluses may be prevented by obstacles to cutting expenditures (as was found in 1957) and by Congressional unwillingness to increase tax rates, at least in time of peace.

Yet an astonishing prejudice still exists against the use of fiscal policy as a regulator whenever it implies deliberately budgeting for a deficit. This prejudice was well illustrated in the national debate during 1962–1964 over the proposal of the Kennedy and Johnson administrations for a cut in federal taxes at a time when a deficit already existed. A fair generalization would appear to be that as of now Congress will neither increase expenditures substantially, nor cut taxes at all, if a deficit is likely to result, unless (1) a serious emergency exists (e.g., war; whether a serious depression would count as such is still uncertain); or (2) simultaneous efforts are made to reduce, if not to eliminate, the deficit (by higher taxes if expenditures are increased, or by expenditure cuts if taxes are cut).

[32] Both Secretaries of the Treasury Humphrey and Anderson clearly felt that a balanced budget should be the objective except in highly unusual circumstances: see, e.g., A. E. Holmans, *United States Fiscal Policy 1945–59* (London: Oxford University Press, 1961), Chs. XII, XIII.

[33] Cf. *ibid.*, Ch. XIV.

[34] "When everyone agrees that there is a recession in progress, the federal budget is allowed to be in deficit, with the size of the tolerable deficit having some weak relation to the severity of the recession; at all other times the federal administrative budget is supposed to be in balance. This constitutes some small triumph for modern fiscal theory, since it keeps the government from making the most egregious errors in recession" (Otto Eckstein, *Review of Economics and Statistics*, XLIV [February 1962], 19).

Clearly this position reflects the principle, if principle it be, that federal deficits should be temporary and should be matched over a period of years by surpluses, so that—serious emergencies apart— the public debt is free from any secular upward trend. Adherence to this condition sharply limits the possible scope of fiscal policy as a regulator of economic activity.

The considerations that make nonsense of these tenets of "sound" finance are familiar to economists and will not be rehearsed in detail here. Suffice it to observe that the absolute size of the gross federal debt (subject to the "debt limit") does not have the significance commonly attached to it by laymen; and that the federal administrative budget offers surplus/deficit figures that in themselves tell us nothing whatever about the soundness of the federal finances.

In the first place, *size* must be distinguished from *burden*. Whatever view one takes of the nature of the debt burden, it is measured by the interest charge on debt held by the public figured as a percentage of gross national product (or of the tax yield from a given tax structure). The *burden* of a public debt of given *size* may therefore be expected to *decline* steadily in the future as GNP increases. Alternatively a steady increase in the debt, i.e., federal deficits in some years uncompensated by surpluses in other years, can occur— within definable limits—*without increasing* the burden.

Second, *total* must be distinguished from *deadweight* debt. The federal government does not separate its capital expenditures from current expenses of government. But public investment in research or physical assets will increase federal revenues because, even if not actually self-liquidating in a financial sense, such expenditures increase tax yields from a given tax structure. It is no more unreasonable for the public sector to finance capital expenditures by borrowing than for the private sector to do so. Moreover in housing and agriculture the Treasury has increasingly engaged in recent years in lending programs through which it acquires financial assets. Thus the public debt to watch (if we are concerned with the "solvency" of the U.S. Treasury) is the figure reached after deduction of (the depreciated value of) physical and other assets held by government. And the surplus or deficit to watch is that obtained after the exclusion of public investment expenditures and lending programs (net of depreciation of existing assets) from the total outgo. In order to show how tax revenues compare with current governmental expenses (and also to measure changes in public wealth), the case for segregation of current from capital expenditures in our national accounts is overwhelming and should have been undertaken long since. This reform is a prior condition for educating the public—to say nothing of public men—in the economics of fiscal policy.

Third, debt held by the *public* is alone relevant to questions of economic policy: debt held by government departments and trust funds and by the Federal Reserve System should be deducted. In the same way the relevant deficit or surplus relates to the cash (or, better, national income accounting) budget, not to the ordinary administrative budget. The cash budget gives a complete picture of payments to or from the public, including transactions of trust funds excluded from the administrative budget. Partly because a balanced administrative budget has usually meant a cash budget in surplus, and partly because public investment and Treasury lending are treated as current expense, such a balanced (administrative) budget (as federal accounts now are compiled) in fact represents a substantial contribution to national saving—and a corresponding reduction in net *deadweight* debt held by the *public*. Such a governmental contribution to the nation's saving may be welcome in some situations, but its size is at no time accurately measured by the state of balance in the *administrative* budget or by what is happening to *total* federal indebtedness.[35]

From one viewpoint the segregation of capital expenditures as a suitable object to be financed by borrowed money may be defended as a concession to the mythology of budget balancing. However, a capital budget may also have other advantages, e.g., for long-range planning of federal activities.[36] At the present time capital expenditures for the acquisition of real assets are included in the administrative and cash budgets, and also (for lack of satisfactory data for their exclusion) in the national income and product version of fed-

---

[35] "Private business could not grow and expand if it practiced the obsolete accounting procedures of the federal administrative budget. . . . That a great country like ours should allow such obsolete accounting concepts to determine far-reaching public policies is beyond belief" (Alvin H. Hansen, "Economic Policy for Fiscal 1963," *Review of Economics and Statistics*, XLIV [February 1962], 11).

[36] There is no more case for earmarking specific tax revenues or loans for meeting capital expenditures than for any other infringement of budgetary unity. Presumably the recent rash of "special funds" (e.g., for highway construction) accounts for lack of enthusiasm for capital budgeting in some quarters: see "Budgetary Concepts: A Symposium," *Review of Economics and Statistics*, XLV (May 1963), 113–47.

eral and state and local budgets. Money lent by the Treasury also represents a capital expenditure; it is included in the administrative and cash budgets, but not in the national income version. Because of their income-generating effects, federal lending activities (like other capital expenditures) should unquestionably be viewed as one aspect of fiscal policy: they are reflected in our federal cash deficit (Fig. 3).

The separation of capital outlays from current expenses of the federal government puts its budgetary situation in a startlingly different light. For example, the federal budget for 1963–1964 envisaged spending of $5½ billion for physical assets, such as office buildings, post offices, power plants, rivers and harbors, and miscellaneous public works; and for financial assets such as home mortgages, loans to small business, and loans for college dormitories. Another $5½ billion went for grants to states and localities for construction of highways, hospitals, and schools, and for urban redevelopment. Research expenditures, mainly for the space program and for medical research, came to $7 billion, not all of which should perhaps be capitalized. All of the above are classified as civilian expenditures; some part of the $50 billion for defense may presumably result in research findings or productive facilities of permanent value. These figures suggest that federally-financed public investment, gross of depreciation, is currently running between $10 and $20 billion annually. Depreciation of existing federal assets may be put at not more than $1 to $2 billion a year. It is thus apparent how large a deficit must appear in the *administrative* budget for any given year, if tax revenues are not to exceed the *current* expenses of the federal government (including depreciation of existing assets). Surpluses figured in this way measure tax revenues used to finance capital outlays and represent the contribution of federal activities to the nation's saving. It is indeed doubtful whether, on this basis, the U.S. Treasury has experienced a single deficit in all the years since the end of World War II. Economists should have made greater efforts to bring home to Congressmen and public officials the extreme conservatism that federal budgetary policy in fact reflects, and the high degree of fiscal responsibility that would still attach to much lower federal revenues, even if combined with present levels of expenditure.

Quite outside the budget lie still other measures of fiscal policy relevant here: federal loan insurance and loan guarantees. Although they, too, influence spending by the public, they do not figure in any budgetary tabulation, nor do they influence the surplus/deficit relationship. Where federal direct lending has run $2 to $3 billion a year, insurance and guarantees (especially in housing) have run to two or three times this figure. Even less than budgetary policy have loan insurance and guarantees been coordinated with monetary policy or in any way regulated with stabilization of the economy in mind.[37]

There is of course no place in fiscal policy for budget balancing as such. The above discussion merely points to the extremely large size of the deficits that would have to be incurred year in year out in our administrative budget before questions of the solvency of the federal government could be raised. The notion that current (as distinct from capital) expenditures should be exactly covered by taxes has in truth no special virtue. Fiscal policy may require that in some years tax revenues exceed, in other years fall short of, the current expenses of government. There is no likelihood that any deficit (however measured) incurred in peacetime as part of a stabilization policy will lead to a secular rise in the burden of the public debt.

Curiously enough the built-in stabilizers, consequences of such innovations as social insurance and pay-as-you-earn taxation, have in some respects made discretionary fiscal policy more difficult to use for stabilization purposes. For they ensure that a tax structure that fails to cover expenditures at a level of GNP below full employment may nonetheless frequently generate a vast surplus at full employment. Built-in stabilizers retard recession but they also dampen recovery. The notion—not too far from the current Congressional consensus—that with a 7% unemployment rate a budget deficit is acceptable, but that with a 5% unemployment rate the budget should be balanced, may imply so large a budget surplus with a 3% unemployment rate as to inhibit expansion and ensure that 3% unemployment never is attained. If a high-employment objective is to be taken seriously, the deficit acceptable in recession should be geared to the budget picture desired and attainable in prosperity. A rational fiscal policy would decide what is an acceptable level of demand or aggre-

[37] Raymond J. Saulnier, H. G. Halcrow, and N. H. Jacoby, *Federal Lending and Loan Insurance* (Princeton: Princeton University Press, 1958), especially Ch. 5.

gate spending and what surplus (or deficit) is desired at that level; the tax structure would then be adjusted to correspond with this latent or implicit "high-employment" surplus (or deficit) and no particular attention would be paid to the actual relation between federal receipts and expenditures at the existing level of demand.[38]

I conclude that the conscious use of fiscal policy, as a means of regulating aggregate spending or effective demand, still is subject— here in the United States in 1964—to severe practical limitations. There can be small doubt that these limitations eventually will disappear, but for the time being they must still be reckoned with. Wilfred Lewis, Jr. concludes his careful study:

> Progress can be discerned over the postwar period, from one recession to the next, in the public and political acceptance of unbalanced budgets as an appropriate means of combating recession. It remains true, however, that balanced budgets and "fiscal responsibility" are powerful ideas. Only for brief periods near the cyclical troughs has opposition been relaxed to deliberate additions to the passive budget deficits that inevitably accompany recession.[39]

As yet discretionary fiscal policy still is not usable as a substitute for or as an adjunct to monetary policy. For the immediate future, at least, the task of managing the economy must continue to be undertaken by monetary policy. It was particularly unfortunate that the use of monetary policy for domestic ends should have been paralyzed during the early 1960's by the balance of payments problem at a time when fiscal policy had not yet been released from the bonds imposed by prejudice and misunderstanding.

The Policy Mix

For the present the major burden of regulating effective demand must fall upon monetary policy: the most that we can hope, serious depression apart, is that fiscal policy will not be used in a destabilizing fashion in the name of budget balancing. Only in a severe and prolonged depression can we at present feel sure that discretionary fiscal policy will be used as a means of stimulating effective

---

[38] On the relation between the latent or implicit and actual budget surplus, see Wilfred Lewis, Jr., *Federal Fiscal Policy in the Postwar Recessions* (Washington, D.C.: Brookings Institution, 1962); also testimony of Walter W. Heller, Chairman of the Council of Economic Advisers, Joint Economic Committee, *January 1961, 1962 and 1963 Economic Reports,* Hearings, 87th Cong. 1st and 2nd Sess. and 88th Cong. 1st Sess., 1961, 1962 and 1963.

[39] *Federal Fiscal Policy in the Postwar Recessions,* p. 275.

demand. The enactment of the 1964 tax cut, after 18 months of Congressional debate, scarcely modifies this conclusion.

Among instruments of monetary policy, open-market operations must take pride of place. This is so, because (1) open-market policy offers a sensitive method of controlling bank reserves, and through bank reserves, bank lending and the volume of money. (2) At the same time open-market operations afford a direct means of influencing interest rates of any given maturity. In normal times arbitrage should secure the diffusion throughout the market of an expansion or contraction of credit, but in case some maturities are sluggish the power to operate in all maturities is valuable. In case arbitrage does not work smoothly, the central bank can use open-market policy to ensure that all rates move in the desired direction. Discount-rate is clearly seen to be an adjunct of open-market policy, and not in any sense an independent instrument. Variations in reserve requirements are large and sudden changes that affect whole classes of banks. They are not suited to day-to-day adjustments, and should be kept for occasions when a semi-permanent shift from one level to another is needed.

As a general rule, selective credit controls are to be avoided. However in case the regulation of interest rates through open-market policy should be found inadequate to stabilize the economy, direct control of consumer credit could be considered as a supplement.

These instruments have been used in the past with such hesitation—especially open-market operations in the long-term end of the market—that it is premature to conclude that they are inadequate to stabilize the economy. The principal doubt of course relates to fiscal policy. If fiscal measures reinforce monetary policy, or even if they are neutral, we may feel rather confident that the Reserve System has in its armory the weapons needed to stabilize the economy. But if the Reserve is called on to neutralize a strongly inflationary or deflationary policy on the part of the Treasury or Congress, the outcome is much more doubtful.

What additional powers might perhaps suitably be given to the System? Standby power to control consumer credit—on the ground that it is insensitive to ordinary interest-rate control—is the most obvious. Another reform to overcome deficiencies in arbitrage would be power to buy and sell marketable corporate as well as government obligations. Finally, to consolidate the System's ability to restrain credit, it should be given power to sell its own debentures in the market.

Eventually, when prejudice against the use of fiscal policy has abated, and monetary and fiscal policies have been subjected to a single source of decisions, a far wider range of policy mix will be available. Only then will it become possible to take advantage of the substitutability of monetary and fiscal measures. If a tight money policy is desired on international grounds, there will then be no difficulty about maintaining effective demand through fiscal means. However, the dilemma of the balance of payments is not necessarily resolved thereby, for a high level of domestic activity may merely increase the deficit on international account. More important, the existence of a wide range of policy mixes that will secure adequate effective demand domestically, will make a choice of objectives possible in other areas. In particular, if a high rate of economic growth is desired, an easy money policy can readily be combined with a tight fiscal policy, yielding budget surpluses that contribute to national saving.

Chapter 14

Some Organizational Matters

> *what in hell*
> *have i done to deserve all these kittens*
> —Don Marquis, Archie and Mehitabel

The Board of Governors has responsibility under the law for numerous matters more or less remote from monetary policy. Some of these are also the concern of the Comptroller of the Currency, the Federal Deposit Insurance Corporation, and even the Department of Justice—not to speak of state supervisory agencies. Proposals have not been wanting to transfer some of these functions from the Reserve System to one or other of these agencies; or to transfer functions in just the reverse direction. Since governors have sometimes complained that they have more than enough to do, it might make most sense to strip the Board of responsibility for banking structure and supervision and allow it to concentrate on monetary policy.

Membership in the System

In form the Federal Reserve System is a cooperative, stock in the Reserve Banks being owned by the member banks. All national (i.e., federally-chartered) commercial banks are required to belong to the System, but membership by state-chartered banks is optional. Only about half of the nation's commercial banks are members, but member banks hold between 80% and 90% of all bank deposits. What are the advantages and disadvantages of membership? Apart from prestige, membership gives access to Reserve credit, simplifies collection of checks, and furnishes free currency shipments. On the other hand member banks must observe reserve requirements which may be more stringent than under state law, must submit to examinations by the Reserve System if required, and must of course pay all items at par without deduction for exchange charges.

Does the existence of numerous nonmember banks limit the System's powers of control? Ignoring Treasury and other minor currency since it is fixed in amount, we may say that nonmember banks are dependent upon Federal Reserve notes for vault cash. The remainder of their reserves they keep on deposit with a member bank, and member-bank deposits are limited by member-bank reserve balances. Apart from a certain looseness of articulation due to pyramiding, since open-market policy controls Federal Reserve notes and member-bank reserves, it must also influence nonmember-bank reserves. Consequently the existence of nonmember banks, at least in their present numbers and importance, does not seriously diminish the ability of the Reserve System to control the money stock and interest rates. At worst, the System might have to operate on a slightly larger scale to achieve a given result.

To be sure a practical limit to reserve requirements of about 25% of member-bank deposits is set by the voluntary nature of System membership. If requirements should be set, with Congressional permission, much higher than this, it is believed that state member banks would give up their membership, and national banks seek state charters.

The existence of the "dual banking system" is so obviously anomalous that great efforts have been made to modify it, if not to bring it entirely to an end. When the Banking Act of June 16, 1933, established insurance of bank deposits, the measure was to cover nonmember banks for three years only. Deposit insurance was a federal measure, and it was felt that the federal government was entitled to lay down conditions that the beneficiaries should fulfill, i.e., that all banks desiring insurance should join the Reserve System. It was rightly supposed that few banks would wish to operate without insurance, and that consequently the vast majority of banks would be forced into the System. But this was not to be. Bankers lobbied so successfully that the deadline for joining the System (or sacrificing deposit insurance) was postponed and finally removed.

In 1940 excess reserves were so large that the Reserve Board felt urgent steps were needed to reduce them. Realizing that reserve requirements of member banks could be increased only if similar requirements were imposed on nonmember banks, the Board asked Congress to enact uniform requirements for all banks, member and nonmember, under the commerce clause. This would not have ended the "dual banking system" as such, but would have eliminated its most crippling feature. But Congress declined to act. In 1944 still another unsuccessful attempt was made at consolidation. The departure from the Federal Deposit Insurance Corporation of Leo Crowley, "strong man" of deposit insurance, suggested the moment had come for its absorption by the Reserve System. Accordingly Chairman Eccles proposed to President Roosevelt that the functions of the Comptroller of the Currency and the Federal Deposit Insurance Corporation should be transferred to the Reserve Board by executive order. Eccles based his case as a war measure upon the manpower savings that would accrue from consolidation of the examination and statistical functions of the three agencies. Had the plan been carried through, the presumption is that the Board could have imposed reserve requirements on nonmember banks—or even required them to join the System—as a condition for continued deposit insurance. But the President was not sure that the order would be legal, and did not feel the manpower savings had been demonstrated. So nothing was done.

In 1949 Senator Douglas' subcommittee made a study of the matter and recommended that all commercial banks be made subject to the same set of reserve requirements and that they all be given access to Federal Reserve credit. The subcommittee did not advocate compelling all banks to become members of the System, but asked further study:

> Federal activities in the chartering, supervision and examination of commercial banks are divided among three federal agencies with overlapping jurisdiction—the Comptroller of the Currency, the Federal Reserve, and the Federal Deposit Insurance Corporation. Owing to voluntary agreements among these agencies and the 48 state supervisory authorities there is less confusion and duplication of effort than might be expected from such overlapping jurisdictions; nevertheless, there is evidence that a thorough study is needed. The present arrangement, though not without its merits, involves an undetermined amount of waste because of duplication of facilities and supervisory personnel; it does not promote the development of uniform supervision and examination policies, and there is evidence that on some occasions the

different agencies have been guided by different concepts as to the purpose of bank supervision and examination; it does not facilitate coordination of policies; and there is evidence of interagency rivalry of types that do not contribute to the development of a better banking system.[1]

Supervision of Commercial Banks

The diversity of bank examinations owes its origin only in part to the "dual banking system." In part it derives from the fact that the Comptroller of the Currency examines national banks and FDIC examines insured banks, and both federal jurisdictions are quite separate from the Reserve System. When the System was founded, the Comptroller (himself a member of the Reserve Board) was well entrenched in the examination function so far as national banks were concerned; and the Board found it convenient in many cases to accept the examination reports for state member banks furnished by state authorities. The System therefore, perhaps wisely, never sought to make of its own examining operations a large-scale or comprehensive enterprise.

A serious difficulty arose during the Great Depression, in that temporary depreciation in the bond market made many banks insolvent in the strict view of bank examiners. The danger was so obvious that the Board under Chairman Eccles was able to obtain the agreement of the Comptroller and the FDIC to a new uniform standard for bank examinations:

> Neither appreciation nor depreciation in . . . marketable obligations in which the investment characteristics are not distinctly or predominantly speculative . . . will be taken into account in figuring net sound capital of the bank.[2]

This "base stock" method of valuing assets was useful also in saving banks from technical insolvency when interest rates rose in the early 1950's.

In campaigning to have a greater, if not indeed the sole, role in bank examination given to the Board—to the exclusion of Comptroller and FDIC—Eccles went far beyond a mere liberalizing of

[1] Joint Committee on the Economic Report, *Money, Credit and Fiscal Policies*, Report pursuant to S. Con. Res. 26, 81st Cong. 2nd Sess., Senate Document 129, 1950, pp. 32–39.

[2] "Revision in Bank Examination Procedure," *Annual Report of the Board of Governors for 1938*, p. 89. See also Marriner S. Eccles, *Beckoning Frontiers* (New York: Knopf, 1951), pp. 266–78.

procedures, and claimed that examinations were an adjunct of monetary control. He sponsored what may be called a cyclical theory of examinations:

> . . . it seems only reasonable to consolidate bank examination and regulatory functions under the single roof of the Reserve System since these functions are directly related to the maintenance of economic stability, with which the System is primarily concerned. Clearly, if the System is committed to a policy of monetary ease in times of depression, then bank-examination policies should follow a similar commitment. Or if the System is committed to a policy of credit stringency in order to curb an imminent inflation, then bank-examination policy should be brought in line with that same intention.[3]

This is to convert bank-examination procedures into an instrument of monetary policy. We may grant that, if bank assets are sound in some sense related to ultimate repayment, their liquidity is unimportant. Collectively bank assets can in any case only be turned into cash through the aegis of the central bank. Granted, too, that cyclical variation in the willingness to lend on the part of the bank would be a useful stabilizing device. Yet variation in examination standards does not seem an appropriate way of inducing banks to expand or contract their lending. The whole proposal asks entirely too much of the bank examiner. To require him not only to apply standards of soundness to assets and procedures, but also to vary these standards according to the state of business—to do this may in theory have merit, but must in practice merely confuse those engaged in the process. One may therefore cordially approve the insulation of marketable assets from market valuation achieved in the 1938 revision of examination standards without seeing virtue in the proposal to vary these standards cyclically.

To arrange for all banks—or at least all insured banks—to be examined by a single agency would appear to make sense. But it is not clear that that agency should be the Federal Reserve. Even were all commercial banks required to become members of the System, their examination by some other agency, e.g., FDIC, could have advantages. For it may well be best for the Board to concentrate upon monetary policy without having its attention distracted by supervisory questions, few of which are related to its main function. Only the regulation of commercial-bank lending as an incident to selective

[3] Eccles, p. 267.

credit control, and the fixing of interest rates payable on deposits, would seem to involve monetary policy—and therefore ought to remain with the Board.

Other supervisory functions relate to mergers, branches, and holding companies. The Board has jurisdiction over mergers involving state member banks (Federal Deposit Insurance Act of 1950), and they require its permission to establish branches (McFadden Act of 1927). Elaborate regulation of bank holding companies under the Acts of 1933, 1935, and 1956 is administered by the Board. The Board also passes upon applications to establish foreign branches and subsidiaries. A check of the Board's *Annual Reports* shows that the burden of its activities—concerned essentially with the control of competition between commercial banks—has been increasing steadily. Much of this work has involved the Board of Governors in extensive litigation to determine the state of the law. One is astonished that the Board had time to grapple with major issues of monetary policy, and was not continually overwhelmed by a mass of administrative detail.[4]

The situation with respect to bank mergers is especially confused, since the Comptroller of the Currency and the FDIC, as well as the Department of Justice and state supervisory authorities, may all be involved and take contradictory positions. It would seem that regulation in this area might well be left to the Department of Justice and state authorities.

Minor Functions of the Board

In its early days the Board lavished immense ingenuity and effort on the development of eligibility standards for commercial paper; another major task was the establishment of par collection upon a firm legal and administrative base. By 1925 statistical research was becoming a large-scale operation, partly for internal use and partly for publication.

Some other more recent developments have affected individual Reserve Banks rather than the Board of Governors. With the Depression came the industrial loan program under Section 13.b—an

[4] Some part of the Board's workload probably results from excessive centralization. For example, the Board has to decide such trivial questions as whether individual member banks may invest more than 100% of their capital in bank premises, and whether or not to waive penalties on temporary reserve deficiencies reported by member banks. See House Committee on Banking and Currency, *Financial Institutions Act of 1957*, Hearings, Part I, 85th Cong. 1st Sess., 1957, pp. 535–43, 562–63.

amendment of the Act made June 19, 1934. Since World War II fiscal agency functions carried out in behalf of the Treasury have much increased, both with respect to the public debt and to foreign operations through the Stabilization Fund. The need for the industrial loan program may be questioned, but to act as fiscal agent for the Treasury clearly is an essential part of central banking. The same may be said of growing operations as agent for foreign central banks and governments that wish to transact business in the American money market. Since 1962 the system has of course acquired substantial foreign-currency holdings for its own account.

Chapter 15

The Personnel of the System

> *A good new chairman of the Federal Re-*
> *serve Board is worth a $10 billion tax cut.*
> —Senator DOUGLAS

What sort of people have been called to service with the Reserve System, and what sort have been attracted by it? How well have its officials been selected? How well have they served it? What organizational or other changes might improve the caliber of the System's personnel?

Occasional black sheep were to be expected. There was the official of the New Orleans branch of the Atlanta Bank who, forgetful when not sober, left the office one evening without closing the vault.[1] And there was the Roosevelt-appointed governor who fled to Mexico, not apparently because of malfeasance during his (necessarily) brief stay with the System.[2] Such cases afford light relief in a story that is mainly one of conscientious officials, often able by native endowment, but equally often ill equipped by training, struggling to meet each new crisis as it developed. To see the forest for the trees, to reach an analysis that would survive in the light of history, to articulate a philosophy that would stand up not only under the current but under the next-succeeding crisis—these have been given to few even of the top officials.

Party Politics

Politics in the narrow sense have played very little role in System appointments, major or minor. Presidents have frequently named to

[1] Hamlin diary, June 20, 1926.
[2] See above, p. 122.

the Board men affiliated with the opposite political party, but very few of them were politically active prior to appointment. Three chief executives of the System have been Democrats, six Republicans.[3]

Attempts to extend the spoils system to Federal Reserve employment were made occasionally. The "merit" principle was established only gradually; in the early days Democratic and Republican administrations alike were tempted. For example, prior to 1935 the office of Federal Reserve Agent at each Bank was a full-time appointment made by the Board and occupants of the White House were apt to feel that their suggestions should be respected. In 1916 Secretary of the Treasury McAdoo (himself a member of the Board ex officio) tried unsuccessfully to have President Wilson's brother-in-law made Federal Reserve Agent of the Richmond Bank.[4]

President Harding's efforts to extend the spoils system were notably blunt and direct: he made it quite clear that he thought his candidates should be appointed, even at the cost of removing the incumbents. Secretary Mellon, however, does not seem to have gone to bat for his chief as did Secretary McAdoo; in any case the Board proved uncooperative.[5] The failure of his namesake in the White House to reappoint W. P. G. Harding Governor of the Board was widely credited to the President's disappointment. To be sure, President Harding's nomination of D. R. Crissinger of Ohio as Governor of the Board may be regarded as a successful piece of spoilsmanship; Crissinger, though conscientious, could scarcely have been more poorly equipped, temperamentally and otherwise, for the role.[6]

There again was trouble when the Democrats returned to Washington. During the summer of 1933 many attempts were made to persuade the Board to appoint spoilsmen, but these efforts appear to have originated mainly with Postmaster-General Farley and to have been called off as soon as the matter was brought to Roosevelt's attention.[7] In addition to his lapse in the case of Morrison (to please Vice-President Garner), Roosevelt appointed the chairman of the Nebraska State Democratic Committee, J. J. Thomas, to the Board.

[3] Governors Hamlin (1914–1916) and Black (1933–1934) and Chairman Martin (1951–present) were Democrats on appointment. Governors Harding (1916–1922), Crissinger (1923–1927), Young (1927–1930), and Meyer (1930–1933), and Chairmen Eccles (1934–1948) and McCabe (1948–1951) were Republicans.
[4] Hamlin diary, February 25, March 6, and July 16, 1916.
[5] Hamlin diary, December 3, 1921; April 28 and May 3, 1922; January 2, 1923.
[6] See above, p. 67.
[7] Hamlin diary, 1933, passim.

Thomas created great offense by refusing to give up his state chairmanship and by seeking to have the Board make political appointments.[8] But Roosevelt's aberrations may well be forgiven when we recall that he appointed Eccles—and over the bitter opposition of Senator Glass! Whether the System was again subjected to similar pressures when the Republicans returned to Washington in 1952 and the Democrats in 1960 is a question I must leave for future historians to settle.

A different and more serious case of political interference seems to have occurred in February 1948 when President Truman failed to reappoint Eccles chairman of the Board of Governors. It has been alleged that the Giannini interests wished to halt antitrust action against the Transamerica Corporation, a bank holding company in California. Eccles himself believes that Senator Sheridan Downey, with this end in view, suggested to Truman that, if he wished to carry California in the fall, he should find another chairman for the Board.[9] That Eccles, demoted, did not resign from the Board, but was around to emancipate the System from the Treasury just three years later, amply testifies to his dedication as a public servant. The incident underscores the disadvantage of charging a single agency both with monetary policy and with the maintenance of competition in the market for banking services.

Qualifications of Appointees

For the Board of Governors the Federal Reserve Act prescribes two qualifications, one formal and the other informal. No two governors may come from the same Federal Reserve district; and in making appointments to the Board, the President "shall have due regard to a fair representation of the financial, agricultural, industrial, and commercial interests, and geographical divisions of the country." It seems unlikely that such broad limitations can have reduced the supply of talent available to the President in making appointments; on the other hand the law gives him no help in deciding what qualifications are appropriate.

There are no restrictions on the choice of Reserve Bank presidents by a Bank's directors, except that the choice must be approved by the Board of Governors. Staffs of the Board and of the Banks are not

[8] See above, p. 122.
[9] Marriner S. Eccles, *Beckoning Frontiers* (New York: Knopf, 1951), pp. 450–53.

subject to civil service methods of recruitment or pay scales, and the Board early set its own standards in these matters. Salaries of governors compare well with those of top federal officials, but are below those in private business. Salaries of Reserve Bank presidents are well above those of governors or other Washington officials, but below those paid to top officials of commercial banks. Salaries of staff compare favorably with, but are somewhat more flexible than, those paid in the federal service. I doubt that it has happened, except perhaps on rare occasions, that inadequate pay has hindered recruitment of suitable personnel, either by the Board or the Banks.

Members of the Board of Governors have predominantly been lawyers or bankers, with a sprinkling of men with other types of business experience. Reserve Bank presidents have in many cases come from commercial banking, but increasingly have had experience within the Reserve Banks themselves. A commercial-banking background could have advantages when it came to dealing with member banks and the money market, but as Benjamin Strong discovered, it was not always easy to convince a man with such a background that a central bank should not be operated for profit,[10] and during the Depression it was even harder to convince such men that a central bank need not hold what are ordinarily considered liquid assets.[11] The carryover of ideas from operating a commercial bank may have had advantages, but it also had disadvantages.

Until Mitchell was appointed governor in 1961 and Daane in 1963, only one top official during the history of the System, Adolph C. Miller, who was a Board member from 1914 to 1936, could stake a claim as a professional economist, although others may of course have had training in economic analysis. Unquestionably the making of Federal Reserve policy, when conducted on almost any criteria and with almost any end in view, requires the economic interpretation of events on a quite sophisticated level. Whether more attention should have been paid to training in economics in the selection of appointees is debatable.

First, the Board and the Banks have from quite early days possessed staffs which have included professional economists and statisticians. To some extent their research divisions, partly because of the limited opportunity for basic research or for publication, have been

[10] See above, p. 68.
[11] See above, p. 107.

staffed by technicians of somewhat limited outlook rather than economists of wide knowledge and experience. This deficiency can be and has been remedied (although to date on a small scale only) through the hiring of outside economists on a consulting basis: one recalls John Williams' work for the New York Bank and Alvin Hansen's for the Board of Governors. It may still be doubted whether a Board member without training will fully understand or appreciate the brief placed before him by an economist, particularly if it runs counter to deep-seated prejudices or fallacious notions that he associates with "common sense." This argues that the policy makers themselves, and not merely their staffs, should be thoroughly grounded in economic analysis.

Second, economics is an uncertain discipline that reaches firm conclusions about policy only with difficulty. Macroeconomic theory and analysis in the 1920's and even in the 1930's was primitive by the standards of today. It is far from clear that the advice, even of the best economists of the time or the leaders of the profession, would necessarily have improved monetary policy at moments when, looking back from our vantage point in the 1960's, we feel it was most deficient. Until very recently Reserve thinking was dominated by the fallacious commercial-loan theory of credit or "real bills" doctrine; but then so also was the thinking of economists. In 1933 many Reserve officials believed that abandonment of gold must inevitably lead to galloping inflation; so did many economists. They believed, too, that in a slump, business recovery could best be promoted by balancing the federal budget at the earliest possible date; so did many economists. In sum, what economists had to offer by way of interpretation and advice was in many cases no better than the highly misleading "common sense" of the average Reserve Board member or Reserve Bank president (governor) of that time. Today we think we have a better understanding of at least some of these matters, so that the innocent Reserve official does not have quite so good an alibi as did his predecessor.

By way of example a few of the more dubious opinions held at one time or another by Reserve officials may be worth quoting, although—as just emphasized—the degree to which the economists of the day could or would have supplied them with superior wisdom is debatable. Board member Adolph Miller, who had taught economics at one time, was a dogmatic exponent of the commercial-loan theory and believed that the risk of inflation lay primarily in the overissue of Federal Reserve *notes*.[12] Governor McDougal of the Chicago Bank was only the most uncompromising among a majority that held the opinion that a central bank had much the same duty to remain liquid —i.e., to hold mainly *short-term marketable* assets—as a commercial bank.[13] In 1932 Board member Hamlin felt that a *rise* in interest rates might expand bank lending owing to its presumed greater profitability to the banks;[14] and a year later, as convertibility was suspended, he was convinced that the dollar was about to go the way of the German mark.[15] When the Gold Reserve bill proposed the transfer of the monetary gold stock from the Reserve Banks to the Treasury in exchange for gold certificates, the Board expected a panic on the ground, according to Hamlin, that gold certificates were "irredeemable."[16] In 1932 Board Governor Eugene Meyer was advocating a balanced budget to restore confidence;[17] and two years later Board Governor Eugene Black, who seems to have regarded Secretary of the Treasury Henry Morgenthau, Jr. as a dangerous radical, still was demanding in mid-1934 that Roosevelt balance the budget at whatever cost.[18]

A comparable collection of opinions held by Reserve officials might quite possibly be assembled for the period since Eccles came to Washington and Sproul to New York. But such a collection for the more recent period would be much more difficult to assemble and the chances are it would not look nearly so foolish. The general level of economic literacy has unquestionably improved with the years.[19]

[12] House Committee on Banking and Currency, *Stabilization*, Hearings on H.R. 7895, 69th Cong. 1st Sess., 1927, pp. 853–54; Hamlin diary, May 10, 1923.

[13] *Ibid.*, January 11 and July 14, 1932.

[14] *Ibid.*, April 29, 1932.

[15] *Ibid.*, April 19, 1933.

[16] *Ibid.*, December 22, 1933.

[17] House Committee on Banking and Currency, *Stabilization*, Hearings on H.R. 10517, 1932, p. 556.

[18] Hamlin diary, July 11 and October 22, 1934.

[19] As late as 1945 some Board members predicted that "the Washington monument would topple" if margin requirements were raised from 40% to 50% (Draper diary, February 2, 1945). Charles R. Whittlesey makes much of the increased influence of economists on System policies since 1950 (*Economica*, N.S. XXX [February 1963], 38–40). It may well be that, with the growing workload, top officials depend more heavily on staff work than formerly; unquestionably the staff work is technically competent. Yet neither the Board of Governors nor individual Reserve Banks normally employ professional economists of the caliber, e.g., of those who have worked in recent years for the Council of Economic Advisers.

The Leading Policy Makers

For most of its history the System's monetary policy has for practical purposes been made by some single dominant individual. When two strong personalities have occupied top positions in the System simultaneously, indecisiveness has frequently resulted. The tendency has been for either the chairman of the Board of Governors or the president of the New York Bank to "run the show." This tendency needs explanation.

In discussing the work of the Board of Governors, Bach has well described one factor in the situation:

> Broad economic experience, understanding of the intricacies of the modern banking and monetary mechanism, awareness of the long history of domestic and international central-banking experience, and some knowledge of the executive processes of government—all important to the formulation and execution of wise credit policy—are qualifications possessed by few men. Most appointees, even those highly successful in other lines, have thus faced a long period of hard work and developing experience before they hope to understand fully the intricacies of monetary policy.
>
> Reflecting this situation, many board members appear never to have contributed importantly to the formation of monetary policy. Thorough understanding of the intricate monetary relationships involved has usually come only with years of service, if at all, and has therefore ordinarily been limited to a small proportion of the board members at any time.[20]

Frequently but not always, officials with most influence were those who worked hardest or had been longest with the System: the newcomer was at a disadvantage. But it was not merely a matter of mastering statistical reports and technical memoranda; a man of strong opinions had to convince his colleagues within the System, and often also the Treasury and other outside agencies. Persuasiveness and strength of personality have counted for much.

The role of the Federal Reserve has been shaped and its policies largely determined by four men whose careers collectively span the half century of its history. These four major figures comprise two presidents of the New York Bank, Strong and Harrison, and two

[20] G. L. Bach, *Federal Reserve Policy-Making* (New York: Knopf, 1950), pp. 121–22.

Board chairmen, Eccles and Martin.[21] Each brought to his position a combination of personality, character, and intellect—but scarcely of background or training—that enabled him to know his own mind and to get his way.

The fact that during its first two decades the System was dominated by the governor of the New York Bank, and since about 1935 has been run chiefly from Washington by the chairman of the Board, is due only in small degree to accidents of personality. The New York Bank was located in the nation's principal money market and was fiscal agent for the Treasury. Unless or until subjected to specific instructions by the Board, it inevitably enjoyed more or less complete freedom of action in dealing with the money market (open-market policy) and negotiating with the Treasury (debt management). Control by the Board was established only slowly and with much friction, as we have seen, and was not fully effective until the 1935 Act gave to the Open Market Committee its present statutory form.

Therefore in the early years any head of the New York Bank could not but be the leading figure in the System's counsels and day-to-day management. Yet the dominance of New York was greatly reinforced by accidents of personality. On the one hand Benjamin Strong would have been a leading figure in almost any sphere of activity; on the other hand the Board in Washington was led by a succession of weak executives. From 1914 to 1916 Hamlin, on his own assessment not well fitted for the position, was governor of the Board. Only from 1916 to 1922 was the Board run by a capable administrator who knew his own mind (W. P. G. Harding, not reappointed in 1922). During nine months in 1922–1923 the governorship of the Board was vacant. Between 1923 and 1934, when Eccles came to Washington, the Board was run by four different governors, none of whom can be described as temperamentally well suited to the position. As a

---

[21] On Strong, see Lester V. Chandler, *Benjamin Strong, Central Banker* (Washington, D.C.: Brookings Institution, 1958); see also the collection of Strong's writings and speeches, *Interpretations of Federal Reserve Policy* (ed. W. Randolph Burgess) (New York: Harper, 1930). On Harrison, his own papers form a valuable source, but have not been collected. Those interested in Eccles should read his autobiograhy, *Beckoning Frontiers* (New York: Knopf, 1951), which is both revealing and full of charm. Martin's character may be studied in the record of his numerous appearances before Congressional committees.

The office occupied by Strong, and by Harrison when he first headed the New York Bank, was called governor; the title was changed to president in 1936. Eccles, too, was known as governor of the Board, rather than chairman, when first appointed.

consequence, the dominance of New York endured far longer than it might otherwise have done. Indeed an oversimplified judgment, not entirely justified, would be that Strong dominated the System from the New York Bank from 1914 to 1928 through his own intellect and strength of purpose; and that Harrison did likewise from 1928 until after Eccles arrived in 1934 through the weakness and division of the Board.

Yet, as Senator Glass so signally failed to understand, a nation's monetary policy must be centralized. Nor could it remain permanently centralized in New York. Both the formal establishment of the Board as the System's top echelon, and the steadily increasing assumption of federal responsibility for economic policy, ensured that the direction of monetary policy would eventually be centralized in Washington rather than in New York. Many of the changes made in the 1935 Act simply represent recognition of this fact. Just as closeness to the money market favored New York in the early days, so the trend toward centralization favored Washington in the later period. Here again accidents of personality reinforced the logic of events. The history of the Board since 1935 is practically spanned by the official lives of two men, Chairman Eccles and Chairman Martin, who, in very large measure, saw to it that New York executed policies laid down in Washington.

It is easy at this distance in time to under-rate the achievement of Benjamin Strong. He believed the Reserve should "follow the market" and failed to grasp the ability of the System to influence interest rates in 1920–1921 until much damage had already been done. As an admirer of the "classical" gold standard his views seem curiously dated today. Yet he had a far clearer view of the nature and needs of central banking than Warburg who, with his European experience, was everywhere accepted as the pundit. Strong's great qualities were his lack of preconceptions and his willingness to learn from experience. To him in large measure is due the discovery and development of open-market policy and the tradition against continuous borrowing. To him, too, we owe the first recognition of the Reserve's ability to influence business conditions.

George Leslie Harrison was a lawyer who had already been in the service of the New York Bank for some years before becoming governor (i.e., president as he would now be called) on Strong's death in 1928. He was on the whole an able executive: he resisted the

Board in the matter of "direct pressure" in 1929; he was responsible for what few open-market purchases were made in late 1929 and 1930; he master-minded the fruitless open-market experiment of the Spring of 1932. But he was strictly an empiricist, quite lacking in any philosophical or theoretical bent. As a result he showed none of Strong's receptivity to new ideas. His lack of imagination is well illustrated by his reaction to the 1931 gold crisis, described in Chapter 5. He could conceive a plan for rounding up commercial paper from the New York banks to defeat the supposed intrigues of the Bank of France, but not as a means of avoiding the destruction of domestic bank credit. It must also be said that Harrison acquired something of a reputation for deviousness; Hamlin calls him "a prince of lobbyists".[22] The times in which he served necessitated extensive dealings with European central banks, and in such negotiations he may have exceeded his authority. Too, he seems to have had extensive traffic with the Treasury without keeping the Board informed.

If Harrison was a lesser man than Strong, and does not rate with Eccles or Martin, there still is no question but that he has to be listed among our four leading policy makers. From Strong's death in 1928 until Eccles' arrival in 1934, he overshadowed all other System officials. To what extent was his dominance simply due to weakness and division at the Board? When Harrison took over the New York Bank in 1928 from the ailing Strong, Roy A. Young was governor of the Board, and he remained so until August 1930, when he resigned to take the more lucrative and less taxing governorship of the Boston Reserve Bank. Young's background was commercial banking. A governor (or chairman) of the Board should be able to carry a majority of the Board with him on important matters, even if unanimity is beyond his reach. Young's lack of leadership is suggested by the rarity during his governorship of a unanimous Board and the frequency with which he is recorded in the minority.[23] In the spring of 1930, Harrison would have liked larger open-market purchases, but it is not clear that the opposition came from Young.

Eugene Meyer, who succeeded Young, was in many respects the

[22] Hamlin diary, August 1, 1935.

[23] Young voted in the minority when the Board ordered "direct pressure," February 2, 1929; voted with the majority disapproving New York's requests for a rate rise in February and March; but voted in the minority again when the Board once more denied New York's request, May 16, 1929. See Hamlin diary.

exact opposite of his predecessor. Formerly with the War Finance Corporation and the Federal Farm Loan Board, Meyer came to the Board with extensive financial and administrative experience. Hamlin describes Meyer as assured and even brusque in handling the Board. More and more in the increasingly difficult months of 1931 and 1932, instead of using the Board as a source of advice or as a lever, Meyer preferred to reach private understandings with Harrison, Mellon, or Ogden Mills, and to neglect the Board. So far as one can judge, Hamlin is right in thinking that Meyer was mostly willing to let Harrison have his way.[24] After the middle of 1932 Meyer's attention was more and more absorbed by his chairmanship of the Reconstruction Finance Corporation. In March 1933 Meyer resigned and was succeeded by Eugene R. Black, Roosevelt's first appointee, a lawyer who had been governor of the Atlanta Reserve Bank. Black's brief time in office was a period of inaction for the Reserve, and the most noteworthy event was the transfer of the monetary gold stock from the Reserve Banks to the Treasury, which Black bitterly resisted. It does not seem that he had important differences with Harrison.

When Black resigned to return to Atlanta, he was succeeded by Marriner S. Eccles, a commercial banker from Utah. Eccles, easily the foremost personality to be associated with the System during its history up to that time, took the position with the understanding that Roosevelt would support an amendment to the Federal Reserve Act that would clarify lines of authority and in some degree centralize power in the Board. The revision of the law and Eccles' role therein were described in Chapter 5. Harrison objected strongly to the centralization of power in the Board, and it is possible that, working through Senator Glass, he was partly responsible for the compromise Open Market Committee.[25] After the passage of the Act there seems to have been no difference of substance between Harrison and Eccles as to the desirability of increasing reserve requirements in 1936 and 1937; but a sharp clash occurred over the speed and extent of the support to be given to the market in March and April 1937 when things went wrong.[26] In the Fall of 1939 there were again differences between New York and Washington as to how the market should be

[24] Hamlin diary, April 29, 1931.
[25] Harrison papers, Discussion notes, February 7, 1935.
[26] See above, Chapter 5.

handled, but in general it may be said that Eccles' views prevailed.[27] In sum, during much of Harrison's period in office his dominance may be not unfairly ascribed to changes in leadership and divided counsel at the Board: once Eccles had taken charge in Washington, his influence declined.

Marriner Stoddard Eccles, a successful banker with wide business experience in the West, brought to the Board much-needed qualities of leadership. Open to ideas from all quarters, and willing to rely heavily on his research people, such as Goldenweiser, his tendency to think aloud sometimes made him appear inconsistent. Eccles' achievements were considerable. Architect of the 1935 revision of the Federal Reserve Act, he made large contributions to System organization and procedures; he struggled manfully against Treasury domination during and after World War II; and it is to him—almost alone—we owe the resuscitation of monetary policy after more than a decade in limbo. The story has been told in detail in Chapters 5 and 6.

At the New York Bank Harrison was succeeded in January 1941 by Allan Sproul, who for a decade had been Harrison's subordinate and who prior to that had worked for the San Francisco Reserve Bank. For the next decade Eccles and Sproul were the two leading figures in the System. The contrast between them was marked. Eccles came fresh to the System's problems; Sproul had been steeped in them for years. Eccles' cast of mind was intuitive and empirical; his inclination was to experiment. Sproul's bent by contrast was more analytical; he had more respect for tradition; temperamentally he was more cautious. It is an oversimplification to describe Eccles as the radical, Sproul as the conservative: but there were moments when such a distinction applied.

Both Sproul and Eccles demonstrated administrative talent and qualities of leadership of a high order. It is a tribute to both men that they worked together so successfully in the manner described in Chapter 6. Even before Pearl Harbor collaboration between the two men, so diverse in character and background, was facilitated by the obvious need to concentrate the resources of the System to limit inflation; unquestionably thereafter the struggle with the Treasury helped to make Washington and New York sink their differences.

[27] See above, Chapter 6.

As head of the New York Bank in an earlier phase of the System's history, Sproul would no doubt have ranked among the System's "leading policy makers." But the centralization embodied in the 1935 Act, together with Eccles' qualities of leadership, ensured that henceforth all major decisions would be made in Washington rather than in New York. Only in the unhappy event that the Board is someday divided or leaderless is there any prospect that the center of power will revert to New York. To be sure, if all major decisions are now made in Washington, New York can still exert an influence. Sproul's analytically-minded opposition to Eccles' highly experimental "special reserves" plan helped to eliminate any prospect of its passage by Congress. Much more recently New York's opposition, initiated by Sproul and continued by Alfred Hayes, to Chairman Martin's "bills only" policy undoubtedly facilitated its partial abandonment by the System in 1961.

Since April 1951, i.e., practically since the Accord which as a Treasury official he helped to bring about, the chairmanship has been occupied by William McChesney Martin. Policies during the Martin regime have been discussed in Chapter 7. It is much too early to attempt a definitive assessment of Martin as a policy maker, but his claim to rank among the System's leading makers of policy is already established. The tendency of other officials to refer questioners to Chairman Martin,[28] his willingness to discuss Federal Reserve policy before the Joint Economic Committee and elsewhere, and his command of the situation when he does so—to say nothing of his survival through changes of administration in 1953 and again in 1961—testify to his capacity for leadership and ability as a diplomat.

To summarize: by and large, policy was made by Strong from 1914 to 1928 and Harrison from 1928 to 1934, both heads of the New York Reserve Bank; and by Eccles from 1934 to 1951 and Martin since 1951, both Reserve Board chairmen.[29] Heads of the Reserve Board prior to 1934 and presidents of the New York Bank since that time have played only a minor role in shaping policy.

[28] See, e.g., Joint Economic Committee, *Review of Annual Report of the Federal Reserve System for the Year 1960*, Hearings, 87th Cong. 1st Sess., 1961, p. 56, 60, 72.

[29] Thomas B. McCabe succeeded Eccles as chairman in 1948, but McCabe's policies were Eccles', and in any case Eccles himself influenced the course of events decisively at the time of the Accord: see above, Chapter 7.

The Also-Rans

The reader will doubtless have remarked the curious fact that, in the course of the above review of System policy making, I have had occasion to mention the name, neither of the head of any Reserve Bank other than New York, nor of any Board member other than the governor (pre-1936) or chairman (post-1936). These others have indeed occasionally influenced policy—almost always by preventing action. Under a weak executive it was sometimes possible to split the Board and put the governor in a minority, as Miller did in 1929 over "direct pressure." Several times in 1930 and 1931 open-market purchases were inhibited or delayed through objections from the Reserve Banks of the interior, especially Chicago. A strong executive on the other hand could always carry with him a majority of the Board, or of the Open Market Committee, as the case might be, even if he could not secure unanimity. Under Eccles and Martin decisions were not always unanimous, indeed, but neither was ever found voting with the minority.

Lack of influence of Reserve Bank presidents outside New York is easy enough to explain. Apart from weakness and division at the Board, New York itself carried weight in System counsels for three main reasons: (1) It was the executant of open-market policy and the largest single source of borrowed reserves. (2) It had direct dealings with the Treasury whenever the latter needed advice on managing the debt. (3) It was the channel through which foreign central bankers sought to deal with their American colleagues, and through which the Board was therefore also forced to deal with foreign central banks. These reasons were lacking in the case of the other eleven Banks. As already explained, since 1936 the factors mentioned have no longer assured New York the same degree of influence as they did formerly.

Lack of influence of Board members other than the governor or chairman is harder to explain. Hamlin and Miller, for example, were Board members continuously from 1914 to 1936 and, after W. P. G. Harding retired in 1922, were senior in point of service to each of the five succeeding Board chairmen with whom they served. Similarly when Martin, new to the Board, was appointed chairman in 1951, Governor Szymczak already had 18 years of Board experience on which to draw. No Board chairman, except

Harding, has been appointed from among existing Board members, so that since 1916 every chairman upon appointment has found himself junior in experience to every one of his colleagues. Yet even with a weak Board chairman—and there have been several— the influence upon policy of other members of the Board has usually been slight. The principal exception was Eccles, who during 1948– 1951, as vice-chairman and former chairman, continued to exercise the leadership that was natural to him.

The explanation seems to be in large part that Board policies, although they do not have to be negotiated in any formal sense, do have to be explained to and cleared with the New York Bank, the Treasury, (since 1947) the Council of Economic Advisers, and (especially if legislation is in view) one or more Congressional committees. This diplomatic function is one that only the chairman can discharge. The point is illustrated by the extreme rarity of those occasions upon which any governor but the chairman chooses, or is called, to testify at Congressional hearings.

The Staff

The System seems to have been well served by its staff. Both the Board and the New York Bank have built up sizable statistical and research divisions, the quality of whose work is partly indicated by the output of financial statistics but also of the well-known indexes of industrial production. The many research and policy memoranda that have circulated unofficially or have been published by the Joint Economic Committee testify to the excellence of the staff work available to policy-making officials. To assess the quality of the staff at different periods or to single out individual contributions is beyond the scope of this study. Yet it is impossible to conclude a chapter dealing with the System's personnel without mentioning Emanuel A. Goldenweiser (1883–1953), who was the Board's Director of Research and Statistics from 1926 to 1945.

Chapter 16

The Present Status of Monetary Management

> *Experience is the name everyone gives to his mistakes.*
>
> —OSCAR WILDE

> *The matters at issue are of an importance that cannot be exaggerated.*
>
> —KEYNES, The General Theory

K eynesian or not, one may agree about the importance of the matters at issue, for they extend to the viability and effectiveness of our entire ways of doing things. These matters will indeed settle the question whether there is a future for the manner in which we in noncommunist countries conduct our economic life. The management of money is central to the survival of our economic system.

Retrospect

From the vantage point of the present, with maximum opportunity for hindsight, the most striking features of our experience with the management of money during a century and a half are the lessons we have learned—and the dreadful slowness with which we have learned them. The mistakes we have repeated have been legion, the failure of our imagination has sometimes been abysmal, and on more than one occasion our loyalty to outworn dogma has proved nothing short of catastrophic. During the first half-century of the Republic we dispatched successively two promising experiments in central banking. Not only did we place the growing burden of monetary management on the Treasury: we surrounded the Treasury with rules and restrictions which ensured that the burden could

368

not be carried. As for the Independent Treasury System, it would have been difficult to devise a plan that could better ensure that the whole structure would collapse periodically in financial crises of maximum severity. Before 1914 several capable Secretaries held office at the Treasury, but only rarely did Congress allow them to take the most elementary precautions against collapse, or to follow the path of common sense in monetary matters.

In 1914 came the great reform. But the reform itself was plagued with the soon-to-be-exploded doctrine of the superiority of commercial loans as central-bank assets; with the mistaken idea that even a manufacturer of liquidity needs to worry about his own liquidity; and with the absurd notion that market rates of interest are data to which the central bank must adapt, rather than the other way around. Since its foundation, the Federal Reserve System has been administered with disinterestedness and a high degree of technical competence in the management of the money market. But with respect to the larger objectives of monetary policy, pusillanimity and myopia are the words that too often spring to mind. Timidity and shortsightedness produced several disastrous failures. Slow to realize the powers it possessed, it was slow to embrace stabilization and high employment as legitimate and desirable objectives for monetary policy.

Among major errors of judgment on the part of the Reserve, all of which have been discussed in previous chapters, may be listed: (1) acquiescence in the Treasury's desire for low interest rates in 1919, which led to the inflation that culminated in the Summer of 1920; (2) maintenance of high interest rates during the last months of 1920 (when the boom was already over) and the first half of 1921, so delaying business recovery; (3) hesitation in making open-market purchases during 1929 and 1930, lack of concern with the bond market during 1930–1933, and failure to include long-term obligations among the securities purchased during these years; (4) unimaginative acceptance policy during the last months of 1931 and failure to treat the resulting credit restriction as a calamity to be avoided at all cost; (5) mistaken increase in reserve requirements of member banks in the Spring of 1937, which played an important role in the subsequent downturn; (6) acquiescence in 1942 in the Treasury's desire to perpetuate the existing "pattern of rates" for the duration of the war; (7) continued subservience to the Treasury's views on interest rates from 1945 until 1951. The above list omits the stock-market boom and collapse (1929), bank failures and the total collapse of the banking system (March 1933), and abandonment of the gold standard (April 1933). These episodes are omitted because I believe that the Reserve had no real responsibility for the stock-market boom; that it had no direct responsibility for bank failures, although it contributed to them indirectly under (3) and (4) above; and that the abandonment of gold (which may not have been the error of judgment many thought it to be at the time) was wholly the responsibility of the Treasury.

All of the seven mistakes listed were subsequently acknowledged as such in varying degrees by officials of the System. While this fact offers hope for the future, it is by no means a guarantee that the same mistakes will not be repeated. Recognition of the error of subservience to the Treasury after World War I did not prevent a similar mistake on a far larger scale after World War II. More interesting is it to inquire to what extent the seven mistakes listed are to be attributed to mediocre personnel on the one hand or to the erroneous doctrines of the time on the other. Such an inquiry is rich in paradox.

The Reserve System has been served by executives of undoubted ability and strong personality: Harding, Eccles, and Martin at the Board; Strong, Harrison, and Sproul at the New York Bank. The first four came to the System with commercial-banking or other outside financial experience; the last two grew up within the System itself. These are men who know their own minds, and when they are in control it is hardly necessary to look further for the source of policy decisions. For our purpose the three heads of the New York Bank almost span its life. At the Board, however, between Harding's departure in 1922 and Eccles' arrival in 1934, a series of undistinguished governors furnished little in the way of leadership. Yet if experience can yield competence, it should not have been lacking even during this inter-regnum: Miller, an economist by profession, and Hamlin, a lawyer, were members of the Board during the entire period 1914–1936. Many mediocrities also served on the Board, some of whom were political appointees: they brought nothing to the System in the way of prior knowledge, and did not serve long enough to acquire a useful understanding of its problems through experience. Nevertheless there were, I believe, available at all times, both in New York and Washington, at least a necessary minimum of talent and capacity to conduct the System's business. Moreover, by the middle 1920's the System already possessed statistical and other research facilities clearly superior to those available at that time to any other government agency. Why then these seven sins, deadly indeed, of commission or omission?

The first and last counts in the indictment—the prolongation of cheap money after World Wars I and II—must be ascribed to the superior power (in the ultimate sense political) and prestige of the Treasury. To let an issue of securities by the Treasury go unsold would lead many to reproach the Reserve with lack of patriotism, even if in truth the cap would better fit the Treasury. Technical issues of this sort are not easily fought out in public, as we all were to learn in 1951. Yet the question still awaits an answer whether the Reserve could or should have taken a firmer line, and have brought both the "pattern" and bond-pegging to an end at an earlier date. It is hard for an outsider not to believe that it could and should.

The second and third counts resulted from a mistaken application of commercial-banking principles to central banking. A commercial bank adapts its rates to the market instead of trying to influence market rates. After the boom was over in the fall of 1920 the System gave no thought to lowering market rates of interest, indeed perhaps had not yet learned how to do so. Liquidity is another matter with which your commercial banker is quite properly concerned. A mistaken application of the same principle to Reserve Banks undoubtedly prevented them from buying long-term obligations during the Great Depression, contributed to the spread between short and long rates, and postponed recovery in the bond market.

The remaining mistakes are perhaps more difficult to explain. I have argued that the gold crisis of September and October 1931, Item (4), was due to lack of imagination. In one sense it came from following tradition—if you lost gold, you raised your discount rate. But the System was no longer bound by this tradition, and the real reason for credit restraint seems rather to have been the shortage of acceptances—a shortage that could have been remedied if sufficient trouble had been taken. Imagination was lacking, for the very measures that were so badly needed in October to avoid a credit restriction—cooperation of member banks in turning acceptances over to the Reserve—were seriously discussed in January 1932 as a means of repatriating the French balances.

Item (5), the increase in member-bank reserve requirements in the Spring of 1937, was as close to a pure error of judgment as can well be. The deflationary fiscal situation was not anticipated as it should have been. The reaction in the bond market was indeed corrected promptly, thanks to Chairman Eccles' insistence, this being the first occasion when the System overcame its scruples and bought long-term bonds. But the damage had been done. The incident illustrates the blunt and unpredictable character of changes in reserve requirements as a weapon of monetary policy, and underscores its inferiority to open-market operations.

The freezing of the existing pattern of interest rates in 1942 for the duration of the war and some time thereafter—Item (6)—resulted from lack of understanding of the fact that rate differentials reflect differences in the market's appraisal of risk. Long-term obligations are priced to yield more than short to compensate their holders against the risk of a future rise in interest rates. As soon as this risk was sharply reduced as a result of the establishment of the pattern, demand shifted toward the long end of the market and "pattern playing" began. Either short rates should have been allowed to rise or long rates to fall, or both. At the time the pattern was established, the Reserve did indeed press for a somewhat higher rate on 3-month Treasury bills, but yielded to the Treasury. Although one cannot be dogmatic, it is probable that the Treasury could have raised the money it needed more cheaply had it not insisted on the pattern, or had it chosen a different pattern—the extent of inflation associated with the war being assumed given.

Since the Accord the Reserve cannot be reproached with major mistakes, although, as we saw in Chapter 7, the timing of its actions could have been improved. The failure, after 1957, to secure full employment is chiefly to be charged to the state of the foreign balance; to liberate monetary policy in these years would have required a different mandate—one not concerned with the convertibility of the dollar into gold.

Prospect

Granted that we desire a high level of employment, a stable price level, and a high rate of economic growth: to what extent should we rely upon monetary policy, and to what extent upon fiscal or other policies, for the attainment of these objectives? I reject stable exchange rates with other currencies, or a stable gold value for the dollar, as an altogether secondary consideration—nice if you can have it but not worth making sacrifices for. It will be difficult enough to attain all three domestic objectives simultaneously; let us not complicate our problem by insisting in addition that the external value of the dollar remain unchanged from one generation to the next. If domestic objectives require that the dollar float freely, so be it. The proper procedure is of course to place an embargo on the sale of gold and to refrain thereafter from adopting any fresh parity. Whether counterspeculation by an official exchange fund is worth while, or whether the exchange market should be left free of official interference, is a question about which I have an open mind. In any case these matters lie beyond the scope of the present study.

We may note first the contributions toward our three major objectives which can, and if possible should, be made by policies other than monetary or fiscal. We saw in Chapter 12 that an adequate level of demand is a necessary but not a sufficient condition for eliminating structural unemployment. Policies to improve labor mobility—particularly retraining—are needed. A stable price level is not likely to be compatible with full employment so long as the cost-push has full rein. The application of antitrust policy both to large-scale business enterprises and to nationwide labor unions may be needed; or as a substitute for the latter a national compact to govern wage policy. Finally, economic growth can be promoted both by government expenditure for research and by a tax structure that favors investment as against consumption.

Let us assume that these other policies are followed; there remains the problem of maintaining an adequate but not excessive level of monetary demand. How much of the burden should be shouldered by monetary, how much by fiscal policy? What will be the most effective policy mix? Analytically we may separate the stabilization problem, primarily concerned with employment and the price level, from the question of the long-run policy mix, which chiefly affects the rate of economic growth. In principle either monetary or fiscal measures may be used for countercyclical purposes, or they may be combined in a wide range of different proportions. In other words an adequate level of demand can be secured from many different policy mixes. On the other hand, to push up the rate of growth, an easy monetary should obviously be combined with a tight fiscal policy.

How then should we divide responsibility when it comes to stabilizing employment and the price level? To be sure, the effectiveness of monetary policy, since its rebirth in 1951, has been questioned from several distinct viewpoints. Friedman believes that the lags with which discretionary monetary policy operates are so serious that it cannot claim to be a stabilizing force at all, but at best has a random impact on the business cycle (Chapter 10). Gurley and Shaw regard the ability of financial intermediaries to supply credit needs outside the banking system, especially by mobilizing idle balances, as a grave obstacle to effective monetary control (Chapter 13). Still other critics have doubted the sensitivity of investment spending to interest-rate changes (Chapter 13). I have argued that none of these lines of criticism represents a fatal—or even a near-fatal—objection to or limitation of monetary policy and that each critic has overstated his case. Nonetheless, even if monetary policy is neither a bull in a China shop, nor a boomerang, nor a broken reed, we have to admit that its use is tricky, its effects not always predictable, and its record far from perfect. What is the alternative?

Automatic fiscal stabilizers have received nearly universal acclaim as a countercyclical weapon; unquestionably they have helped to moderate and shorten recent business recessions (Chapter 7). They represent, too, our first line of defense against any recession leading to such an economic collapse as occurred a generation ago. Yet to depend upon automatic stabilizers exclusively would be to set our sights too low, for they can only slow down a decline in business but cannot reverse such a decline; nor can they begin to ensure that demand is maintained at an adequate level. Consequently the practical alternative to discretionary monetary policy is discretionary fiscal policy.

From the purely economic standpoint the inauguration of budget surpluses and deficits has at least as powerful, if not a more powerful effect upon output, employment, and the price level than has monetary policy. The time lag between a budgetary turnaround and its effects upon demand is shorter than it is for monetary policy and the magnitude of the result is mostly more predictable. In a rationally organized society these advantages would be decisive, and extensive use would unquestionably be made, especially, of variations in tax rates as a means of securing the desired level of aggregate demand. But our society is not rationally organized.

I have argued that during the 1920's and the 1950's monetary policy had some stabilizing effect, but the influence of the federal budget has been predominantly destabilizing.[1] If we consider practical future potentials I would say the contrast is even more marked. Monetary discretion is confided to a conscientious and able group of men with ample intelligence facilities who in a comparable situation are most unlikely to repeat the mistakes of the 1930's and who on the whole have been steadily improving their record. By contrast, fiscal discretion is jealously guarded by Congress—no suitable body for exercising it. Except in case of extreme emergency—and most business-cycle situations do not wear this air—the time required for Congress to vote a tax cut or increase, or a public-works program, runs to many months and almost guarantees that the ultimate effects of the measure will be wide of the mark. Unless or until Congress is willing to vote "formula flexibility," or still better, limited Presidential discretion, we may as well write off discretionary fiscal policy except in case of severe depression.

Quite apart from the necessarily ponderous nature of Congressional decision making, the use of fiscal policy has to cope with the most serious kind of ideological lag. Economists by and large now hold the view that balancing the federal budget is a highly qualified objective; at the very least they consider that the fiscal year has no special virtue as an accounting period over which to achieve a balance; many if not most would go further in suggesting the income-and-product rather than the tax-collection-and-appropriation basis for judging the degree of balance; and almost all feel that federal expenditures of a long-term investment character, especially when made for the purpose of acquiring self-liquidating assets, may justifiably be met from borrowed funds rather than tax collections. Some members of our profession would indeed go much further and claim that budget balancing is in no sense an appropriate or proper objective of economic policy, and that fiscal policy should be judged exclusively by other criteria, such as the need to maximize employ-

[1] See Otto Eckstein, "The Federal Budget," *Review of Economics and Statistics*, XLIV (February 1962), 17–20. A. E. Holmans would make a somewhat kinder judgment: see his *United States Fiscal Policy 1945–1959* (London: Oxford University Press, 1961), p. 301.

ment or to stabilize the price level. If this more radical position should lead to rather regularly recurring deficits—which is far from obvious—its upholders would urge that not all debt is publicly held, that the burden even of publicly-held debt has been greatly exaggerated, and that in a growing economy the absolute size of the publicly-held debt can increase with no rise in its burden. It is obvious that even the most "conservative" of the positions favored by economists sets little or no store by any attempt to balance the administrative (as distinct from the cash or income-and-product) budget each fiscal year, but offers scope for the use of fiscal policy as a stabilizing medium.

Congressional attitudes on this question are very different, nor can it seriously be argued that they fail to reflect the opinion of the public at large. A chasm gapes between the economist's view and that of the layman. The fatal and wholly fallacious analogy between the federal and the family budget still dominates public ideology; you should never "spend money you don't have"; deficits when long continued necessarily lead to inflation and even to "national bankruptcy." Ideas change, but at a snail-like pace. President Hoover, Secretary of the Treasury Mills, and even President Roosevelt in the 1932 campaign, all felt it politic to proclaim (no doubt sincerely) their belief that balancing the budget was the greatest help that the federal government could give toward business revival. Few but politicians of the stamp of Senator Byrd or Representative Cannon would endorse this doctrine in a depression today, nor would Congress be likely to legislate such savage tax increases in any comparable situation as it did in 1932. The idea that a genuine effort should be made to balance the federal budget each fiscal year, no matter what the state of the economy, is now held only by such eccentrics as Representative Patman or the late Senator Bridges.

Despite these slight advances, Congressional—and public—opinion still holds to notions that represent a major obstacle to the rational use of fiscal policy as a means of managing the economy. Experience in the recessions of 1954 and 1958 shows that it is politically much easier to increase expenditures, on unemployment compensation or on public works, than to cut taxes; yet the latter has much the more useful and immediate impact. Public discussion in 1961–1962 showed that much political credit may still be garnered from attempts to balance the budget and political discredit from attempts to unbalance it. By and large the American public now seems willing to accept deficits in periods of recession, provided such deficits result from the recession, are not deliberately created to deal with it, and are accompanied by measures designed to produce a returning surplus within a year or two. But recent experience demonstrates that the deliberate creation of a deficit for stabilization purposes is still taboo—except perhaps in the case of a deficit resulting from public-works expenditures undertaken with a view to relieving unemployment. The notion that deficits and surpluses should be varied countercyclically, or that regular federal expenditure of an investment character may suitably be met from borrowed funds—such notions are still far from acceptance. In 1964 a tax cut could at long last be enacted only on the promise of substantial reductions in federal expenditure.

To overcome the worst effects of this lag in public ideology, certain administrative changes may be helpful. The use of the income-and-product basis in the *Economic Report of the President* for presenting figures for the federal budget, which tends to reveal a surplus when the conventional administrative budget is still in deficit, is a distinct advance, both in rationality and in public relations. A logical extension would be for the Treasury to incorporate at least some features of income-and-product accounting in its regular reporting of the budgetary situation. For instance if tax receipts were reported on an accrual rather than a collection basis, the federal deficit would disappear at an earlier date as business recovers from a recession, thus easing pressure on legislators for restrictive budgeting that could bring the recovery prematurely to an end. A further much-needed reform is the separation of federal expenditures of an investment nature from the ordinary expenses of government; the former could then be met by borrowing, at times when such borrowing was desirable from the viewpoint of fiscal policy, with less risk of a charge of "fiscal irresponsibility."

To sum up: fiscal policy, unquestionably the most rational and effective means of controlling economic activity, suffers from two grave weaknesses. First, long lags at present exist between the need for action and the taking of action. The variation of tax rates is somewhat less subject to lags than the variation of expenditures; but so long as Congress is unwilling to vote formula flexibility or limited discretion to the President, for example to vary tax rates, serious delays seem inevitable, except in case of extreme emergency. Second, public and consequently Congressional thinking on these matters is so far behind what, I think, must be called expert opinion in this connection that the outlook for suitable discretionary action, even after long delay, is not good. The forum granted to economists by the Joint Economic Committee must have done something to enlighten Congressmen. As for public opinion, the courageous stand taken by the Commission on Money and Credit in favor of giving the President power to vary tax rates is to be applauded. The Committee for Economic Development has endorsed tax cuts to deal with recession. But the National Association of Manufacturers and the United States Chamber of Commerce still remain to be converted.

The net of the situation early in 1964, as we approach the fiftieth anniversary of the founding of the Federal Reserve, is that heavy reliance must still be placed upon monetary policy in regulating employment, price levels, and the rate of economic growth. And particularly in regulating employment and price levels, for growth can be promoted by long-range tax and expenditure policies that have little or no application to the stabilization problem (Chapter 12). What is the outlook for achieving high employment and a stable price level through monetary policy? Suppose the two objectives conflict?

Where employees demand, and employers are willing to pay, wages which rise—for the economy at large—more rapidly than productivity is increasing, the purchasing power of the dollar must decline. The same is true where monopolists or oligopolists arbitrarily raise product prices. The condition for the success of such a "cost-push" is of course that demand—for labor and for final products—shall be strong. The acquiescence of the monetary authority is necessary. But the maintenance of employment at an acceptable level may require a monetary policy that also encourages the cost-push. We should surely bring this contradiction out into the open. Possibly it can be resolved by a national wage policy acceptable to business and labor alike. Certainly we need a vigorous antitrust policy, and perhaps a change in the legislative framework which surrounds collective bargaining—a new Taft-Hartley to weaken the short-run bargaining power of organized labor. The promotion of guidelines for noninflationary wage increases by the Kennedy Administration in 1961–1962 is a step along this road, but many more steps may be required.

Within the confines of our existing situation, in which we have to depend upon monetary policy, and the cost-push is still with us, a narrower question needs an answer. If faced with a conflict of objectives, which should we prefer—full employment or a stable price level? Toward which horn of the dilemma should we lean?

It is a matter of some concern that the Federal Reserve has not even publicly admitted the existence of the dilemma. Its position is that for high employment to be sustainable the price level must be kept stable. While extreme price-level instability is obviously damaging to employment, there is some reason to think that average unemployment might have been raised during 1957–1964 at the cost of a somewhat more rapid rise in the price level. There is some evidence that the higher levels of unemployment in recent years result rather from larger deficiencies of demand than from heavier structural unemployment (Chapter 12).

In my opinion the public at large is far more concerned about unemployment than about inflation. In the decade following the outbreak of World War II we saw the dollar lose half its purchasing power. Times were good; protest was confined largely to the few groups whose income lagged. By contrast in 1954, and again in 1958, a rise of one or two percentage points in unemployment led to widespread outcry and filled the headlines. I judge that the public at large is far more concerned about unemployment than about inflation. The conclusion is reinforced by negative evidence. The public currently is willing to hold record amounts of fixed-money obligations: life insurance, savings bank deposits, savings and loan association shares, not to speak of commercial-bank deposits and government bonds. No flight from the dollar is in prospect. Yet fractional increases in the consumer price index are announced almost monthly. I conclude that the public is less afraid of inflation than of unemployment: that, indeed, it prefers "moderate" inflation to "moderate" unemployment.

If this assessment is correct, it would seem that policy should lean somewhat more toward the employment objective and somewhat less toward the price-level objective than it has in recent years. This judgment can of course be upset, for example, if it develops that the amount of inflation required to produce short-run full employment leads sooner or later to instability destructive of the original aim—either because sooner or later a crisis supervenes, the resulting recession destroying the full employment; or because sooner or later moderate or "creeping" inflation seriously threatens to slide off into hyperinflation, also destroying the full employment. On the first count, much modern thinking and some postwar experience have tended to downgrade crises as serious obstacles to full employment; they now seem rather easily and quickly overcome. On the second count, we have to reckon with the remarkable vitality and persistence of the money illusion. For example, in France continuing inflation at a moderate pace has been a safe prediction for decades; here and there among the French the money illusion is a little tattered, yet no signs of approaching hyperinflation are visible.

To be sure it may be questioned whether an appeal to implied or expressed social preference is the right way to settle the issue—especially since such preference is so difficult to measure. There is the matter of honesty of intention. Since money is issued and monetary policy determined by the same sovereign power, inflation is dishonest, involving a partial repudiation of the public debt. Yet deliberately to deprive individuals of job opportunities, and the community of output, by permitting underutilization of resources, is also dishonest. An appeal to moral principle is not helpful here. Nor are welfare considerations decisive. The burden inflicted on the many through inflation may or may not exceed the (individually greater) burden inflicted on the few through unemployment. A balance must be struck. My subjective judgment is that, so far as monetary policy is concerned, we would have done better, at least since early 1957, to have placed more emphasis on raising GNP and less on fighting inflation.

So much for the objectives of monetary policy. I have argued that the instruments already are reasonably well adapted to the needs of the situation (Chapter 13). General credit controls are powerful and well coordinated, and the modern emphasis on open-market operations is unquestionably sound; personally I share the view of many critics that recent reductions of reserve requirements have been a mistake. The case for selective credit controls is not made out. The thought that sectors out front in a boom might helpfully be curbed by such controls grossly over-rates the authorities' ability to determine which sectors are out front. If a case is made out for selective controls it will rather be because the sectors to be controlled have shown themselves insensitive to general controls. The structure of the Reserve System should be improved by reducing the number of persons involved in making decisions (Chapter 11).

If and when remedies are found for the defects of fiscal policy reviewed above, monetary policy may be able to take a back seat: the same dilemma—whether to fight hardest against unemployment or against inflation—will face fiscal policy. For the present, having to rely upon monetary policy, we may as well make it as efficient as possible. Our major need is for top-level coordination (Chapter 11). Monetary management cannot achieve its potential unless the debt-management policy of the Treasury is integrated with the open-market policy of the Reserve System. The various lending programs over which the Treasury has ultimate jurisdiction also need coordinating with other elements in the picture. The need for unified direction of the nation's macroeconomic policy will become even more urgent as and when fiscal policy begins to play a stabilizing role. I have argued that only the President can achieve such unification, and that for staff work he should rely principally upon the Council of Economic Advisers.

Appendix I

Bibliography

A. Sources for Part I

This selective bibliography is intended to supplement the footnote references in Part I. Its purpose is to indicate the relative worth of different sources. Confined to books and Congressional documents, it does not cover periodicals.

Three books cover the whole or a substantial part of our period. *A Monetary History of the United States, 1867–1960,* by Milton Friedman and Anna J. Schwartz (Princeton: Princeton University Press, 1963), appeared as the manuscript of this volume was on its way to the printer. Obviously a work of the greatest interest to the student of monetary management, its emphasis and many of its interpretations differ markedly from my own. Comment must be postponed for another occasion. A second book that covers the period from the close of the Civil War through 1960 is Tilford C. Gaines, *Techniques of Treasury Debt Management* (Glencoe: The Free Press, 1962): within its province it can be warmly recommended. Taking in a still longer span, a third book, *Federal Budget and Fiscal Policy, 1789–1958* by Lewis H. Kimmel (Washington, D.C.: Brookings, 1959) surveys public attitudes toward deficit financing and the federal debt, but the opinions quoted are of very uneven interest.

Chapter 2. For the functioning of the First and Second Banks, Bray Hammond's *Banks and Politics in America from the Revolution to the Civil War* (Princeton: Princeton University Press, 1957) is easily the most useful source. In assessing the central-banking functions, such as they were, of the Second Bank, I consulted Walter B. Smith's *Economic Aspects of the Second Bank of the United States* (Cambridge: Harvard University Press, 1953), especially Chapter II. Ralph C. H. Catterall, *The Second Bank of the United States* (Chicago: University of Chicago Press, 1903) is distinctly less useful. Quite indispensable are Albert Gallatin's two pamphlets: *Considerations on the Currency and Banking System of the United States* (Philadelphia: Carey and Lea, 1831) and *Suggestions on the Banks and Currency of the Several United States* (New York: Wiley and Putnam, 1841); both pamphlets are of course reprinted in the Henry Adams edition of Gallatin's *Writings* (Philadelphia: Lippincott, 1879), Vol. III.

For the whole of the nineteenth century, two most useful studies are: Margaret G. Myers, *The New York Money Market,* Vol. I, *Origins and Development* (New York: Columbia University Press, 1931) and Esther R. Taus, *Central Banking Functions of the United States Treasury, 1789–1941* (New York: Columbia University Press, 1943). Indispensable are the reports (usually annual) of the Secretary of the Treasury. The regular series of such reports begins in 1849; earlier reports appeared in a somewhat haphazard fashion under the imprint of John C. Rives and other Washington printers. David Kinley's *History, Organization and Influence of the Independent Treasury of the United States* (New York: Crowell, 1893) is a useful summary. Good studies of nineteenth-century crises are conspicuously lacking: J. S. Gibbons, *The Banks of New York and the Panic of 1857* (New York: Appleton, 1858) and the *History of Crises under the National Banking System* (61st Cong., 2nd Sess., Sen. Doc. 558, 1910), written by O. M. W. Sprague for the National Monetary Commission, are descriptive rather than analytical. George W. Van Vleck's *The Panic of 1857* (New York: Columbia University Press, 1943) is more useful.

Chapter 3. For the period covered by the Federal Reserve System, the *Federal Reserve Bulletin* (monthly) and *Annual Reports* of the Federal Reserve Board (since 1936, Board of Governors) are indispensable. Main source for the establishment of the System must remain H. Parker Willis, *The Federal Reserve System* (New York: Ronald Press, 1923), despite the author's many prejudices and misconceptions. Still more personal (and to some extent conflicting) accounts of the authorship of the Federal Reserve Act are: Carter Glass, *An Adventure in Constructive Finance* (New York: Doubleday Page, 1927); J. Lawrence Laughlin, *The Federal Reserve Act* (New York: Macmillan, 1933); Robert L. Owen, *The Federal Reserve Act* (New York: Century, 1919); and Paul M. Warburg, *The Federal Reserve System* (New York: Macmillan, 1930).

Original sources for the System's operations during its early years are: W. P. G. Harding, *The Formative Period of the Federal Reserve System* (Boston: Houghton Mifflin, 1925), and the diary of Charles Sumner Hamlin (MSS, Library of Congress). Lester V. Chandler, *Benjamin Strong, Central Banker* (Washington, D.C.: Brookings, 1958) and Willis may also be consulted. Much valuable detail will be found in Benjamin H. Beckhart, *The Discount Policy of the Federal Reserve System* (New York: Holt, 1924).

Chapter 4. Prime sources for the period 1920–1929 are the *Annual Reports of the Federal Reserve Board,* testimony of System officials before Congressional committees, and the Hamlin diary. Published writings of Reserve officials or former officials are sparse and not too helpful. Among these may be mentioned Benjamin Strong, *Interpretations of Federal Reserve Policy,* ed. W. Randolph Burgess (New York: Harper, 1930), a collection of reprinted papers, most of which are available elsewhere. Mr. Burgess' own *Reserve Banks and the Money Market* (New York: Harper, 1927; revised, 1936) is in the nature of a textbook and well reflects many of the views and preoccupations of the era. E. A. Goldenweiser's *American Monetary Policy* (New York: McGraw-Hill, 1951) is uneven, and its usefulness is limited by its author's excess of discretion and desire to defend System policies. Except for a few sidelights, Herbert Hoover's *Memoirs* (New York: Macmillan, 1952) have little value for our purpose.

A wealth of monographs is available, the best being probably (from widely differing standpoints) Charles O. Hardy, *Credit Policies of the Federal Reserve System* (Washington, D.C.: Brookings, 1932) and Chandler's *Benjamin Strong*. Beckhart's *Discount Policy* brings the story only to mid-1923. Seymour E. Harris' *Twenty Years of Federal Reserve Policy* (Cambridge: Harvard University Press, 1933), while encyclopedic, is extremely uneven in value. Harold L. Reed, *Federal Reserve Policy, 1921–1930* (New York: McGraw-Hill, 1930), although marred by the author's sympathy for the commercial-loan theory, is useful as a contemporary document. William O. Weyforth, *The Federal Reserve Board* (Baltimore: Johns Hopkins, 1933), is an excellent study of the distribution of power within the System prior to the revision of 1935; see also Karl R. Bopp, "The Agencies of Federal Reserve Policy," *University of Missouri Studies*, X, No. 4 (October 1935).

Among Congressional documents the most interesting are the various *Stabilization* hearings before the House Committee on Banking and Currency between 1923 and 1928; and the hearings pursuant to S. Res. 71, *Operation of the National and Federal Reserve Banking Systems,* before the Senate Committee on Banking and Currency in 1931.

Chapter 5. For the period of the Great Depression, valuable unpublished materials are the Hamlin diary (through January 1936; increasingly illegible in the last months, but see the typewritten index-digest) and the George Leslie Harrison papers (Columbia University). Beginning in 1935, the papers of Marriner Stoddard Eccles (in his possession in Salt Lake City) were found to be an extremely valuable source. The papers of Emanuel Alexander Goldenweiser (Library of Congress) are also useful, but more for office memoranda than for personal papers. The Ogden Livingston Mills papers (Library of Congress) are voluminous but disappointing. Memoirs by former Reserve officials include the invaluable *Beckoning Frontiers,* by Marriner S. Eccles (New York: Knopf, 1951), and the less useful *Ended Episodes,* by George W. Norris (Philadelphia: Winston, 1937). Whatever the Henry Morgenthau, Jr., papers may eventually be found to contain, as scholars are permitted to examine them, John M. Blum's *From the Morgenthau Diaries,* Vol. I, *Years of Crisis, 1928–1938* (Boston: Houghton Mifflin, 1959) is almost without interest.

Among secondary sources, H. Parker Willis and John M. Chapman, *The Banking Situation* (New York: Columbia University Press, 1934) contains much on banking structure, bank failures, and such, and a good account of the legislative history of the Banking Act of 1933. *Monetary Policies of the United States, 1932–1938* by James D. Paris (New York: Columbia University Press, 1938), actually confined to the gold and silver policies, is useful for a chronology and texts of official documents. Kenneth D. Roose, *The Economics of Recession and Revival, An Interpretation of 1937–1938* (New Haven: Yale University Press, 1954) is indispensable. Among Congressional documents the most useful are the House and Senate hearings on the Banking Act of 1935.

Chapter 6. For the period of domination by the Treasury, unpublished sources are the George L. Harrison papers (but only through the end of 1940) and, above all, the Marriner S. Eccles collection. For this period, the Goldenweiser papers contain little of interest; and the diary of Ernest Gallaudet Draper (MSS, Library of Congress), which covers the period May 1941 to November 1949, though titled "Stirring Times," is practically valueless. The most useful published primary source is Eccles' *Beckoning Frontiers*. Goldenweiser's *American Monetary Policy* is useful, subject to qualifications already mentioned. Henry C. Murphy, *National Debt in War and Transition* (New York: McGraw-Hill, 1950) gives the Treasury's viewpoint. In *Economics in the Public Service* (New York: Harcourt Brace, 1953), Edwin G. Nourse has some interesting recollections, but surprisingly little to say about monetary policy; the *Memoirs* of Harry S. Truman (Garden City, N.Y.: Doubleday, 1956) also have little to contribute.

Secondary sources include Lester V. Chandler, *Inflation in the United States, 1940–1948* (New York: Harper, 1951) and the excellent if extremely detailed *The Federal Reserve System, 1945–1949,* by J. S. fforde (London: Oxford University Press, 1954). The growing importance of fiscal policy during this period is discussed by A. E. Holmans in the earlier chapters of his most useful *United States Fiscal Policy, 1945–1959* (London: Oxford University Press, 1961).

With the establishment of the Joint Economic Committee in 1947 (known until 1956 as the Joint Committee on the Economic Report), the Congressional literature is vastly enriched. Of special interest are the hearings on *Monetary, Credit and Fiscal Policies* held by a subcommittee under the chairmanship of Senator Douglas in the Fall of 1949.

Chapter 7. For the period since 1951, reliance must necessarily be placed upon published sources, but these are fortunately abundant. Primary material is the record of meetings of the Federal Open Market Committee and of the Board of Governors in *Annual Reports of the Board of Governors of the Federal Reserve System.* The Joint Economic Committee has supplemented its annual hearings on the *Economic Report of the President* by such special inquiries as those concerned with *Monetary Policy and the Management of the Public Debt* in 1952 and *Employment, Growth and Price Levels* in 1959–1960. From time to time, important hearings have also been held by the House and Senate Committees on Banking and Currency and by the Senate Finance Committee. Few memoirs are yet available; Dwight D. Eisenhower's *Mandate for Change* (New York: Doubleday, 1963) is without interest for our purpose.

Several monographs are available, including three published as Congressional documents: Senate Committee on Banking and Currency, *Federal Reserve Policy and Economic Stability, 1951–1957*, by Asher Achinstein, Senate Report No. 2500, 85th Cong., 2nd Sess., 1958; and Joint Economic Committee *Employment, Growth and Price Levels*, Study Paper No. 1, "Recent Inflation in the United States," by Charles L. Schultze, 86th Cong., 1st Sess., 1959, and Study Paper No. 19, "Debt Management in the United States," by Warren L. Smith, 86th Cong., 2nd Sess., 1960. Two excellent studies of fiscal policy have also appeared: Holmans' *United States Fiscal Policy, 1945–1959* and Wilfred Lewis, Jr., *Federal Fiscal Policy in the Postwar Recessions* (Washington, D.C.: Brookings, 1962).

B. Select List of Congressional Documents

U.S. National Monetary Commission, *Letter . . . transmitting . . . the report of the Commission*, 62nd Cong., 2nd Sess., Sen. Doc. 243, 1912 (reprinted in J. L. Laughlin, *Federal Reserve Act*, pp. 295–349). Discusses the defects in the banking system as the Commission saw them and contains the text of the Aldrich bill for a National Reserve Association.

Senate Committee on Banking and Currency, *Banking and Currency*, Hearings on H.R. 7837 (S. 2639), 63rd Cong., 1st Sess., 1913. The Federal Reserve Act.

Joint Commission of Agricultural Inquiry, Hearings, 67th Cong., 1st Sess., 1922; and Report, 67th Cong., 2nd Sess., 1922. Valuable testimony by W. P. G. Harding and Benjamin Strong.

House Committee on Banking and Currency, *Stabilization of Purchasing Power of Money*, Hearings on H.R. 11788 (first Goldsborough bill), 67th Cong., 4th Sess., 1923. See Chapter 4.

House Committee on Banking and Currency, *To Stabilize the Purchasing Power of Money*, Hearings on H.R. 494 (first Goldsborough bill revised), 68th Cong., 1st Sess., 1925. See Chapter 4.

House Committee on Banking and Currency, *Stabilization*, Hearings on H.R. 7895 (first Strong bill), 69th Cong., 1st Sess., 1927. See Chapter 4.

House Committee on Banking and Currency, *Stabilization*, Hearings on H.R. 11806 (second Strong bill), 70th Cong., 1st Sess., 1928. See Chapter 4.

House Committee on Banking and Currency, *Branch, Chain and Group Banking*, Hearings pursuant to House Res. 141, 71st Cong., 2nd Sess., 1930. Extended discussion of the case for and against branch banking; testimony mainly by John W. Pole, Comptroller of the Currency, and Roy A. Young, Governor of the Federal Reserve Board. Other topics: bank failures, brokers' loans.

Senate Committee on Banking and Currency, *Operation of the National and Federal Reserve Banking Systems*, Hearings pursuant to S. Res. 71, 71st Cong., 3rd Sess., 1931. The most important single source on monetary policy during the 1920's. See Chapter 4.

House Committee on Banking and Currency, *Liberalizing the Credit Facilities of the Federal Reserve System,* Hearings on H.R. 9203 (Glass-Steagall bill), 72nd Cong., 1st Sess., 1932. Governor Meyer and Secretary Mills explain the need for the legislation.

Senate Committee on Banking and Currency, *Restoring and Maintaining the Average Purchasing Power of the Dollar,* Hearings on S. 4429 (Fletcher bill), 72nd Cong., 1st Sess., 1932. Interesting for Representative Strong's report on Governor Strong's views; and for Miller's account of past Reserve policy. See Chapter 4.

House Committee on Banking and Currency, *Stabilization of Commodity Prices,* Hearings on H.R. 10517 (second Goldsborough bill), 72nd Cong., 1st Sess., 1932.

Senate Committee on Banking and Currency, *Operation of the National and Federal Reserve Banking Systems,* Hearings on S. 4115, 72nd Cong., 1st Sess., 1932. Interesting only in regard to banking reform: branch banking, security affiliates, reserve provisions. Testimony by many commercial bankers, and by Meyer and Pole.

Senate Finance Committee, *Investigation of Economic Problems,* Hearings, 72nd Cong., 2nd Sess., 1933. Interesting only for Eccles' early views.

Senate Committee on Banking and Currency, *Gold Reserve Act of 1934,* Hearings on S. 2366, 73rd Cong., 2nd Sess., 1934.

House Committee on Banking and Currency, *To Establish the Federal Monetary Authority,* Hearings on H.R. 7157, 8780, 73rd Cong., 2nd Sess., 1934. The third Goldsborough price-stabilization bill was supported by Willford I. King, Irving Fisher, Frank A. Pearson, and Frank A. Vanderlip; also Father Coughlin. Testimony against the bill was given by Secretary Morgenthau, Governor Black, and Benjamin M. Anderson.

House Committee on Banking and Currency, *Banking Act of 1935,* Hearings on H.R. 5357, 74th Cong., 1st Sess., 1935. Eccles and Goldenweiser defend the bill; Fisher advocates 100 per cent money; Spahr says bill will enable administration to dominate System.

Senate Committee on Banking and Currency, *Banking Act of 1935,* Hearings on S. 1715, 74th Cong., 1st Sess., 1935. Testimony for the bill by Morgenthau, Hamlin, Miller, Szymczak, and Sprague; against the bill by B. M. Anderson, Kemmerer, Warburg, and Willis.

House Committee on Banking and Currency, *To Extend the Period during which Direct Obligations of the United States may be used as Collateral Security for Federal Reserve Notes,* Hearings on S. 417, 75th Cong., 1st Sess., 1937.

Senate Special Committee to Investigate Unemployment and Relief, *Unemployment and Relief,* Hearings pursuant to S. Res. 36, 75th Cong., 3rd Sess., 1938. Contains a defense by Chairman Eccles of Federal Reserve policy during 1937; otherwise uninteresting.

House Committee on Banking and Currency, *Government Ownership of the Twelve Federal Reserve Banks,* Hearings on H.R. 7230 (Patman bill),

75th Cong., 3rd Sess., 1938. The last of the stabilization bills. See Chapter 5.

Senate Committee on Banking and Currency, *Full Employment Act of 1945,* Hearings on S. 380, 79th Cong., 1st Sess., 1945.

Joint Committee on the Economic Report, *Anti-Inflation Program,* Hearings, 80th Cong., 1st Sess., 1948. Eccles defends the special-reserves plan.

Joint Committee on the Economic Report, *Credit Policies,* Hearings, 80th Cong., 2nd Sess., 1948. Defense of pegging long-term bonds by Eccles and Sproul. Discussion of reform of reserve requirements by Thomas and Bopp.

Joint Committee on the Economic Report, *Monetary, Credit, and Fiscal Policies,* Hearings, Collection of statements, and Report (Douglas Subcommittee), 81st Cong., 1st Sess., 1949. Important testimony by Eccles and Sproul. The Report favors the revival of monetary policy and "independence" for the Reserve.

Joint Committee on the Economic Report, *January 1949 Economic Report of the President,* Hearings, 81st Cong., 1st Sess., 1949. Chairman McCabe's views, especially in favor of consumer credit regulation.

Joint Committee on the Economic Report, *January 1950 Economic Report of the President,* Hearings, 81st Cong., 2nd Sess., 1950. The Council of Economic Advisers argues against the revival of monetary policy proposed by the Douglas Subcommittee.

Joint Committee on the Economic Report, *Compendium of Materials on Monetary, Credit, and Fiscal Policies: A Collection of Statements,* Sen. Doc. 132, 81st Cong., 2nd Sess., 1950. Useful summaries of recent policies by Chairman McCabe, Secretary Snyder, and Reserve Bank presidents.

Joint Committee on the Economic Report, *January 1951 Economic Report of the President,* Hearings, 82nd Cong., 1st Sess., 1951. Eccles pleads for the unpegging of long-term bonds; Representative Patman accuses the Reserve System of "sabotaging" Treasury debt-management policy.

Joint Committee on the Economic Report, *January 1952 Economic Report of the President,* 82nd Cong., 2nd Sess., 1952. Uninteresting.

Joint Committee on the Economic Report, *Monetary Policy and the Management of the Public Debt,* 82nd Cong., 2nd Sess., 1952. Hearings; Replies to Questions, Parts 1 and 2; Report (often known as the Patman Report). These documents are basic for an understanding of the philosophies of the Federal Reserve and the Treasury in the period following the Accord.

Joint Committee on the Economic Report, *January 1954 Economic Report of the President,* Hearings, 83rd Cong., 2nd Sess., 1954. Riefler and others discuss the availability of credit and the elasticity of demand for capital.

Joint Committee on the Economic Report, *United States Monetary Policy: Recent Thinking and Experience,* Hearings, 83 Cong., 2nd Sess., 1954. Important for genesis of the "bills only" doctrine.

Joint Committee on the Economic Report, *January 1955 Economic Report of the President,* Hearings, 84th Cong., 1st Sess., 1955. Uninteresting.

Joint Committee on the Economic Report, *January 1956 Economic Report of the President*, Hearings, 84th Cong., 2nd Sess., 1956. See Martin on consumer credit and interest rates, and Eccles' criticism of "bills only."

Joint Committee on the Economic Report, *Conflicting Official Views on Monetary Policy: April 1956*, Hearings, 84th Cong., 2nd Sess., 1956. Throws light on Treasury–Federal Reserve relations at this period.

Joint Committee on the Economic Report, *Monetary Policy: 1955–56*, Hearings, 84th Cong., 2nd Sess., 1957.

Joint Economic Committee, *January 1957 Economic Report of the President*, Hearings, 85th Cong., 1st Sess., 1957. Contains an early discussion of the cost-push by economists; also valuable for Martin's views on recent monetary policy.

House Committee on Banking and Currency, *Financial Institutions Act of 1957*, Hearings on S. 1451 and H.R. 7026, 85th Cong., 1st Sess., Part 1, 1957; 2nd Sess., Part 2, 1958. Testimony by Chairman Martin and Governor Robertson; mainly about interest on deposits, exchange charges, par collection, and bank supervision.

Senate Committee on Finance, *Investigation of the Financial Condition of the United States*, Hearings, 85th Cong., 1st and 2nd Sess., 1957–1958. A transcript running to more than 2,000 pages, the value of which falls far short of its volume.

Joint Economic Committee, *January 1958 Economic Report of the President*, Hearings, 85th Cong., 2nd Sess., 1958. Uninteresting.

Joint Economic Committee, *Relationship of Prices to Economic Stability and Growth*, Hearings, 85th Cong., 2nd Sess., 1958; same, Compendium of Papers submitted by Panelists, 1958. Extensive and useful discussion mainly by academic economists.

Senate Committee on Banking and Currency, *Federal Reserve Monetary Policies*, Hearings, 85th Cong., 2nd Sess., 1958. Testimony by Chairman Martin.

Joint Economic Committee, *Fiscal Policy Implications of the Current Economic Outlook*, Hearings, 85th Cong., 2nd Sess., 1958. Concerned mainly with proposals for a tax cut to deal with the recession.

Senate Committee on Banking and Currency, *Federal Reserve Policy and Economic Stability, 1951–57*, by Asher Achinstein, Report No. 2500, 85th Cong., 2nd Sess., 1958. A useful summary.

Joint Economic Committee, *January 1959 Economic Report of the President*, Hearings, 86th Cong., 1st Sess., 1959. Valuable post mortem on the 1958 recession; testimony by Martin, as well as Seymour Harris and Paul Samuelson; also interesting for Patman's views.

House Committee on Government Operations, *Amending the Employment Act of 1946*, Hearings on H.R. 1225, etc., 86th Cong., 1st Sess., 1959. A proposal to add price-level stabilization to the objectives listed in the Employment Act. Although opposition was now half-hearted, the proposal was not enacted.

Senate Committee on Banking and Currency, *Member Bank Reserve Requirements*, Hearings on S. 860 and S. 1120, 86th Cong., 1st Sess., 1959.

House Committee on Banking and Currency, *Member Bank Reserve Requirements,* Hearings on H.R. 5237. 86th Cong., 1st Sess., 1959.

House Committee on Ways and Means, *Public Debt Ceiling and Interest Rate Ceiling on Bonds,* Hearings, 86th Cong., 1st Sess., 1959.

Joint Economic Committee, *Employment, Growth and Price Levels,* Hearings, Staff report, 23 study papers, and Report, 86th Cong., 1st and 2nd Sess., 1959–1960. The hearings and several of the study papers are an indispensable source.

Joint Economic Committee, *January 1960 Economic Report of the President,* Hearings, 86th Cong., 2nd Sess., 1960. Important for Chairman Martin's views.

Joint Economic Committee, *1960 Joint Economic Report,* S. Rep. 1152, 86th Cong., 2nd Sess., 1960. Recommends the abandonment of "bills only," the purchase of long-term bonds, and the use of open-market operations rather than the lowering of reserve requirements to expand the money supply.

Senate Committee on Banking and Currency, *Employment Act Amendments,* Hearings on S. 64 and S. 2382, 86th Cong., 2nd Sess., 1960. Mainly a discussion of a proposal for public hearings on price and wage increases; also contains a useful collection of documents relating to the Accord of 1951.

Joint Economic Committee, *A Study of the Dealer Market for Federal Government Securities,* 86th Cong., 2nd Sess., 1960.

Joint Economic Committee, *Current Economic Situation and Short-run Outlook,* Hearings, 86th Cong., 2nd Sess., 1961. Mainly interesting for Triffin's views on the gold situation.

Joint Economic Committee, *January 1961 Economic Report of the President,* Hearings, 87th Cong., 1st Sess., 1961. Important testimony by Martin; also contains Tobin's paper denying that structural unemployment had increased.

Joint Economic Committee, *Review of the Annual Report of the Federal Reserve System for 1960,* Hearings, 87th Cong., 1st Sess., 1961. One of Mr. Patman's better efforts.

Joint Economic Committee, *Review of Report of the Commission on Money and Credit,* Hearings, 87th Cong., 1st Sess., 1961. A miscellany.

Joint Economic Committee, *Unemployment: Terminology, Measurement and Analysis,* 87th Cong., 1st Sess., 1961. A useful contribution by the U.S. Bureau of Labor Statistics.

Joint Economic Committee, *Higher Unemployment Rates, 1957–1960: Structural Transformation or Inadequate Demand,* 87th Cong., 1st Sess., 1961. A staff paper broadly supporting the Tobin thesis.

Joint Economic Committee, *Employment and Unemployment,* Hearings, 87th Cong., 1st Sess., 1962. Mainly devoted to measurement problems.

Joint Economic Committee, *January 1962 Economic Report of the President,* Hearings, 87th Cong., 2nd Sess., 1962. Further discussion of structural unemployment, and of difficulties created by the deficit in the balance of payments.

House Committee on Banking and Currency, *Higher Interest Rates on Time Deposits of Foreign Governments*, Hearings on H.R. 12080, 87th Cong., 2nd Sess., 1962.

Joint Economic Committee, *State of the Economy and Policies for Full Employment*, Hearings, 87th Cong., 2nd Sess., 1962.

Joint Economic Committee, *Factors Affecting the United States Balance of Payments*, Compilation of studies, 87th Cong., 2nd Sess., 1962.

Joint Economic Committee, *The Federal Budget as an Economic Document*, Study paper, Hearings, and Report (S. Rep. 396), 87th Cong., 2nd Sess., and 88th Cong., 1st Sess., 1962–1963. Report endorses usefulness of concept of full-employment budget, but does not discuss differing measures of deficit/surplus.

Joint Economic Committee, *Outlook for United States Balance of Payments*, Hearings, 87th Cong., 2nd Sess., 1963.

Joint Economic Committee, *January 1963 Economic Report of the President*, Hearings, 88th Cong., 1st Sess., 1963. Testimony by Chairman Martin, Governor Mitchell, and President Swan of the San Francisco Reserve Bank.

Joint Economic Committee, *1963 Joint Economic Report*, S. Rep. 78, 88th Cong., 1st Sess., 1963. Chiefly interesting for wide variety of views as to the desirability of a tax cut.

Joint Economic Committee, *Measuring Employment and Unemployment*, Hearings, 88th Cong., 1st Sess., 1963.

House Committee on Banking and Currency, *Conflict of Federal and State Banking Laws*, Hearings, 88th Cong., 1st Sess., 1963.

House Committee on Banking and Currency, *Recent Changes in Monetary Policy and Balance-of-Payments Problems*, Hearings, 88th Cong., 1st Sess., 1963.

Appendix II

Biography

The intention has been to list some information, at least, about all officials or legislators who played a role in our story.

Allen, Carl E. 1905–
Born in Illinois; educated at Dartmouth; with National City Bank of New York, 1926–1950; President of Campbell Wyant, 1950–1956; President, Reserve Bank of Chicago, 1956–   .

Anderson, Robert Bernard. 1910–
Texas lawyer (Weatherford College, University of Texas); Texas legislature, 1932; various state offices 1932–1936; Secretary of the Navy, 1953–1954; Deputy Secretary of Defense, 1954–1955; Secretary of the Treasury, 1957–1961.

Balderston, C. Canby. 1897–
Pennsylvania born; Vice Chairman of the Federal Reserve Board (until 1966), has been with the Board since 1954; attended Pennsylvania State College 1915–1917; B.S., M.A., Ph.D. from the University of Pennsylvania; Dean of Wharton School, 1941–1954; Director, Reserve Bank of Philadelphia, 1943–1953.

Biddle, Nicholas. 1786–1844
Financier; born in Philadelphia; President, Second Bank of the United States, 1822–1839.

Black, Eugene Robert. 1873–1934
Banker-lawyer Black, Sr., was born in Atlanta, attended the University of Georgia, served as Governor of the Reserve Bank of Atlanta 1933, and as Governor of the Federal Reserve Board 1933–1934 (resigned).

Bopp, Karl Richard. 1906–
Born in Missouri; educated at University of Missouri and taught there, 1931–1941; with Reserve Bank of Philadelphia since 1941, President since 1958; author of *Agencies of Federal Reserve Policy* (1935); *Hjalmar Schacht, Central Banker* (1939).

Boutwell, George Sewall. 1818–1905
Lawyer; born in Massachusetts, self-educated. In Massachusetts legislature, 1842–1850 (Democrat); Governor 1851–1852; admitted to the bar,

1862; Commissioner of Internal Revenue, 1862–1863; in Congress 1863–1869; helped to frame the Fourteenth Amendment; led movement to impeach Johnson; Secretary of the Treasury under Grant; United States Senator, Massachusetts, 1873–1877; then practiced law.

Broderick, Joseph A. 1881–1959

Born in New York City, educated at New York University; bank examiner, 1910–1918; Vice President of the National Bank of Commerce, New York, 1919–1928; Superintendent of Banks, New York, 1929–1934; Federal Reserve Board, 1936–1937; East River Savings Bank, New York, 1937–1957.

Bryan, Malcolm Honore. 1902–

Born in Illinois; educated at University of Illinois; taught economics at the University of Georgia, 1925–1936; with Reserve Bank of Atlanta since 1938; President, 1946– .

Burgess, Warren Randolph. 1889–

Born in Rhode Island; educated at Brown and Columbia Universities; with Reserve Bank of New York from 1920; Deputy Governor and Open-Market Account Manager, 1930–1938; National City Bank of New York, 1938–1952; Federal Advisory Council, 1947; Deputy Secretary of the Treasury, 1953–1954; Under Secretary 1955–1957; United States Ambassador to NATO, 1957–1961; author of *The Reserve Banks and the Money Market* (1927).

Campbell, Milo D. 1851–1923

Federal Reserve Board, March 14–22, 1923 (died).

Carlisle, John Griffin. 1835–1910

Lawyer; born in Kentucky. Kentucky legislature, 1859–1871; Democratic Congressman, 1877–1890; Cleveland's Secretary of the Treasury, 1893–1897; gold Democrat; practiced law in New York City, 1897–1910.

Case, James Herbert. 1872–

New Jersey banker; Deputy Governor, New York Reserve Bank, 1917–1930; Chairman, 1930–1936; Director, National War Fund, 1942–1946.

Clay, George Harry. 1911–

Kansas-born lawyer; educated at University of Missouri; practiced law, 1934–1944; airline executive, 1944–1958; with Reserve Bank of Kansas City since 1958, President since 1961.

Clayton, Lawrence. 1891–1949

Born in Utah; educated at the University of Michigan, Stanford; LL.B., Harvard; First National Bank of Ogden, Utah, 1924–1934; staff, Federal Reserve Board, 1934–1945; Board of Governors, 1947–1949 (died).

Cobb, Howell. 1815–1868

Lawyer; born in Georgia; educated at University of Georgia; Democratic Congressman, 1842–1857; Buchanan's Secretary of the Treasury, 1857–1860; subsequently general in the Confederate Army.

Crissinger, Daniel Richard. 1860–1942

Ohio lawyer-banker; Comptroller of the Currency, 1921–1923; Governor of the Federal Reserve Board, 1923–1927 (resigned).

Cunningham, Edward Henry. 1869–1930
Iowa farmer; Wisconsin born; served three terms in the Iowa House of Representatives, becoming Speaker in 1913; Federal Reserve Board, 1923–1930 (died).

Daane, James Dewey. 1918–
Born in Michigan; educated at Duke University (B.A., 1939), Harvard, 1945–1947; statistician, Reserve Bank of Richmond, 1939–1947; monetary economist, 1947–1952; Assistant Vice President, 1952–1963; Board of Governors, 1963–   .

Davis, Chester Charles. 1887–
Born in Iowa; educated at Grinnell College; agricultural expert; AAA Administrator, 1933–1936; appointed to seat on Federal Reserve Board earmarked for a farmers' spokesman, 1936–1941 (resigned); President, Reserve Bank of St. Louis, 1941–1951; Professor of Agricultural Economics, University of California, Berkeley, 1955.

Dawes, Henry May. 1877–1952
Ohio oil man; educated at Marietta College; Comptroller of the Currency, 1923–1924 (resigned); became utility executive.

Delano, Frederick Adrian. 1863–1953
Hong Kong born, Harvard-educated railroad man (President of Wheeling and Lake Erie, 1905–1908); appointed to the Federal Reserve Board for six-year term in 1914; Vice Governor 1914–1916; resigned 1918 to enter U.S. Army Engineers; Chairman, National Resources Planning Board, 1934–1943.

Deming, Frederick Lewis. 1912–
Born in Des Moines; educated at Washington University; insurance agent, 1936–1941; with Reserve Bank of St. Louis, 1941–1957; President, Reserve Bank of Minnesota, 1957–   .

Douglas, Paul Howard. 1892–
Senator; economist; born in Salem, Massachusetts; educated at Bowdoin College and Columbia University; taught at the University of Chicago, 1920–1948; Democratic Senator from Illinois since 1948.

Draper, Ernest Gallaudet. 1885–1954
Born in District of Columbia; educated at Amherst (where he got his M.A. 30 years after graduation); switched from manufacturing to public service in the thirties; New York State Commission on Unemployment, 1930–1935; Assistant Secretary of Commerce, 1935–1938; Federal Reserve Board of Governors, 1938–1950 (term expired); author of *Can Business Prevent Unemployment* (1925), and MSS diary, Library of Congress.

Eccles, Marriner Stoddard. 1890–
Financier, banker, and business executive; born and educated in Utah (Brigham Young College); Assistant to the Secretary of the Treasury, 1934; Federal Reserve Board of Governors, 1934–1951 (Chairman, 1938–1948; Vice Chairman, 1948 to resignation in 1951); Chairman, First Security Bank of Utah since 1955; author of *Beckoning Frontiers* (1951).

Ellis, George Hathaway. 1920–
Born in Maine; educated at Harvard; taught economics, 1948–1951; with Reserve Bank of Boston since 1951; President, 1961–   .

Evans, Rudolph Martin. 1890–1956
Iowa farmer and livestock raiser; educated at Iowa State College; Assistant to the Secretary of Agriculture, 1936–1938; AAA Administrator, 1938–1942; Federal Reserve Board of Governors, 1942–1954 (term expired).

Fairchild, Charles Stebbins. 1842–1924
Lawyer; born in Madison County, New York; educated at Harvard; Attorney General of New York, 1875–1877; Cleveland's Secretary of the Treasury, 1887–1889; later entered commercial banking.

Folger, Charles James. 1818–1884
Lawyer; born in Nantucket; educated at Hobart College; judge, 1844–1855; Republican state senator, New York, 1861–1869; judge, New York Court of Appeals, 1870–1881; President Arthur's Secretary of the Treasury, 1881–1884.

Forgan, James Berwick. 1852–1924
Born and educated in Scotland; President, First National Bank of Chicago, 1892–1924; President, Federal Advisory Council, 1914–1920.

Fulton, Wilbur Dutton. 1898–
Born in Cleveland; educated at Western Reserve University; with savings banks, 1916–1929; with Reserve Bank of Cleveland since 1933; President, 1953–   .

Gilbert, Seymour Parker. 1892–1938
New Jersey lawyer; educated at Rutgers University; Assistant and Under Secretary of the Treasury, 1920–1923; Agent General for German Reparations, 1923–1924; with J. P. Morgan and Co., 1924–1938.

Glass, Carter. 1858–1946
Longtime Virginia Congressman (1902–1919) and Senator (1924–1946); Secretary of the Treasury, 1918–1920; father of Federal Reserve Act; vehement opponent of New Deal fiscal policies; author of *An Adventure in Constructive Finance* (1927).

Goldenweiser, Emanuel Alexander. 1883–1953
Russian-born, American-educated economist (B.A., Columbia; M.A., Ph.D., Cornell); Assistant Statistician, Federal Reserve Board, 1919–1924; Director, Research and Statistics, 1926–1945; Economist, Federal Open Market Committee, 1936–1945; author of *American Monetary Policy* (1951); papers, Library of Congress.

Goldsborough, Thomas Alan. 1877–1951
Born in Maryland; educated at Washington College, University of Maryland; lawyer, Congressman (1921–1939) with debt phobia, monetary reformer; resigned from Congress to accept United States District judgeship in Washington, D.C., 1939.

Guthrie, James. 1792–1869
Lawyer, railroad promoter; born in Kentucky; Secretary of the Treasury,

1853–1857, under Pierce; later returned to Louisville and Nashville Railroad; Unionist during the Civil War.

Hamlin, Charles Sumner. 1861–1938

Boston-born, Harvard-educated lawyer; twice Assistant Secretary of the Treasury, 1893–1897, 1913–1914; Federal Reserve Board, 1914–1936 (term expired); Board Governor, 1914–1916; widely considered painstaking and patient but not a fighter; inveterate diarist; papers, Library of Congress.

Harding, William Proctor Gould. 1864–1930

Alabama banker; University of Alabama, B.A., 1880, M.A. 1881 (youngest graduate in history); in 20 years rose from bank clerk (1882) to President of the First National Bank of Birmingham, 1902–1914; Federal Reserve Board, 1914–1922 (term expired); Board Governor, 1916–1922; Governor, Federal Reserve Bank of Boston, 1923–1930; Director, War Finance Corporation, 1918–1919; author of *Formative Period of the Federal Reserve System* (1925).

Harrison, George Leslie. 1887–1958

San Francisco-born; Yale- and Harvard-educated lawyer; with Federal Reserve Board, 1914–1920; with New York Reserve Bank, 1920–1941 (Governor, 1928–1936; President, 1936–1941); with New York Life Insurance Co. 1941–1954; papers, Columbia University.

Hayes, Alfred. 1910–

Banker; born in Ithaca, N.Y.; studied at Harvard (1926–1927), Yale (B.A., 1930), and New College, Oxford (Rhodes Scholar, B.Litt., 1933); commercial banker in New York City, 1933–1956; President, Reserve Bank of New York, 1956–   .

Houston, David Franklin. 1866–1940

Born in North Carolina; educated at South Carolina College; taught political science at the University of Texas, 1894–1902; President, University of Texas, 1905–1908; Chancellor, Washington University, St. Louis, 1908–1916; Secretary of Agriculture, 1913–1920; Secretary of the Treasury, 1920–1921.

Humphrey, George Magoffin. 1890–

Michigan-born and educated (University of Michigan, LL.B., 1912); General Attorney, The M. A. Hanna Company, 1918, President, 1929, Chairman of the Board, 1952; Secretary of the Treasury, 1953–1957.

Irons, Watrous Henry. 1903–

Born in Atlanta; educated at University of Pennsylvania; taught finance at University of Texas, 1937–1945; with Reserve Bank of Dallas since 1945, President since 1954.

James, George Roosa. 1866–1937

Outspoken, down-to-earth, Memphis manufacturer and commission broker; President, State National Bank of Memphis, 1910; Federal Reserve Board, 1923–1936 (term expired).

Jay, Pierre. 1870–1949

Yale-educated (B.A., 1892) banker, born in Warwick, N.Y.; Bank Commissioner of Massachusetts, 1906–1909; Chairman, Reserve Bank of New York, 1914–1926; Agent for Reparation Payments under Dawes Plan, 1927–1930.

King, George Harold, Jr. 1920–
  Born in Louisiana; educated at Louisiana State University; in lumber business, 1946–1959; Federal Reserve Board of Governors, 1959–1963 (resigned).

Leffingwell, Russell Cornell. 1878–
  Lawyer; born in New York City; educated at Yale and Columbia Universities; practiced law, 1907–1917; Assistant Secretary of the Treasury, 1917–1920; with J. P. Morgan and Co., 1923–1940.

McAdoo, William Gibbs. 1863–1941
  Born in Georgia; educated at University of Tennessee; Secretary of the Treasury, 1913–1918; led California delegation which swung nomination to Roosevelt in 1932; in 1932 elected Senator, defeated in 1938; Chairman, American President Lines, 1939.

McCabe, Thomas Bayard. 1893–
  Born in Maryland; educated at Swarthmore (B.A., 1915); through being topnotch salesman, reached Presidency of Scott Paper Company, 1927; Director, Reserve Bank of Philadelphia, 1938–1948; Chairman, Federal Reserve Board of Governors, 1948–1951 (resigned).

MacDougal, James Barton. 1866–1948
  Born in Peoria; with Peoria Central National Bank, 1887–1901; bank examiner, 1906–1914; Governor, Reserve Bank of Chicago, 1914–1934.

McGarrah, Gates W. 1863–1940
  Banker; born in Monroe, N.Y.; President, Goshen National Bank, 1881–1904; Chairman, Executive Committee, Chase National Bank, 1926–1927; Chairman, Reserve Bank of New York, 1927–1930.

MacIntosh, Joseph Wallace. 1873–1952
  Born in Illinois; commercial banker in Nebraska and Illinois, then in private business; Comptroller of the Currency, 1924–1928.

McKee, John Keown. 1891–
  Born in Pittsburgh; educated at the University of Pittsburgh; People's National Bank, Pittsburgh (later consolidated with First National Bank), 1907–1931; Federal Reserve Board of Governors, 1936–1946 (term expired). President, Director, Continental Bank and Trust Company, New York City, 1946–1948.

Magee, Wayland Wells. 1881–
  Born in Chicago; educated at University of Chicago; studied law at Harvard and Northwestern Universities; Member, Advisory Board, Omaha branch of Reserve Bank of Kansas City, 1927–1930; Director, 1930–1931; Federal Reserve Board, 1931–1933 (term expired).

Manning, Daniel. 1831–1887
  Journalist; born in Albany, N.Y.; self-educated; New York State Democratic Committee, 1874–1884; helped elect Cleveland; Secretary of the Treasury, 1885–1887.

Martin, William McChesney, Jr. 1906–
  Born in St. Louis; graduated from Yale in 1928; became President of
  the New York Stock Exchange before he was 30 (1935–1938); Chairman, Export-Import Bank, 1946–1948; Assistant Secretary of the Treasury,
  1949; Chairman, Federal Reserve Board of Governors, 1951 (reappointed
  1956–1970); Martin's father helped Carter Glass draft Federal Reserve
  Act, later became President of the Reserve Bank of St. Louis.
Mellon, Andrew William. 1855–1937
  Pittsburgh industrialist; educated at Western University of Pennsylvania
  (now University of Pittsburgh), class of 1873; President, Mellon National
  Bank until 1921; Secretary of the Treasury under Presidents Harding,
  Coolidge, and Hoover, 1921–1932; Ambassador to Great Britain, 1933–
  1937.
Meyer, Eugene. 1875–1959
  Los Angeles-born; Yale-educated (B.A., 1895); at 26 started his own in-
  vestment house, bought a seat on the Stock Exchange within a few years;
  Director, War Finance Corporation, 1918–1925; publisher, later Chairman,
  The Washington Post, from 1933; Governor, Federal Reserve Board, 1930–
  1933 (resigned).
Miller, Adolph Caspar. 1866–1953
  San Francisco economist; educated at the University of California (B.A.,
  1887) and Harvard (M.A., 1888); Flood Professor of Economics and
  Commerce, University of California, 1902–1913; autocratic, cantankerous
  member of Federal Reserve Board, 1914–1936 (term expired); testified
  frequently before the House and Senate Committees on Banking and
  Currency.
Miller, Paul Emmert. 1888–1954
  Agronomist; born in Iowa; educated at Iowa State College; taught at
  the University of Minnesota, 1911–1954; Federal Reserve Board of Gov-
  ernors, August 13–October 21, 1954 (died).
Mills, Abbot Low, Jr. 1898–
  Harvard-educated (B.A., 1920) banker from Oregon; Director, United
  States National Bank, Portland, Ore., 1939–1952; Federal Reserve Board
  of Governors, 1952 (reappointed 1958–1972).
Mills, Ogden Livingston. 1884–1937
  Lawyer from Newport, R.I.; B.A. Harvard, 1904, LL.B., 1907; New York
  state senator, 1914–1918; United States representative, 1921–1927; Under-
  Secretary of the Treasury, 1927–1932; Secretary of the Treasury, 1932–
  1933; papers, Library of Congress.
Mitchell, George Wilder. 1904–
  Economist; born in Wisconsin; educated at the University of Wisconsin;
  with Illinois Tax Commission, 1933–1943; with Reserve Bank of Chicago,
  1944–1961; Federal Reserve Board of Governors, 1961–   .
Mitchell, John Raymond. 1868–1933
  Minneapolis banker; born in Pennsylvania; educated at Yale (Ph.B.,
  1889); President, Capital National Bank, St. Paul, 1906–1920; Federal

Reserve Board, 1921–1923 (resigned); Chairman, Reserve Bank of Minneapolis, 1924–1933.

Moehlenpah, Henry A. 1867–1944
Illinois banker; educated at Northwestern University, 1890–1894; President, Citizens Bank in Wisconsin; Federal Reserve Board, 1919–1921 (term expired); President, Bankers Finance Corporation, 1921.

Morgenthau, Henry, Jr. 1891–
Born in New York City; educated at Cornell (1909–1910; 1912–1913); publisher, *American Agriculturalist*, 1922–1933; conservation commissioner, state of New York; Secretary of the Treasury, 1934–1945; papers in the Franklin D. Roosevelt Library, Hyde Park, N.Y.

Morrill, Chester. 1885–
Missouri-born public servant; received LL.B., Georgetown University, 1909; with U.S. Department of Agriculture, 1914–1924; General Counsel, War Finance Corporation, 1925–1931; Secretary, Federal Reserve Board, 1931–1945; Secretary, Federal Open Market Committee, 1936–1950; Adviser to Minister of Finance, Nationalist China, 1951.

Morrison, Ralph Waldo. 1878–1948
Born in Missouri; a St. Louis salesman and 32nd-degree Mason who made a fortune in Texas real estate and utilities; Federal Reserve Board of Governors, February 10–July 9, 1936 (resigned); one of Roosevelt's less happy choices.

Norris, George Washington. 1864–1942
Lawyer-banker; born in San Francisco; educated at the University of Pennsylvania; Philadelphia law practice, 1886–1894; Vice Chairman, Reserve Bank of Philadelphia, 1916; Federal Farm Loan Commissioner, 1916–1920; Governor, Reserve Bank of Philadelphia, 1920–1936; author of *Ended Episodes* (1937).

Norton, Edward Lee. 1892–
Realtor and broadcasting executive; Alabama-born and educated at Birmingham Southern College (B.S., 1913); Federal Reserve Board of Governors, 1950–1952 (resigned).

O'Connor, James Francis Thaddeus. 1886–1949
Lawyer; born Grand Forks, N.D.; educated at University of North Dakota, Yale; Comptroller of the Currency, 1933–1938; United States District Judge, 1940–1949.

Owen, Robert Latham. 1856–1947
Virginian; educated at Washington and Lee University (M.A., 1877); began practice of law, 1880; Indian agent, 1885–1889; President, First National Bank of Muskogee, 1890–1900; Democratic National Committee, 1892–1896; three-term Senator from Oklahoma, 1907–1925; helped draft Federal Reserve Act; author of *The Federal Reserve Act* (1919).

Patman, Wright. 1893–
Congressman; lawyer; born in Texas; LL.B. Cumberland University, 1916; served as district attorney and member of Texas legislature; has

represented Texas' 1st District (Northeastern Texas) since 1928; Chairman of House Committee on Banking and Currency since 1963.

Platt, Edmund. 1865–1939

Journalist; born in New York; Harvard-educated (B.A., 1888); Editor, *Poughkeepsie Eagle*, 1907–1920; New York Congressman from 26th District (1913–1921); Member, Federal Reserve Board, 1920–1930 (resigned); Vice President, Marine Midland Corporation, 1930–1939.

Pole, John William. ? –1958

Engineer; born in England; national bank examiner, 1915–1928; Comptroller of the Currency, 1928–1932 (resigned).

Powell, Oliver Stanley. 1896–

Minneapolis banker of long tenure with Reserve System; born in South Dakota; B.A. University of Minnesota, 1917; various banking positions; Reserve Bank of Minneapolis, 1920–1936; First Vice President, 1936–1950; Federal Reserve Board of Governors, 1950–1952 (resigned); President, Reserve Bank of Minneapolis, 1952–1957.

Ransom, Ronald. 1882–1947

Atlanta lawyer; born in South Carolina; educated at the University of Georgia (LL.B., 1903); President, Atlanta Clearing House Association, 1929; President, Georgia Bankers Association, 1931–1932; Federal Reserve Board of Governors, 1936–1947 (died).

Reuss, Henry Schoellkopf. 1912–

Congressman, lawyer; born in Milwaukee; educated at Cornell and Harvard Law School; has represented Wisconsin's 5th District (Milwaukee) as Democrat since 1954.

Richardson, William Adams. 1821–1896

Lawyer; born in Massachusetts; educated at Harvard; Secretary of the Treasury under Hayes, 1873–1874; Court of Claims, 1874; taught law, Georgetown University, 1879–1894.

Riefler, Winfield William. 1897–

Buffalo-born economist; educated at Amherst with Ph.D. from Brookings; Department of Commerce, 1921–1923; Division of Research and Statistics, Federal Reserve Board, 1923–1933; Central Statistical Board, 1933–1935; Minister to London, 1942–1944; Assistant to Chairman, Federal Reserve Board of Governors, 1948–1959; Secretary, Federal Open Market Committee, 1952–1959; author of *Money Rates and Money Markets* (1930).

Robertson, James Louis. 1907–

Government official from Nebraska; educated at George Washington University and Harvard (LL.B., LL.M.); FBI Agent, 1932–1933; Assistant Counsel, Comptroller of the Currency, 1933–1942; Deputy Comptroller, 1944–1952; Federal Reserve Board of Governors since 1952 (reappointed 1964–1978).

Roosa, Robert Vincent. 1918–

Born in Michigan; educated at University of Michigan; taught economics, 1939–1943; with Reserve Bank of New York, 1946–1960; Undersecretary of the Treasury for Monetary Affairs, 1961– .

Scanlon, Charles Joseph. 1915–
  Born in Chicago; educated at Northwestern University; with Reserve Bank
  of Chicago since 1933, President since 1962.
Shaw, Leslie Mortier. 1848–1932
  Lawyer; born in Vermont; educated at Cornell College, Iowa; Governor
  of Iowa, 1898–1902; champion of gold standard; Roosevelt's Secretary
  of the Treasury, 1902–1907; then commercial banker.
Shepardson, Charles Noah. 1896–
  Agronomist; born in Colorado; educated at Colorado State University
  (B.S., 1917) and Iowa State College (M.S., 1924); Dean of Agriculture,
  Texas A & M, 1944–1955; Director, Houston Branch, Federal Reserve
  Bank of Dallas, 1950–1955; Federal Reserve Board of Governors, 1955–
  (to 1968).
Snyder, John Wesley. 1895–
  Arkansas-born banker; educated at Vanderbilt University; National Bank
  receiver, Office of the Comptroller of the Currency, 1931–1937; Recon-
  struction Finance Corporation, 1937–1944; Vice President of First Na-
  tional Bank of St. Louis, Mo., 1943–1945; Secretary of the Treasury,
  1946–1953.
Sproul, Allan. 1896–
  Banker; born in San Francisco; with Federal Reserve System from graduation from University of California in 1919; Chief, Analysis and Re-
  search, Reserve Bank of San Francisco, 1920–1924; Federal Reserve
  Agent and Secretary, 1924–1930; from Assistant Deputy Governor to First
  Vice President, Reserve Bank of New York, 1930–1941; President, 1941–
  1956 (resigned).
Strauss, Albert. 1864–1929
  New York City banker; educated at the College of the City of New York;
  appointed in 1918 to succeed Paul Warburg as Vice Governor of the
  Federal Reserve Board; resigned in 1920 to return to private banking.
Strong, Benjamin Jr. 1872–1928
  Brilliant, persuasive Governor of the Reserve Bank of New York, 1914–
  1928; born in Fishkill-on-Hudson, N.Y.; attended public schools in Mont-
  clair, N.J.; became President of Bankers Trust Company.
Strong, James George. 1870–1938
  Lawyer, businessman, farmer, Congressman; born in Illinois; educated
  at Baker University, Kansas; House of Representatives, 1919–1933; author
  of the stabilization bills bearing his name.
Swan, Eliot James. 1911–
  Born in Minneapolis; educated at the University of California; taught
  economics, 1937–1941; with Reserve Bank of San Francisco since 1941;
  President, 1963–   .
Szymczak, Matt Stephen. 1894–
  Banker, educator; educated at St. Mary's College, Ky. (B.A., M.A.);
  taught business administration and economics at De Paul University, 1923–

1933; Comptroller of Chicago, 1931–1933; Federal Reserve Board of Governors, 1933–1961 (resigned).

Thomas, John Jacob. 1869–1948
Lawyer and Democratic politician from Nebraska; LL.B. from University of Michigan, 1890; Member and Vice Governor, Federal Reserve Board, 1933–1936 (term expired); Director and Chairman, Federal Reserve Bank of Kansas City, Mo., 1937–1938; Director and Deputy Chairman, 1938–1941.

Thomas, Woodlief. 1897–
Economist from Tennessee with lifetime career in Federal Reserve; B.S., University of Pennsylvania; Ph.D., Brookings; Research Assistant, Federal Reserve Board, 1922–1933; Assistant Director, Division of Research and Statistics, Reserve Board of Governors, 1934–1945; Director, 1945–1949; Economic Adviser to Board, 1949–1962 (retired).

Traylor, Melvin Alvah. 1878–1934
Banker; born in Kentucky; practiced law in Texas, 1901–1905; with commercial banks in Texas and Illinois, 1905–1934; President, First National Bank of Chicago, 1925–1934.

Vardaman, James Kimble, Jr. 1894–
Mississippi-born banker; educated at University of Mississippi and Millsaps College; President Truman's Naval Aide (1945) and first appointee to Federal Reserve Board of Governors, 1946–1958 (resigned).

Vinson, Frederic Moore. 1890–1953
Kentucky-born and educated lawyer; United States Congressman, 1923–1929, 1931–1938 (resigned); United States Court of Appeals, 1938–1943; Director of Economic Stabilization, 1943–1945; Secretary of the Treasury, 1945–1946; Chief Justice of the Supreme Court, 1946–1953.

Warburg, Paul Moritz. 1868–1932
German-born and educated, and Reichsbank trained; member of Kuhn, Loeb and Company; Federal Reserve Board, 1914–1918 (term expired); Vice Governor, 1916–1918; introduced bank acceptance to United States; author of *The Federal Reserve System* (1930).

Williams, John Skelton. 1865–1926
Self-righteous financier, publicist, and railway executive; born in Virginia and educated at University of Virginia; First Assistant Secretary of the Treasury, 1913; Comptroller of the Currency, 1914–1921 (resigned); President, Richmond Trust Company, 1924–1926.

Willing, Thomas. 1731–1821
Banker; born in Philadelphia; educated in England; member of the Continental Congress; President of the First Bank of the United States, 1791–1797.

Willis, Henry Parker. 1874–1937
Massachusetts-born economist; B.A., Ph.D., University of Chicago; Professor of Finance, George Washington University, 1905–1912; Secretary, Federal Reserve Board, 1914–1918; Director of Research, 1918–1922;

Professor of Banking, Columbia University, 1917–1937; author of *The Federal Reserve System* (1923).

Wills, David Crawford. 1872–1925

Self-made banker from Pittsburgh; worked his way up from bank messenger (1889) to President of Citizens National Bank in Bellevue, Pa., 1914–1917; Chairman of Federal Reserve Bank of Cleveland and Federal Reserve Agent, 1914–1920; Federal Reserve Board, 1920–1921 (term expired).

Windom, William. 1827–1891

Lawyer, legislator; born in Ohio; Republican Congressman from Minnesota, 1858–1869; United States Senator, 1870–1881, 1881–1883, and 1889–1891; Secretary of the Treasury under Garfield, 1881; bimetallist.

Woodin, William Hartman. 1868–1934

Manufacturer; born in Pennsylvania; educated at Columbia University; Secretary of the Treasury, March 4–December 31, 1933 (resigned).

Young, Owen D. 1874–1962

Lawyer; educated at St. Lawrence and Boston universities; Chairman, General Electric Corporation, 1922–1927; Director, Reserve Bank of New York, 1923–1940; gave name to Young plan for German reparations.

Young, Ralph Aubrey. 1901–

Wyoming-born economist; educated at Ohio Wesleyan and the University of Pennsylvania; National Industrial Conference Board, 1928–1934; National Bureau of Economic Research, 1938–1946; Professor, University of Pennsylvania, 1931–1945; Division of Research and Statistics, Federal Reserve Board, 1946–1959; Adviser to Board, 1960– .

Young, Roy Archibald. 1882–1961

Born in Marquette; commercial banker in Michigan, 1900–1917; Governor, Federal Reserve Board, 1927–1930 (resigned); President, Reserve Bank of Boston, 1930–1942.

Appendix III

Statistics

As explained in the Preface, I have made no attempt to supply tabular material to illustrate the text of this book. Figures 1 to 3, together with the few tables in the text, should suffice to make the narrative intelligible. The numerical data on which the three charts are based come so readily to hand that it would be absurd to reproduce them here. Therefore, with two exceptions, this Appendix is confined to a listing of sources, together with a few explanatory notes.

The exceptions are as follows. For the years 1932–1936, Figure 2 is partly drawn from unpublished material shown in Table A below. Second, discount rate changes are shown in Figures 1 and 3, and open-market operations in Figure 1. However, use made of the third main policy instrument, variation of member-bank reserve requirements, does not lend itself to diagrammatic representation. Especially important in the period since World War II, changes in the level of reserve requirements will be found in Table B.

SOURCES AND NOTES

Figure 1   (Production, Prices and Money-Market Data, 1919–1941)

Industrial production: This is the most comprehensive Federal Reserve index, seasonally adjusted. See *Federal Reserve Bulletin;* also *Survey of Current Business.* The monthly series is available complete in a single table in Board of Governors of the Federal Reserve System, *Industrial Production, 1957–1959 Base* (Washington, D.C.), p. S-148.

Wholesale prices: This is the index for "all commodities" published by the United States Bureau of Labor Statistics. See *Monthly Labor Review;* also *Survey of Current Business.*

Member-bank reserves, Change in monetary gold stock, Open-market purchases and sales, Bond yields, Customer-loan rates in New York City, and Discount rate of the Federal Reserve Bank of New York: All are from the *Federal Reserve Bulletin;* complete tabulations are available in Board of Governors of the Federal Reserve System, *Banking and Monetary Statistics* (Washington, D.C., 1943). Open-market purchases and sales include acceptances as well as United States government securities. Aaa and Baa yields relate to corporate bonds; the Baa yield reached a peak—not shown—of 11.6 per cent in May 1932.

Figure 2 (System Holdings of U.S. Treasury Obligations, 1932–1963)

The earliest published distribution by maturity is for the end of July 1936 (see *Banking and Monetary Statistics,* p. 344). The distribution for the period January 1932 through February 1936 is from the George L. Harrison papers and is reproduced in Table A below with the permission of the Federal Reserve System. The distribution from September 1936 to December 1963 is from the *Federal Reserve Bulletin;* see also *Banking and Monetary Statistics* and *Supplement* thereto. Through April 15, 1953, the System defined maturity as first call date; since then classification has been based upon date of final redemption.

Figure 3 (Production, Prices and Money-Market Data, 1941–1963)

Industrial production: See notes to Figure 1. Data for 1962–1963 were taken directly from the *Federal Reserve Bulletin.*

Wholesale prices: See notes to Figure 1.

Consumer prices: This is the index for "all items" published by the United States Bureau of Labor Statistics. See *Monthly Labor Review;* also *Survey of Current Business.*

Net free reserves (all member banks), Change in monetary gold stock, Customer-loan rates (seven northern and eastern cities), Bond yields, Yield on three-month Treasury bills, and Discount rate of the Federal Reserve Bank of New York: All are to be found in the *Federal Reserve Bulletin;* see also *Supplements to Banking and Monetary Statistics,* issued by the Board of Governors during 1962 and 1963.

Federal cash deficit, twelve-month (centered) moving average: See *Treasury Bulletin;* also *Federal Reserve Bulletin.* Data are for net payments ($+$) to, or net receipts ($-$) from the public, other than debt.

TABLE A

SYSTEM ACCOUNT AND TOTAL HOLDINGS OF U.S. TREASURY
OBLIGATIONS, 1932–1936
$ million; end of month

	System account						Total
	Maturing			Callable bonds	Other bonds	Total	
	within 1 year	1 to 2 years	2 to 5 years				
1932							
J	355	–	–	212	–	567	746
F	375	–	–	212	–	587	740
M	475	–	–	212	–	687	872
A	778	1	–	239	–	1 018	1 228
M	1 058	57	–	290	–	1 405	1 549
J	1 106	67	64	322	–	1 559	1 784
J	1 098	69	132	336	–	1 635	1 841
A	1 029	165	110	336	–	1 640	1 852
S	998	172	134	336	–	1 640	1 854
O	1 051	178	75	336	–	1 640	1 851
N	1 046	181	77	336	–	1 640	1 851
D	1 021	182	101	336	–	1 640	1 855
1933							
J	903	204	116	336	–	1 559	1 763
F	856	234	203	336	–	1 629	1 866
M	856	234	203	336	–	1 629	1 838
A	725	233	335	336	–	1 629	1 837
M	823	139	384	336	–	1 682	1 890
J	879	238	335	336	–	1 788	1 998
J	903	240	341	336	–	1 820	2 028
A	1 025	166	394	336	–	1 921	2 129
S	1 102	176	452	336	–	2 066	2 277
O	1 257	186	498	252	–	2 193	2 421
N	1 235	200	511	252	25	2 223	2 432
D	1 216	210	520	252	25	2 223	2 438
1934							
J	1 216	210	520	252	25	2 223	2 434
F	1 190	225	531	252	25	2 223	2 432
M	1 034	253	659	252	25	2 223	2 447
A	1 008	468	488	195	64	2 223	2 431
M	991	484	489	195	64	2 223	2 430
J	972	382	550	195	124	2 223	2 432
J	939	382	583	195	124	2 223	2 432
A	1 018	347	539	195	124	2 223	2 432

TABLE A

SYSTEM ACCOUNT AND TOTAL HOLDINGS OF U.S. TREASURY
OBLIGATIONS, 1932–1936
$ million; end of month

	System account						*Total*
	Maturing			*Callable bonds*	*Other bonds*	*Total*	
	within 1 year	*1 to 2 years*	*2 to 5 years*				
S	868	390	646	195	124	2 223	2 431
O	964	378	647	110	124	2 223	2 430
N	968	381	640	110	124	2 223	2 430
D	953	452	584	110	124	2 223	2 430
1935							
J	950	444	595	110	124	2 223	2 430
F	950	510	529	110	124	2 223	2 430
M	889	490	603	56	185	2 223	2 437
A	1 087	437	519	–	180	2 223	2 430
M	976	440	615	–	192	2 223	2 430
J	887	394	748	–	194	2 223	2 433
J	829	404	796	–	194	2 223	2 430
A	856	325	848	–	194	2 223	2 432
S	850	343	836	–	194	2 223	2 430
O	871	342	816	–	194	2 223	2 430
N	871	342	816	–	194	2 223	2 430
D	913	253	863	–	194	2 223	2 431
1936							
J	912	253	864	–	194	2 223	2 430
F[a]	971	249	809	–	194	2 223	2 430

[a] February 19, latest date for which data are given in source.

Source: George L. Harrison papers, "Federal Open Market Committee," Vol. III; re-produced by permission. "Callable bonds" were callable—and were mostly called—within a few months of the date reported. "Other bonds" mostly had maturities between 10 and 15 years. The difference between the System Account total and the total for the System consisted of holdings by individual Reserve Banks for their own account; such holdings were consolidated into the System Account as of June 30, 1936.

TABLE B

MEMBER-BANK RESERVE REQUIREMENTS
% of deposits

Date made effective	Net demand deposits			Time deposits
	Central reserve city banks	Reserve city banks	Country banks	
Nov. 1914	18	15	12	5
June 1917	13	10	7	3
Aug. 1936	19½	15	10½	4½
Mar. 1937	22¾	17½	12¼	5¼
May 1937	26	20	14	6
Apr. 1938	22¾	17½	12	5
Nov. 1941	26	20	14	6
Aug. 1942	24	–	–	–
Sep. 1942	22	–	–	–
Oct. 1942	20	–	–	–
Feb. 1948	22	–	–	–
June 1948	24	–	–	–
Sep. 1948	26	22	16	7½
May 1949	24	21	15	7
June–July 1949	–	20	14	6
Aug. 1949	23½	19½	13	5
Aug. 1949	23	19	12	–
Aug. 1949	22½	18½	–	–
Sep. 1949	22	18	–	–
Jan. 1951	23	19	13	6
Jan. 1951	24	20	–	–
Feb. 1951	–	–	14	–
July 1953	22	19	13	–
June 1954	21	–	–	5
July–Aug. 1954	20	18	12	–
Feb. 1958	19½	17½	–	–
Mar. 1958	19	17	11½	–
Apr. 1958	18½	–	11	–
Apr. 1958	18	16½	–	–
Sep. 1960	17½	–	–	–
Nov.-Dec. 1960	16½	–	12	–
Oct.-Nov. 1962	–	–	–	4
In effect Jan. 1, 1964	–	16½	12	4
Present legal requirements:				
Minimum	–	10	7	3
Maximum	–	22	14	6

Source: *Supplement to Banking and Monetary Statistics*, Sec. 10, p. 62; also *Federal Reserve Bulletin*.

Notes to Table B:

Net demand deposits equal total demand deposits minus cash items in process of collection and demand balances due from domestic banks. From April 1943 to June 1947, war loan and Series E bond accounts were also excluded from net demand deposits.

From August 1935 to July 1959 minimum and maximum requirements allowed by law were 13% and 26% respectively for central reserve city banks; and maximum requirements for reserve city banks were 20%; except that from August 1948 to June 1949 maximum requirements against demand deposits were 30% for central reserve city, 24% for reserve city, and 18% for country banks, and against time deposits 7½%. On July 28, 1962, the central reserve city was merged with the reserve city classification.

From June 1917 until late 1959 all required reserves were held on deposit with Federal Reserve Banks. Since Nov. 24, 1960, member banks have been allowed to count all vault cash as part of required reserves.

Index